Not an Eas

Some Transitions in Baptist Life

■ ■ ■

by
WALTER B. SHURDEN

■ ■ ■

MERCER UNIVERSITY PRESS
MACON, GEORGIA USA

ISBN 0-86554-933-8   MUP/P289

Library of Congress Cataloging-in-Publication Data

Shurden, Walter B.
Not an easy journey : some transitions in Baptist life /
by Walter B. Shurden.-- 1st ed.
p. cm.
Includes bibliographical references and indexes.
ISBN 0-86554-933-8 (pbk. : alk. paper)
1. Baptists--Doctrines. 2. Southern Baptist Convention--History.
3. Cooperative Baptist Fellowship--History.
4. Baptists--United States--History. I. Title.
BX6331.3.S58 2005
286'.173--dc22

2005002535

Contents

3. Baptists and Cooperative Baptist Fellowship History

4. A Bibliography

For five grandchildren

Emily Shurden Brewer
Audrey Wilson Batts
Benjamin Harrison Brewer
Samuell Callaway Batts
Langley Wilson Shurden

whose consciences, I pray,
will always be free from domination of any kind;
whose lives, I pray,
will always be in the service of God and humankind.

Baptists
History, Literature, Theology, Hymns

General editor: *Walter B. Shurden* is Professor of Christianity in the Roberts Department of Christianity and executive director of the Center for Baptist Studies, Mercer University.

John Taylor. *Baptists on the American Frontier: A History of Ten Baptist Churches*. Edited by Chester Young (1985).

Thomas Helwys. *A Short Declaration of the Mystery of Iniquity (1611/1612)*. Edited by Richard Groves (1998).

Roger Williams. *The Bloody Tenant of Persecution for Cause of Conscience*. Historical introduction by Edwin Gaustad. Edited by Richard Groves (2001).

James A. Rogers. *Richard Furman: Life and Legacy* (1985; reprint with new forewords, 2002).

Lottie Moon. *Send the Light: Lottie Moon's Letters and Other Writings*. Edited by Keith Harper (2002).

James P. Byrd, Jr. *The Challenges of Roger Williams: Religious Liberty, Violent Persecution, and the Bible* (2002).

Anne Dutton. *Selected Spiritual Writings of Anne Dutton, Eighteenth-Century, British-Baptist, Woman Theologian*. Volume 1. *Letters*. Edited by JoAnn Ford Watson (fall 2003).

David T. Morgan. *Southern Baptist Sisters: In Search of Status, 1845–2000* (fall 2003).

William E. Ellis. *"A Man of Books and a Man of the People": E. Y. Mullins and the Crisis of Moderate Southern Baptist Leadership* (1985; reprint, fall 2003).

Jarrett Burch. *Adiel Sherwood: Baptist Antebellum Pioneer in Georgia* (winter 2003).

Anthony Chute. *A Piety above the Common Standard. Jesse Mercer and the Defense of Evangelistic Calvinism* (spring 2004).

William H. Brackney. *A Genetic History of Baptist Thought* (September 2004).

Henlee Hulix Barnette. *A Pilgrimage of Faith: My Story* (November 2004).

Walter B. Shurden. *Not an Easy Journey: Some Transitions in Baptist Life* (2005)

Also by Walter B. Shurden

Editor. *Perspectives on Theological Education. Essays in Honor of C. Penrose St. Amant* (1989).

Editor. *The Struggle for the Soul of the SBC. Moderate Responses to the Fundamentalist Movement* (1993).

Coeditor, with Randy Shepley. *Going for the Jugular. A Documentary History of the SBC Holy War* (1996).

Preface

Marc Jolley, director of Mercer University Press, is the catalyst for this book. I was in his office one day to discuss the publication of another research project in which I was engaged. While encouraging the latter, a project in which I had invested considerable time, Dr. Jolley suggested that I needed to pull together a book of some of my previously published as well as unpublished writings. His nudging coalesced with some long-time encouragement from my wife Kay and a few close friends. One expects a spouse and friends to "urge," but Marc Jolley's nudge was unexpected and decisive. Over the years, a friend or student occasionally would ask, "Where can I find a copy of that presentation you made at such and such a place on such and such a topic?" Often, I would have to search to find the item and not without some expenditure of time. I hope this volume helps meet some of those needs. Personally, it has been a help to me to pull these varied writings together in one place.

When I began to compile these essays that span a twenty-five-year period, I expected to discover a good bit of diversity in the themes I had treated in my speaking and my writing. Indeed various themes and approaches do appear. However, as I read back through the material, I became aware that a Baptist thread inexorably winds its way through most of the writings. It is the thread of the Baptist identity and how that identity played a crucial role in the Fundamentalist-Moderate Holy War that dominated white Baptist life in the South from 1979 to 1990. Before the war actually erupted, I was writing on some of the themes that would be controversial later in the struggle. For example, that was the case with the article on "Southern Baptist Responses to Their Confessional Statements," published in the winter issue of *Review and Expositor* and republished here. That article, as I suggest later in this volume, needs desperately to be updated, but the trends about which I wrote in 1979 came to dominate much of the discussions about the role of confessions of faith in the next twenty-five years of Baptist life in the South.

You will find several different genre of writings in this volume. Some are academic articles published in professional journals. Most of these were requested pieces. I hope that even these articles are user-friendly for the reader. I have always made a sustained effort to write and speak for the educated layperson when writing about historical or theological issues. Indeed, I have wished many times over the past two and a half decades that

Baptists had been a more historically curious people. That curiosity, I believe, would have saved us from much heartache. The articles in this volume entitled "The Priesthood of All Believers and Pastoral Authority in Baptist Thought," "The Origins of the Southern Baptist Convention: A Historiographical Study," "What 'Being Baptist' Meant for Southern Baptists during World War II," and "The Baptist Identity and the Baptist Manifesto" are not, I know, usual fare for Baptist laity. I hold out hope, however, that they contain some help for the people who occupy the pews of Baptist churches each Sunday.

In addition to the more academic articles, you also will find brief, popular articles in this collection. This is especially true of some of the selections under the section entitled "Baptists and CBF History." Some of these I wrote because I had been invited to speak at a gathering of some kind, such as the tenth anniversary of *Baptists Today* or the third anniversary of Smyth & Helwys Publishing Inc. They are intentionally interpretive with, I hope, a bit of inspiration.

Some of the chapters here take the form of what Fred Craddock appropriately designated as "prectures," a dab of lecturing and a bit of preaching. These, too, initially were most often delivered in oral form. "Precture" may be an apt description of "A Decade of Promise," the address I delivered at the banquet celebrating the tenth anniversary of the formation of the Cooperative Baptist Fellowship. I also gave two "prectures" for the Carver-Barnes lectures at Southeastern Baptist Theological Seminary in 1980. These are printed here unchanged and are known as "The Southern Baptist Synthesis: Is it Cracking?" and "The Inerrancy Debate: A Comparative Study of Southern Baptist Controversies." I have done a good bit of "precturing" in my life. It is one of my favorite things to do. A "precture" both frees one from the formality of an academic article while holding one accountable for what is said.

Others of the offerings here, however, are brief, journalistic, advocacy pieces, such as "Twenty Reflections after Twenty Years." This was an effort, after two decades, to reflect on the Southern Baptist Holy War between the fundamentalists and the moderates. By the way, I claim no disengaged neutrality about what I have said in that little piece and others of my writings regarding the controversy. Without apology, I am a partisan, a moderate when I write about the SBC controversy. I do not buy into the historiography that says that real objectivity is found only by those who write at a distance or who write without passion. War journalists describe something about conflict that later historians will never capture. And those in the middle of conflict are no more blinded by their prejudices than those who have no stake in the struggle. I have been amused by a few Baptists and non-Baptist historians who think that real "objectivity" belongs to them because they were not part of the argument or that they have a point of view different from either the fundamentalists or the moderates. For me, all of these claims, spoken or unspoken, of "transcendent objectivity" smack of one of the worst forms of self-righteousness.

As much as possible I have intentionally left the presentations as I originally wrote or spoke them. It is very important for me, therefore, to urge you to read the articles within the historical context of the times in which I wrote them. I was sorely tempted to update some of the articles, if for no other reason than to make my past judgments and assertions look less foolish. I thought it best, however, to leave them untouched and take my deserved lumps.

Precisely because these essays have been left essentially as first published or presented, bibliography as well as content need to be updated. Much has happened since some of these presentations were made and the articles were written. And much has been written about what has happened. Indeed, it would please me much if some eager student or students tackled some of these topics in an effort to update them.

As always, I am in debt. I am grateful that I work in one of the freest Baptist environments anywhere, Mercer University. That environment has been nurtured and guarded by R. Kirby Godsey, president of Mercer. Mercer University Press is one of President Godsey's "free children" and it is under the direction of Marc Jolley, another free Baptist and someone I have already mentioned as important to this volume. I requested of Marc Jolley that he please put Mercer University Press's senior editor, Edd Rowell, on this manuscript. Edd knows secrets about editing that few others know, and I am deeply in his debt as my editor and friend.

Greg Thompson, my initial colleague at the Center for Baptist Studies, has saved me time and effort by showing me mysterious things about the computer, scanning articles for this volume, and breaking up the seriousness of life with some robust humor. Bruce Gourley, my present associate at the Center, gave me valuable proofreading time while healing from a fractured back and during his holidays.

My wife Kay is a bibliophile, a faithful and good proofreader, and a gentle critic, and I am deeply in her debt for almost everything I have ever written. She also suggested the title for this book, taking her cue from the first book I ever wrote, *Not a Silent People: Controversies That Have Shaped Southern Baptists*. Baptists, like other Christians, have not had an easy journey. They have wrestled with the state, other religious groups, and with each other. Transitions in Baptist life have come often and with much turbulence, even in my lifetime.

Like most professors and professional people of all kinds, I have done my work often at the expense of family time. I am, therefore, happy to complete this project prior to Christmas 2004.

Walter B. Shurden

Baptists and Their Distinctives

■ ■ ■

Second Baptist Church, Greenville, Mississippi[1]

Filled with very common people with untrained voices, the robeless choir hummed in the background while M. E. Perry leaned into the microphone, almost whispering with that godlike bass voice.

> Welcome to the Sunday morning broadcast of the Second Baptist Church in Greenville, Mississippi. We are glad you have joined us by radio and invite you to come worship with us in person at 907 South Theobald Street. We are the church "where friends meet friends and sinners meet Christ" and where you are always welcome.

After a few more sentences of trying to entice "radioland" to come our way, he would close:

> Once again, we are the Second Baptist Church, 907 South Theobald, Greenville, Mississippi, M. E. Perry, pastor.

Turning from the microphone toward the choir, he slipped out of his preacher role and into his minister of music portfolio, conducting the choir as they began singing the lyrics they had been humming. It was the Second Baptist Church's call to worship. M. E. Perry wrote it, and I have hummed and sung it to myself for fifty years.

> Because Christ Jesus died for me,
> because he suffered on a tree,
> because he lived and died for me,
> I consecrate my all.

In that simple manner I was introduced into the immeasurably rich liturgy of the Christian tradition. It was also my introduction into the Baptist tradition.

Surely the unstated assumption in a book with the title *Why I Am a Baptist* (see fn. 1) is that, after extolling Baptist ideas and ideals, I will eventually get around to telling you that I am a Baptist because of "Baptist beliefs." The most vulgar form of that is, "Baptists are closer to the New Testament than others, so I joined and stayed on." A more palatable form

---

[1]This essay was first published in a slightly different form in *Why I Am a Baptist*, ed. Cecil P. Staton, Jr. (Macon GA: Smyth & Helwys Publishing Inc., 1999) 143-56. It is reprinted here with permission of Smyth & Helwys.

goes like this: "I am a Baptist because I grew up Baptist, but in my mature years I also learned the truthfulness of Baptist ideas." None of the first and only a bit of that latter kind of thing is in my story, and I will get around to it in time. But honesty compels me to start at a very different point.

"Second"

I am a Baptist of the South partly because of economics. My mother finished the tenth grade. My daddy quit after the fourth. At the time of his death my daddy's eighty-four-year-old crusty and gnarled hands testified that he had worked long and hard as a welder and pipefitter. He could barely read the words in the hymnbook. I was the first person in my nuclear family to graduate from college and the first in my extended family to receive a doctorate.

My family was what I braggingly described as "lower middle class." Truth be told, we were probably one rung below that! The only time I remember really being embarrassed by our standing in life was in my early years of high school. Our family had one car—an old blue Chevrolet with one black fender. My brother and I would ask our mother and daddy to let us out a block or two from high school. We needed exercise, we said. As now, status mattered then to adolescents.

Move me a tad down the socioeconomic ladder in the Delta of Mississippi in the 1950s, and I would probably have ended up with the Church of God or the Pentecostals, which would have been fine, I am sure. For certain I would not have been an Episcopalian or Presbyterian, not even a Methodist. They had too much money. As it was, I first experienced the Holy in life in my dormitory room in the spring of my first year of college. I committed my life to Christ and promptly asked for membership in the Second Baptist Church of Greenville, Mississippi, my parents' home church.

Don't let the "Second" part of that church name slip by you. We were "second" not merely in terms of chronology; we were "second" in terms of zip codes, the vehicles we drove, the English we spoke, and the jobs we worked at. We worked for the folks at "First" Baptist Church. Baptists are stratified sociologically just as denominations are.[2] The people at "First

---

[2]If you want evidence of the socioeconomic stratification of Christian denominations, visit church parking lots on a Sunday morning at 11:30 and do a quick survey of the vehicles. You will not find many pickups or Chevrolets at the Episcopal Church or many Cadillacs or Lexuses at the Pentecostal churches. You will notice something of the same difference, though maybe not as great, if you

Church," people I later admired, had a beautiful carpeted sanctuary with plush cushions in the pews and beautiful robes on the choir members. But at Second Baptist Church we knew liberalism when we saw it! We had concrete floors, hard wooden pews to punish the body for the sins of the soul, and nobody in our choir wore a robe. Formalism, we said at Second Baptist, was the death of the spirit. Being antiformal was one way we had of being spiritually superior!

Our beloved preacher, "Brother" M. E. Perry, pranced up and down the rostrum, occasionally strayed into the church aisles, clapped his hands, and preached six octaves louder than "Dr." Perry Claxton at First Baptist Church. Both Perrys, thankfully, became fathers-in-God to me. As with most ecclesiastical stratification, economics, not theology, served as the primary wedge between First and Second Baptist Churches in Greenville, Mississippi. At Second Baptist Church we *accepted* our "second" status. We accepted it socially, economically, and educationally. But we took second place to no group religiously.

In his well-used history of Baptists, Robert G. Torbet attributed Baptist growth in America to its appeal to "plain people." Please do not mistake this description for an inverted social elitism. It is not. But to be sure, some Baptists have wallowed in their "plainness." You know, "Aw shucks, I am just an old country boy," when what they really mean is, "I am just a *good* ole country boy!" But to say as Torbet did that Baptist growth was due to its appeal to "plain people" is not sociological brag; it is historical truth, especially in the Southern part of the United States.

I once asked Emmanuel McCall, an African-American Baptist friend, what he and I, so different in our background and culture, had in common as Baptists. He answered, "We are common folks." Let's be sure of what we are talking about and describing here. We are talking "Once upon a time. . . . "

White Baptists of the South have pulled a massive comeuppance in the world of American religion.[3] We now have some Episcopalian money, and

---

compare the parking lots of First Baptist Church and Second Baptist Church in the average size town in the South.

[3]To tell the historical story accurately, one has to acknowledge that not all Baptists, even from their beginning, came from the lower strata of society. The phenomenal progress of Baptists on the American frontier and especially in the rural South has left a sociological imprint on Baptists in America, especially in the South. W. W. Sweet's once-popular historical treatment of Baptists and the importance of the frontier Baptist preacher intensified this portrayal. See his *Religion on the*

a few Baptists have Book-of-Common-Prayer liturgies. We even have some Presbyterian education! (We had much more superb education before the fundamentalists among us tried choking the life out of the University of Richmond, Wake Forest, Furman, Stetson, Baylor, Carson-Newman, and a few others. Consequently, these stellar schools exited the Baptist scene.) And we have Catholic influence. Look at the faces that dominate Washington, D.C.: Bill Clinton, Al Gore, Trent Lott, Newt Gingrich, Strom Thurmond, Robert Byrd, Jesse Helms, and Jesse Jackson.[4] They are all Baptists! Blaming the Jews in New York or the liberals in the Ivy-League East for the mess in the country simply no longer works!

But the issue is more than denominational; it is personal. I now prefer stately anthems to some of the down-home gospel singing I cut my teeth on at Second Baptist, though those gospel songs can still stir my heart. I prefer silence and a richer liturgy to the boisterous fellowship and simple worship of earlier years. And I prefer to hear the pulpit struggle with the ambiguities and contradictions of life rather than to proclaim, however so enthusiastically, the simplicities I first confused with the gospel. For me, this is not comeuppance; it is spiritual growth and discovery, the discovery of *mystery*.

My saga in Baptist churches is—again thankfully—as diverse as Baptist life itself. I've worshiped "high," "low," "broad," and what my friend Bill Leonard calls "charismatic lite" (hands but no tongues!). I've sung out of both the front and back of the *Baptist Hymnal* and from every kind of hymnbook, including Stamps-Baxter. I've preached in coatless short-sleeve dress shirts in rural frame buildings and in Geneva gowns in urban cathedrals; spotted lots of "first" folks in "second" churches and lots of "second" folks in "first" churches; baptized in cow ponds, cold rivers, and warm "indoor" baptismal pools; and been part of Sunday morning worship that closed with as much as forty-three verses of "Just As I Am" and as little as a brief benediction.

I came out of Second Baptist Church in Greenville, Mississippi, but I spent several years at St. Charles Avenue Baptist Church in New Orleans, Louisiana, Crescent Hill Baptist Church in Louisville, Kentucky, and even

---

American Frontier: The Baptists, 1783–1830 (New York: Cooper Square Publishers, Inc., 1964). But as E. Brooks Holifield demonstrated in *The Gentleman Theologians: American Theology in Southern Culture, 1795–1860* (Durham NC: Duke University Press, 1978), Sweet's depiction is not the whole picture.

[4]This was the political situation in 1999 when I wrote this essay.

a couple of months at the cathedral at Myers Park Baptist Church in Charlotte, North Carolina. To say it historically for those who know the references, I came out of Sandy Creek, but I've been to Charleston.[5] I apologize for neither and am grateful that Baptists have been "catholic" enough to have both and all shades in-between.

Indeed, I am glad that at the beginning of a new millennium we Baptists have churches of all kinds. Rich kids need to know that Jesus loves them just as do "lower-middle-class" kids. But being lower middle class, I started at "Second" Baptist. Economics is partly responsible for my Baptist beginnings.

"Church"

I am Baptist partly because of emotions. We were "Second" Baptist Church on South Theobald in Greenville, Mississippi, but we were also Second Baptist "Church." Sociologists delight in telling you that the "Second" part of our name probably made church out of us more than the "Church" part of our name. To say it another way, people choose the churches they do because of acceptance and a sense of belonging.

H. Richard Niebuhr made that point way back in 1929 in *The Social Sources of Denominationalism*. Now read Niebuhr's title again. *The Social Sources of Denominationalism*! There is truth in it! Christian denominations have social, not just theological, differences. At Second Baptist we were "Church" because we accepted each other, cared for each other, and belonged to each other. And doubtless our ease of belonging, what we called our "fellowship," surely had something, as Niebuhr said, to do with our "second" status. We were with our kind. We may have been "Second" to those on the outside, but we were "Church," to each other on the inside.

After he announced his intention not to seek the presidency a second term and so to return to his ranch in Texas, Lyndon Johnson was asked by someone why he was leaving the power and pomp of Washington to return to Texas. He said, "Because out there they ask about you when you are sick, and they cry when you die." That's what those plain people did at Second "Church."

Even though I did not grow up at the church's altar, the plain people at Second Baptist Church in Greenville, Mississippi, became "church" to me when I was age eighteen. That is the second reason I am a Baptist.

---

[5]See my essay in this volume entitled "The Southern Baptist Synthesis: Is It Cracking?"

Economics may have been an unconscious force in my becoming a Baptist, but I was totally conscious of being loved. I am a Baptist partly because of emotions. Baptist people were the first Christians to love me. Had I gone to a Church of God or a Methodist church and had they loved me as did those wonderful people down on South Theobald, I doubtless would have ended up one of them rather than a Baptist.

Along with those carpetless concrete floors at Second Baptist church, we had rip-roaring gospel singing (much of which I can still do pretty well at from memory), revved-up evangelistic preaching, hugs and tears, and a place that *felt* unspeakably, indescribably good to me. The only appropriate word to describe the place is one we would have never used at Second Baptist, even if we had known it—"sanctuary"! A sanctuary is a holy or sacred place, a refuge, an asylum, a shelter. More than anything else, this particular "sanctuary" on South Theobald consisted of a somewhat uneducated, more than somewhat unwealthy, lily-white, uncritical people who claimed to hate sin and Satan but love God, Jesus, the Bible, each other, and *me*.

What made Second Baptist Church feel unspeakably and indescribably good, of course, was overwhelmingly personal. Either those people loved me, believed in me, wanted the best for me, or they have deceived me to this very moment. I will always believe the former. Looking back over my shoulder after almost a half a century, I realize how much at eighteen I resembled all eighteen-year-olds, thinking secretly that I was nobody and wanting so very much to be somebody.

Reverberating within the walls of that simple but blessed sanctuary of Second Baptist Church on South Theobald in Greenville, Mississippi, I heard the affirming whispers of those plain people, "You are somebody. You really are somebody!" Fortunately, it is difficult, even impossible, to get over being loved. And those people launched me with love! They launched me not only into life but also into the ministry of Jesus Christ. For the three years I was at Mississippi College (a Baptist college) in undergraduate school, that struggling little Baptist church sent a check every month for thirty-five dollars (good money during the years 1955–1958) to the college's finance office to help pay my tuition. Moreover, they did it for the other seven preacher-boys who came out of that church during the same period of time.

(Incidentally, a church that is not appealing enough to produce women and men for the ministry needs to check its spiritual pulse.)

"Baptist"

I am a Baptist first because of economics and second because of emotions. But third, I am a Baptist because I was educated to be one. I am a Baptist because I learned to be a Baptist. The first Baptist book I ever read was Joe T. Odle's *A Church Member's Handbook*, replete with historical, theological, and denominational silliness, for example, "successionism." Successionism is the perverse idea that Baptists are the true church because they can trace themselves back to the Jordan River and John the Baptist. That's where I began Christian nurture, being taught the theological tribalism that Baptists are the true church.

I was a heretic from the beginning; I never believed it. However, while I may never have believed we were the only ones, I snuggled up pretty close to the absurdity that we were the best ones, but I have repented of that a thousand times and with good reason. Tribalism, like all other provincialisms, has to die. I do not decry the death of tribalism, but neither do I deny the pull of home. For me, the larger Baptist family has been my home and my little corner of the forty-acre field of Christendom. I hope I am not flirting again with tribalism when I say that at the center of my being there is something about being Baptist as I understand it that is both freeing and fulfilling. What is that?

It is the principle of voluntarism. My wife tells me not to use that word because it does not communicate. But the abortion debate has conscripted the word "choice." And when I tried using the word "freedom" for a synonym, a few Baptists thought that I was shucking responsibility while others accused me of being, as they said, "too anthropocentric rather than theocentric." Both had misunderstood, of course. But let's try voluntarism this time.

> Voluntarism—Authentic faith is chosen as God works through the individual's will.
> Voluntarism—Coercion of any kind and all kinds is out.
> Voluntarism—If faith is to be valid, it must be uncoerced.
> Voluntarism—The only conversion that counts is conversion by conviction.
> Voluntarism—Where there is no autonomy, there is no authenticity.
> Voluntarism—Cramming a creed down a person's throat is rape of the soul.

We Baptists do not distinguish ourselves from other Christian groups by our concepts of God, Christ, the Holy Spirit, and other such cardinal Christian emphases. We don't have a Baptist bible, separate from other

Christians. Nor do we identify ourselves by certain theological approaches, for example, Calvinism with its stress on the sovereignty of God or Arminianism with its emphasis on human free will. Both Calvinism and Arminianism have long and noble histories among Baptists, but one can be either or neither and still be a Baptist. Nor are we distinguished by popular theological labels. Among Baptists you will find fundamentalists, conservatives, liberals, evangelicals, and everything in between. But it is a serious mistake and gross misrepresentation of our history to equate "Baptist" with any of these. One can be a Baptist and be any of these.

I am a Baptist because the core value of the Baptist vision of Christianity is voluntarism. Freedom. Choice. The following is what voluntarism means for me in relation to the individual, the church, the state, and religious authority.

In terms of Christian discipleship, this means that I personally, individually, and voluntarily choose to follow Christ. No one imposes this on me—not God, the church, my family, or the state. Saved completely by God's grace and not by my doings, I accept God's grace, submit to God's will, and with other believers start my Christian journey. Negatively, this means that I do not believe that one becomes a Christian automatically, sacramentally, or institutionally through baptism or the Lord's Supper. I am drawn to the Baptist insistence on believer's baptism because it stems from the belief that baptism, representing one's commitment to Christ, is freely chosen. On the other hand, Baptist opposition to infant baptism stems from the belief that infants cannot choose and that proxy faith is no faith at all. I am a Baptist because I believe that the Christian faith is personal, experiential, and voluntary.

In terms of the church, Baptist voluntarism means that I voluntarily covenant with others who have trusted Christ as Savior and Lord, and under God's Spirit we create together a believers' church. Faith begins privately, in the lonely soul of the individual, but it is rooted in a congregation of believers. I like the idea that Baptist Christians who voluntarily covenant with each other to form a local church are free, under the lordship of Christ, to determine our membership, which we insist should be of believers only. Calling this a "regenerate church membership," we seek to safeguard that membership through believer's baptism by immersion. The "believers" part of the baptism is far more important to me than the "immersion" part. Moreover, in our churches we Baptists choose our leadership, order our worship and work, ordain whom we wish, and voluntarily participate in the larger body of Christ. Without priesthood or hierarchy, we affirm that all members of the churches stand on equal footing and serve as priests before God, to the church, and for the world.

As a local Baptist church under the lordship of Christ and the word of Holy Scripture, we are an autonomous, self-governing body. We practice congregational church polity. We are also an independent body, fully the church without reference to some larger institution. However, we Baptists voluntarily unite with other churches in covenant relationships through associational, regional, and national denominational bodies. Moreover, we Baptists see our churches and all other Christian churches as part of the universal Church of Jesus Christ. I am a Baptist because I believe the local church is a covenanted community of believers responsible under God for its life and faith, but I also believe the universal church of Jesus Christ includes all of God's people everywhere.

In terms of the state, Baptist voluntarism makes me an ardent advocate of liberty of conscience and opinion, including freedom of religion, freedom for religion, and freedom from religion. We Baptists have championed religious liberty because of our belief that God alone is lord of the conscience. Also, we have led the religious liberty parade because we have insisted that if faith is to be genuine, it must be free. Because this kind of voluntarism works best where religion and government are separate, Baptists have argued historically for the separation of church and state. I am a Baptist because I believe in liberty of conscience for every human being and because I oppose the entanglement of government and religion, recognizing, of course, that complete separation is impossible.

In terms of religious authority, Baptists, as do most other Christians, point to the authority of scripture for faith and practice. Unlike many other Christians, however, Baptists do not invest the final interpretation of the Bible in creeds, councils, or clergy. Certainly the interpretations of creed, councils, and clergy cannot be imposed. We Baptists leave the Bible where it belongs. It belongs in the hands of the individual believer, who interprets it within the trusting relationship of a local congregation of believers. This does not mean that Baptists can believe anything they want and remain Baptists. It does mean, however, that the Bible is a dynamic, not a static or closed, book. Its final interpretation is not locked up in ancient creeds or confessions or in hands of a few ecclesiastical specialists. I am a Baptist because, as anticreedalists, Baptists believe in an open Bible and an open mind, both working in the context of trusting relationships in a local church.

All of these distinctives and some I have not listed are vulnerable to the "Confuser," Clarence Jordan's word for Satan. The authority of scripture can be tragically distorted into blind biblicism and excessive subjectivism. Baptist individualism can be transformed into the sovereignty of self and narcissistic privatism, and the independence and autonomy of the local church into ecclesiastical lone rangerism. Liberty of conscience can easily degenerate into expediency rather than principle, prostituting itself into freedom for "us" or for "Christians" or "Americans."

These distortions are not only possible; sadly, they have occurred in Baptist history. This important principle of freedom or voluntarism can easily get lost. It can be sacrificed on the altars of political ideology that are only inches from governmental tyranny. It can get so enmeshed in culture that it never recognizes that it has become a ruthless system of domination. It can be conscripted as a code word for self-serving caucuses and one-eyed movements. It can lose itself, as Langdon Gilkey said, in the trivia of self-indulgence.[6] It can get lost in corporatism and a pack mentality. Voluntarism—freedom—the Baptist vision—is an exceedingly fragile commodity.

But I live with the conviction that voluntarism represents the Baptist heritage. I am hopeful that the core value of voluntarism will survive and triumph as the prevailing Baptist vision. Philipp Jakob Spener, the spearhead of German Pietism and a resounding critic of German Lutheranism of the seventeenth century, requested a few days before his death that he be buried in a white rather than a black coffin. He had lamented sufficiently the condition of the church while on earth, he said. In dying he wanted a white coffin, symbolic of his hope for a better church on earth. I have that kind of optimism for Baptists.

At bottom I believe that "voluntarism" or "freedom" or "choice"—call it what you will—is temporarily conquerable and subject to perversion. I also believe, however, that it is an ultimately imperishable moral commodity. That is why I believe that, even if Baptists sacrifice the spirit of voluntarism on pagan altars, it will rise again in some wing of the Christian church. I am a Baptist because I learned that voluntarism is the core value of Baptists.

"Greenville, Mississippi"

Had I been born and reared in Boston, Massachusetts, I might be a Congregationalist or a Catholic. Had I grown up in Minneapolis, Minnesota, I would probably be a Lutheran. But I am a Southerner, born in

---

[6]Langdon Gilkey, "The Threshold of a New Common Freedom," *Criterion* (Divinity School, University of Chicago) 37/3 (Autumn 1998): 19.

Greenwood, Mississippi, where we lived until we moved fifty-five miles far away to Greenville, Mississippi. Other places of residence included Clinton, Mississippi; Lake Village, Arkansas; New Orleans, Louisiana; Ruston, Louisiana; Jefferson City, Tennessee; Louisville, Kentucky; and Macon, Georgia. Look at that! Mississippi, Arkansas, Louisiana, Tennessee, Kentucky, and Georgia! When the Southeastern Conference plays, I can't lose! But neither do I know for whom to cheer! But more to the point, it is difficult to grow up where I grew up or live all your life where I have lived without either being a Baptist, being witnessed to by a Baptist, being influenced by Baptists, or downright despising Baptists.

In a cry of despair a rather irreligious gubernatorial candidate in Mississippi, who was taking a pummeling from Baptists, once said, "Johnson grass and Baptists are taking over this state." He obviously did not know that by the time he uttered his lament, Baptists had already taken over the South. The South is my home. Environment has something to do with why I am a Baptist.

Actually my wife, three children, and I lived one exceedingly happy year in Hamilton, Ontario, Canada where Ivan Morgan, Gerry Harrop, Russell Aldwinckle, Jim Perkins, and a few others broadened my Baptistness and challenged my Southernness. If they had needed a Church History professor at McMaster Divinity School, we probably would have stayed and become Canadians, people we came to love and admire. But Providence or the tug of home—probably economics—shuttled us back south. A twenty-nine-year-old with a wife and three children tends to go where the work is, though those of us in the ministry downplay economics and call it the "will of God"!

I came home to the South; I was a Southern Baptist. I served as pastor of the First Baptist Church of Ruston, Louisiana (note the upward mobility from "Second Baptist" to "First Baptist"), taught seven wonderful years at a Baptist college in East Tennessee (Carson-Newman College), taught and served as an administrator in a Baptist seminary (the Southern Baptist Theological Seminary), and taught at a Baptist university (Mercer). If all that does not make one a Southern Baptist, what does?

But in June 1987 I divorced the Southern Baptist Convention when its fundamentalist leaders stopped being Baptist. They trashed the cardinal Baptist concept of the priesthood of all believers, subjugated women, idolized the Bible, crucified freedom, baptized the right wing of the Republican Party, and in general moved the Southern Baptist Convention just to the right of every place I wanted to be. But they had already accused me and my friends of moving to the left of every place they thought we should be! Probably we were both overaccused and misaccused.

The divorce, as divorces often do, liberated me. It did not send me scurrying toward the broader, more catholic Baptist tradition and toward the broader more catholic Christian church. I had been there for a long time. But it liberated me from having to defend such a decent and legitimate posture to my own denomination.

Through the years people, institutions, books, human hurts and joys, good jobs, Holy Scriptures, and Holy Spirit have worked diligently to extricate me from my parochial Southern environment, my restricted Baptist education, my rustic Second Baptist Church liturgy, and my lower-middle-class economics. They have helped me to see that being a Christian means taking seriously what Jesus took seriously. What Jesus took seriously was not believer's baptism by immersion, congregational church government, the priesthood of all believers, and the symbolic view of the ordinances. I do think that Jesus took voluntarism seriously, but what Jesus took really seriously was including the excluded, healing human hurts, confronting the exploiters, sharing what you have, living a life anchored in and under God, and being obedient to God even in the face of death. It is much easier to be a Baptist than it is to take Jesus seriously.

I have walked much closer to the Baptist ideals than to the Jesus ideals. But those "people, institutions, books, human hurts and joys, good jobs, Holy Scriptures, and Holy Spirit" have been successful enough that I hardly ever brag on being a Baptist anymore. But while I seldom brag, I cannot forget. To some small degree Baptists set me free, but they never set me adrift. As long as I can find a Baptist church that will take me and one that I can take, I'll be a Baptist. Their acceptance of me and my stewardship to them is part of the covenant. If they or I ever break that covenant, I'll pack up and move out. But I could never move on without packing some Baptist stuff—golden Baptist stuff—to carry with me.

I would pack "memories," especially memories of relationships with people of the Second Baptist Church in Greenville, Mississippi; the First Baptist Church in Ruston, Louisiana; St. Charles Avenue Baptist Church in New Orleans, Louisiana; the First Baptist Church in Jefferson City, Tennessee; Crescent Hill Baptist Church in Louisville, Kentucky; and the First Baptist Church of Christ at Macon, Georgia.

I would pack one other thing. I would pack several extra portions of voluntarism, for I think it is not only essential to good religion but also necessary to being fully human.

But I'm not packing . . . yet.

Turning Points in Baptist History[1]

In the year 2009 Baptists will celebrate a huge 400th birthday party. Born in 1609, Baptists began, as all infants, struggling to survive. Today, however, Baptists number forty-three million people in more than 200 countries in every continent of the world. Hassled, heckled, and persecuted both in England and America in the seventeenth century, Baptists of the twenty-first century have become the largest Protestant denominational family in North America. Baptists have come a very long way!

A diverse group from their beginning, Baptists express themselves today in such a variety of ways that many who claim the Baptist name will not claim others who claim the very same name! Baptists differ today—and they did from their beginning—in what they believe, how they worship, their attitudes toward other Christians, and their understanding of what is important in Christian discipleship. A history of four centuries of fragmentation and controversy has only compounded the complex appearance of the Baptist family. It is, therefore, impossible to speak of Baptists as a monolithic group. No single tradition or group of Baptists captures the enormous variety in Baptist life.

One can, however, identify some of the more prominent "convictional genes" of Baptists generally. One way of identifying these genes is to understand some of the pivotal turning points in the history of the Baptist people. The following describes six such pivotal points which go a long way in characterizing many of the people called Baptists.

The Turn toward a Believers' Church: 1609

The Lutherans have Martin Luther. Presbyterians have John Calvin. Methodists have John Wesley. But whom do Baptists have? In keeping with their description as a "common" people, Baptists appropriately trace their

---

[1] I wrote this brief essay as the introductory pamphlet to the pamphlet series entitled *The Baptist Style for a New Century*. It is reprinted by permission of the Baptist History and Heritage Society, Brentwood, Tennessee, and of the William H. Whitsitt Baptist Heritage Society, Atlanta. It is printed here essentially unaltered except that endnotes have become footnotes. To order copies of pamphlets in the series, contact the Baptist History and Heritage Society, P.O. Box 728, Brentwood TN 37024-0728.

origin to an Englishman with the most common of names: John Smyth (Smith).

A clergyman of the Church of England and a graduate of Cambridge University, Smyth pioneered the Baptist tradition. Thomas Helwys, a wealthy layman, worked side by side with Smyth. Eventually Helwys became even more important for later Baptists than Smyth.

Reared as Anglicans (Episcopalians), Smyth and Helwys, like many Christians in the early seventeenth century, wanted genuine reform in their church. Using the Bible as their guide, they sought to restore what they believed to be the biblical model of the church. They wanted to "purify" the Church of England, as did other Puritans, of all traces of Roman Catholic practices. So Smyth and Helwys were Anglicans who became Puritans. But they even went beyond Puritanism.

Some Puritans became so impatient with the church's reforms that they "separated" from the Church of England, setting up independent congregations of believers. Smyth and Helwys became part of such a group of Separatists in Gainsborough, England, in 1606. These Separatists had three beliefs which shaped later Baptists.

First, they believed that the Bible, not church tradition or religious creeds, was their guide in all matters of faith and practice. Second, they believed that the church should be made up of believers only, not all people born into the local parishes. Third, they believed that the church should be governed by those believers, not by church bishops.

Harassed and hounded by both the Church of England and the civil government for their beliefs, Smyth and Helwys, along with their small congregation of believers, sailed in 1607 to Holland to breathe the fresh air of religious freedom. There, Baptists met and were influenced by Anabaptists. While in Holland Baptists experienced their first major turning point. In fact, the Baptist movement marks its beginning in Amsterdam.

In 1609 John Smyth performed a radical and scandalous act. He baptized himself by pouring water on his head! In turn he baptized Helwys and others of the congregation. Smyth, Helwys, and their church came to believe that their infant baptism was no baptism at all. Why? Because, they said, it was performed by a false church, and it was performed on infants—people who *could not* believe.

Many people think that the single most important characteristic of Baptists is the way they baptize—by immersion. However, when Baptists began in the early seventeenth century, they were first concerned with *whom* rather than *how* they baptized. Baptists wanted churches made up of people who sincerely, deliberately, and freely affirmed Christ as the Lord of their lives. They wanted a Believers' Church.

The Separatists had also wanted a church made up of only "saints." But they did so by retaining infant baptism. Smyth and Helwys left the Separatists and began the Baptist movement when they rejected infant baptism in 1609. They concluded that believer's baptism was the best way to guarantee a Believers' Church.

In the tradition initiated by Smyth and Helwys, only believers made up the churches. But for these Baptists, believers alone also governed the churches. Separatists had believed in congregational church government, but they often gave a superior role to the clergy over the laity. Not Baptists! Each believer had an equal voice in the affairs of the church.

Likewise, each believer was looked upon as a minister within the church. Known as the universal ministry or the priesthood of all believers, Baptists utilized this concept to argue that the work of Christ belonged to all Christians, not merely the clergy. In Baptist life the "clergy" have a respected place but not a unique place, for all Christians are ministers.

The Turn toward a Free Conscience: 1612

Religious fussing and fighting dominated the seventeenth century. Contention led to division. As Smyth and Helwys had separated first from the Anglicans, next the Puritans, then the Separatists, they finally ended by separating from each other. Why was this? Because Smyth eventually questioned the authenticity of his self-administered baptism because it had no succession with the larger Christian church. Helwys and a few others disagreed, thinking that succession of baptism was not necessary. They retained their newfound baptism, nurtured their small church fellowship, and courageously returned to England and established the first Baptist church on English soil in 1612.

The return of Thomas Helwys to his native England cost him his life. Just as John Smyth had the audacity to baptize himself, Thomas Helwys had the spunk to write a fiery little book on freedom of conscience in an era when freedom was scarce and individual conscience suppressed. Brashly, Helwys autographed a personal copy and sent it to, of all people, the king of England!

The publication in 1612 of Helwys's book, *A Short Declaration of the Mystery of Iniquity*, was the second turning point in Baptist history. Based upon Paul's phrase in 2 Thessalonians 2:7, Helwys interpreted "the mystery of iniquity" as the spirit of domination and oppression in matters of conscience which existed in his native land.

Lauded as the first full plea for religious freedom in the English language, Helwys's *Mystery of Iniquity* is surely one of the classics of Baptist history. It contains one of the most oft-quoted passages from Baptist history. Said Helwys:

> For we do freely profess that our lord the king has no more power over their consciences [Roman Catholics] than over ours, and that is none at all. For our lord the king is but an earthly king, and he has no authority as a king but in earthly causes. And if the king's people be obedient and true subjects, obeying all human laws made by the king, our lord the king can require no more. For men's religion to God is between God and themselves. The king shall not answer for it. Neither may the king be judge between God and man. Let them be heretics, Turks, Jews, or whatsoever, it appertains not to the earthly power to punish them in the least measure. This is made evident to our lord the king by the scriptures.[2]

With such strong language, one is not surprised to discover that Helwys died in prison.

In this Baptist classic, Helwys moved in and out of several other themes related to the Baptist emphasis on freedom of conscience. Among those themes were the freedom of the local congregation to mind its own affairs; the freedom of individuals to interpret scripture; the importance of believer's baptism and the freedom of the individual to choose that baptism; the freedom of and the need for the churches of Jesus Christ to live from voluntary support of its members; the freedom from coerced uniformity in worship practices; and the freedom of the churches to acknowledge Christ as the sole "King" of the church, rather than being bound by creed or clergy or civil government.

During the first half of the seventeenth century, Baptists in England peppered both royalty and religion with some of the first and most forceful tracts ever written on religious liberty. Baptists in America, especially Roger Williams and John Clarke, joined their English counterparts in this war on religious tyranny. Baptists led the parade for universal liberty of conscience. Thomas Helwys, Roger Williams, John Clarke, and a host of

---

[2]Thomas Helwys, *A Short Declaration of the Mystery of Iniquity (1611/1612)*, edited and introduced by Richard Groves, Classics of Religious Liberty (Macon GA: Mercer University Press, 1998) 53.

other Baptist leaders were the Baptist drum majors for freedom in the seventeenth century!

The Turn toward Believer's Baptism by Immersion: 1641

The earliest Baptists, the Helwys group, came to be known as General Baptists. They believed that the death of Christ was effective for any and all people who claimed Christ as Lord. Another group, known as Particular Baptists, developed shortly after Helwys returned to England in 1612. Particular Baptists got their name from the fact that they believed that the death of Christ on the cross was only for the predestined or elect. The Particular Baptists were Calvinists while the General Baptists rejected Calvinism.

Whereas the General Baptists had affirmed believer's baptism, they had done so without practicing it by immersion. By 1641, however, the Particular Baptists of England took another momentous step regarding baptism. They began to practice believer's baptism *by immersion*. This is the third turning point in Baptist history.

Baptists began to practice believer's baptism by immersion for the same reason they had affirmed their belief in a believer's church and freedom of conscience. They thought the New Testament taught immersion as the form of baptism. Willing to be corrected from scripture, early Baptists would not have any belief imposed upon them but that commanded by Christ. They said that they would never go "against the least tittle of the truth of God, or against the light of our own conscience."[3] Baptists wanted to be free to follow their consciences in obeying Holy Scripture.

Following their reading of scripture, especially Colossians 2:12 and Romans 6:4, Baptists concluded that the manner of believer's baptism should be by dipping the body into water, resembling death to self and resurrection to the Christian life. To this day all Baptist churches practice believer's baptism by immersion, though some Baptist churches will accept Christians from other churches who have been baptized by other modes.

The Turn toward Cooperative Christianity: 1707

Baptists from their beginnings cherished congregational church govern-ment. Often referred to in Baptist life as the "autonomy" (self-rule) of the

---

[3]As cited in William L. Lumpkin, *Baptist Confessions of Faith*, rev. ed. (Valley Forge PA: Judson Press, 1969) 149.

local church or as the "independence" of the local church, congregational church government simply meant that the congregation of believers was the final authority in determining the will of God in Baptist church life. No bishop or pastor or pope or conference of churches or civil government had a say-so over the religious affairs of a Baptist congregation.

A fourth major turning point for Baptists in America occurred in 1707. In that year Baptists formed the Philadelphia Baptist Association, the first major Baptist organization through which several local churches worked together without compromising their congregational independence. Baptists in England, both General and Particular, had organized associations as early as the 1640s.

With the formation of the Philadelphia Baptist Association, Baptists in America, therefore, affirmed their belief in the interdependence as well as independence of local churches. Following the basic pattern of organization laid down by the Philadelphia Association, Baptist associations evolved all over America. Later, Baptists formed other Baptist organizations such as societies, state conventions, national conventions, and the Baptist World Alliance through which they cooperated and pooled their resources.

Baptists often vaguely defined the purposes of Baptist associations in such language as "to promote the interest of the Redeemer's kingdom and the good of the common cause." Usually one could identify four main objectives of these nonlocal-church Baptist organizations. These were (1) to promote fellowship among the churches; (2) to affirm commonly held beliefs; (3) to provide counsel and assistance to local churches; and (4) to establish a structure through which churches could cooperate in their broader ministries, ministries such as theological education, publications, and mission work.

In terms of church government, Baptists viewed associations and other such Baptist organizations as autonomous bodies functioning in an advisory role for the churches. Baptists, however, have always been far more interested in the freedom and independence of the local churches than in extending the powers of associations and other denominational bodies. On the other hand, Baptists in America began stressing in 1707 the interdependence of the churches and denominational cooperation. Additionally, English Baptists, American Baptists, and several of the black Baptist groups in America have cooperated extensively with other Christian denominations in ecumenical activities. Christian cooperation does not begin and end with Baptists.

The Turn toward Missionary Responsibility: 1792

During the 1700s Baptists in both England and America profited from the spirit of revivalism that dominated much of that century. In England the Wesleyan revival led by Methodists John and Charles Wesley indirectly helped to revitalize the Calvinistic Particular Baptists and virtually resurrected the dying General Baptists.

George Whitefield, an associate of the Wesleys and maybe the greatest English preacher of the eighteenth century, toured America seven times, fanning the fires of revivalism begun under Jonathan Edwards. Baptists in America varied in their reactions to the emotional preaching of Whitefield, but when the revivalistic fires waned, Baptists had reaped as many benefits from revivalism as any denomination in America. No Christian has symbolized the continuing emphasis of revivalism as has evangelist Billy Graham, a Baptist.

While revivalism massaged a somewhat sagging Baptist denomination in the eighteenth century, global missions fired the Baptist spirit near the end of that century. Christian denominations at this time were not taking seriously the missionary mandate of the New Testament. But a poor shoe cobbler by the name of William Carey could not get Jesus' words of "Go ye into all the world" off his heart and mind. Preaching, pleading, sometimes nagging, Carey urged Particular Baptists to "expect great things from God" and "attempt great things for God."

As a result of Carey's influence, Baptists in England formed a missionary society in the town of Kettering on October 2, 1792. The purpose was simple: to take the gospel of Christ to people in distant lands. This is the fifth significant turning point in Baptist history. This act on the part of British Baptists revolutionized Baptist life and influenced much of the rest of Protestant Christianity toward missions.

William Carey sailed as a missionary to India in 1793 where he devoted the rest of his life. His letters aroused the missionary ardor of Baptists in both England and America. By the end of the century Baptists in America began organizing and contributing in support of foreign missions. In 1814, under the leadership of Luther Rice, Baptists in America formed their first national convention whose sole purpose was to send missionaries overseas. Since the time of Carey and Rice, Baptists have been at the forefront of sharing the gospel and ministering in Christ's name throughout the world. A famous German Baptist, Johann Oncken, adopted as his motto "Every Baptist a missionary."

The Turn toward Social Justice: 1955

In 1955 a bright, young Baptist preacher in Montgomery, Alabama, led a bus boycott that turned into a national struggle for racial justice. Martin Luther King, Jr., pastor of the Dexter Avenue Baptist Church, symbolized the Baptist struggle for social justice as much as Billy Graham personified evangelism, William Carey embodied foreign missions, and Thomas Helwys and Roger Williams incarnated liberty of conscience.

One should not assume by any means, however, that all Baptists agreed with King. Many of his white Baptist kinfolk, especially in the South, and some of his black Baptist brothers and sisters resisted King's efforts and strategies to rid the nation of racial segregation. But as King moved the conscience of the nation, he also moved the hearts of many of his Baptist people. Arrested twenty-nine times for challenging the cultural status quo in America and winner of the Nobel Peace Prize in 1964, King died of the hatred of an assassin's bullet in Memphis, Tennessee, in 1968.

The Baptist concern for social justice reached its apex with King, but it did not begin with him. Even his strategy of civil disobedience had been practiced by Baptists such as Isaac Backus in the struggle for religious justice in America years before King came on the Baptist scene. Also, Roger Williams and John Clarke served as prophets for justice in the seventeenth century.

Walter Rauschenbusch, a New York Baptist with a warm evangelical faith, was the father of the Social Gospel in America. Before he died in 1918 he had advocated, among other things, social reform of poverty and economic injustice based upon biblical and theological principles. Likewise, the Baptist World Alliance, founded in 1905, has put much of its energy and effort in the struggle for human rights around the world. No Baptist, however, had been the cheerleader for justice as had Martin Luther King, Jr.

Conclusion

No Christian denomination is well served by thinking it is the only one God has. No denomination is well served by wallowing in delusions of its own righteousness while minimizing the values of other religious groups. Baptists, like other Christian groups, have suffered from those delusions periodically. We Baptists have our sins to confess.

But Baptists also have some significant gifts to bring to the larger Christian table. Among those gifts are our struggle for a believers' church, our devotion to liberty of conscience, our desire for a baptism freely chosen and reflective of biblical teachings, our confession of both the independence and interdependence of local churches, our commitment to the missionary mandate, and our commitment, though checkered, to social justice. Upon these hinge issues, Baptist history has turned.

Questions for discussion

1. Can one have a Believers' Church without the practice of baptism by immersion? Does the act of baptizing young children threaten the concept of a Believers' Church? How many nonresident members does your church have? What does that say about the struggle for a Believers' Church?
2. The Baptist emphasis on liberty of conscience has issued into the separation of church and state. At what points in American society are these twin Baptist emphases endangered?
3. What are the current dangers to the independence of local Baptist churches?
4. How can Baptists regain the missionary passion of William Carey?
5. How can Baptists continue the legacy of Martin Luther King, Jr. regarding racial justice?

The Baptist Identity and the Baptist Manifesto[1]

Baptists do not agree on where they came from, who they are, or how they got that way. In other words, Baptists do not agree on their historical origin, their theological identity, or their subsequent denominational history. The widely circulated and highly stimulating document "Re-Envisioning Baptist Identity: A Manifesto for Baptist Communities in North America"[2] surfaces yet again for Baptists the important issues of origin, identity, and history. The Manifesto's primary concern appears to be the theological identity of Baptists at the end of the twentieth century, but theological identity for the Manifesto, and for the rest of us, is inevitably related to historical origins and subsequent history.

James McClendon, the theological father of the Manifesto, suggested that the Manifesto is a "conversation among friends." Count this article as a friendly talk back to the Manifesto about the Baptist identity. It is important that I talk back because some people assumed, correctly or not, that the original draft of the document was to some degree directed at my 1993 book *The Baptist Identity*. Robert P. Jones's careful and critical contrast and critique of both the original draft of the Manifesto and *The Baptist Identity* appeared to document this assumption.[3] But Baptists, especially Baptist historians, should study the Manifesto and talk back to it, not only because they have been invited to do so, but because profiling the Baptist identity in a so-called postdenominational era and at the beginning of a new millennium is no minor matter. In my talk back that follows I have sincere affirmations to share, serious reservations to voice, and honest questions to ask. Focusing my talk back primarily on Baptist history, I want first to visit briefly the issue of Baptist identity. Following

---

[1]This article first appeared in *Perspectives in Religious Studies* 25/4 (Winter 1998): 321-40, and is now also available online at <http://www.mercer.edu/baptist studies/addresses/Baptist%20Manifesto.htm>. It is reprinted here with the permission of *Perspectives in Religious Studies*.

[2]"Re-Envisioning Baptist Identity: A Manifesto for Baptist Communities in North America," *Perspectives in Religious Studies* 24/3 (Fall 1997): 303-10. Hereafter, Manifesto.

[3]See Robert P. Jones, "Re-Envisioning Baptist Identity from a Theocentric Perspective: An Essay on the Occasion of James M. Gustafson's Gift to the McAfee School of Theology at Mercer University," unpublished paper, Emory University, 29 June 1998.

that I will address two of the major emphases of the Manifesto: the individual-communal nature of Baptist life and the notion of freedom in Baptist history. The historical issues, namely, those of Baptist origins and the historical development of Baptists, important as they are, must wait for another day.[4]

Interpretations of the Baptist Identity

What is it that lies at the *center* of the Baptist vision of Christianity? Do Baptists have a *core value* from which the rest of their life emerges? What is our essential spiritual significance, our interior determinant? Is there a singular Baptist idea, ethos, or impulse out of which we live our lives of faith? The late Robert G. Torbet, revered American Baptist historian, suggested that, rather than pointing to one integrating factor, one must identify a group of principles that constitutes the Baptist identity. In the end, he may have been correct.[5]

A number of other Baptist historians and theologians, however, I included, have sought to discover a "core value" or a single hermeneutical motif around which one can cluster and interpret the several Baptist distinctives. Some of these motifs have been developed expansively and related comprehensively to Baptist theology, while others have simply been noted without much elaboration. Examples of some twentieth-century inter-

---

[4]For an interpretation of the historical development of Baptists from the *Manifesto* perspective, see Curtis W. Freeman, "Can Baptist Theology Be Revisioned?" *Perspectives in Religious Studies* 24/3 (Fall 1997): 273-302.

[5]See Robert G. Torbet, *A History of the Baptists* (Philadelphia: Judson Press, 1950) 15-34. Torbet listed the following as Baptist principles: the Bible as the norm for faith and practice, the church as composed of baptized believers, the priesthood of believers and the autonomy of the local congregation, and religious liberty and the separation of church and state. Others before and after Torbet have taken the same approach of delineating the Baptist identity by listing a group of principles. While often the lists of principles vary, they do not do so in major ways. See, as examples, William Bullein Johnson, *The Gospel Developed through the Government and Order of the Churches of Jesus Christ* (Richmond: H. K. Ellyson, 1846) 16; A. H. Newman, *A History of the Baptist Churches in the United States* (New York: Scribner's, 1894) 1-8; Henry Cook, *What Baptists Stand For* (London: Carey Kingsgate Press, 1947), and "Towards a Baptist Identity: A Statement Ratified by the Baptist Heritage Commission of the Baptist World Alliance," July 1989, in Walter B. Shurden, *The Baptist Identity* (Macon GA: Smyth & Helwys Publishing Inc., 1993) 66.

preters and their "core values" are as follows: E. Y. Mullins, "soul competency"; James D. Freeman, "the sovereignty of Christ" and "His personal, direct, and undelegated authority over the souls of men"; Walter Rauschenbusch, "experimental religion"; W. T. Whitley, "the doctrine of the church"; H. Wheeler Robinson, "spiritual individualism"; a British Baptist Statement of 1948, "the evangelical experience"; James Wm. McClendon, Jr., "shared awareness of the present Christian community as the primitive community and the eschatological community"; William H. Brackney, "believers' baptism by immersion" and "the voluntary spirit"; Eric H. Ohlmann, "soteriology"; E. Glenn Hinson, "voluntarism"; Glen Stassen, "the Lordship of Christ"; and Philip Thompson, "the two-fold freedom of God."[6]

Significantly, while many of these interpreters utilized a single hermeneutical theme, they often began or concluded by listing a set of

---

[6]For these interpreters and their interpretations in the order listed above, see E. Y. Mullins, *The Axioms of Religion* (Philadelphia: American Baptist Publication Society, 1908); John D. Freeman, "The Place of Baptists in the Christian Church," in *The Life of Baptists in the Life of the World*, ed. Walter B. Shurden (Nashville: Broadman Press, 1985) 19-29; Walter Rauschenbusch, "Why I Am a Baptist," in *A Baptist Treasury*, ed. Sydnor L. Stealey (New York: Thomas Y. Crowell Company, 1958) 163-84; W. T. Whitley, *A History of British Baptists*, 2nd ed. (London: Kingsgate Press, 1932) 4; H. Wheeler Robinson, *The Life and Faith of the Baptists*, rev. ed. (London: Kingsgate Press, 1946) 123; "The Baptist Doctrine of the Church," in Shurden, *The Baptist Identity*, 94; James Wm. McClendon, Jr., *Systematic Theology: Ethics* (Nashville: Abingdon Press, 1986) 31; William H. Brackney, " 'Commonly (Though Falsely) Called . . . ': Reflections on the Search for Baptist Identity," *Perspectives in Religious Studies* 13/4 (Winter 1986): 67-82, and "Voluntarism Is a Flagship of the Baptist Tradition," in *Defining Baptist Convictions: Guidelines for the Twenty-First Century*, ed. Charles W. Deweese (Franklin TN: Providence House Publishers, 1996) 86-94; Eric H. Ohlmann, "The Essence of Baptists: A Reexamination," *Perspectives in Religious Studies* 13/4 (Winter 1986): 83-104; E. Glenn Hinson, "The Changing Face of Baptists: A Global Perspective," *The Whitsitt Journal* 5/2 (Winter 1998): 7-10, and Hinson's four chapters in *Are Southern Baptists "Evangelicals"?* by James Leo Garrett, Jr., E. Glenn Hinson, and James E. Tull (Macon GA: Mercer University Press, 1983) 131-94; Glen Stassen, "Finding the Evidence for Christ-Centered Discipleship in Baptist Origins by Opening Menno Simons's *Foundation Book*," unpublished paper; Philip E. Thompson, "People of the Free God: The Passion of Seventeenth-Century Baptists," *American Baptist Quarterly* 15/3 (September 1996): 223-41.

principles very similar to Torbet's.[7] Most such integrative approaches have been more of an effort to construct a door of entrance to understanding the Baptist identity than a crusade to define dogmatically the denominational identity in any singular or exclusive way. The motif, in other words, functions in a hermeneutical, not reductionistic, fashion. In truth, I find myself nodding affirmatively in reading most of the interpretations, much at some of them, only some at a few of them. Surely personal preferences will pull a Baptist toward one motif or another, but one can, in my judgment, take any number of these several approaches as long as one draws near to the cluster of remarkably similar "principles" Torbet and so many others have identified.

In *The Baptist Identity* I utilized the category of "freedom" as an integrative motif for understanding Baptist life,[8] coming down unhesitatingly on the importance of the individual in Baptist life and speaking of "individualism" as a proper component of the Baptist identity. In doing so,

---

[7]Illustrative of this pattern are Mullins, McClendon, Stassen, and Shurden, among others.

[8]Like most everything else, my selection of the word "freedom" has a history. It came as a result of a 1985 book I compiled, consisting of addresses delivered at the Baptist World Congresses from 1905 to 1985. In my judgment, if you want to know the essence of Baptist Christianity today, you must transcend national, regional, theological, and ethnic peculiarities; the best, and maybe *only*, place to accomplish that is to go to the proceedings of the Baptist World Alliance. In going there I of course assumed some general continuity of the BWA in the twentieth century with the previous three centuries of Baptist life. In the conclusion of that book I wrote, "So if there is a single, recurring, and almost monotonous theme in these BWA documents, it is that of *freedom*." See Shurden, ed. *The Life of Baptists*, 255. Frankly, I preferred then and prefer now the word "voluntary" or "voluntarism" to describe the central motif of Baptist life. But a careful student of the English language cautioned against the use of the word, saying, "The average person will not know what 'voluntarism' means." I think that is probably correct. But I am not at all sure the average person knows what the word "freedom" means either. I also considered using the word "choice" as a motif but discarded it because of its association with the abortion debate. So I settled on "freedom" and used the word to describe, not a single Baptist distinctive, but a specific *style* of faith, a distinctive *posture* of faith, a particular *attitude* toward the issues of faith. In *The Baptist Identity* I applied "freedom" (voluntarism) to the Baptist view of salvation, which I called "Soul Freedom," to the Baptist view of religious authority ("Bible Freedom"), to the Baptist view of church ("Church Freedom"), and to the Baptist view of the state ("Religious Freedom").

however, I very deliberately sought to cast the concepts within polarities.[9] Not one but several polarities are necessary if one is to understand properly the Baptist identity: faith and freedom, freedom and responsibility, liberty and loyalty, the sovereignty of God and human freedom, independence and interdependence, and the individual and community. Regarding the latter, I said that Baptist life historically affirms the theme of "the individual *in* community." The Baptist vision of Christianity certainly does not envision individuals apart from churches, and it is impossible to conceive of the churches apart from individuals. Even when gladly siding with Stewart A. Newman on the centrality of the freedom and responsibility of the individual in the Free Church tradition, I quickly added:

> This is not, however, spiritual lone rangerism. While the individual is central, the individual is always an "individual in community." Baptists do not understand the story line of the Bible as simply the heroic achievements of isolated individuals. Abraham, Moses, David, Jeremiah, Peter, and Paul are not pictured in the Bible as invincible individualists who, in their isolation, whipped the forces of evil. They are portrayed as people in community—Israel in the Old Testament and the Church in the New Testament—who are aware of historical identity and treasured traditions. They are in need of the genuine value of relationships.[10]

So, while utilizing the concept of "freedom" as one approach to understanding the Baptist vision, I did so by beginning with the individual and

---

[9]This is no novel approach to be sure. For an explicit but abbreviated example of the use of polarities and one that also utilized the individual-community motif, see Stanley Grenz's presidential address at the 1990 National Association of Baptist Professors of Religion (NABPR) meeting in New Orleans, "Maintaining the Balanced Life: The Baptist Vision of Spirituality," *Perspectives in Religious Studies* 18/1 (Spring 1991): 59-68. The late Penrose St. Amant appropriated often and extensively the polarities approach in his writings about Baptists: see my "C. Penrose St. Amant: Interpreter of the Baptist Vision," in this volume and also in *Perspectives in Religious Studies* 16/4 (Winter 1989): 73-87.

[10]Shurden, *The Baptist Identity*, 34; see also 4, 26, 27, 56; and see Walter B. Shurden, ed., *Proclaiming the Baptist Vision: The Church* (Macon GA: Smyth & Helwys, 1996) 9; "Southern Baptist Theology Today: An Interview with Walter Shurden," *The Theological Educator* 36 (Fall 1987): 27. Stewart A. Newman's book is *A Free Church Perspective: A Study in Ecclesiology* (Wake Forest NC: Stevens Book Press, 1986).

deliberately sought to encase the emphasis on individualism within the polarity of "individuals-in-community."

The Manifesto, proposing a Baptist "vision of freedom, faithfulness, and community," has different emphases. It calls Baptists to faithful discipleship, stressing "community" as the "core value" of Baptists while taking pains to describe what freedom is and is not. After an introduction that stresses the nature of freedom, the Manifesto makes five affirmations, concluding each affirmation with a "call" to other Baptists for adopting a free, faithful, and communal identity. The five affirmations are followed as a group by a conclusion. The Manifesto's first affirmation deals with the Bible, the second with discipleship, the third with the church, the fourth with the ordinances, and the fifth with a disestablished church that witnesses publicly to society.

The Individual/Communal Polarity and the Baptist Identity

The Manifesto stresses the "communal" nature of Baptist Christianity over against the individual dimension. In reading the Manifesto I often find myself saying, "I second the motion—some!" I "second the motion—some" in relation to the emphasis on community. In the first place, one can and should argue for the centrality of the church in Baptist life. Indeed, one may accurately say that what Baptists have given to the Christian world is an ecclesiology, not a theology. For someone to stress a "believers'-church theology" as basic to Baptist life should not be mysterious to any Baptist historian.[11] The church is an altogether valid hermeneutical "core value" for understanding the Baptist identity as long as one does not ignore the role of the individual.

Second, the Manifesto has touched an extremely vulnerable point in Baptist Christianity specifically and in Protestant Christianity generally. The Roman Catholic Church, however, has been making this very point ever since the Protestant Reformation. Without question, Baptists have often drifted into a perverted privatistic faith. One can find all types of narcissism in Baptist life—political, economic, romantic, liturgical, vocational, and spiritual. The Baptist tendency toward the privatizing of faith surely does not need to be documented for the readers of this journal [*Perspectives in Religious Studies*, wherein this essay first appeared].

---

[11]See, for example, Ernest A. Payne, *The Fellowship of Believers: Baptist Thought and Practice Yesterday and Today* (London: Carey Kingsgate Press, 1952).

With all the dangers Baptists face in privatizing and overly individualizing discipleship, the Manifesto, because of its studied, strained, and unfortunate deemphasis on the role of the individual, nonetheless fails to paint a balanced picture of the Baptist identity. Present throughout the document, this recurring antithesis of the concept of community over against that of the individual occurs most clearly in the first two affirmations, those dealing with the Bible and discipleship. I shall address these below.

The Manifesto says: "We affirm Bible study in reading communities rather than relying on private interpretation or supposed 'scientific' objectivity." Later in the same affirmation: "Scripture wisely forbids and we reject every form of private interpretation that makes Bible reading a practice which can be carried out according to the dictates of individual conscience (2 Peter 1:20-21)." And further: "We therefore cannot commend Bible study that is insulated from the community of believers or that guarantees individual readers an unchecked privilege of interpretation."[12]

My first response on reading this was to ask very earnestly as some others have done, "Are you serious or are you just pulling our Baptist legs?" Here appears part of the enormous influence of Stanley Hauerwas on the Manifesto. Hauerwas, professor at Duke Divinity School and one of the most creative and provocative ethicists/theologians working today, suggested taking the Bible out of the hands of individual Christians. Hauerwas says that "No task is more important than for the church to take the Bible out of the hands of individual Christians in North America."[13] Hauerwas continued, horrendously to my Baptist ears:

> I certainly believe that God uses the Scripture to help keep the church faithful, but I do not believe, in the church's current circumstance, that each person in the church thereby is given the right to interpret the Scripture. Such a presumption derives from the corrupt egalitarian politics of democratic regimes, not from the politics of the church. The latter, as I will try to show, knows that the "right" reading of Scripture depends on having spiritual masters who can help the whole church stand under the authority of God's Word.[14]

---

[12]*Manifesto*, 304-305.

[13]Stanley Hauerwas, *Unleashing the Scripture: Freeing the Bible from Captivity to America* (Nashville: Abingdon, 1993) 15.

[14]Hauerwas, *Unleashing the Scripture*, 16.

Hauerwas fails to make clear which "politics of the church" he means, but the appropriate Baptist response to this kind of theologizing is that Baptists were born reacting to and rejecting the idea of "spiritual masters." The right and responsibility of private interpretation of Scripture is most certainly part of the "politics" of Baptist church polity. One may argue that Baptists, along with many other Protestants, are theologically wrong in calling for the personal interpretation of Scripture, but one cannot argue that Baptists historically have not embraced the idea. The fact of the matter is that Baptist history contradicts this kind of theologizing. While the Manifesto is not nearly as bold or extreme in its statement as Hauerwas, both Hauerwas and the Manifesto are very far in this regard from what I understand both the Protestant and the historical Baptist point of view to be. In this connection, I am not sure I have ever seen a statement on the Baptist identity proposing the denial of private interpretation of Scripture prior to the Manifesto.

Seventeenth-century Baptists on both sides of the Atlantic were unmistakably clear about their right and responsibility to go to Scripture for themselves. The Second London Confession [1677] argued that Scripture should be translated from Hebrew and Greek because "these original tongues are not known to all the people of God, who have a right unto, and interest in the Scriptures, and are commanded in the fear of God to read and search them."[15] In the colonies John Clarke, the most significant Baptist in seventeenth-century New England, admonished the individual Christian "to search the Scriptures and therein to wait for the power and glory of the spirit of God."[16] Obadiah Holmes, Clarke's successor and friend at Newport, while urging his church members to honor their future clergy, said:

> Be much with God in secret; try what you hear whether it be according to truth, and take nothing from any man until you have tried it and well

---

[15]As cited in William L. Lumpkin, *Baptist Confessions of Faith*, rev. ed. (Valley Forge PA: Judson Press, 1969) 251. See also Thomas Helwys, *A Short Declaration of the Mystery of Iniquity (1611/1612)*, edited and introduced by Richard Groves, Classics of Religious Liberty 1 (Macon GA: Mercer University Press, 1998) 15, 42-43, 55.

[16]John Clarke, *Ill Newes from New-England, or, A Narrative of New England's Persecution* (1652), as reprinted in *Colonial Baptists, Massachusetts and Rhode Island*, Baptist Tradition series, Edwin S. Gaustad, advisory editor (New York: Arno Press, 1980) 21.

digested it by a good understanding. Often examine yourselves, and lean not to other men's judgments; beware of falls; endeavor and see that your evidence be good, which is alone the Spirit of God with your own spirit according to the Scriptures. Be much in holy meditation; read the Scriptures carefully.[17]

A casual reading of Obadiah Holmes's seventeenth-century document, "Testimony to the Church," reveals the clear sanctioning of private interpretation of Scripture, a substantial dose of healthy individualism, and a firm commitment to the local community of believers, all within the context of a theological Calvinism so strict that most Baptists today would have difficulty squeezing into it. For Baptists, private interpretation of Scripture is not a post-Enlightenment appropriation of democratic individualism and egalitarianism; it is part of their earliest seventeenth-century heritage.[18]

The Manifesto, in its zeal for advocating a legitimate role for the community of believers, negates a powerful part of the Baptist heritage concerning the individual. Not only so, but the Manifesto references a highly questionable verse of Scripture (2 Peter 1:20-21) in doing so. No part of the Baptist tradition that I am familiar with proposes that final, ultimate, and absolute authority is invested in individual interpretation. The individual is always an "individual-in-community" in Baptist life. So while agreeing that no Baptist individual has papal-like freedom to interpret Scripture in any final sense, one seriously wonders what "community of believers" the Manifesto would authorize to "check" the individual's interpretation.

---

[17]Cited in Edwin S. Gaustad, ed. *Baptist Piety: The Last Will and Testament of Obadiah Holmes* (Grand Rapids MI: Christian University Press, 1978) 109-10; see also 80, 111. Historian Edwin S. Gaustad said of Holmes's words that "much of Christian liberty and Baptist polity can be read in these words" (107). For further examples of the role of individual judgment and interpretation of scripture, see "The Baptist Debate of April 14-15, 1668," ed. William G. McLoughlin and Martha Whiting Davidson, in *Colonial Baptists, Massachusetts and Rhode Island*, Edwin S. Gaustad, advisory editor (New York: Arno Press, 1980) 111, 113, 119, 133; and John Russel, "A Brief Narrative," in *The History of the First Baptist Church of Boston, 1665–1689*, ed. Nathan E. Wood (New York: Arno Press, 1980) 159-60.

[18]While I personally admire but would not list Anabaptist Balthasar Hubmaier among "Baptist" theologians, my sense is that the *Manifesto* might want to do so. So hear Hubmaier on the issue of interpretation of Scripture: "Since every Christian believes for himself and is baptized for himself, everyone must see and judge by the Scriptures whether he is being properly nourished by his pastor." Cited in Lumpkin, *Baptist Confessions of Faith*, 21.

Frankly, I hope it is the local congregation of believers and that the Manifesto is not suggesting an authoritarian connectionalism in Baptist life that our congregationalism will not support.[19] It would help if the Manifesto unpacked the meaning of "community" as it relates practically and in polity-issues to Baptist life.

If the fear driving the Manifesto's statement is the idea that any Baptist can believe anything she or he wishes and remain in a local congregation of Baptist believers, one has some sympathy. Baptists have never endorsed or embraced that kind of theological anarchy. However, the importance of the individual, including the individual's free access and encouragement to read and interpret the Bible, while admittedly freighted with difficulties, as the Catholic Church has long and rightly claimed,[20] is basic to an understanding of the Baptist identity. Moreover, one has the sense that the Manifesto is concerned more with "authority" and "order" than with "freedom." This is a long-standing tension in Baptist life.

Two relatively recent statements on the Baptist identity, one from Europe and one from America, reflect a far more balanced approach than that exhibited in the Manifesto. The statement known as "Baptist Distinctives and Diversities," drafted in 1964 not by one but by *six* different Baptist denominational bodies in North America said, "The Christian is free to read the Bible and be guided to its meaning by the Holy Spirit. In becoming a part of the witness of a local church, however, one's freedom in doctrinal interpretation and personal behavior is tempered by the convictions and needs of the community of believers."[21] In a similar vein, a study paper issued by the Division for Theology and Education of the European Baptist Federation as recently as 1993 said, "While individual believers must always allow their interpretation of Scripture to be illuminated by the understanding of the wider Christian community, they

---

[19]McClendon was most certainly correct to state that "local church" is a redundancy. See James Wm. McClendon, Jr., *Systematic Theology: Doctrine* (Nashville: Abingdon, 1994) 366.

[20]See Daniel Donavan, *Dintinctively Catholic: An Exploration of Catholic Identity* (New York: Paulist Press, 1997) for an interesting Catholic comparison to the *Manifesto*. In his exposition of the Catholic identity, Donavan titled his first chapter "An Emphasis on Community." Like the *Manifesto*, Donavan emphasizes "community" throughout the book. However, Catholic Donavan appears surprisingly more sensitive than the *Manifesto* to what I am calling the Baptist emphasis on the individual. See Donavan, 30-31, 167.

[21]As cited in Shurden, *The Baptist Identity*, 72.

have the final right to discern for themselves what God is saying to them through the word and by the Spirit."[22] These two statements taken together suggest an accurate Baptist limitation on individual freedom. Given Baptist polity, however, only one of the limitations, the first, could be enforced.

In its second affirmation the Manifesto says: "We affirm following Jesus as a call to shared discipleship rather than invoking a theory of soul competency." And in the next paragraph it states: "We reject all accounts of following Jesus that construe faith as a private matter between God and the individual or as an activity of competent souls who inherently enjoy unmediated, unassailable, and disembodied experience with God."[23] Again, "I second the motion—some."

The Manifesto's rather harsh exclusion of "soul competency" and "all accounts" of following Jesus "as a private matter between God and the individual" is understandable on the one hand and troubling to the point of perplexity on the other. It is understandable because the privatization of faith appears on every hand in American culture today. Baptists, as stated above, are not now nor have they ever been exempt from such privatization. A church in my city recently sponsored a "JAM" session, a "Jesus and Me" seminar. It sounded too much like "He walks with *me* and talks with *me* and tells *me I* am His own."

But the Manifesto's statement on "shared discipleship" is troubling because of what it minimizes. Intended or not, there appears to be a lessening of the direct, personal nature of faith, the singular idea standing behind the concept of soul competency. What gives dynamism to the life of a Baptist church is the deep and devoted personal faith that individuals bring to the corporate body of believers. One hopes that the Manifesto is saying that faith is more than private rather than implying that it is not profoundly personal and deeply individualistic.

A personal faith born in the privacy of the human heart is of the essence of both Baptist and Protestant life. Carlyle Marney, another individualistic Baptist if ever there was one, spoke correctly when he denounced "bastard individualism." On the other hand, Marney never tired

---

[22]"What Are Baptists?: On the Way to Expressing Baptist Identity in a Changing Europe," A Study Paper issued by the Division for Theology and Education of the European Baptist Federation (1993) 4-5. (This study paper is conveniently available online at <http://www.rpc.ox.ac.uk/ohp/ebf_ident/ident_00.htm>.)

[23]*Manifesto*, 305.

of telling the story of the rabbi, the priest, and the average Protestant. Said Marney, "The rabbi begins, 'Thus saith the *Lord!*' The priest begins, 'As the *Church* has always said. . . . ' The average Protestant begins, 'Now, brethren, it seems to *me*. . . . ' " Marney said that the story was told as a joke at a Jewish-Christian dialogue. Then he added, "But I take it as a serious distinction! This is legitimate. The Protestant affirms his being, his selfhood. For it matters as to what 'it' seems to him. It is the thrust of his 'I am.' "[24] One may only add that most historians, non-Baptists as well as Baptists, have viewed Baptists as among the most individualistic of Protestants.

Long before Marney, however, Baptists uttered such experiential, individualistic, and private understandings of faith. Article XXV of the First London Confession of 1644 captures something of this when it said:

> That the tenders of the Gospel to the conversion of sinners, is absolutely free, no way requiring, as absolutely necessary, any qualifications, preparations, terrors of the Law, or preceding Ministry of the Law, but onely and alone the naked soule, as a sinner and ungodly to receive Christ, as crucified, dead, and buried, and risen againe, being made a Prince and a Saviour for such sinners.[25]

Thomas Helwys, and other seventeenth-century Baptists, stiff-armed the intervention of civil government in the life of the soul partly on the grounds that "men's religion to God is between God and themselves." Individuals, therefore, were accountable to God alone.[26] On this side of the

---

[24]Carlyle Marney, *Priests to Each Other* (Valley Forge PA: Judson Press, 1974) 42.

[25]Cited in Lumpkin, *Baptist Confessions of Faith*, 163.

[26]Helwys, *A Short Declaration of the Mystery of Iniquity*, 53. Something of this same argument may be seen among New England Baptists. See John Clarke, *Ill Newes from New-England*, 37; and "The Baptist Debate of April 14-15, 1668," 119, 133. Isaac Backus echoed Helwys in the eighteenth century: "Religion is a concern between God and the soul with which no human authority can intermeddle." As cited in William Gerald McLoughlin, *New England Dissent, 1630–1833: The Baptists and the Separation of Church and State*, 2 vols. (Cambridge MA: Harvard University Press, 1971) 1:559. A century later, historian A. H. Newman's interpretation of the Baptist heritage coincided with both Helwys's and Backus's argument. Said Newman in 1894, "Believing that faith is a matter between the individual man and God, Baptists have, from the beginning of their denominational history, regarded as an enormity any attempt to force the conscience." See Newman,

Atlantic, Obadiah Holmes's faith was so personal and private that his biographer, Edwin Gaustad, suggested that Holmes flirted with the temptation of dispensing with all the externals of "churches, ministers, ordinances, and even scriptures." But in the end, Gaustad added, Holmes steered a middle course between those who placed too much emphasis on forms, such as the Seventh Day Baptists, and those who placed too little, such as the Quakers.[27] In their 1948 statement on the church, British Baptists said:

> The basis of our membership in the church is a conscious and deliberate acceptance of Christ as Saviour and Lord by each individual. There is, we hold, a personal crisis in the soul's life when a person stands alone in God's presence, responds to God's gracious activity, accepts His forgiveness, and commits to the Christian way of life.[28]

To insist that saving faith is personal not impersonal, relational not ritualistic, direct not indirect, private not corporate has never meant for Baptists that the Christian life is a privatized disengagement from either the church or society. Indeed, those notable Baptist voices insisting the loudest on the experiential and private nature of faith were the very ones who argued vigorously for the communal and public nature of discipleship. John Clifford of England, loyal pastor of Praed Street Baptist Church in London for almost six decades, twice president of the British Baptist Union, the first elected president of the Baptist World Alliance, and the president of the National Free Church Council, could hardly, given this record of "community" participation, be accused of spiritual privatism. Yet Clifford described Baptists as advocates of "an eager, intense, and sanctified individualism," saying that "spiritual experience" was "the basis of our free and voluntary association as churches."[29] Likewise, Walter Rauschenbusch, father of the Social Gospel and devoted churchman, gave "experimental religion" as his first reason for being Baptist. Immediately, however, Rauschenbusch followed up his discussion of "experimental religion" by saying, "But religion is not a purely individual matter."[30]

A History of the Baptist Churches in the United States, 3.

[27]Gaustad, *Baptist Piety*, 71.

[28]As cited in Shurden, *The Baptist Identity*, 89.

[29]John Clifford, "The Baptist World Alliance: Its Origin and Character, Meaning and Work," in *The Life of Baptists in the Life of the World*, ed. Walter B. Shurden (Nashville: Broadman Press, 1985) 37-38. Also see "The Baptist Doctrine of the Church," in Shurden, *The Baptist Identity*, 89.

[30]Rauschenbusch, "Why I Am a Baptist," 165-70.

"Soul Competency" as Mullins used the term,[31] "Soul Liberty" as Clifford used the term, and "Soul Freedom" as I have used the term never restricted discipleship to a "disembodied experience with God," whatever that is! Both Mullins and Clifford did mean to say, however, and I and most Baptist historians gladly join them, that discipleship begins with an awareness of God that is intensely personal, private, and uncoerced, allowing no proxies, and where each individual is accountable to God.

Surely "faith as a private matter between God and the individual" is not the whole of discipleship. But neither is what Baptists have meant by private faith a mindless sashay into some type of deviant New-Age individualism, void of any sense of church. It is, according to the Baptist tradition, where discipleship begins and where it returns again and again for much of its staying power. It is also where the church, according to Baptists, is born.

Glenn Hinson, one of our few Baptist mystics, has warned Baptists repeatedly of the dangers of individualism, but he was also correct when he said,

> If one ranged church groups across a spectrum from extreme individualism and voluntarism, where the Holy Spirit is seen to effect obedience through the individual will, to extreme corporatism and intentionalism, where the Holy Spirit is seen to effect obedience through the corporate will, at the beginning Baptists would have occupied the extreme individualist/voluntarist end of the spectrum and Roman Catholics the extreme corporatist/intentionalist end. . . . Most Baptists have remained near the individualist/voluntarist pole throughout their history.[32]

---

[31]Those who suspect Mullins of a hyperindividualism that undercuts church life need both to reflect on Mullins's life more critically and read him more carefully. For example, he included a chapter in *The Axioms of Religion* entitled "Institutional and Anti-Institutional Christianity," in which he decried the tendency toward "churchless Christianity." Recognizing what he called "the peril of mere individualism in religion and the rejection of all church life," Mullins quoted Sabatier approvingly: "The Protestant Christian who isolates himself, believing that he can draw all religious truth from the Bible for his individual inspiration, lives and thinks in unreality. . . . We have need one of another. . . . Only in this social solidarity can the Christian life blossom out, and find at once health and security. An unsocial Christianity is a stunted and sterile Christianity." See *The Axioms*, 252.

[32]E. Glenn Hinson, "Baptists and Spirituality: A Community at Worship," *Review and Expositor* 84/4 (Fall 1987): 656.

The Baptist Notion of Freedom and the Baptist Identity

The Manifesto, as do most statements on the Baptist identity and as did I in *The Baptist Identity*, profiles the Baptist identity in light of the historic Baptist concern for freedom. Describing itself as a Baptist vision of "*freedom,* faithfulness, and community," the Manifesto uses the word "freedom" some fifty times or more. The freedom factor—its source, its meaning, and its applications—is viewed as an integral component of the Baptist identity in the Manifesto.

As I could conscientiously "second the motion—some" in talking about the Manifesto's understanding of community, I can also "second the motion—some" regarding the Manifesto's concept of freedom. Indeed, at several points in speaking of freedom, the Manifesto speaks powerfully and with relevance to the beginning of a new century. Let me identify a few of these quickly.

First, the Manifesto underscores rightly that for early Baptists God is the true source of all freedom.[33] The Manifesto wants to be certain that the reader understands that freedom is theologically, not humanistically, rooted; freedom originates in God's will, not the human will. Actually, Baptists grounded their contention for liberty of conscience in several arguments,[34] but behind all of these lay the belief in God's sovereignty. Early Baptists, without question, rooted religious freedom in the nature of God.

A sovereign God who dared to create people as free beings is portrayed in the Bible as a liberating deity. Throughout the Old Testament, God is set against persons and institutions that restricted the freedom of God's people. And the complete thrust of Jesus' ministry was to free people from all that would hold them back from obedience to God. Freedom for Baptists was far more than a constitutional right or a governmental gift. God, not nations or courts or human law, is the ultimate source of liberty. The same line of argument, I contend, in contrast to the Manifesto, has been true for later Baptists as well, including Isaac Backus, John Leland, and E. Y. Mullins.

---

[33]*Manifesto,* 303, 309.

[34]I have tried to summarize the major arguments in my essay, "How We Got That Way: Baptists on Religious Liberty and Separation of Church and State." See that essay in this volume and also in *Proclaiming the Baptist Vision: Religious Liberty,* ed. Walter B. Shurden (Macon GA: Smyth & Helwys Publishing Inc., 1997) 19-25.

Said Mullins, echoing the Second London Confession and later incorporating it into the SBC Baptist Faith and Message, "The great principle underlying religious liberty is this: God alone is Lord of the Conscience."[35]

One of the glories of the Baptist heritage has been the advocacy and protection of human rights, just as one of the tragedies of our Baptist heritage is the way we Baptists have, in too many instances, resisted human rights. In 1980 the Baptist World Alliance adopted a statement from its Commission on Freedom, Justice, and Peace on human rights chaired by William W. Pinson, Jr. Rather than basing the statement on some humanistic notion of an autonomous self, the Commission rooted it theologically. "Human rights are derived from God—from his nature, his creation, and his commands," said the BWA's Commission.[36]

Second, the Manifesto insists that freedom is not a license, "something that we possess for ourselves to use for our own ends."[37] A good seventeenth-century Baptist prooftext for such an emphasis may be found in the third section of article 21 of the Second London Confession.[38] That kind of call to responsible discipleship abounds in early Baptist writings. Baptists, of course, must not permit their profile of the Baptist identity regarding freedom to be sketched apart from the corresponding note of responsibility and accountability.

Third, the Manifesto affirms that authentic freedom is found in the Jesus way of living and being. Gospel freedom, it says, cannot be defined "as the pursuit of self-realization apart from the model of Jesus Christ." This theme echoes throughout the document. "By following the call to discipleship we discover true freedom," it says. And again, "God therefore calls us to the freedom of faithful discipleship by participating in the way

---

[35]E. Y. Mullins, *Baptist Beliefs* (Valley Forge PA: Judson Press, 1912) 73. Those who accuse Mullins of anthropocentrism fail to notice that his very first "axiom" of religion was that "The Holy and Loving God Has a Right to Be Sovereign."

[36]Cited in Shurden, *The Life of Baptists in the Life of the World*, 244.

[37]*Manifesto*, 303.

[38]"They who upon pretence of Christian Liberty do practice any sin, or cherish any sinfull lust; as they do thereby pervert the main design of the Grace of the Gospel to their own Destruction; so they wholly destroy the end of *Christian* Liberty, which is, that being delivered out of the hands of all our Enemies we might serve the Lord without fear in Holiness and Righteousness before him, all the days of our Life." As cited in Lumpkin, *Baptist Confessions of Faith*, 280.

of Jesus."[39] While these statements appear to be more characteristic of the broader Christian identity than the specific Baptist identity, they certainly constitute significant notes for Baptists to strike at the beginning of a new millennium. The Christocentric character of the Manifesto, so prevalent at many points, is highlighted in these quotations. The Manifesto's call to "faithful" discipleship is certainly one of the strengths of the entire document.

Fourth, one of the most prophetic statements in the Manifesto appears in the final affirmation where it speaks of the disestablishment of the church:

> We further believe that in order for our free church witness to be faithful we must do more than seek institutional independence of civil authorities. We must also continue to press for the independence of the church from the idols of nationalism, racism, ethnocentrism, economic systems, gender domination, or any other power that resists the Lordship of Jesus Christ.[40]

The Manifesto goes on to say, "Nor can we accept terms of agreement with nation-states which sequester the authority of faith to a private, internal, individual, and narrow sphere." While I agree that the Manifesto sounds far too optimistic about the possibility of political and cultural independency,[41] one must certainly identify with the Manifesto, in light of the Baptist heritage, and reject "any attempt to establish a vision of the church, whether Baptist or any other, by means of civil or political power." The Baptist identity surely demands that we disavow, in the words of the Manifesto, "all . . . constantinian strategies."[42]

I come away from the Manifesto, despite its many strengths in speaking of freedom, with serious reservations regarding its description of the Baptist identity vis-à-vis the concept of freedom. Most significantly and inexplicably, the Manifesto contains at best a muted emphasis on liberty of conscience for all people. Can the Baptist identity be appropriately sketched by any group, Baptist or otherwise, apart from the loud trumpeting of this principle? I doubt it. In light of the enviable and courageous history of Baptists on this point, a history acknowledged by non-Baptists as well

---

[39]*Manifesto*, 306, 305.

[40]*Manifesto*, 308.

[41]Robert P. Jones, "Re-Envisioning Baptist Identity from a Theocentric Perspective," 30.

[42]*Manifesto*, 309.

as Baptists and by secular as well as church historians, one can only be surprised that a statement on the Baptist identity virtually bypassed the theme of freedom of conscience for all.

Specifically, three dimensions of the Manifesto's discussion of freedom are problematic in light of my reading of Baptist history. First, the Manifesto stresses the freedom that comes in redemption and neglects the freedom that comes with creation. Second, and closely related, the Manifesto stresses the freedom that comes to the church and neglects the freedom that comes to individuals. Third, the Manifesto stresses the disestablishment of the church while minimizing freedom of conscience for all.

Regarding the first issue, the Manifesto seems to restrict freedom to the people of God who have been redeemed rather than to all who have been created. In making the point that freedom is a gift of God, the Manifesto seems to say that such freedom is restricted to Christians. Does it intend this? It speaks of "the freedom graciously given by God in Jesus Christ" and of "freedom in Christ" and "the gift of freedom in Jesus Christ." "Human freedom exists," it says, "only in relationship with the Triune God. . . . " Granted, one must insist that "freedom in Christ" is a gift, but is this the distinctive idea that shaped the Baptist identity among early Baptists? I think not. Rather, what distinguished early Baptists was the conviction that *all* human beings, redeemed or not, have a God-given freedom to follow conscience in matters spiritual and religious. Early Baptists, as did other Christians of the their time, assumed that freedom for living fully, authentically, and genuinely was found in Jesus Christ. Where Baptists differed with their culture was believing that people had as a gift from God the right to choose that path. Freedom came with creation, as well as with redemption.

Glen Stassen has made this point crisply with his most significant but relatively unknown essay, "The Christian Origin of Human Rights." Insisting rightly that the origin of human rights is not found in the rationalism and individualism of the Enlightenment but in the free churches at the time of the Puritan Revolution, Stassen described seventeenth-century Baptist Richard Overton as the "pioneer of human rights." Basing his arguments for human freedoms on reason, experience, and Scripture, Overton did not limit his concerns to religious or political liberties. All such liberties, however, came with being human. Stassen says of Overton, "The rights Overton is advocating clearly belong to all because all persons are created in the image of God and all are the objects of God's love shown in Christ's sacrificial death on the cross."[43] Roger Williams, who drew from earlier Baptist tracts on religious liberty and influenced later ones, said, "It is the will and command of God that, since the coming of his Son the Lord Jesus, a permission of the most Paganish, Jewish, Turkish, or anti-Christian consciences and worships be granted to all men in all nations and countries."[44] John Clarke made something of the same point by insisting that deprivation of religious freedom was not only unbiblical, un-Christlike, and unspiritual, but it was also unnatural.[45]

Secondly, the Manifesto, in keeping with its communal focus, underscores the gift of freedom that comes to the church and neglects unnecessarily and out of hand the gift of freedom that comes to each individual. In somewhat repetitive fashion, freedom, says the Manifesto, is for "the new creation," it "cannot be understood apart from the fellowship of the Holy Spirit," it is "the freedom of God's people," and it is something "we encounter through the divine community of the triune God and with the Christian fellowship that shares in this holy communion."[46] Understandably fearful of "modern notions of freedom" that lead to excessive individualism and in which "the mere expression of the will is the greatest good" and believing that such notions have affected contemporary Baptists in North America, the Manifesto overlooks the vast Baptist heritage which identifies freedom with individuals, especially freedom of conscience.

Seventeenth-century Baptists in England and America were stalwart advocates of individual freedom. Does one really need to document that fact with the writings of Smyth, Helwys, Busher, Murton, Roger Williams, John Clarke, Obadiah Holmes, to say nothing of Isaac Backus and John Leland and others? Of course they believed that the ultimate source of freedom was divine, not human. Of course they (except for the later Williams) believed that the Christian life centered in the community of believers. But they also believed in and were advocates for individual freedom. John

---

[43]Glen H. Stassen, *Just Peacemaking* (Louisville KY: Westminster/John Knox Press, 1992) 148. Summarizing Overton at another point, Stassen said, "Overton says all are equally born to natural rights 'delivered of God by the hand of nature.' . . . He argues that everyone has an individual selfhood by nature, because without this we could not be ourselves. God delivers all of us equally into this world with a selfhood that is naturally free." (152)

[44]As cited in H. Leon McBeth, *A Sourcebook for Baptist Heritage* (Nashville: Broadman Press, 1990) 83.

[45]See John Clarke, *Ill Newes from New-England*, 101.

[46]*Manifesto*, 303.

Clarke argued in *Ill Newes from New-England* on multiple grounds for liberty of conscience. But one of these grounds was the idea that "the voice of each man's conscience [was] to him as the voice of his God."[47]

William G. McLoughlin argued, persuasively but not conclusively, that pietism is the "key" to the American character. He was certainly correct, however, in identifying two kinds of pietism in seventeenth-century America. "Conservative Pietists," the Congregationalists, represented the established church. "Liberal Pietists," the Baptists and Quakers, represented dissenters and those struggling for freedom of individual conscience. The first, said McLoughlin, were concerned with moral order; the second with moral freedom. The first wanted to keep the society moral; the second wanted to keep the society moral while protecting individual freedoms.[48]

The Manifesto is concerned that freedom is imperiled in contemporary denominational life by some Baptists "who would sever freedom from . . . membership in the body of Christ and the community's legitimate authority."[49] That is exactly what the seventeenth-century establishment in England and America said of Baptists of their day.[50] And how did the Baptists answer? They said that they were only trying to escape the tyranny of the community so as to have genuine freedom for individuals and the church to be obedient to God's Spirit and Holy Scripture. John Smyth, who never rose to the heights of freedom of conscience as did some of his Baptist successors, said that the magistrates were "to leave Christian religion free, *to every man's conscience.*" Why? Because "Christ only is the king, and lawgiver of the church and *conscience.*"[51]

In the important debate of 1668 the Puritans made numerous accusations against the Baptists, one of which was the incredible idea that Baptists believed in liberty of conscience for "every single person."[52] During that debate Thomas Shepard, a Puritan clergy, sounded the

---

[47]Clarke, *Ill Newes from New-England*, 113.

[48]William G. McLoughlin, "Pietism and the American Character," in *Modern American Protestantism and Its World; Historical Articles on Protestantism in American Religious Life: Trends in American Religion and the Protestant World*, ed. Martin E. Marty (Munich, Germany: K. G. Saur, 1992) 122.

[49]*Manifesto*, 304.

[50]See for example "The Baptist Debate of April 14-15, 1668."

[51]As cited in Lumpkin, *Baptist Confessions of Faith*, 140; italics mine. This statement, attributed to Smyth, actually came from his followers after his death as they were seeking admission to the Waterlanders.

[52]"The Baptist Debate of April 14-15, 1668," 118.

communitarian note when he said, "A particular person may not judge the whole: but is to be subject to the whole." Thomas Goold, founding pastor of the First Baptist Church of Boston, responded with both the individual's right to personal interpretation of Scripture and the individual's freedom to judge the church according to Scripture, saying, "a private member may cast them off." Responding to Goold, one Puritan said, "A dangerous inference. Because the all-seeing God may do it: therefore Goodman Goold a fallible judge and running to many errors may."[53]

Three, the Manifesto stresses the disestablishment of the church while minimizing freedom of conscience for all. In its fifth and final affirmation the Manifesto makes a powerful and relevant case for the disestablishment of the church, not only from the control of the state but from the domination of culture.[54] The latter point may derive from the Manifesto's fondness for the Anabaptist tradition. But the historic Baptist concern to affirm "freedom and renounce coercion" was not simply a sectarian concern that the church be disestablished from the civil, political, and cultural forces, as important as that was and is. Rather, seventeenth-century Baptists, when it came to the freedom issue, were concerned primarily that all human beings be free to embrace what Leonard Busher called in *Religion's Peace* "a meek and gentle lamb." That "meek and gentle lamb" was permission of conscience. In fact, a case can be made that Baptists' initial concern was for freedom to believe, worship, and live according to conscience. That was the Baptist struggle of the seventeenth century. As they moved into the eighteenth century Baptists began pulling down the establishment and plugging away at separation of church and state.[55]

---

[53]"The Baptist Debate of April 14-15, 1668," 111, 112. A close reading of the debate demonstrates the individualism of Baptists.

[54]The *Manifesto*'s concern for Baptist freedom from cultural captivity is, as I have said earlier, one of its strongest points. Few could doubt that Baptists, who began as a minority movement and cultural critics, evolved into a majority movement captive to their culture. This is most especially true of white Baptists in the South, those whom I take to be the primary audience of the *Manifesto*. One must ask again, however, Is cultural disestablishment central to the *Baptist* identity or is it part of the *Christian* identity? Have Baptists in the past, no matter how much they called for "separation from the world," seen this as one of their identifying marks? Again, I doubt it.

[55]Compare William Henry Brackney, *The Baptists* (New York: Greenwood Press, 1988) 95. The struggle of Baptists for liberty of conscience is not a pure or even one. As McLoughlin demonstrated regarding New England Baptists in his

I am not even close to suggesting that the authors of the Manifesto do not believe in religious freedom for all people. I know better. What I am suggesting, however, is that I do not know of a description of the Baptist identity anywhere that would not place universal freedom of conscience and religious liberty at the very center of the Baptist identity. But not only was this not a cardinal theme of the Manifesto's reenvisioning of the Baptist identity, it was, it seems, only reluctantly mentioned in the document.

A major part of this reluctance, it seems to me, is the Manifesto's concern that "some Baptists . . . [have] embraced modernity by defining freedom in terms of the Enlightenment notions of autonomous moral agency and objective rationality."[56] While I doubt seriously the historical accuracy of the description, let's say, for the sake of argument, it is correct. Should we, therefore, minimize a historic characteristic of the Baptist people simply because we think that some of their successors got it from the wrong source?

Are we not all acquainted with the story of how Baptists in America united with those of diverse religious views, many of whom were exceedingly rationalistic, to move closer to the idea of freedom of conscience for all? What Stassen observed about human rights in general can be applied to the Baptist drive in America for liberty of conscience in particular: "The ethic of human rights can be a universal ethic, not because its *source* is a common philosophy believed by all people but because its *intention and application* affirm the rights of all persons."[57] No wonder Helwys said, "Let them be heretics, Turks, Jews, or whatsoever, it appertains not the earthly power to punish them in the least measure."[58] The Baptist identity statement issued by the Commission on Baptist Heritage of the Baptist World Alliance in 1989 said, "Baptists were among the first to campaign for liberation of opinion and religious practice, not only for themselves but for all people, including the unbeliever, for they believed

---

two-volume *New England Dissent* and as H. Leon McBeth showed concerning English Baptists in *English Baptist Literature on Religious Liberty to 1689* (New York: Arno Press, 1980), Baptists stubbed their freedom toes at times, restricting their call for freedom occasionally to Christians or orthodox Christians. But on the whole, Baptists came forth in the seventeenth century screaming for freedom for all because they did not have freedom at all.

[56]*Manifesto*, 309-10.

[57]Stassen, *Just Peacemaking*, 156.

[58]Helwys, *A Short Declaration of the Mystery of Iniquity*, 53.

that each individual needed to be free to make choices about faith and commitment unfettered by any outside agency."[59] Maybe the most serious oversight in the Manifesto's effort to reinterpret the Baptist identity is its neglect of one of the major tiles in the mosaic of the Baptist identity. I am not suggesting that there is only one way to talk about freedom of conscience as a part of the Baptist identity. I am suggesting, however, that one cannot talk about the Baptist identity without talking about freedom of conscience for all.

Conclusion

Is it possible, as the Manifesto wishes to do, to reenvision the Baptist identity? Not only is it possible, it is necessary. Baptist life is dynamic, not static. Every generation of Baptists must seek to make the essence of Baptist life understandable to its day. Many have attempted during the four hundred years of Baptist Christianity to reinterpret the denominational identity. When in 1908 E. Y. Mullins wrote his now classic *The Axioms of Religion*, he subtitled it *A New Interpretation of the Baptist Faith*. Baptists do not have an unchanging "Deposit of Truth" as the Catholics once claimed for themselves.

On the other hand, I agree with Robert Torbet that Baptists possess some principles—distinctives—traditions, what an American Baptist statement called "convictional genes," that anchor the Baptist identity. These "genes" transcend generational, national, regional, ethnic, and theological preferences. Again, this is precisely why I think in the twentieth century one does well to go to the proceedings of the Baptist World Alliance to find these genes. These "genes" may be placed under the theological microscope and interpreted from various angles, and that is why we come up with different "visions" of the Baptist identity. When I stare at these Baptist genes through the lenses of four centuries of Baptist history, I see "voluntarism" as the glue that holds the "convictional genes" together.

For me, one of those genes has to do with the centrality of the individual, the individual's religious experience with God, the individual's freedom from God, the individual's freedom of conscience. To stress the individual is not to suggest that Baptists are Roger Williams-like seekers, untethered to the church. I think, however, that Edwin Gaustad was right when he said that "Baptists indeed stand for individualism above institu-

---

[59]As cited in Shurden, *The Baptist Identity*, 65-66.

tionalism, for the reforming prophet more than the conforming priest, for a pietism that is private and personal before it can properly become public and social."[60] The Manifesto, fearing rightly the perversions of individualism in modern culture and religion, failed to distinguish sufficiently the modern perversions from the historic Baptist affirmations. Consequently, the Manifesto could not appreciate adequately the importance of the individual in reenvisioning the Baptist identity.

A second Baptist gene has to do with the centrality of the church, especially the local church, its regenerate nature, its final authority in the life of believers, its congregational polity, its fear of external authorities, and its call to minister freely but responsibly in its setting. While I assume the Manifesto meant primarily "church" when it used "community," I wish it, and all the rest of us, would work harder at making this point clearer. Specifically, I would like to hear more from the authors of the Manifesto about how "community" actually works itself out in Baptist life. For example, when the Manifesto speaks of "the community's legitimate authority," what "community" and what "authority" does it reference for Baptist life?

On the whole, however, the *Manifesto* helps us to understand that the "church gene" in Baptist life does not simply consist of hundreds or thousands of independent molecules "doing their own thing." Baptist individuals live out their faith in local churches. Beyond the local communities of faith, a very important part of the "church gene" in Baptist history has to do with the universal body of believers. This part of the Baptist gene deals more, of course, with attitudes than with polity, with ideals than with function.

A third Baptist "gene," as most all my writings attest, is the "freedom" gene. I interpret it as central to the Baptist identity. The Manifesto contains, as I have said, some needful and relevant ideas on freedom. I wish it had a much stronger statement on freedom of conscience and religious liberty. Also, I must confess that when reading the *Manifesto*, I get an uneasy feeling about its commitment to Baptist freedom in general. I subtitled my book on Baptist identity *Four Fragile Freedoms*. After studying the Manifesto, I quite honestly wonder if Baptist freedom is not more fragile than I first thought.

---

[60]Edwin S. Gaustad, "Toward a Baptist Identity in the Twenty-First Century," in *Discovering Our Baptist Heritage*, ed. William H. Brackney (Valley Forge PA: American Baptist Historical Society, 1985) 88.

For me, the strength of the Manifesto's threefold call to Baptists of "freedom, faithfulness, and community" is clearly in the "faithfulness" dimension of the call. The Manifesto breathes a seriousness about following Jesus. Whatever it means to be a Baptist Christian, or a Christian of any kind for that matter, it means surely to take seriously what Jesus took seriously, to be committed to what Jesus was committed to. When we take seriously what Jesus took seriously, we often transcend the preoccupation with denominational distinctives. I am of the opinion that this is what the Manifesto does. In truth, Jesus' words on baptism—its mode, subject, and administrator—are about as plentiful as his words on circumcision, the priesthood of all believers, and the appropriate form of church government, which are nonexistent.

While the document by title and intent focuses on denominational identity, the Manifesto manifests concerns for a serious Christian discipleship that transcend the primary subject of the document—reenvisioning the *Baptist* identity. The Manifesto's concerns for "peace" and "justice" are doubtless rooted in its fondness of Anabaptism. While Baptists have never been numbered among the historic "Peace Churches," the call for peace and justice is a noble one. In this connection, one may not be too far off base saying, as Fisher Humphreys said and in a positive rather than pejorative vein, that the Manifesto is "an Anabaptist tract for the times."[61] For me, the document reinterprets the Baptist identity too much in terms of the Anabaptist identity, though I also acknowledge a strong Calvinistic emphasis in the document as well.

I could not in my voluntaristic-freedom-loving-Thomas Helwys-Leonard Busher-John Murton-John Clarke-Obadiah Holmes-Isaac Backus-John Leland-E. Y. Mullins-Baptist fashion sign the document. On the other hand, I revel in the Baptist freedom that no ecclesiastical community can tell a group of Baptists, including the authors of the Manifesto, what they can say and cannot say, what they can sign or not sign. That is part of what I mean by voluntarism.

---

[61]Fisher Humphreys, "How Shall We Re-Envision Baptist Identity"? An unpublished paper.

How We Got That Way:
Baptists on Religious Liberty
and Separation of Church and State[1]

In the United States one can count 28,921,564 individual Baptists in 122,811 local churches in sixty-three different denominational bodies.[2] Worldwide one can identify 37,334,191 Baptists in 157,240 local Baptist churches.[3] Those are impressive statistics of no small measure. So why then does that idiosyncratic Baptist Farmer-Preacher, Will Campbell, say in several of his books that not many Baptists exist any longer? What Campbell means, I gather, is that not many Baptists continue to act out of the muscular Baptist tradition of freedom, including religious liberty and separation of church and state.

How is it in your part of the country? Are Baptists widely and popularly recognized today as the "stout champions of freedom"? Or is the popular image of Baptists in your part of the world by non-Baptists what it is in mine? And that is that we are narrow, provincial, even reactionary Christians, not freedom-loving freedom fighters. Baptists in many places today are not seen as those who keep a sickle in their hands to root out the weeds of oppression and totalitarianism in the garden of life.

Walker Percy, the psychiatrist turned novelist, was, for my money, one of the most prophetic and perceptive readers of American life in the last half of the nineteenth century. Here is what Percy said about the Baptists he knew in the deep South. He said they are a group of evangelistically

---

[1]I first presented this address at a conference in Washington, D.C. celebrating the 60th anniversary of the Baptist Joint Committee on Public Affairs. The conference met Octoger 6-8, 1996. The Baptist Joint Committee later published the address in pamphlet form and online at <http://www.bjcpa.org/Pages/Resources/Pubs/shurden.html>. It also appeared in Walter B. Shurden, ed., *Proclaiming the Baptist Vision: Religious Liberty* (Macon GA: Smyth & Helwys, 1997) 13-29, and is reprinted her with permission from Smyth & Helwys.

[2]For the U.S. statistics, see Robert Gardner, "Baptist General Bodies in the USA," *Baptist History and Heritage* 31/1 (January 1996): 50.

[3]For world statistics, see Albert W. Wardin, ed., *Baptists around the World* (Nashville: Broadman & Holman Publishers, 1995) 473.

repulsive anti-Catholics who are political opportunists advocating scientific creationism in the public school system.[4]

Surely one must not swallow uncritically Walker Percy's assessment. But I concede that he was in fact describing what many *assume* the Baptist identity to be today. Baptists are simply not perceived as freedom-lovers and freedom-givers and freedom-protectors by many persons in America today. If that is the case, and I think to a great degree it is, it is sad, sad, sad.

It means that Baptists have come a long, long way from home, from their humble beginnings and struggling origins. Most of us when we think of Baptists and freedom in the last half of the twentieth century could probably point to only three movements: (1) African-American Baptists and the struggle for civil rights in America; (2) the Baptist World Alliance and its involvement in religious liberty and human rights issues around the globe; and (3) The Baptist Joint Committee in Washington, D.C., and its pit-bulldog defense of religious freedom and separation of church and state in the United States.

We can thank God for all three because, each in its own way, has rung sharply and loudly the note of freedom, a note which has become fainter and fainter for some Baptists in the last half of this century. Today many Baptists know the words of freedom, but they have forgotten the music. But both the music and the words in the Baptist heritage speak words and make melodies of no uncertain sound. Both the lyrics and the tunes in the Baptist past speak harmoniously and unambiguously of absolute religious liberty based upon principle, not expediency. And they speak of the political derivative of religious liberty, the separation of church and state.

How did we Baptists get to these ideas of absolute religious liberty and separation of church and state? There is no doubt that we did. Even some of our fiercest historical opponents affirm this. So how did Baptists get beyond "establishmentarianism," which was so much a part of the concept of Christendom in Europe and England and New England and in most of the American colonies?

And how did Baptists get beyond mere "tolerationism"? Tolerationism, while a gigantic step beyond establishmentarianism, never discovered the spacious land of freedom of conscience. And how did Baptists get beyond

---

[4]For references in Walker Percy's writings see his novels: *The Second Coming* (New York: Washington Square Press, 1980) 218; *Love in the Ruins* (New York: Avon Books, 1971) 22; *Thanatos Syndrome* (New York: Farrar, Straus, and Giroux, 1987) 347.

"accommodationism"? Accommodationism—the seductive idea that all Christian denominations would share equally in the bounty of the state—how did Baptists get beyond that one?

In some instances, as Baptist history will document, we sputtered at times in getting beyond accommodationism, but in the end our forebears recognized its inadequacies and inequities and "leveller" heads prevailed. How did Baptists get to these heady ideas of religious freedom for absolutely everybody and separation of church and state for both the good of the church and the good of the state? As I said, there is no question that Baptists got there. How did they?

I will suggest that Baptists finally got that way because of three factors. First, Baptists got that way because they were *birthed in adversity*. Second, Baptists got that way because *their peculiar Christian convictions and common sense encouraged theological diversity*. Third, Baptists got that way on religious liberty and separation of church and state because, birthed in adversity and with Christian convictions encouraging theological diversity, *they inevitably sealed their convictions by engaging in political activity*. They got that way because of their *birthing*, their *believing*, and their way of *being* in the world.

Baptists Birthed in Historical Adversity

Baptists came from the womb of the seventeenth-century English Reformation and landed immediately in hostile territory. Almost twenty-five years ago I published a little book entitled *Not A Silent People: Controversies That Have Shaped Southern Baptists.*[5] Some may recall that I entitled the very first chapter "Here Come the Battling Baptists." After twenty-five years I remain convinced of the appropriateness of the title of the first chapter to describe the emergence of Baptists as a distinct denomination.

Baptists emerged as a specific body in the midst of a crippling adversity. They came battling! If you ever write a historical essay on early Baptist life in either England or the American Colonies, a good place to begin your research is in the records of court proceedings, search warrants, and prison records. While that story of repression and oppression may be overdramatized, and even skewed in a comprehensive retelling of the Baptist story, it is nonetheless a fact that Baptists bled in their earliest years

---

[5]Originally published in 1972 by Broadman Press in Nashville, a revised edition was issued in 1995 by Smyth & Helwys Publishing Inc. of Macon GA.

of the seventeenth century, and they remained handcuffed in much of the eighteenth century. They bled from the whip of religious oppression, and they were constricted by the arms of both church and state and of the two acting in concert.

The historical context is crucial. Queen Elizabeth reigned in England from 1558 to 1603, the last half of the sixteenth century, and she tried valiantly to settle the problem of an emerging religious pluralism in England. The Queen attempted to build a tent big enough to accommodate a passionate, powerful, and proliferating pluralism. She failed. The old dream of the Medieval Synthesis with all of life united around a single ruler and a single expression of religion was slowly crumbling in the dust of blazing individual freedoms. In the end, the so-called Elizabethan Settlement settled nothing.

When Elizabeth died in 1603, James I, formerly James VI of Scotland, came to the throne, stirring hope in the hearts of Puritans and more radical dissenters. After all James was coming from the Church of Scotland. But Puritans and nonconformists hoped in vain. James's immediate and persistent remedy for the knotty problem of religious fragmentation in England was simple: forced uniformity!

James I and Charles I, who succeeded James and who reigned till 1649, both reacted with horror to the idea of liberty of conscience. Rather, James and Charles affirmed the divine right of kings and the divine right of bishops as one and the same. It was a scrambled-eggs society. Church and State came on the same plate and all mixed together. Baptists, virtual babies on the religious scene, tried to unscramble the political-ecclesiastical eggs, maintaining, among other things, that the state has no say-so over the soul of a person.

During James's reign from 1603 to 1625, the Separatists, from whom the Baptists would themselves eventually separate, multiplied. The Separatists had no reason to be surprised, however, when the king's fist came down hard on them. Less than a year after coming to the throne, James I called the Hampton Court Conference in January 1604 to deal with the petitions made by the Puritans, a people not nearly so liberal as the Separatists, for reform in the church. When the Puritans demanded modification of the episcopacy, James declared, "No bishop, no king." And then reacting to the slightest tinge of religious liberty, James said in kingly fear and sarcasm:

> Jack and Tom and Will and Dick shall meete, and at their pleasure censure me and my Councell and all our proceedings. Then Will shall stand up and

say it must be thus; then Dick shall reply and say, nay, narry, but we shall have it thus.[6]

James I, like so many of his age, caricatured religious pluralism because he simply could not imagine a society built on the freedom to choose one's faith. And so that there could be no mistake of the king's point of view, James declared of the Puritans at Hampton, "I shall make them conforme themselves, or I wil harrie them out of the land, or else doe worse."

It was during James's reign that the little group at Gainsborough, led by John Smyth and Thomas Helwys, pioneers of the Baptist movement, left their homeland of England in 1608 to find religious refuge in Holland.

And it was during Charles's reign that folks swarmed to New England to escape the merciless hand of Archbishop William Laud. Laud, who became archbishop of Canterbury in 1633, and Charles I, the monarch who favored him so, would in the end both feel the sting of political and religious persecution in their own executions.

And it was during both reigns of James and Charles that Baptists peppered both royalty and religion with some of the first and most forceful tracts ever written on religious liberty.

John Smyth's 1612 "Propositions and Conclusions . . . " was according to William Lumpkin, "perhaps the first confession of faith of modern times to demand freedom of conscience and separation of church and state."[7] Said Smyth, "[T]he magistrate is not by virtue of his office to meddle with religion, or matters of conscience, to force or compel men to this or that form of religion, or doctrine: but to leave Christian religion free, to every man's conscience . . . for Christ only is the king, and lawgiver of the church and conscience (James 4:12)."[8]

Thomas Helwys, upon returning to England with a remnant of Smyth's group, released in 1612 his document entitled *A Short Declaration of the Mistery of Iniquity*. He was rewarded with a prison sentence, but not before

---

[6]As cited in H. Leon McBeth, *English Baptist Literature on Religious Liberty to 1689* (New York: Arno Press, 1980) 4. (This book, the published version of McBeth's 1961 doctoral dissertation at Southwestern Baptist Theological Seminary in Ft. Worth TX, is a marvelous resource for the subject at issue.)

[7]William L. Lumpkin, *Baptist Confessions of Faith*, rev. ed. (Valley Forge PA: Judson Press, 1969) 124.

[8]Lumpkin, *Baptist Confessions of Faith*, 140.

this pioneer Baptist freely professed of the Roman Catholics of England that

> our lord the King hath no more power over their consciences then ours, and that is none at all: for our Lord the King is but an earthly King, and if the Kings people be obedient & true subjects, obeying all humane lawes made by the King, our lord the King can require no more. For mens religion to God, is betwixt God and themselves; the King shall not answer for it; neither may the King be judg betwene God and man.
>
> Let them be heretikes, Turks, Jewes or whatsoever, it apperteynes not to the earthly power to punish them in the least measure.[9]

First, Smyth; second, Helwys; and then Leonard Busher. Busher wrote *Religion's Peace: A Plea for Liberty of Conscience*, which Leon McBeth called "the first Baptist treatise devoted exclusively to religious liberty."[10] Published in 1614, Busher asserted that "as kings and bishops cannot command the wind, so they cannot command faith." He continued, writing the following in capital letters: "IT IS NOT ONLY UNMERCIFUL, BUT UNNATURAL AND ABOMINABLE; YEA, MONSTROUS FOR ONE CHRISTIAN TO VEX AND DESTROY ANOTHER FOR DIFFERENCE AND QUESTIONS OF RELIGION."[11]

And then John Murton in *Persecution for Religion Judg'd and Condemn'd* (1615, 1620, 1662) confessed he was compelled to write because of "how heinous it is in the sight of the Lord to force men and women by cruel persecution, to bring their bodies to a worship whereunto they cannot bring their spirits."[12] Starkly, he wrote, "that no man ought to be persecuted of his religion, be it true or false. . . . "[13]

It is important to pause and remember that Baptists in the seventeenth century confronted religious restrictionism from both the courthouse and the church house, from both the monarchs of England and the bishops of the Church of England. It did not end there, however. Neither the Puritans, the Presbyterians, nor the Separatists in England advocated complete soul liberty. And things were no better in New England. There Obadiah Holmes was publicly whipped on the streets of Boston. And as a result, John

---

[9]H. Leon McBeth, *A Sourcebook for Baptist Heritage* (Nashville TN: Broadman Press, 1990) 72.

[10]McBeth, *English Baptist Literature*, 39.

[11]As cited in McBeth, *A Sourcebook*, 74.

[12]McBeth, *A Sourcebook*, 75.

[13]McBeth, *A Sourcebook*, 75.

Clarke, pastor of the First Baptist Church in Newport, Rhode Island, sent a document back to England with the ominous title of "Ill Newes from New-England." There, in the New World, Isaac Backus had to write as late as 1773 a pleading work entitled "An Appeal to the Public for Religious Liberty." Two decades later John Leland (1791) wrote a pamphlet, "The Rights of Conscience Inalienable," saying that "Government has no more to do with the religious opinions of men, than it has with the principles of mathematics." Leland continued, "Let every man speak freely without fear, maintain the principles that he believes, worship according to his own faith, either one God, three Gods, no God, or twenty Gods; and let government protect him in so doing."[14]

So born in the midst of great pain with freedom denied, Baptists, a minority people, grounded their affirmation for religious freedom to some degree in their own historical experience of deprivation. There is nothing quite so strong as the testimony of the oppressed, unless it is the testimony of the oppressed which has gone public so that all can see and hear. You will remember that Martin Luther King, Jr. was criticized because, as some said, "He was simply trying to attract the media." King responded that such was precisely what he was trying to do. He sought to attract a crowd to expose to the nation and the world the denial of basic human rights. Helwys, Busher, Murton, Clarke, Williams, Backus, and Leland penned their fiery tracts and pamphlets for precisely the same reason. As the Civil Rights Movement of the 1960s was born from freedoms denied, just so the Religious Rights Movement of the seventeenth and eighteenth centuries. Baptists "got that way" on religious liberty and separation of church and state because they were born in adversity.

Baptists: Christian Convictions Which Encouraged Diversity

Second, Baptists got that way on these issues because their Baptist interpretation of the Christian faith and human life encouraged theological diversity. Let us be sure of what I am saying. To say that their convictions encouraged diversity does not suggest in the least that Baptists had no firm certainties regarding cardinal Christian truths, nor is it to say that their opinions were flabby with an "anything goes" approach to the Bible and theology. They were as certain, even dogmatic, about their views as the most fervent bishop in the Church of England. The difference, however,

---

[14]L. F. Greene, ed., *The Writings of John Leland* (New York: Arno Press, 1969) 184.

was that the bishop's commitments led to uniformity while the theological approach of Baptists' led to diversity.

What do I mean when I say that Baptists' convictions encouraged theological diversity and ultimately religious liberty and the separation of church and state? Recently I encountered a gripping and felicitous phrase in Charles Talbert's commentary on Luke's gospel. Writing about the parable of the Good Samaritan, Talbert quoted W. A. Beardslee who spoke of "The way the world comes together again through the parables."[15] If you want to know "how the world came together" for Jesus, you have to read his parables. If you want to know "how the world came together" for disciples of Jesus, you have to read the parables. "How the world comes together!" Simple but descriptive words.

"How the world came together" for Baptists—their inner life, their thought processes, their inner spiritual world—in the seventeenth century issued in freedom of conscience. Baptists grounded their lives in a view of the world that led inevitably to soul liberty. Their commitment to religious liberty and separation of church and state did not come simply from their historical circumstances of adversity. Indeed, had Baptists never felt the sting of religious and civil oppression, the distinct way "the world came together," if logically followed, would have still led to religious liberty and separation of church and state.

Of course, Baptists are as riddled by sin as any group that ever lived. We are as liable to conscript the Bible and theology in the service of self-interest as anybody. Baptists have been vulnerable, therefore, to build their case for religious freedom on mere expediency. At times they have done exactly that. Indeed what worries one about some contemporary Baptists in America is that principle has been sacrificed upon the altar of expediency.

It is easy to "holler" freedom when you are the one who does not have it. It is a more principled position, however, to cry for freedom when you are in the majority but now lift your voice on behalf of new minorities. All of Baptists' moral shortfalls notwithstanding, when one reads the entire historical record of Baptists, one sees that Baptists committed themselves to ideas that compelled them to plead for religious liberty and separation of church and state on the basis of principle, not expediency.

---

[15]See Charles H. Talbert, *Reading Luke: A Literary and Theological Commentary on the Third Gospel* (New York: Crossroad, 1988) 124.

How *did* "the world come together for Baptists"? Very quickly, I want to approach the topic from five directions, all of which overlap and all five of which state why Baptists "got that way" on religious liberty and separation of church and state.

First, how did the world come together for Baptists biblically? That is, how did they read their Bibles?

Second, how did the world come together for Baptists theologically? How did they think about God and humanity?

Third, how did the world come together for Baptists ecclesiologically? How did they think about the church?

Fourth, how did the world come together for Baptists philosophically? With what kind of common sense did they approach life in general?

And fifth, how did the world come together for Baptists historically? How did they read human history?

Baptists planted their convictions concerning religious liberty in all five soils. A brief word about each of the five.

First, Baptists called for religious freedom because of the way they read the bible. Like all people, Baptists went to the Bible with lenses that refracted the truth of God to them in a certain way. Leon McBeth pointed out that seventeenth-century Anglicans tended to read church-state issues in light of the Old Testament. They liked, for example, the king motif in the history of Israel. Even some Separatists, such as John Robinson, spoke of the godly magistrate and the magistrate's authority to punish religious error, basing this on the power of Old Testament kings. Baptists, on the other hand, spent almost all their time interpreting the New Testament.

Baptists, for example, went to the New Testament to persuade others of the separation of the civil and spiritual kingdoms. Advocating religious liberty never meant that Baptists denied proper authority to civil rulers. In fact, Baptists were Romans 13 people, fond of quoting "let every person be subject to the governing authorities." McBeth was right when he said, "The fact that many Englishmen associated Baptists with . . . Anabaptists who disdained magistracy, plus the thought that spiritual liberty would lead to political anarchy, helps explain the frequent and insistent professions of civil loyalty by Baptists."[16]

But Baptists saw two spheres in the Bible. Romans 13 was for the civil, but James 4:12—"There is one lawgiver and judge"—that is, the Lordship of Christ, was for the church. Thomas Helwys in *The Mistery of Iniquity*

---

[16]McBeth, *English Baptist Literature*, 52.

clearly set out the concept of the two spheres, civil and spiritual. He used Luke 20:25 as his prooftext and says he is willing to render obedience to Caesar in matters of the temporal order but he adds, "farr be it from the King to take from Christ Jesus anie one part of that power & honor which belongs to Christ in his kingdome."[17] Roger Williams used this two spheres model in his famous ship metaphor.[18]

Another favorite biblical text for Baptists was Matthew 13:24-30, the parable about the tares and the wheat growing together. Both should be tolerated until the judgment day, they argued.[19]

Moreover, Baptists said the apostles did not use force but they endured scourging and stonings and the like. The worst they did to those who would not receive the gospel was to shake the dust off their feet (Matt 10:14; Luke 10:11; Acts 13:51).[20] Also, the New Testament, said Baptists, stressed that we are not to lord it over one another (Mark 10:35ff.).[21]

Second, Baptists called for religious liberty because of the way the world came together for them theologically. I mention only three theological themes. Baptists anchored their passion for religious liberty to (1) the nature of God, (2) the nature of humanity, and (3) the nature of faith.

Religious freedom, said the early Baptists, is rooted in the nature of God. A Sovereign God who dared to create people as free beings is portrayed in the Bible as a liberating Deity. Throughout the Old Testament, God is set against persons and institutions that restricted the freedom of God's people. And the complete thrust of Jesus' ministry was to free people from all that would hold them back from obedience to God. Freedom for Baptists was far more than a constitutional right or a governmental gift. God, not nations or courts or human law, is the ultimate source of liberty.

While early Baptists, especially General Baptists, stressed free will, they also emphasized the Sovereignty of God. Richard Overton wrote a satirical and humorous masterpiece in the seventeenth century entitled "The Arraignment of Mr. Persecution." Personifying the practice of religious oppression, Overton places "Mr. Persecution" on trial. At the preliminary

---

[17]Cited in McBeth, *English Baptist Literature*, 33.

[18]See Anson Phelps Stokes, *Church and State in the United States*, 3 vols. (New York: Harper & Bros., 1950) 1:197.

[19]Glen H. Stassen, *Just Peacemaking: Transforming Initiatives for Justice and Peace* (Louisville: Westminster/John Knox Press, 1992) 146.

[20]Stassen, *Just Peacemaking*, 147.

[21]Stassen, *Just Peacemaking*, 150.

inquest ten persons bring charges. "Mr. Sovereignty of Christ" is the first to testify against Mr. Persecution, saying he is an "arch-traitor" to the rule of Jesus Christ over the consciences of humankind.[22] One can render unto Caesar what belongs to Caesar but the soul, said Baptists, belongs to God alone.

Baptists also based their call for religious liberty on the biblical view of persons. Created in the image of God, a human being is the crowning work of God's creation (Ps 8). Human personality is sacred and life's highest value. To deny freedom of conscience to any person is to debase God's creation.

Third, and I think here we come to the essence of how the world came together for them, Baptists insisted on soul liberty because of their understanding of faith and the nature of the spiritual life. "To be authentic," Baptists yelled, "faith must be free." Backus spoke for all the Baptists who had gone before him and all who would come after him, "True Religion is a voluntary obedience to God." Baptists have said it in many ways, but it lies at the heart of how the world comes together for them.

> "Where there is no autonomy, there is no authenticity."
> "If faith is to be valid, it must be voluntary."
> "To cram a creed down a person's throat is rape of the soul."
> "The only conversion that counts is conversion by conviction."

Martin E. Marty called it "Baptistification." It is an approach to life that underscores freedom, choice, and voluntarism in matters of faith. This is, in my judgment, the core value of the Baptist people.

Third, Baptists called for religious freedom because of their ecclesiologial convictions. "The world came together" for them with a certain view of church. Just as salvation was the work of God but never imposed, the church was the work of the Holy Spirit but one was never coerced in it. Helwys had an ecclesiology, says McBeth, where the church was "primarily spiritual rather than organizational. Response to God was highly personal and individualistic. Not only was it impractical and unscriptural to attempt to legislate such a spiritual relationship, it would be completely impossible to do so."[23] And in the opening paragraph of Leonard Busher's 1614 *Religion's Peace: A Plea for Liberty of Conscience*, Busher argued

---

[22]Stassen, *Just Peacemaking*, 145.
[23]McBeth, *English Baptist Literature*, 33.

that the church is created not by being born into it but by being reborn, a matter of personal, spiritual response to God.[24]

In his 1615 Confessional Statement Richard Overton argued that "Christ allowed full power and authority to his church, assembled together, *cordially* and *unanimously*, to choose persons to bear office in the church. And these and no others are to be included, viz. [the offices], of pastors, of teachers, of elders, of deacons, of sub-ministers, who, by the Word of God, from every part are qualified and approved."[25]

Overton is arguing against the power of the bishops over the churches and he is giving a definition of the church as a "gathered church." One of Overton's recurring themes was "the sole authority of Jesus Christ versus ecclesiastical hierarchy."[26]

Fourth, the world came together for Baptists philosophically in a natural and commonsense sort of way. Early Baptists used exceedingly practical arguments in support of their contention for freedom of conscience. Thomas Helwys, for example, claimed that religious persecution was both unnecessary and ineffective. The spiritual kingdom does not need the aid of the state, he said. Moreover, rather than producing religious uniformity and protecting civil loyalty, persecution drives people to do the opposite, confirming them more solidly in their judgments. Forcing religion upon people only makes hypocrites out of them. Another practical issue, said Helwys, one that surely did not set well with the likes of James I, was that civil rulers usually are not spiritually fit to preside over religion.[27]

Listen to this natural rights argument! The use of force in matters of religion, said Busher, "is not only unmerciful, but *unnatural. . . .*" Equality in matters of the heart, he contended, was the only path to civil tranquility. Injustice breeds disorder.[28] Further, Leonard Busher argued in *Religion's*

---

[24]Cited in McBeth, *A Sourcebook*, 73.

[25]Cited in Benjamin Evans, *The Early English Baptists*, 2 vols. (London: J. Heaton & Son, 1862) 1:255.

[26]Stassen, *Just Peacemaking*, 143.

[27]McBeth, *English Baptist Literature*, 37.

[28]McBeth, *A Sourcebook*, 74. John Clarke used the same argument in *Ill Newes from New-England* when writing to the civil and religious authorities of Massachusetts after they had imprisoned him, John Crandall, and Obadiah Holmes. Clarke said, "As touching the wrong and injury done to us, you having thereby much more wronged your own souls in transgressing the very law, and light of Nations, doing as you would not be done unto." See this quotation in *Ill Newes from New-England* as reprinted in *Colonial Baptists, Massachusetts and Rhode Island*, Baptist

Peace, as Thomas Helwys before him, that quite apart from the question of right and wrong, coercion in religion is simply not effective in stamping out heretics. Heresies cannot be killed by fire and sword, Busher said, but only by the word and spirit of God.[29]

In what I take to be a most significant but relatively unknown essay, Glen Stassen in "The Christian Origin of Human Rights," argues that the origin of human rights is not found in the rationalism and individualism of the Enlightenment but in the free churches at the time of the Puritan Revolution, a good half century prior to the Enlightenment.[30] Free churches, Stassen argues, based their arguments on biblical, theological, and rational grounds. While reason was not the primary grounding of the Baptist argument, it was certainly present.

Stassen uses Richard Overton, a seventeenth century General Baptist, to make his point. In Overton's "The Arraignement of Mr. Persecution," which I have already referred to, Overton has a mock trial for Mr. Persecution. The trial ends with a concluding statement from Justice Reason. Not Justice Bible, mind you, or Justice Theology, or Justice Christ, but Justice Reason! Justice Reason, in his conclusion, says that Mr. Persecution threatens "the general and equal rights and liberties of the common people . . . their native and just liberties in general."[31] Baptists distinguished religious liberty and religious freedom as belonging to all persons as persons and not to Christianity or to people of a particular brand of Christianity.

Grounding the argument for religious liberty in natural reason is important because it gives Christians the opportunity to identify with non-Christians in the struggle for human rights. All of us know the story of how Baptists in America united with those of diverse religious views, many of whom were very rationalistic, to move closer to the ideal of religious liberty.[32] What Stassen observed about human rights in general can be applied to the Baptist drive for religious liberty in particular: "The ethic of

---

Tradition series (New York: Arno Press, 1980) 16.

[29]McBeth, *English Baptist Literature*, 44.

[30]While not arguing precisely as does Stassen, E. Glenn Hinson maintains something of the same in James Leo Garrett, Jr., E. Glenn Hinson, and James E. Tull, *Are Southern Baptists "Evangelicals"?* (Macon GA: Mercer University Press, 1983) 178.

[31]Stassen, *Just Peacemaking*, 148.

[32]Robert T. Handy, "The Principle of Religious Freedom and the Dynamics of Baptist History," *Perspectives in Religious Studies* 13/4 (Winter 1986): 28.

human rights can be a universal ethic, not because its *source* is a common philosophy believed by all people but because its *intention and application* affirm the rights of all persons."[33] No wonder Helwys said, "Let them be heretikes, Turks, Jewes, or whatsoever, it appertynes not to the earthly power to punish them in the least measure."

Fifthly, while not a major argument, Baptists called for religious liberty on the basis of history itself. Busher chided proud old England by comparing it to Muslim Constantinople. "I read that Jews, Christians, and Turks, are tolerated in Constantinople," he said, "and yet are peaceable, though so contrary the one to the other."[34] And Richard Overton, taking the historical evidence in another direction, pointed to historical examples in Germany, Holland, France, Scotland, and Ireland, and asked what caused that civil unrest but "this devilish spirit of binding the conscience."[35]

So the world came together for Baptists biblically, theologically, ecclesiologically, philosophically, and historically in such a way that it drove them to a "theology of pluralism." Birthed in adversity, Baptist convictions issued in diversity.

Baptists: Engaged in Political Activity

It is obvious from all that I have said that Baptists were far from passive observers in their quest for religious freedom. They got that way on issues of conscience because their convictions issued into activity. To *say* something is one thing; to *act* on what you say is quite another thing. Actions confirm and deepen rhetoric. You believe it more once you do something about it.

Back several years ago when the "Honk if you love Jesus" bumper stickers were popular, I heard of a clunker of a car hobbling down the interstate. Bent up, broken down, with several colors of paint on it, and puffing down the road, the bright new bumper sticker read, "If you love Jesus— Push!" Honking is not enough! Baptists certainly "honked" about religious liberty; they did more than "honk," however.

They lobbied with their lives and pens, and they lobbied *together* as a denomination, not simply as lone individuals howling in the night against the cold winds of constrictionism. When one starts pushing at whatever she is honking about, the thing tends to get positioned firmly in the soul. There

---

[33]Stassen, *Just Peacemaking*, 156.
[34]McBeth, *A Sourcebook*, 74.
[35]Stassen, *Just Peacemaking*, 146.

was a Baptist joint committee long before there was a Joint Committee in 1936. Baptists lobbied jointly with their pens and lives for religious liberty. They even broke laws deliberately and premeditatively.

Thomas Helwys spoke not only for himself, but for his little band of believers when he wrote *The Mistery of Iniquity*. Near the close of his document, Helwys uses the plural in more than an editorial way:

> Let none thinke that we are altogether ignorant, what . . . war we take in hand, and that wee have not sitt downe and in some measure throughly considered what the cost and danger may be: and also let none thinke that wee are without sense and feeling of our owne inability to begin, and our weaknes to endure to the end, the weight and danger of such a work: Lett none therefore despise the day of small things.[36]

Let none despise the day of small beginnings, indeed!

In no place in Baptist life does one see political engagement by the entire denomination better than in America in the work of Baptist associations in the eighteenth century. The temptation in Baptist historiography has been to isolate the accomplishments of salient individuals without recognizing and giving due credit to the denominational context within in which the individuals worked. John Leland cannot be understood apart from his work on behalf of associations in both Virginia and New England. Isaac Backus, likewise, cannot be properly appraised apart from the Warren Association.

In its 1791 circular letter the General Committee of Virginia described itself as the "political mouth"[37] of the Baptists of Virginia, a heritage I would suggest that the Baptist Joint Committee has perpetuated in grand style. And the Warren Association of Rhode Island adopted in 1769 a "plan to collect grievances" on issues of religious freedom.[38]

The Warren Association subsequently appointed a personal agent to act for the association. The agent became the voice of the Warren Association on behalf of religious liberty. The first agent was Hezekiah Smith, the incomparable pastor of the Haverhill Baptist church in Haverhill, Massachusetts. The second was John Davis, pastor of the Second Baptist Church in Boston, who was selected to act for "Baptists as a denomination." Had

---

[36]Cited in McBeth, *English Baptist Literature*, 38.

[37]See Walter B. Shurden, *Associationalism among Baptists in America: 1707–1814* (New York: Arno Press, 1980) 208.

[38]Shurden, *Associationalism among Baptists*, 212.

Davis not died suddenly, he might have become one of American Baptists' greatest champions of religious freedom. Immediately before his selection as agent for the Warren Association, Davis had taken a strong stand for religious liberty in Boston. This incident had brought him to the attention of the Warren Association. And except for Davis's sudden death Baptists may have never heard of Isaac Backus as a great activist for religious liberty.

Backus became the third agent of the Warren Association. Most of Backus's treatises and sermons on religious freedom were written after he assumed the office of "agent" of the Warren Association. His petitions, memorial, and remonstrances were usually signed, "Isaac Backus, Agent of the Baptist Churches."

Here is my point: the Baptist fight to disestablish state churches was not a political fray which courageous individuals entered alone; it was a melee in which the entire denomination was involved. Many Baptists in America may have forgotten that it was the struggle for religious liberty and the struggle for an educated ministry which first brought Baptists in America together. Foreign missions is often given that credit, but that is to read later affections back into early Baptist history. Not until William Carey and 1792 did Baptists get together on global missions. Years prior to Carey Baptists had been plugging away for soul liberty.

Interestingly, it is on issues of religious liberty that Baptists of America still cooperate more than they do on any other issue. It has been an ecumenical force for Baptist life for most of Baptist history. Their denominational cooperation in lobbying on behalf of religious liberty and separation of church and state has made them more committed to the concepts for which they lobbied.

Conclusion

Groucho Marx once said, "I didn't like the play, but then I saw it under adverse conditions—the curtain went up!" And so the Baptist people. They did not like what they saw in England and the colonies in the seventeenth and eighteenth centuries, but they had no choice. The curtain had gone up. They were birthed in adversity. And that historical experience, plus the way the theological world came together for Baptists and the fact that they would not remain passive in the face of freedoms denied—those were the factors that explain how Baptists "got that way" on issues of the freedom of conscience and separation of church and state.

I would only add of our time: if we love freedom, we are going to have unite with the Baptist Joint Committee and push—HARD!

The Priesthood of All Believers and Pastoral Authority in Baptist Thought[1]

Much of the Baptist world was shocked when the historic Baptist doctrine of the priesthood of believers was revised to the point of repudiation in 1988 with the adoption of "Resolution 5" by the fundamentalist majority at the Southern Baptist Convention in San Antonio, Texas. Surrounded by fiery debate, the resolution read as follows.

WHEREAS, None of the five major writing systematic theologians in Southern Baptist history have given more than passing reference to the doctrine of the Priesthood of the Believer in their systematic theologies; and

WHEREAS, The Baptist Faith and Message preamble refers to the Priesthood of the Believer, but provides no definition or content to the terms; and

WHEREAS, The high profile emphasis on the doctrine of the Priesthood of the Believer is a term which is subject to both misunderstanding and abuse; and

WHEREAS, The doctrine of the Priesthood of the Believer has been used to justify wrongly the attitude that a Christian may believe whatever he so chooses and still be considered a loyal Southern Baptist; and

WHEREAS, The doctrine of the Priesthood of the Believer can be used to justify the undermining of pastoral authority in the local church.

Be it therefore, RESOLVED, That the Southern Baptist Convention meeting in San Antonio, Texas, June 14-16, 1988, affirm its belief in the biblical doctrine of the Priesthood of the Believer (1 Peter 2:9 and Revelation 1:6); and

Be it further RESOLVED, That we affirm that this doctrine in no way gives license to misinterpret, explain away, demythologize, or extrapolate out elements of the supernatural from the Bible; and

Be it further RESOLVED, That the doctrine of the Priesthood of the Believer in no way contradicts the biblical understanding of the role, responsibility, and authority of the pastor which is seen in the command of the local church in Hebrews 13:17, "Obey your leaders, and submit to them; for

---

[1]This article first appeared in *Faith and Mission* 7/1 (Fall 1989): 24-45. It later appeared in Walter B. Shurden, editor, *Proclaiming the Baptist Vision: The Priesthood of All Believers* (Macon GA: Smyth & Helwys Publishing Inc., 1993) 131-54. It is reprinted here with the permission of Smyth and Helwys.

they keep watch over your souls, as those who will give you an account;" and

Be it further RESOLVED, That we affirm the truth that elders or pastors are called of God to lead the local church (Acts 20:28)[2]

The central issue posed by the resolution is the relationship of the Baptist doctrine of the priesthood of believers to the concept of pastoral authority. The underlying issue, therefore, becomes the locus of authority within a local Baptist congregation. What is the nature and authority of church officers, especially pastors, in relationship to the congregation as a whole? What, specifically, is meant in Baptist thought by the "authority of the pastor"?

My primary purpose in this article is investigative in nature. I have attempted to survey Baptist thought chronologically to detect development, patterns, and emphases concerning the topic. This proved valuable. My secondary purpose is explanatory. I have sought to explain language, ideas, and concepts as they relate to pastoral authority in Baptist history. In the "Summary" I have tried to identify the most important historical considerations.

Baptist Thought in the Seventeenth Century

Any effort to understand the first principles and foundation of Baptist thought must begin with John Smyth. Fortunately he wrote much, and we have much of what he wrote.[3] Because of his own spiritual saga and the pressing ecclesiological issues of his day, Smyth often confronted the question of the relative authority of pastors over against the congregation as a whole. A casual reading of Smyth's writings would dispel any doubts regarding the historical rootage of the priesthood of all believers among early Baptists.[4]

Smyth, and all subsequent Baptists, stress that the church is fundamentally a Christocracy. Baptists have no monopoly on this idea, however. All Christian denominations argue that Jesus is the ultimate

---

[2]*SBC Annual 1988*, 68, 69.

[3]For Smyth's writings, see W. T. Whitley, ed., *The Works of John Smyth*, 2 vols. (Cambridge: Cambridge University Press, 1915). For the life of Smyth see vol. 1 of Whitley and the excellent article on Smyth by James Tull, *Shapers of Baptist Thought* (Valley Forge PA: Judson Press, 1972; repr.: Reprints of Scholarly Excellence [ROSE] 8, Macon GA: Mercer University Press, April 1984).

[4]Whitley, *The Works of John Smyth*, 1:274-75.

source of the church's power and authority. The differences in polity emerge when this basic principle is translated into practice. In other words, how is the rule of Christ delegated to and through the church? The question is crucial to this essay and four answers are possible.

Roman Catholicism, believing that the rule of Christ is processed through the pope, practices autocracy. Anglicanism, affirming that the authority of Christ is channeled through the bishops, practices oligarchy. Presbyterianism, or at least "the main Presbyterian tradition,"[5] believes that Christ rules through the ministers of the church. This is aristocracy. Congregationalism, which includes Baptists, asserts that Christ invests all authority in the congregation where believers share equally in power, privilege, and responsibility. This is democracy, sometimes caricatured as "mobocracy."

Smyth wrote at length on what he called "Christ's ministerial powre" and the way that power is delegated to the church. Insistent that this power is given not to clergy "but to the body of the church," Smyth said that "the Church or two or three faithful people Separated fro [from] the world and joyned together in a true covenant, have both Christ, the covenant, and promises, and the ministerial powre of Christ given to them."[6]

Smyth did not, Quaker-like, dismiss or even disregard the elders or pastors. Important for "order sake," they are to "lead" and "goveme." Smyth did not even dispute "whither the Elders must rule or not," but he wanted to clarify what all such language meant. Elders act "for the body," not on their own. With emphasis he wrote that "the definitive sentence, the determining powre, the negative voice is in the body of the church, not in the elders."[7]

Prominent among the differences between the Smyth-Helwys group and some other Separatists was the authority of elders. Separatists such as Francis Johnson elevated pastors above the congregation, while Smyth subordinated church leaders to the congregation. Over against pastoral authority Smyth contended that "the brethren joyntly have all powre both of the Kingdom and Priesthood immediately from Christ."[8] Articulating a

---

[5]Harry G. Goodykoontz, *The Minister in the Reformed Tradition* (Richmond: John Knox Press, 1963) 137.

[6]Whitley, *The Works of John Smyth*, 2:403.

[7]Whitley, *The Works of John Smyth*, 416-17. For Smyth's treatment of Hebrews 13:17, see 434, 435.

[8]Whitley, *The Works of John Smyth*, 1:315.

point of view which became dominant in the Baptist tradition, Smyth put it bluntly, "The presbytery hath no powre, but what the church hath and giveth vnto it: which the Church vppon just cause can take away."[9]

W. T. Whitley, British Baptist historian and Smyth's biographer, accurately described Smyth's understanding of pastors as "creatures of the church."[10] While not without a leadership role in the church, pastors added nothing but "order" to the church. The subordination of pastors to congregations is unmistakable in Smyth's thought. General Baptists in sixteenth-century England tended to adhere to Smyth's understanding.[11]

Turning from General to Particular Baptists, one finds the same basic pattern with a slightly different emphasis. Smyth emphasized the authority of the congregation while affirming a distinctive role for the pastor. Calvinistic Baptists also emphasized the congregation as the centerpiece of church authority, but in addition they *stressed* that pastors were gifts of God to the churches. The difference is one of degree, not kind. Among Particular Baptists the congregation suffered no diminishment, but the place of ministers became more prominent. This difference was partially due to diverse origins.[12]

The Particular Baptist position can be illustrated with "The First London Confession of 1644," the theological document that set the normal pattern of future Calvinistic Baptist church life.[13] Based upon a 1596 Separatist statement known as "A True Confession," the basic ecclesiology in the two confessional documents was the same. But as British Baptist historian B. R. White noted, there were also "significant differences." One of those differences was that in the Baptist Confession of 1644 "the

---

[9]Whitley, *The Works of John Smyth*, 1:315.

[10]Whitley, *The Works of John Smyth*, 1:lxix.

[11]For Thomas Helwys' position, see his confession of faith in William L. Lumpkin, ed., *Baptist Confessions of Faith* (Valley Forge PA: Judson Press, 1959) 120. Three other seventeenth-century General Baptist confessional statements add nuances of their own. See Lumpkin, 185, 229, 322, 332.

[12]See Winthrop Still Hudson's lead article in his *Baptist Concepts of the Church: A Survey of the Historical and Theological Issues Which Have Produced Changes in Church Order* (Chicago: Judson Press, 1959) 12, 13. See also B. R. White, *The English Separatist Tradition* (Oxford: Oxford University Press, 1971) 165-69. While acknowledging the differences in origin, White wisely balances this interpretation by pointing to the Separatist antecedents to Particular as well as General Baptists.

[13]See Lumpkin, *Baptist Confessions of Faith*, 144-47.

ministry was firmly subordinated to the immediate authority of the covenanted community."[14]

Several articles in the 1644 Confession refer either explicitly or implicitly to both the Priesthood of Believers[15] and to the role of the pastor.[16] Hebrews 13:17 is used twice to prooftext ministerial authority, but never with the connotation of domination. Pastors are certainly "speciall men over the church," but they labor alongside the members who share both the authority and duty "to watch over one another." The Confession is lucid on how the power of Christ is processed. It is delegated "to every particular Congregation, and not one particular person, either member or Officer of the whole."[17] The 1644 Confession enunciated the equality of all believers, while holding up the pastor as "special." All are equal. And pastors are first among equals. This became the prevailing pattern in Baptist life.

As in England, Baptists in seventeenth-century America were far more interested in the freedom that flowed from the equality of believers than from any control that evolved from pastoral authority. Their circumstances argued for such. With only twenty-four small and struggling churches by 1700, they were harassed by the establishment and lacking in trained ministerial leadership. Their primary concern was survival, not the authority of pastors. Indeed, in many (maybe most) cases, church leadership was essentially lay in character.

John Clarke, pastor of the First Baptist Church of Newport, Rhode Island, was correctly described by A. H. Newman as "the most important American Baptist of the century in which he lived."[18] Writing from a

---

[14]See White, *English Separatist Tradition*, 62, 63. See also Murray Tolmie, *The Triumph of the Saints* (Cambridge UK: Cambridge University Press, 1977) 57.

[15]See Lumpkin, *Baptist Confessions of Faith*, 161 (article XVII), 164 (XXVII), 165 (XXXIII), 166 (XXXV), 168 (XLII, XLIII, XLIV).

[16]Lumpkin, *Baptist Confessions of Faith*, 166 (articles XXXVI, XXXVII), 168 (XLIV).

[17]Lumpkin, *Baptist Confessions of Faith*, 168. Space forbids further development of the English Particular Baptist viewpoint in the seventeenth century. Local church records, however, as well as the thought of prominent individual ministers support the general profile drawn here. See Roger Hayden, ed., *The Records of a Church of Christ in Bristol, 1640–1687*, Bristol Record Society Publications 27 (Gateshead, England: printed for the Bristol Record Society, 1974) and Pope A. Duncan, *Hanserd Knollys: Seventeenth-Century Baptist* (Nashville: Broadman Press, 1965) 28-35.

[18]Albert Henry Newman, *A History of the Baptists of the United States* (New

Boston jail in 1651, Clarke testified to his faith in the freedom of the individual believer to develop spiritual gifts and to "speak by way of prophecy for the edification, exhortation, and comfort of the whole [congregation], and to act with free conscience in spiritual matters."[19]

Obadiah Holmes, celebrated sufferer for Baptist principles, succeeded Clarke as pastor at Newport. His writings, often beautiful and moving, reflect a deep concern for the role and respect of ministers. Probably with Hebrews 13:17 in mind, Holmes said, "Honor them . . . that labor in the word and doctrine of Christ, those that are over you in the Lord and watch over yourselves as they that must give an account of stewardship."[20]

If one quoted only the statements above as representative of Holmes's convictions on pastoral authority, one would egregiously misrepresent him. Describing Holmes's point of view on this issue, his biographer said, "The minister, however, is but a single and imperfect instrument. *Even more significant* in God's grand scheme is the ministry of the congregation."[21]

Like Clarke, Holmes believed that individual believers "are under duty" not only to speak their convictions in worship, but to judge critically what they hear.[22] He added, "Take nothing from any man until you have tried it and well digested it by a good understanding."[23] Concerning this last admonition, Edwin Gaustad said, "Indeed, much of Christian liberty and Baptist polity can be read in these words."[24] Surely Obadiah Holmes would agree. After all, he became a Baptist because his former Congregationalist pastor "had assumed a presbyterial power over the church."[25]

York: Charles Scribner's Sons, 1894) 108.

[19]This is found in John Clarke, *III Newes from New-England* (1652) as reprinted in *Colonial Baptists, Massachusetts and Rhode Island*, Baptist Tradition series (New York: Arno Press, 1980) 37. For important elaborations and explanations of Clarke's confession see 96, 97, and 103.

[20]As cited in Edwin S. Gaustad, *Baptist Piety: The Last Will and Testimony of Obadiah Holmes* (Grand Rapids MI: Christian University Press, 1978) 109.

[21]Gaustad, *Baptist Piety*, 109.

[22]As cited in Gaustad, *Baptist Piety*, 91. For another example see Nathan E. Wood, *The History of the First Baptist Church of Boston* (New York: Arno Press, 1980) 65.

[23]As cited in Gaustad, *Baptist Piety*, 109-10.

[24]Gaustad, *Baptist Piety*, 107.

[25]Isaac Backus, *Your Baptist Heritage, 1620–1804* (Little Rock AR: Challenge Press, 1976) 56. This book was originally published in 1844 as *Church History of New England from 1620 to 1804, Containing a View of the Principles and Practice,*

Baptist Thought in the Eighteenth Century

Three patterns of authority relative to pastors and congregations developed among Baptists in the eighteenth century. The first, represented by John Gill (1697–1771) of England, was "a clergy-centered congregationalism." Probably nowhere else in Baptist history is pastoral authority more pronounced than in the writings of John Gill. Because of his voluminous publications and theological erudition, he has been dubbed "the Baptist Origen."[26] A hypercalvinist, Gill labored in the light of eighteenth-century rationalism, Deism, and numerous other theological aberrations. If his intellectual milieu helped drive him to theological extremes, it may have caused him to accentuate the authority of the clergy as a control factor in a freewheeling century.[27]

If, in fact, he does not, Gill comes uncomfortably close to altering the flow of authority in Baptist life from Christ → Congregation → Clergy to Christ → Clergy → Congregation. Appearing to be influenced almost as much by a Calvinistic ecclesiology regarding pastors as a Calvinistic theology concerning grace, Gill wrote, "They [pastors] are under Christ, and are subject to him, but are over the churches by his appointment . . . and obedience to them is required."[28] Gill's language would be shocking to most Baptists. Pastors have "preeminence," are "the highest officers," are

---

Declensions and Revivals, Oppression and Liberty of the Churches, and a Chronological Table. With a Memoir of the Author (Philadelphia: American Baptist Publ. and S.S. Society, 1844). See also Doug Adams, *Meeting House to Camp Meeting: Toward a History of American Free Church Worship from 1620 to 1835* (Saratoga CA: Modern Liturgy-Resource Publications, 1981) 90. Adams says: "Among the seventeenth-century Congregationalists were numerous ministers and laity of Presbyterian persuasion. Presbyterians both inside and outside the Congregational churches influenced an increase of ministerial prerogatives at the expense of lay participation in worship." This was precisely what Holmes rebelled against.

[26]John W. Brush, "John Gill's Doctrine of the Church," in Hudson, *Baptist Concepts of the Church*, 54.

[27]Brush ("John Gill's Doctrine of the Church," 56), along with other Baptist historians, argues that Gill was a theological extremist. For the opposite point of view, see Thomas J. Nettles, *By His Grace and for His Glory* (Grand Rapids MI: Baker Book House, 1986) 73-107.

[28]John Gill, *A Complete Body of Doctrinal and Practical Divinity: or, A System of Evangelical Truths Deduced from the Sacred Scriptures*, 2 vols., a new edition (London: printed for Thomas Tegg, 1839) 2:558.

"set in the first and most eminent place," have "superiority" over church members, and should be esteemed above "common Christians." For Gill, the pastor did not simply possess spiritual gifts; he had "office power." And the professional ministers were not "only convenient" but "absolutely necessary" to the church.[29]

Unquestionably, Gill's rhetoric moves pastoral authority dangerously near the usurpation of congregational rule. But Gill should be read with care, and his comments regarding the pastor interpreted contextually. For example, the Greek scholar in Gill quickly explains that the same word for "feed" is used for "rule."[30] Pastors who "rule" the church "feed" the church. That ministry is never "exercised in an arbitrary way." Pastors are not to "lord it over God's heritage" because they do not have dominion over the faith of church members. Pastors cannot "create" rules. They "rule well" only when they teach according to scripture.

The crucial question, therefore, is who decides when or if pastors teach scripturally? Gill intimates his answer with these words:

> Indeed, none are obliged to receive and obey their [pastors'] word or doctrine, but as it appears to be agreeable to the sacred scriptures, . . . every spirit is not to be believed, but to be tried, . . . and, indeed, every thing delivered by pastors to churches is not binding on churches; nor are they obliged to receive it, but as it accords with the word of God.[31]

Interpretation of scripture rests finally where all decisions and conclusions in Baptist church life are to be found—with the congregation. Gill, for all his lofty language regarding pastors, seems to have recognized this fact clearly.

Whereas Gill taught a clergy-centered congregationalism, his younger colleague in America, Isaac Backus (1724-1806), energetically advocated a "lay-centered congregationalism." Gill, in his context, was primarily concerned with authority and, therefore, wanted a strong clergy. Backus, in his environment, was focused on freedom and, therefore, lobbied for a weak clergy. Coming out of New England Congregationalism that had become "presbygationalism," Backus feared the abuse of civil authority (the state), ecclesiastical authority (synods and associations), and ministerial authority (clergy).

---

[29]Gill, *A Complete Body*, 588, 593, 595, 595, 595, 592.
[30]Gill, *A Complete Body*, 588.
[31]Gill, *A Complete Body*, 597.

When writing about the church, the apostle Peter, said Backus, rested the cause of truth not on pastors but "on the shoulders" of the "holy priesthood." And then, quite accurately, Backus adds, "Saints are often called *priests*, but ministers as distinguished from other Christians are never once . . . called priests in the New Testament."[32] Rather than elevating the clergy over the laity, Backus would not even permit separating the two. He believed that the "core" of the Great Awakening was that common people claimed "as good a right to judge and act for themselves in matters of religion as civil rulers or the learned clergy."[33]

But just as Gill did not overlook the authority of the congregation of believers, Backus did not totally ignore a special role for clergy. The "rule of the pastor" was not language foreign to Backus. But he carefully described its meaning and consistently circumscribed its authority.[34] Pastors "rule" over the church, according to Backus, only by word and example. They "have no power to make rules nor to govern others' judgments but only to explain the rules which are made and labor to move others to regard them." While believers should follow pastoral teaching, they are not to "obey and follow them in an implicit or customary way." Rather "each one" must evaluate pastoral teaching in light of biblical teaching. To follow pastors uncritically, thought Backus, is to "incur guilt."[35]

Theologically, Backus was a staunch Calvinist and drank deeply from the well of John Gill. It is fair to say that Backus's concern for preserving the congregational autonomy of the church was only exceeded by his defense of the monarchical authority of God.[36] While agreeing with Gill on the latter, he dared to differ with him on the former, especially as it touched the issue of pastoral authority. Backus was adamant about the hierarchy of

---

[32]Isaac Backus, "A Fish Caught in His Own Net," in *Isaac Backus on Church, State, and Calvinism: Pamphlets, 1754–1789*, ed. William G. McLoughlin (Cambridge MA: Harvard University Press, 1968) 275.

[33]Backus, "A Fish Caught in His Own Net," 273.

[34]See Edwin S. Gaustad, "The Backus-Leland Tradition," in Hudson, *Baptist Concepts of the Church*, 117. Gaustad's article is a good discussion of Backus' ecclesiology. For a superb study, see also Stanley Grenz, *Isaac Backus—Puritan and Baptist. His Place in History, His Thought, and Their Implications for Modern Baptist Theology*, NABPR Dissertation Series 4 (Macon GA: Mercer University Press, 1983) 126-50.

[35]Backus, "A Fish Caught in His Own Net," 224, 225. Also see Grenz, *Isaac Backus*, 280.

[36]McLoughlin, ed., *Isaac Backus on Church, State, and Calvinism*, 37.

authority in a local Baptist church. It was Christ, congregation, and clergy—always in that order.

In between Gill and Backus, a *via media* developed in the eighteenth century. Embodied in the Philadelphia Association, this third tradition spread rapidly in America. It appears more in keeping with seventeenth-century Baptist thought than either the clergy-centered congregationalism of Gill or the lay-centered congregationalism of Backus. How does one describe this middle way? It is a "first-among-equals congregationalism."

Rooted in the "Second London Confession of 1677" and transported from Philadelphia to the South primarily through the Charleston Association, this approach is spelled out in two significant documents. One is the "Philadelphia Confession of Faith," adopted with slight alterations by Charleston in 1767. The second is "A Summary of Church Discipline," published in 1774 and adopted by the Charleston Association a year previously. According to the Confession, ultimate power in the church is, of course, vested in "the Lord Jesus Christ," the head of the church. But penultimate power, or the execution of the power of Christ, is entrusted to local congregations. "To each of these churches," confesses the Confession, Christ "hath given all that power and authority, which is any way needful."[37] Echoing the same truth, the Summary used the metaphor of "the keys," affirming that "a church has the keys, or power of government, *within itself*, having Christ for its head, and his law for its role."[38] The congregation, not the pastor, has "the keys" of the church.

According to this tradition, pastors have no monopoly on the preaching ministry,[39] nor are they essential for organizing a church.[40] But they deserve "all due respect" because they have been appointed by Christ, gifted by the Spirit, and chosen by the church to the "highest office in the church."[41]

The Summary devoted one entire section to the "duties incumbent on all members of churches" toward ministers. Composed of seven obligations and documented with scriptural citations, this section encourages members to esteem, respect, support, and assist ministers. Moreover—and most

---

[37]As cited in Lumpkin, *Baptist Confessions of Faith*, 287.

[38]"A Summary of Church Discipline" in *Baptist Confession of Faith: And a Summary of Church Discipline* (Charleston SC: printed by W. Riley, 1831) 5.

[39]See Lumpkin, *Baptist Confessions of Faith*, 228.

[40]"A Summary of Church Discipline," 5.

[41]See Lumpkin, *Baptist Confessions of Faith*, 287, and "A Summary of Church Discipline," 7.

pastors will be delighted with this one—members should not "expose" the minister's infirmities. Reminiscent of Gill, members are even "to obey and submit" themselves to their ministers.[42] One cannot read this document without sensing a deep respect for the pastor's role. But the tone suggests just that—respect for the role by the people, not the assertion of authority by the pastor.

The closest one comes to pastoral authority in this tradition relates to the church's discipline. Pastors are administrators of church discipline, especially excommunication. But unilateral and arbitrary action is, of course, forbidden. Pastors may act only "with the consent of members." The power of church discipline lies in the congregation as a whole; "the authority of executing it lies in the elders."[43]

This "first-among-equals congregationalism" posits church authority with the people, not the pastor. Because the church polity is congregational, all believers are equal. Because the pastor is a uniquely gifted believer, he is "first among equals." Pastoral authority, where it is present, is always derivative, delegated by the people.

Southern Baptist Thought in the Nineteenth Century

For a couple of reasons, the rest of this paper will concentrate on Baptists in the South. For one thing, Baptists in America and England had grown so phenomenally by 1800, and their publications were so numerous in the nineteenth century, that one could not do justice to the topic in a paper of this length without narrowing the focus. Second, and more importantly, because "Resolution 5" of San Antonio came from a group of Southern Baptists, it is important to see what, if any, historical antecedents the resolution has. Because John L. Dagg was Southern Baptists' first systematic theologian, and because William Bullein Johnson was the first president and a major influence in organizing the Southern Baptist Convention, they will function as my major sources for a study of the nineteenth century.

University president and professor of theology during the years 1844–1856, J. L. Dagg wrote four influential books in his retirement. Dagg published the second of these, *A Treatise on Church Order*, in 1858. One

---

[42]"A Summary of Church Discipline," 17.

[43]See "A Summary of Church Discipline," 21, and Lumpkin, *Baptist Confessions of Faith*, 287.

entire chapter deals with "The Ministry," and other parts of the book relate to issues touching pastoral authority and the equality of all believers.

If Gill tended to separate clergy into an elitist class from ordinary Christians and if Backus leaned toward no significant separation at all, Dagg had a view of "separate but equal." Separated by a special calling to a special service, ministers appear among the people of God "like the mountains on a continent, forming a part of it, and closely united with surrounding lands." Distinguished by their spiritual gifts, pastors are none-theless endowed by the "the same spirit" that "pervades the whole body of Christ." Unique ministerial gifts constitute a divine call and a solemn duty, not mere privilege.[44]

The special work of ministers, according to Dagg, is preaching. He elevates the proclamation of scripture above all other ministerial tasks. From among these "ministers of the Word," who, interestingly, are officers of the universal church, the churches should choose bishops or pastors "to teach and rule them." "The term bishop signifies overseer and implies authority to rule," he said.[45]

What is meant by "the ruling authority of a pastor"? Dagg is better, as are most Baptist sources that use this language, at telling us what it is *not*. It is "peculiar in its kind" and "while bearing some analogy to that of a father in his family, or of a governor in civil society, it differs from these." And what are the peculiarities? It is noncoercive, voluntary, with the consent of the people, and restricted to scripture.[46]

Indeed, Dagg does speak of pastoral authority. But he spends far more time setting the boundaries to that authority than he does in explicating it. In a later discussion of "scriptural church order," however, Dagg gives needed perspective and a more detailed explanation of what he means by pastoral authority.

After lamenting that "immense mischief has resulted from the ambition of the clergy" and that such mischief needs unscriptural centralization to sustain it, Dagg follows with a paragraph on Baptist church order weighted with the concept of the Priesthood of Believers. Local church independence

---

[44]John Leadley Dagg, *A Treatise on Church Order* (Charleston SC: Southern Baptist Publication Society, 1858) as reprinted as part 2 of *Manual of Theology* (with "A Treatise on Christian Doctrine" [part 1, 1857] and "Autobiography of Rev. John L. Dagg" [1886]) 3 vols. in 1 (Harrisonburg VA: Gano Books, 1982) 241-43.

[45]Dagg, *A Treatise on Church Order*, 263.

[46]Dagg, *A Treatise on Church Order*, 264-65.

and the democratic form of church government "appeal strongly to individual responsibility" and, therefore, "every man feels that the cause of Christ is in some measure committed to him." "This doctrine of individual responsibility," says Dagg, coupled with the concept of a regenerate church membership, bring glory to Christ.[47]

Dagg proceeds with a brilliant refutation of "some objections" to Baptist church polity. In Dagg's words, "Objection 1" is as follows:

> The independent form of church government does not allow sufficient influence to the ministerial office. Learned divines may be outvoted by ignorant laymen; and pastors, who ought to rule their flocks, may have their peace and reputation destroyed by their churches, without any right of appeal.[48]

Dagg's response to this objection clarifies his understanding of pastoral authority. "The objection supposes," said this Southern Baptist theologian, "some other than *moral power* to be needful for ministers." Authentic piety and a sincere "call of God to the ministry" that express themselves in selfless service to church members are rewarded with an influence over the church that is "almost unbounded." "God's truth, and a holy life, have rendered the ministry invincible," Dagg said, quickly adding, "and *the minister who asks for other power, mistakes the nature of his office*."[49]

Utilizing words as surgical tools, Dagg continued to eviscerate his objectors. His words are too precise to paraphrase.

> It is alleged, that a learned divine may be outvoted by ignorant laymen; and what then? Do truth and holiness lose their power, by being outvoted? The learned divine may be in the wrong; or he may arrogantly claim a deference to which he is not entitled. In this case, to give him governing power would be a sad remedy for the supposed evil. Perhaps he is in the right, and possesses the meekness and gentleness of Christ. In this case, he will teach us how to answer the objection now before us. He will choose in meekness to instruct those that oppose themselves, rather than prevail over them by authority.[50]

Drawing his rebuttal to a close, Dagg warned, "When a pastor seeks defence *from* his people, by entrenching himself in official authority, or

---

[47]Dagg, *A Treatise on Church Order*, 276.

[48]Dagg, *A Treatise on Church Order*, 277.

[49]Dagg, *A Treatise on Church Order*, 277; italics mine for emphasis.

[50]Dagg, *A Treatise on Church Order*, 277-78.

appealing to a higher tribunal, there is a radical evil which needs some other remedy."[51]

To summarize, Dagg was not anticlerical. He wrote with warmth and appreciation about the role and authority *of* pastors. But Dagg could never be used as a prooftext for dismantling believers' rights and inserting a constituted clerical authority. Respect for the pastoral role without abdicating Baptists' time-honored tradition of "individual responsibility" and participatory church life was the Dagg approach.

What about W. B. Johnson, one of the nineteenth-century architects of Southern Baptist life? What did he teach about the relative authority *of* congregation and clergy? In 1846, the year after he led in the formation of the Southern Baptist Convention, Johnson published a valuable little book entitled *The Gospel Developed through the Government and Order of the Churches of Jesus Christ*. Opposing confessions of faith as a basis for union,[52] advocating women deacons,[53] describing the church as "a holy priesthood,"[54] lobbying for the principle of "equal rights" in the church,[55] and devoting an entire chapter to "The Rulers of a Church,"[56] Johnson is primarily concerned to explain what he calls a "Christocratic" form of church government.[57] In the introduction of the book, Johnson identified "Baptist Distinctives," which he called "the true fundamental principles of Jesus Christ." He listed five specific convictions that apparently characterized Southern Baptists in the mid-nineteenth century. These Baptist convictions were (1) the sovereignty of God in salvation, (2) the supreme authority of the Bible, (3) "the right of each individual to judge for himself in his views of truth as taught in the scriptures," (4) "the independent, democratical, Christocratic form of church government," and (5) "the profession of religion by conscious subjects only."[58] Points 3 and 4 on Johnson's list of Baptist distinctives relate directly to the doctrine of the Priesthood of all Believers.

---

[51]Dagg, *A Treatise on Church Order*, 278.

[52]William Bullein Johnson, *The Gospel Developed through the Government and Order of the Churches of Jesus Christ* (Richmond: H. K. Ellyson, 1846) 197, 200.

[53]Johnson, *The Gospel Developed*, 93, 97.

[54]Johnson, *The Gospel Developed*, 159.

[55]Johnson, *The Gospel Developed*, 202, 224, 195.

[56]Johnson, *The Gospel Developed*, 75-91.

[57]Johnson, *The Gospel Developed*, 134.

[58]Johnson, *The Gospel Developed*, 16.

Johnson also wrote an entire chapter on the nature and function of the pastor, whom he prefers to call "overseer." His language sounds somewhat stern and rigid, if one does not permit Johnson to interpret. "Rulers" are provided by Christ "whom he clothes with authority, and to whom he requires that obedience and respect be rendered."[59] And the disciples who obeyed Peter's instruction set an important pattern that all churches should follow.[60] Quoting Hebrews 13:7, 17, 24 and several other scriptures, Johnson describes the titles and duties of "these rulers."

After quoting the scriptures, Johnson presented his interpretation as to their meaning. Johnson believed that each church in the New Testament had not a single leader, but "a plurality of rulers," designated variously as "elder, bishop, overseer, pastor." Equal in rank, "no one having a preeminence over the rest," the church leaders shared pastoral responsibility according to gifts. (Modern-day church staff members have labored, usually in vain, for that point of view!) Their duties were "to feed the members with spiritual food, to watch for their souls, and to supervise the whole body," all of which has the contemporary sound of preaching, pastoral care, and administration. Great responsibility on the part of the clergy called for great respect from the church, especially liberal financial support. But what about pastoral "authority"? "This authority," stressed Johnson, involved no *legislative* power or right but . . . was *ministerial and executive* only, and . . . the rulers were not to lord it over God's heritage" but were to lead by example.[61]

What we have here in Johnson's teaching is not constitutional authority of office before whom people bowed, but a high calling to service, which, if done right, caused the people to obey, submit, and follow. The plurality of pastors composed "a council of advisers" to the church collectively and to members individually.[62] The bishops are "gifts of Christ."[63]

In truth, W. B. Johnson was not nearly so concerned with either pastoral authority or the Priesthood of all Believers as he was with the rule of Christ in the church. He wanted a Christocracy! He wanted Christ to be Head, and he wanted Christ's power "manifested in perfect accordance with the freedom of his people." With an exemplary idealism, Johnson

---

[59]Johnson, *The Gospel Developed*, 75.
[60]Johnson, *The Gospel Developed*, 134.
[61]Johnson, *The Gospel Developed*, 77, 78.
[62]Johnson, *The Gospel Developed*, 85.
[63]Johnson, *The Gospel Developed*, 36.

stubbornly longed for a church where things were done "not according to our preconceived notions . . . but in obedience to the will of Christ."[64]

An important question, therefore, is: How does a local congregation of believers discern the will of Christ? Is it told them by their pastor? Does the plurality of bishops "hand down" such spiritual truth to the people? As a Christocracy, "*they* are to learn his will" by studying scripture under the influence of the Spirit.[65]

One of the advantages of the Christocratic form of government, Johnson reasoned, was that it freed churches from "human customs and the authority of men." While a strong propensity to submit to human authority exists in people, the "Christocratic form of government does not treat the members of the churches as mere machines but as rational, moral beings, the free exercise of whose powers is required in ascertaining and per-forming their duty." Christocracy provides for the exercise of voluntary, independent and democratic principles. In theory, Johnson desired an infallible Christocracy; in practice, he settled for a fragile and fallible democracy. He believed "the noble principle of equal rights" could be maintained and guarded in perfect consistency with "submission to the authority of the King in Zion."[66]

If Dagg and Johnson represent the normative pattern for Baptists in the nineteenth century South on the issues of pastoral and congregational authority, we have a continuation of the Philadelphia-Charleston Tradi-tion.[67] Clearly, it is a tradition where authority in the church proceeds from Christ to the congregation to the clergy. Pastors are respected for the calling they have, the work they do, and the service they render. They do not have authority by command for they work in a congregational polity among fellow believers, their equals in Christ. The "first-among-equals congrega-tionalism" continued among Southern Baptists in the nineteenth century.

Southern Baptist Thought in the Twentieth Century

To examine twentieth-century Southern Baptist thought, I will draw from four diverse sources. These are: (1) a manual of ecclesiology, (2) official statements adopted by the SBC, (3) publications from two

---

[64]Johnson, *The Gospel Developed*, 35.

[65]Johnson, *The Gospel Developed*, 221.

[66]Johnson, *The Gospel Developed*, 201-202.

[67]My preliminary research in other sources would appear to sustain this argument.

systematic theologians, and (4) publications of two prominent pastor theologians. What do these reveal concerning the Priesthood of Believers vis-à-vis pastoral authority?

E. C. Dargan (1852–1930), seminary professor, prominent pastor, Sunday School Board editor, and SBC president, published *Ecclesiology: A Study of the Churches* in 1897. Revised in 1905, this popular volume reflected and influenced Southern Baptist ecclesiological theory and practice during the first quarter of the twentieth century. Some of the themes in E. Y. Mullins's 1908 *The Axioms of Religion* are found here. Among them are the equality of all believers and the freedom and responsibility of individual Christians.

With Dagg and W. B. Johnson before him, Dargan emphasized that a plurality of elders existed in most New Testament congregations.[68] These elders, Dargan believed, were accorded "a certain amount of authority," but it was "moral and executive rather than governmental or judicial."[69] Relating pastoral authority to congregational authority in the Baptist churches of his day, Dargan observed, "The churches recognize these officers as executive only. The seat of authority is in the church, and to the church all its officers are directly responsible."[70]

By no means, however, did Dargan demean the authority or office of pastor. He pointed out that the very name "elder" or "bishop" denoted some type of authority. It was the *nature* of that authority that he underscored. Mild in leadership and nondespotic, this authority accrued to the pastor who manifested "high character" and "superior wisdom."[71]

---

[68]This point is not made as clearly or emphatically by subsequent Southern Baptist sources. "Resolution 5," while citing Hebrews 13:17 that uses the plural ("leaders"), alludes to "authority" of *the* pastor.

[69]Edwin Charles Dargan, *Ecclesiology: A Study of the Churches*, 2nd and "carefully revised" ed. (Louisville: Charles T. Dearing, 1905) 32.

[70]Dargan, *Ecclesiology*, 170.

[71]Dargan, *Ecclesiology*, 94. In a smaller, more popularized book, Dargan said of New Testament churches, "They had no governing board or ruler within themselves." See E. C. Dargan, *The Doctrines of Our Faith* (Nashville: Sunday School Board, Southern Baptist Convention, 1905) 168. Dargan dedicated this book to F. H. Kerfoot, James P. Boyce's successor in Systematic Theology and Dargan's colleague at Southern Seminary. An appendix in the book contains a statement by Kerfoot entitled "What We Believe according to the Scriptures." Kerfoot lists "individual responsibility or privilege" as the second of five Baptist distinctives. Concerning church officers, Kerfoot said that a local church "recognizes no such

In his discussions of church polity, Dargan certainly interpreted ecclesial authority as emanating from Christ to the congregation to the pastors. Without minimizing the pastoral role, Dargan at no point placed that role above the community of believers. He continued to perpetuate a "first-among-equals congregationalism."

Unquestionably, the Baptist Faith and Message (BFM) has been the single most influential theological document adopted by the Southern Baptist Convention. Initially approved in 1925 and revised in 1963, it enunciates the principles of the Priesthood of Believers at three points. First, the 1963 "Preamble" isolated cardinal Baptist distinctives in saying that "Baptists emphasize the soul's competency before God, freedom in religion, and the priesthood of the believer."[72] Second, the article on the church relates the Priesthood of Believers to church polity. A New Testament church, states the confession, is an autonomous body, operating through democratic processes under the Lordship of Jesus Christ. In such a congregation members are equally responsible.[73] Finally, the article on religious liberty reflects the Priesthood of Believers as it is related to the state. The article affirms that "God alone is Lord of the conscience."[74] It may be of some significance that the Baptist Faith and Message contains absolutely no reference to pastoral authority in Baptist life. In fact, pastors are not mentioned beyond the identification of them as "scriptural officers."[75]

While not a formal confessional statement, the Southern Baptist Convention approved a statement in 1938 on "Interdenominational

---

thing as priestly or papal domination nor any authority in its own officers to be in any way lords over God's heritage" (233).

[72]*SBC Annual 1963*, 270. Herschel Hobbs, chairman of the committee that presented the 1963 confession, was also the primary composer of the document. Hobbs said, "The committee was careful to include the safeguards of the individual conscience in the interpretation of scripture. With few exceptions, as much time was spent on this preamble as upon any other article in the statement." See Herschel H. Hobbs, "The Baptist Faith and Message-Anchored But Free," in *Baptist History and Heritage* 13/3 (July 1978): 36.

[73]*SBC Annual 1963*, 275.

[74]*SBC Annual 1963*, 281.

[75]*SBC Annual 1963*, 275. Although not a major development, it is of interest to note that Hebrews 13:17, used by "Resolution 5" to bolster the claim of pastoral authority, while used as a proof text in the 1925 BFM, was dropped in 1963 in favor of 1 Peter 5:1-4 which speaks of "not domineering."

Relations" that ought not be overlooked. Explaining Baptist ecclesiology, the statement said, "We believe that a church is a sure democracy, and cannot subject itself to any outside control, nor bend to a superior clergy." Employing language often used by Baptists to underscore the Priesthood of Believers, the document added, "We here declare our unalterable belief in the universal, unchangeable, and undelegated sovereignty of Jesus Christ."[76] No reference is made in the document to pastoral authority.

The two systematic theologians exerting the most influence, by far, on Southern Baptists in the twentieth century were E. Y. Miullins and W. T. Conner. Mullins believed that the single most distinguishing Baptist principle was "the competency of the soul in religion."[77] This concept, for Mullins, led "directly to democracy in church life and the priesthood of all believers."[78] Also, from this "mother principle" of Baptists there emerged six "axioms" or self-evident truths about the Christian faith. Four of the six relate to the Priesthood of All Believers, but for our purposes the most important was the third. Declaring that "all believers have a right to equal privileges in the church," Mullins called it the "ecclesiological axiom."[79]

As with the preponderance of the Baptist tradition preceding him, Mullins interpreted ecclesial authority as paradoxically an absolute monarchy and a pure democracy.[80] From Christ the King to the people of the congregation all power flowed. Developing the biblical metaphor of the church as the Body of Christ, Mullins said, "The blood flows directly from head to members." Believers in a congregation, therefore, have a twofold relationship. They have "a direct relation to the head and a relation of equality to other members of the body."[81] So intent on establishing the equality of all believers, Mullins failed completely, in his chapter on Baptist ecclesiology, to even discuss the role of the pastor.

The subordination of clergy to congregation in Mullins's thought is impossible to dispute. When, in another book, Mullins described the pastor's role, he said simply, "His authority is that of influence and leadership rather

---

[76]*SBC Annual 1938*, 24.

[77]Edgar Young Mullins, *The Axioms of Religion: A New Interpretation of the Baptist Faith* (Philadelphia, New York: American Baptist Publication Society, 1908) 53.

[78]Mullins, *The Axioms of Religion*, 55.

[79]Mullins, *The Axioms of Religion*, 73.

[80]Mullins, *The Axioms of Religion*, 129.

[81]Mullins, *The Axioms of Religion*, 130.

than official."[82] Even though the pastor "has no authority to lord it over God's heritage," the church still owes the pastor "loyalty and support."[83]

Serving for thirty-nine years as professor of systematic theology at Southwestern Seminary, Conner, a student of Mullins, has been called the Baptist "theologian of the Southwest." He may have exceeded his old professor in trumpeting the competency of the individual before God and the equality of all believers in the church. With both emphases, he relegated officers of the church to a role secondary to the people. Rather than arguing on the basis of Hebrews 13:17 for the accountability of church leaders, Conner chose to highlight Romans 14:9-12 and the accountability of each believer to the Lord. No person should try to come between the individual believer and the Lord because "every one of us shall give account of himself to the Lord, . . . not to pastor, priest, nor the bishop."[84] In church polity, the Southwestern theologian rejected any idea that clergy constituted an official class that "managed the affairs of the churches."[85]

Since about 1960, pastor-theologians have probably exerted more influence on Southern Baptists than have academic theologians.[86] Two of the most illustrious pastor-theologians of this era are Herschel H. Hobbs and W. A. Criswell, both former presidents of the Southern Baptist Convention. In 1978 Hobbs produced a thoroughly revised edition of E. Y. Mullins's interpretation of Baptist distinctives.

Continuing the structure and spirit of the original work, Hobbs, nevertheless, made the book his own, using language often more expressive and direct than Mullins. For example, Hobbs declared, "When church leaders presume to monopolize for themselves authority and privileges or when they usurp spiritual authority to become lords over the faith and life of others,"[87] they have violated the first axiom of religion. That axiom is

---

[82]Edgar Young Mullins, *Baptist Beliefs*, 4th ed. (Philadelphia: Judson Press, 1925; 1st ed.: Louisville KY: Baptist World Pub. Co., 1912) 67.

[83]Mullins, *Baptist Beliefs*, 67.

[84]Walter T. Conner, *The Gospel of Redemption*, "A revision and enlargement of some things I published . . . in *A System of Christian Doctrine*" (Nashville: Broadman Press, 1945) 275.

[85]W. T. Conner, *Christian Doctrine* (Nashville: Broadman Press, 1937; originally *A System of Christian Doctrine*, 1924) 266.

[86]For the development of this interpretation see my "The Pastor as Denominational Theologian in Southern Baptist History" in this volume.

[87]Herschel H. Hobbs and E. Y. Mullins, *The Axioms of Religion*, rev. ed. (Nashville: Broadman Press, 1978) 76.

that "all men have an equal right to direct access to God."[88] Moreover, in the church "no one believer should enjoy special privilege or sit in authority over another fellow believer, for only Jesus Christ is Lord."[89] About pastoral authority, Hobbs, like Mullins, insisted that it was restricted to "leadership and service." In fact, to attach official authority to the pastoral position "is to misread the New Testament."[90]

In two of his books,[91] Criswell may have developed the concept of the Priesthood of Believers more thoroughly than Hobbs or even Mullins before them. Criswell pointed out the various dimensions to the doctrine when he said, "The belief that every believer is a priest is functional in Baptist worship services, church government, and ministry."[92] Demonstrating the relationship of church polity to the Priesthood of Believers in Baptist life, Criswell argued, "In contrast with the Episcopalian and Presbyterian forms of church government, the congregational form is used in Baptist churches to enhance our belief in the priesthood of every believer."[93] Criswell was following Mullins's ecclesiastical axiom that all believers are equal in the church when he said that in the New Testament the government of the local church "was in the hands of all the people rather than in the hands of a small group of rulers."[94]

When explaining the three titles of "pastor," "elder," and "bishop," Criswell provides an excellent description of the pastoral role.[95] In one place Criswell argued that strong churches do not exist with weak, ineffectual pastors.[96] Eldership is an office of leadership. At another point the Dallas pastor used Hebrews 13 to confirm the prominence of the pastor.[97] At no point in these writings, however, does Criswell suggest that individual believers are subject to the principle of pastoral authority.

---

[88]Hobbs and Mullins, *The Axioms of Religion*, rev. ed., 75.

[89]Hobbs and Mullins, *The Axioms of Religion*, rev. ed., 91.

[90]Hobbs and Mullins, *The Axioms of Religion*, rev. ed., 94.

[91]See Wallie A. Criswell, *The Doctrine of the Church*, Church Study Course: Baptist Doctrine (Nashville: Convention Press, 1980) 46-47, 65-76, and his *Ecclesiology*, Great Doctrines of the Bible 3, ed. Paige Patterson (Grand Rapids MI: Zondervan, 1983) 17, 96-104.

[92]Criswell, *The Doctrine of the Church*, 47.

[93]Criswell, *The Doctrine of the Church*, 47.

[94]Criswell, *The Doctrine of the Church*, 67.

[95]Criswell, *The Doctrine of the Church*, 69-76.

[96]Criswell, *The Doctrine of the Church*, 74.

[97]Criswell, *Ecclesiology*, 101-102.

Pastors deserve respect, even reverence, Criswell said, and they will be followed when they lead as caring shepherds.

Based on the sources researched for this section, one comes away from twentieth-century Southern Baptist thought with the sense that the "first-among-equals congregationalism" continues. Although milder language is used to describe it, the pastoral role has suffered no significant loss of respect. Neither, however, has it been allowed to rise above its traditional leadership role and be transformed into official authority.

Summary

Stewart A. Newman, a former distinguished professor of theology at Southeastern Seminary, published a marvelous little book in 1986 called *A Free Church Perspective: A Study In Ecclesiology*. His magnificent chapter entitled "The Church and Its Leaders: First among Equals" deserves wide dissemination among Baptists. Essentially theological in his approach, Newman is solidly anchored in the history of Baptist polity by describing church leaders as "first among equals." Newman recognized that free-church ecclesiology does not suggest that all believers are of equal capacity and ability. But he insisted, "It does mean that no one of the group is quali-fied to exercise authority per se over others of the congregation."[98] With these emphases he represents the continuation of a long tradition in Baptist life, reaching back to eighteenth-century Charleston and beyond that to England.

Sadly, and unnecessarily, "Resolution 5" perverts, rather than perpetu-ates, this tradition. In terms of Baptist history, it perverts in at least two ways. First, it perverts by distorting the historical record concerning the Priesthood of Believers. The first "whereas" of the resolution leaves the reader with the *impression* that "the five major writing systematic theo-logians in Southern Baptist history"[99] *minimized* the Priesthood of Believers. This simply is not the case.

As demonstrated in the section on the nineteenth century, J. L. Dagg, in the second part of his *Manual of Theology*, came down much more firmly on the principles of the Priesthood of Believers than on pastoral authority. And James P. Boyce states explicitly in the preface to his

---

[98]Stewart A. Newman, *A Free Church Perspective: A Study in Ecclesiology* (Wake Forest NC: Stevens Book Press, 1986) 64.

[99]The resolution apparently refers to those listed by H. Leon McBeth, *The Baptist Heritage* (Nashville: Broadman Press, 1987) 675-76.

systematic theology that he was not addressing the subject of ecclesiology,[100] where normally a discussion of the issues in "Resolution 5" might
occur. Dale Moody, it is true, did not describe the Priesthood of Believers
extensively in *The Word of Truth*. Anyone who knew Dale Moody's
teaching would not have to be told that the resolution misrepresents him by
its implication. And even to hint that Mullins and Conner were not ardent
advocates of the Priesthood of Believers is either to distort intentionally or
to profess publicly that one has not read the writings.

The distortion of the historical record continues in the second
"whereas" of "Resolution 5." Again, a false *impression* is conveyed. But
in this instance the impression is that the Baptist Faith and Message had
little interest in the doctrine of the Priesthood of Believers. After all, says
the resolution, the Baptist Faith and Message "refers to" but "provides no
definition or content" to the doctrine. No Southern Baptist in the last
twenty-five years has given more emphasis to this historic doctrine than
Herschel Hobbs, and Herschel Hobbs's was the primary hand behind the
1963 version of the BFM. As indicated earlier, the Baptist Faith and
Message has three references, at least, to the Priesthood of Believers and
not a single one to pastoral authority.

Second, in light of Baptist historical thought, "Resolution 5" perverts
by exaggeration. It exaggerates the role of pastoral authority. To juxtapose
pastoral authority alongside the Priesthood of Believers affords a prominence to pastoral authority absolutely unwarranted by Baptist history.
While the resolution is fraught with theological, biblical, and historical
difficulties, one of the major problems is linguistic. That is, it provides "no
definition or content" to pastoral authority. The resolution and the explanation of the resolution are both ambiguous.[101]

Baptist history, however, is clear on the following: the church is a
priesthood of believers, with no separated order of priests;[102] pastors are

---

[100]James Petigru Boyce, *Abstract of Systematic Theology*, revised by Franklin
Howard Kerfoot (Philadelphia: American Baptist Publication Society, 1899; [1]1887)
v. That Boyce would have included such in a book on ecclesiology is suggested by
the fact that E. C. Dargan, successor to Kerfoot and Boyce in teaching the course
at Southern on ecclesiology, included such in his later *Ecclesiology: A Study of the
Churches* (1897; [2]1905).

[101]Jerry Sutton, "Author Details Rationale for SBC Priesthood of Believers
Resolution," in *SBC Today* 6/5 (August 1988): 6.

[102]Robert G. Torbet, *The Baptist Ministry: Then and Now* (Philadelphia: Judson
Press, 1953) 12.

called of God and gifted by the Spirit, but they lack authority of any kind until calling and gifts are confirmed by a local church; pastoral authority is, therefore, always derived from the church and not inherent in a clerical office; the "keys" of the church (its authority and power) are given by Christ to the Priesthood of Believers and leaders; the authority of pastors is "moral," "ministerial," "administrative," and "executive," but in no sense "judicial" or "legislative"; pastoral authority, always derived from the church, is the result of commitment, caring, and faithful teaching and shepherding, and, to repeat the quote from Dagg, "The minister who asks for other power, mistakes the nature of his office." The evidence of Baptist history is that faithful pastors, always respected as "first among equals," do not have to assert or ask for power. It comes with the work.

Church and Association: A Search for Boundaries[1]

The complex and knotty issue which this paper addresses may be stated at the outset in the form of a question: How can one autonomous body be joined with another autonomous body without one of the two giving up autonomy? Local Baptist churches rightly claim, because of their congregational form of church government, to be independent and autonomous. Baptist associations, composed of Baptist churches or of messengers from those churches,[2] make the same claim to self-government. To complicate matters, each recognizes the other's right to make the claim.

C. E. Colton served as chairman of the Credentials Committee of the Dallas Baptist Association in 1975 when two charismatic churches were excluded from the association. After making the motion to exclude the churches, Colton said:

> I would like for you to understand that the action that we are suggesting here today is not designed in any sense of the word to presume to exercise authority over anybody's church—we believe in the autonomy of the local church, and we would not want to be a part of any program that would violate the autonomy of any local church (we have been accused of doing so) but this is not the case. Every Baptist church has the right to do what it feels led of the Lord to do, and we would not violate that privilege in

---

[1]I presented a version of this address at the joint annual meeting of the Historical Commission of the Southern Baptist Convention and the Southern Baptist Historical Society in Nashville, Tennessee, in April 1979. Published later in *Baptist History and Heritage* 14/3 (July 1979): 32-40, 61, it is reprinted by permission of the Baptist History and Heritage Society, Brentwood, Tennessee. Since presenting this paper, the issue of the relationship of associational authority to local Baptist churches has become increasingly important in both the American Baptist Churches, USA and the Southern Baptist Convention. I believe that basic principles of local church-associational relationships enunciated in the article continue to be applicable today.

[2]This article will not deal with the question of what is the true constituency of a Baptist association. Some interpreters have argued that associations are composed only of *messengers* from the churches. Others contend that associations are composed of *churches* themselves. While the problem of associational constituency does not significantly affect the thrust of this paper, my view on the subject is already spelled out. See Walter B. Shurden, *Associationalism among Baptists in America: 1707–1814* (New York: Arno Press, 1980) 51-58.

any sense of the word. But let us also remember that the Dallas Baptist Association is also an autonomous body, and that it also has the right to do what it feels it is led of the Lord. It has the right to determine with whom it shall have fellowship.[3]

Was Colton giving voice to ecclesiastical mumbo-jumbo? Are these simultaneous claims actually in conflict? If so, or if not, where are the boundaries between associational authority and local church authority? While the broad topic here concerns the nature of Baptist polity, the specific problem is that of authority within Baptist polity. From the beginning of associational life among Baptists in America, the issue of associational-church relationship has refused to go away. Unless Baptists become something other than Baptists, in terms of church government, the problem will never disappear. It is built into the fabric of Baptist ecclesiology.

During times of relaxed uniformity in Baptist denominational life, the question of the relationship of churches to associations is little more than an ecclesiological itch. In times of growing diversity and controversy, however, it is more like a case of churchly poison ivy. You "claw" one spot only to have it become a pain all over. The "clawing" has become real in Baptist life in recent years. This paper will do three things: describe some of the issues in recent Baptist life which give rise to the issue of church-association conflict; make a historical excursus in search of guidelines for church-association relationships; and include some personal observations, based upon both the past and the present.

Issues Which Raise the Issue

The question of local church authority versus associational authority has been raised often in recent Baptist life, and because of a variety of issues. Three such issues, among others, have been the charismatic movement, the ordination of a woman minister, and problems related to baptism. Perhaps a feel for the nature of the problem can come through if I isolate a few examples.

Beginning in 1975, certain Baptist associations in Texas, Ohio, Louisiana, and California excluded charismatic churches from their associational fellowship. Among the most publicized of these was that of the Dallas Association in Texas. In 1975 this association excluded the Beverly

---

[3]*Minutes*, Dallas Baptist Association, Texas (1975), 32, 33.

Hills and Shady Grove churches. The resolution which called for this action stressed that the two churches had

> openly practiced the present-day phenomena of glossolalia and public faith-healing services in which people are declared healed, exercises which mark a radical departure from what Southern Baptists have historically believed are valid biblical gifts and doctrines, thus indicating that they are in doctrinal error and are no longer in harmony with our historic Baptist practices, and. . . .
> Whereas because of these departures from historic Baptist practice other churches have been adversely affected, resulting in a breach of fellowship among our churches,
> Be it therefore resolved that the messengers of these above named churches be not seated in this associational meeting and that they be no longer considered as cooperative bodies in our Association.[4]

In the same year the Cincinnati Association in Ohio excluded the Oak Hills and Sayer Park Churches. Three charges were brought against the churches: the practice of unknown tongues, the promotion of the baptism of the Holy Spirit as a second work of grace, and the practice of baptizing people who did not join a Southern Baptist church but who remained in other denominations.[5] One of the charismatic pastors denied the second accusation and declared that the other two accusations were not contrary to Scripture. The association remained firm in its action, however. Similar actions have been taken by the Trenton and Plaquemines Associations in Louisiana, while Harmony Association in California experienced disharmony over the same issue.

In 1977 a Baptist association in Kentucky excluded a church from its membership for ordaining a woman to the gospel ministry. By a vote of 96 to 64 the South District Association excluded the Beech Fork church which had ordained Suzanne Coyle to the gospel ministry.[6] A two-hour debate preceded the association's action. Some messengers questioned the validity of such action by pointing to article 4 of the association's constitution. Article 4 says, "This body is no 'Court of Appeals' and should exercise no ecclesiastical authority." The moderator of the association gave the following interpretation of article 4:

---

[4]*Minutes*, Dallas Baptist Association, Texas (1975), 31-32.
[5]*Minutes*, Cincinnati Baptist Association, Ohio (1975), 31.
[6]*Minutes*, South District Association of Baptists, Kentucky (1977), 10.

To say that we are no "Court of Appeals" means that we are prohibited from functioning as a body to whom disagreeing parties within a local church present their arguments, receive a judgement, and return to implement that judgement. To say that we "shall exercise no ecclesiastical authority" means that we are prohibited from forcing any member church to believe or act according to any judgement the Association might render concerning their doctrine or practice. Both are intended to insure that this body does not violate the autonomy of the local church. . . . The Association and each member church are separate organizations. This article does not refer to or regulate the internal affairs, including membership, of the Association itself.[7]

While some argued that the association acted injudiciously and violated Baptist polity, others insisted that the association was obligated to act since the church, in ordaining a woman, acted contrary to Scripture. Subsequent letters to the editor of the *Western Recorder* revealed how diverse and contradictory the thinking among Kentucky Baptists regarding this kind of associational action. When the issue of the ordination of women to the ministry came before the Kentucky Baptist State Convention, the convention refused to make a ruling, declaring ordination to be a local church prerogative.

Neither the charismatic movement nor the ordination of a woman minister has elicited as much direct associational action as the issue of baptism. In North Carolina, South Carolina, Kentucky, and Arkansas, associations since the mid-1960s have excluded churches for baptismal practices which were considered unorthodox. In some instances, associations disfellowshipped churches for accepting alien immersion. That is, these churches had received members into their church who had been immersed as believers in other denominations.[8] Other associations have excluded churches accepting alien baptism and pedobaptism.[9]

In 1978 Robert E. Wiley sent 825 directors of associational missions a "Questionnaire Concerning the Role of the Association in Determining Doctrinal Unity within the Association." The results merit close study and

---

[7]*Minutes*, South District Association of Baptists, Kentucky (1977), 11.

[8]*Minutes*, Upper Cumberland Baptist Association, Kentucky (1974), 26, 27.

[9]*Minutes*, Mecklenburg Baptist Association, North Carolina (1967), 39, 45-47; ibid. (1968), 31. This action excluded St. John's and Myers Park Baptist Churches. See also *Minutes*, Saluda Baptist Association, South Carolina (1976), 29. This action excluded First Baptist Church, Clemson, S.C.

wider circulation among Baptists. Of the 300 responses which Wiley received, eighty-three indicated some conflicts over doctrine or polity during the five-year period 1973–1978. Seventeen associations indicated that they had actually withdrawn fellowship from churches during that period. The "search for boundaries" in church-associational relationships is obviously a live issue.

The Local Church in Historical Perspective

The search for boundaries can go in many different directions. This search will move in a historical direction, seeking to uncover church-associational relationships in early American Baptist history prior to 1814. First, the concept of the local church in early American Baptist ecclesiology will be examined.

Local Church Independency. Baptists of the twentieth century are accustomed to well-worn phrases such as "congregational polity," "democratic church government," and "local church autonomy." All such terms reflect the relationship of a local church to extralocal organizations and persons. Associational documents of the eighteenth century preferred to speak of the "independency of local churches," but the point was precisely the same.

"Independency," like "autonomy," can lead to a serious misunderstanding of the Baptist point of view if the words are taken to mean a raw and rugged individualism. Baptists never meant that their churches were independent of God, of Christ, of the leadership of the Holy Spirit, or of the counsel of other Christians and churches. Emphasis on independency never excluded interdependency. By "independency" Baptists meant they could order the lives of their churches according to the will of God *as they understood it*. No agency of the state, no pope, bishop, or civil ruler, and no other ecclesiastical organization could impose a decision on the church without the church's permission.

The theological rationale for independency resided in the belief that God invested each local congregation of Christians with complete and sufficient power to guide its own affairs. Christ gave to each church all authority needful for fulfilling Christian worship and discipline.[10] According to the *Charleston Church Discipline*, a regularly constituted

---

[10]See William L. Lumpkin, *Baptist Confessions of Faith*, rev. ed. (Valley Forge: Judson Press, 1969) 286, 287.

local church had "the keys, or power of government, within itself," because it had "Christ for its head, and his law for its rule."[11]

Exclusive Powers of a Local Church. Baptists spoke often of local church independency and insisted that associations could not interfere in the "internal affairs" of a particular congregation. With this insistence, they meant especially three things. First, they intended for all to know that local churches were independent in determining their constituency.[12] A local church had the exclusive prerogative to say who could be received as members of the visible church of Christ. The writer of one associational circular letter argued convincingly that the goals of a local church could not be achieved without fellowship and that fellowship could not possibly exist if the church was deprived of the freedom to determine its membership.[13]

The second exclusive prerogative of the local church was that of disciplining its membership. In his famous 1749 essay on "The Power and Duty of an Association of Churches," Benjamin Griffith said that "each particular church hath a complete power and authority from Jesus Christ. . . . to receive in and cast out. . . . and to exercise every part of gospel discipline."[14] Disciplinary powers were to be exercised prudently; nevertheless, churches asserted the right to mete out discipline independent of any other religious group. If councils, synods, or associations assumed the power of judging decisively in cases of church discipline, they became "*mere usurpers* and *intruders* upon the government of the church."[15]

The third area in which churches maintained sole authority was in the selection of church officers. Baptists believed that a person entered the ministry not by personal choice but in response to two "calls." One call was internal, the other external. The internal call came when Christ "appointed" one to the ministry. Local churches issued the "external call" when

---

[11]Cited in James Leo Garrett, Jr., *Baptist Church Discipline* (Nashville: Broadman Press, 1962) 30.

[12]Benjamin Griffith, *A Short Treatise of Church Discipline* (Philadelphia: printed by B. Franklin, 1743) 18-19, 58.

[13]*Minutes*, Cumberland Association, Maine (1811), 10.

[14]See A. D. Gillette, *Minutes of the Philadelphia Baptist Association from A.D. 1707 to A.D. 1807* (Philadelphia: American Baptist Publication Society, 1857; repr.: Baptist Book Trust, Otisville MI, 1976) 61.

[15]Stephen Wright, *History of the Shaftsbury Baptist Association from 1781 to 1853* (Troy NY: A. G. Johnson, 1853) 32.

requesting a person to assume responsibilities. Each church had power from Christ to "call" and "ordain" its leadership.[16]

The historical background of Baptists helps in explaining their preoccupation with local church independency in the preceding areas. Baptists in England had learned by experience to be wary of ecclesiastical tyranny in all forms. They had witnessed the results of the arbitrary imposition of bishops and synods. Protecting themselves from similar future circumstances, Baptists affirmed the independence of the congregation in determining membership, disciplining membership, and selecting leadership.

Associational Protection of Local Church Independency. Baptist polity has often been described as a government of checks and balances, but Paul M. Harrison was correct when he concluded that early Baptists were "primarily interested in checks."[17] Extensive reading in early associational documents is not required for one to be convinced that Baptists were more interested in the freedom of the local church than in extending the powers of the association. Most associational constitutions consumed far more space indicating what an association could not do than clearly stating what it could do. Even those who worked vigorously in support of associational activities never relinquished the idea that the local church, not the association, was the paramount unit in Baptist ecclesiology.[18]

In the face of some recent interpretations of Baptist ecclesiology, this last point, the preeminence of the local church in early Baptist ecclesiology, must be underscored. Some have seen, and legitimately so, a theological erosion of Baptist connectionalism in eighteenth- and nineteenth-century Baptist life in America. This erosion, so the argument goes, was precipitated by several factors: Separate Baptist revivalism as expressed in the individualistic theology of Isaac Backus and John Leland; the legacy of the Enlightenment with its philosophy of individualism; and the popularity of the New Hampshire Confession of Faith with its stark omission of the universal church. But the incomparable villain was Landmarkism.[19]

---

[16]Griffith, *A Short Treatise of Church Discipline*, 57.

[17]Paul M. Harrison, *Authority and Power in the Free Church Tradition* (Princeton NJ: Princeton University Press, 1959) 78.

[18]For documentation see Shurden, *Associationalism among Baptists in America: 1707–1814*, 121-24.

[19]For this interpretation see Howard R. Stewart, *Baptists and Local Autonomy* (Hicksville NY: Exposition Press, 1974).

Few historians, if any, in Baptist life would want to speak a good word in public on behalf of Landmarkism. The faults of Landmarkism, however, must not be allowed to blind Baptists to a basic truth in their heritage. Landmarkism, with its emphasis on localism, was not so much an innovation as it was a perversion by intensification. What was wrong with Landmarkism was not the idea of local church autonomy but the implications which Landmarkers derived from it. Their use of localism to justify denominational exclusivism was new in the nineteenth century. J. R. Graves's fixation on the local church blinded him to the universal church as a legitimate part of the Baptist heritage. The evidence is not convincing that Landmarkism caused a decline in associational connectionalism. As a matter of fact, a case may be made that Graves used connectionalism at the associational level to reinforce and perpetuate Landmarkism. After all, when he was excluded from First Baptist Church in Nashville, the first thing he did was to persuade the Concord Association to censure R. B. C. Howell, the pastor, and to refuse a seat in the association to the delegates from First Church. The basic point is a simple one: the prominence of the local church in Baptist ecclesiology did not begin with J. R. Graves; it was perverted by Graves. Care must be taken not to let go of a legitimate Baptist emphasis because of Landmarkism's overemphasis. Early Baptist associations in America supported, in theory and in practice, the centrality of the local congregation in Baptist polity.

Associational Authority in Historical Perspective

To say that early Baptist associations supported, in theory and practice, the centrality of the local church in Baptist polity is not, however, the whole story. The theory and practice of associational authority among early Baptists often contradicted the claims made concerning local church independence.

What was the nature of associational authority among early Baptists? To answer that question one must *study* official associational statements, constitutions, confessions of faith, statements of discipline, and essays, explicating associational authority, but one must also *observe* associational practice. Theory and practice were not always the same. There were at least three levels of associational authority. These represent something of an ascending power structure and are noticeable when an association is viewed as an autonomous body, an advisory council, and an autocratic assembly. No one concept or level of authority was practiced alone. Variations of all three levels of authority might appear in the same association. This diversity ought to give a clue about the difficulty of this search. The history of associational polity is freighted with ambiguity.

The Association as an Autonomous Body. In his essay of 1749 Benjamin Griffith thoroughly rejected the idea that Baptist associations were powerless. Declaring that an association was "not to be deemed a superior judicature, as having superintendency over the churches," he nevertheless stated "that an association of the delegates of associate churches have a very considerable power in their hands, respecting those churches in their confederation."[20] The power of which he spoke was the power of self-rule. Just as local churches had certain powers over their members, so associations, as autonomous bodies, had certain authority over the churches composing their organization.

The autonomous powers of associations can be listed under five categories: the right of admitting into membership, the right of investigating membership, the right of excluding from membership, the right of working on behalf of membership, and the right of regulating annual meetings. Clearly, the most powerful weapon which associations possessed was that of determining membership.

Application for membership into an association was more than procedural. If a church lacked an acceptable doctrinal statement or had disorderly practices, it was not given associational membership. After becoming a member of the association, a church was expected to conform to the previously agreed upon policies. If disorders arose, associations reserved the right of investigation. If necessary, they could follow up with exclusion. Discipline was as vital a part of eighteenth-century associational life as it was of church life. Associations excluded churches for theological heresy, irregular church practice, lack of participation in associational life, and failure to follow associational advice.

If one looks to Baptist history to answer the question, "Can associations legitimately exclude churches from their associations?" the answer is, a resounding "Yes." If one looks to Baptist history to answer the question, "On what issues can associations exclude churches?" the answer is, "Over any issue they wish." It is part of the right of an association as an autonomous body to determine its own membership.

The Association as an Advisory Council. Inherent within the concept of the association as an autonomous body was the right of associations to advise member churches. Numerous associational documents indicated that

---

[20]As cited in Gillette, *Minutes of the Philadelphia Baptist Association*, 61.

the association had legitimate authority to offer advice. Ample justification exists for isolating and studying the advisory authority of associations. For one thing, the concept of an association as an advisory council appeared prior to that of the association as an autonomous body. Secondly, it was more common. Thirdly, associations exerted more power over local churches by means of their advisory functions than by any other means. "Advice" was more than objective suggestions or innocent guidelines. Often it was little less than ecclesiastical law.

Undergirding the concept of a Baptist association as an advisory council lay a strange polarity of ideas. From one perspective, it constituted a determined effort to insure the independency of local churches. Associations could "advise" but they could not "coerce" or "impose." They also gave advice because of the frank recognition that local churches were interdependent as well as independent.

On one occasion the Ketocton Association in Virginia was asked to define the particular areas in which an association could make pronouncements and give advice. The answer was that the association "may and ought to give advice in all cases that respect the glory of God, and the peace and prosperity of Zion."[21] If the answer was evasive, it was also comprehensive. It epitomized an attitude prevalent among associations that they could freely pontificate on any issue.

Associations made no secret of the fact that they expected their counsel to be followed. While there are instances where it was not, associational advice usually prevailed. The willingness of the churches to conform is to be found in three factors. One, Baptists sent their wisest leaders to associational meetings, and deference was shown for their decisions. Second, the social pressure attached to associational directions was real. Prior to the time of state conventions and national conventions, a church, cut off from the association, was cut off from the denomination. Three, churches were unwilling to be "dropped from the minutes" and that was the result of recalcitrance. Through their advice to the churches, associations often indirectly determined membership, disciplined membership, and selected leadership of the local churches. As indicated earlier, these were supposedly exclusive prerogatives of the churches.

The Association as an Autocratic Assembly. On a few occasions associations made authority claims which obviously exceeded the general Baptist opinion concerning associational power. In these instances associa-

---

[21]*Minutes*, Ketocton Association, Virginia (1872), 7.

tions assumed preeminence over the churches. The theoretical presupposition of this "high" Baptist ecclesiology was that local churches could transfer their authority to an association. One of the most famous examples of this was the Sandy Creek Association of North Carolina. Morgan Edwards said that "they had carried matters so high as to leave hardly any power in particular churches."[22]

This particular idea of associational authority constituted an anomaly within the Baptist tradition. It appeared only in scattered instances and in every case for only a brief period. Baptists were not always careful in defining associational authority. However, when they discovered that language had been used which magnified associational powers, they promptly made amendments.

The Continuing Search

A study of church-association relationships in Baptist history only serves to underscore that the search is an old one. That fact, in itself, might be helpful. At least it shows that the problem under consideration is not brand new. Tensions in congregational-associational relationships go back to the beginning of associational life. Baptists should not, therefore, throw up their hands in despair as though they are confronting a problem which comes out of the present time. In the search for boundaries today, the following observations are in order.

First, the centrality of the local congregation within Southern Baptist life ought to be reaffirmed carefully and clearly. This can be done on biblical, theological, and historical grounds. It ought also to be done, however, on the basis of denominational experience. A continuing openness to the Word of God has come as often from the local congregation of believers as it has from denominational institutions, if not more so. Creativity for ministry and insight into biblical teachings flow out of an atmosphere of freedom more often than they do out of denominational control.

This call for a reaffirmation of local church independency is certainly not a desire to encourage ecclesiastical lone-rangerism. In fact, Southern Baptists, especially, need to find a way to give expression to the idea of the

---

[22]Morgan Edwards, "Materials towards a History of the Baptists in the Province of North-Carolina" (1772), 115-16, in *Materials towards a History of the Baptists*, 2 vols., "prepared for publication by Eve B. Weeks and Mary B[ondurant]. Warren" (Danielsville GA: Heritage Papers, 1984) 2:103.

universal church which their 1963 confession included and their 1925 confession omitted. But giving expression to the universal church goes far beyond mere unity in denominational organizations such as Baptist associations. In fact, the application of the concept of the universal church to denominational structures alone serves only to support a denominational chauvinism which needs badly to be rethought.

Second, Southern Baptists need to reaffirm the right of associations to regulate their own membership. The argument that associations are *merely* for fellowship and that they have no grounds for excluding churches is a specious one. In fact, the opposite is true. Baptist associations, like all other Baptist connectional bodies, have the privilege of determining their membership.

What must not be assumed, however, is that the specific issues which have caused associations to exclude churches have always been uniform. They patently have not been uniform in Baptist history, and, as a matter of fact, they still are not. For example, all associations—in fact most associations—have not excluded charismatic churches or churches which have ordained women to the ministry or churches which accept alien immersion.

What Southern Baptists need, of course, is a covenantal and confessional basis of associational membership which is narrow enough to permit some theological and ecclesiastical unity and broad enough to obstruct disharmony over minutiae. That is to do little more, however, than to restate the problem, for what some consider minutiae, others consider essential. Given the problem there may now be as much unity and breadth already as is possible in congregational church government.

While associations may determine their own membership, they should not allow themselves to be used to determine the legitimacy of a church's membership in state conventions or in the Southern Baptist Convention. The point is relevant because of some recent indications that some would like to predicate a church's membership in the state convention upon satisfactory associational membership. In the face of the pluralism in Southern Baptist life, that process would place unfortunate authority within regional associations.

Third, one has difficulty finding in Baptist history a theology of church order beyond the local church. That is not the same, however, as saying that one has difficulty finding a theology of the church beyond the local church. With the difficulty in finding a theology of church order beyond the local church level, there is double difficulty in finding a singular theology of associational authority. Hugh Wamble, in his study of early English Baptist associationalism, demonstrated that.[23] My personal research of Baptist associations in America convinces me that Regular Baptists and Separate Baptists did not approach it the same way.[24]

This diversity is both bane and blessing. Its disadvantage is that it leaves Baptists without a thoroughly thought-out, clearly defined, and uniform ecclesiology beyond the local church. Its advantage is that it leaves them free to explore possibilities for extralocal connectionalism.

Fourth, some would argue for a tighter denominational connectionalism and increased associational authority by arguing for the need of confessional uniformity. No one who has read the history of Baptist associations in America can doubt that confessionalism became a significant component of associational unity. No single confessional statement, however, has ever been adopted by Baptist associations as a whole. The same continues to be true today. Earlier in this paper several contemporary associations were mentioned which have excluded churches in recent years. Interestingly, not one of those associations had exactly the same confessional statement.

If, in their search for boundaries, Baptists stress confessionalism as a means of preserving denominational integrity and increasing associational authority, which confession do they use? More importantly, who in Baptist life has authority to tell associations what confessional statement they must use? Also, what confession deals explicitly with such issues as the charismatic movement, the ordination of women, and alien baptism? The associations need freedom to hammer out their faith for themselves, and Baptists will do well to live with the diversity inherent in such an approach.

---

[23]See G. Hugh Wamble, "The Concept and Practice of Christian Fellowship: The Connectional and Interdenominational Aspects Thereof, among Seventeenth-Century English Baptists" (Ph.D. diss., Southern Baptist Theological Seminary, Louisville KY, 1955).

[24]See Shurden, *Associationalism among Baptists in America: 1707–1814*.

John E. Steely: On Being Baptist[1]

This article is an exercise primarily in Baptist historiography, secondarily in Baptist biography. It is an analysis of what John Steely, long-time professor of Historical Theology at Southeastern Baptist Theological Seminary in Wake Forest, North Carolina, *said* about what it means to be Baptist. In the strictest sense, therefore, this is a historiographical study. However, most of what Steely wrote said volumes about who Steely himself was and what he really cared about. Thus, biography is inevitably involved in any analysis of Steely's historiography.

Who was John Edward Steely and what did he care about? If judged by his literary legacy, one would answer in two ways. He was a *translator* and he was a *Baptist church historian*. Because of his linguistic skills that enabled him to translate some eighteen books from German and Dutch into English, those in scholarly circles will doubtless remember this dimension of Steely's significant work, a work which certainly deserves remembrance.

Some, even among those who knew him well, may be surprised to note that the vast majority of what Steely himself wrote, however, concerned Baptist history. In addition to the book which he coauthored with Brooks Hays, Steely wrote more than twenty articles in which he delineated the Baptist identity, always indicating the implications for contemporary Baptists and contemporary society. To speak of Steely as a Baptist church historian is altogether appropriate, not only because he was a Baptist and a historian, but because most of what he wrote focused on a historical inter-

---

[1]This article represented a combination of my personal interests in biography, historiography, and the Baptist identity. It first appeared in *Perspectives in Religious Studies* 20/4 (Winter 1993): 431-46, and is reprinted here with the permission of that journal. I never studied under John Steely, and I knew him only modestly well. However, I had enormous respect for him as a Christian scholar, a traditional Baptist, and a devout churchman. He taught at Southeastern Baptist Theological Seminary in Wake Forest, N.C. for thirty years, from 1956 to 1986, prior to the fundamentalist takeover of that school. He was a major shaper of that school in its early years. In his writings, especially his articles, he identified the dangers facing Southern Baptists before the fundamentalist triumph in Southern Baptist life. For a brief biography of Steely, along with his bibliography, see Morris Ashcraft, "John Edward Steely," *Perspectives in Religious Studies* 20/4 (Winter 1993): 331-40.

pretation of Baptists. His magnificent works of translation should never obscure his insightful descriptions of the meaning of being Baptist.

Most of Steely's Baptist writings could be subsumed under three categories, each of which concerned him enormously as a Baptist, an academician, and a churchman. These three subjects are (1) diversity and freedom in Baptist life, (2) the nature of the church, and (3) the nature of the ministry. In the following pages I have tried to describe what Steely thought and said about what it means to be a Baptist in relation to these three topics. In addition, I have included a fourth section on the Bible, not only because Southern Baptists have been embroiled in the inerrancy controversy for the last decade, but because some of Steely's best and last articles addressed this issue.

Being Baptist . . . Diversity and Freedom

Along with former Unites States congressman and Southern Baptist Convention president, Brooks Hays, John Steely coauthored *The Baptist Way of Life*, published in 1963. In fact, "coauthored" borders on inaccuracy. Speaking of the book, Hays wrote, "It represents our joint efforts only in a very general sense. His [Steely's] contribution has been so much greater than mine that I take this opportunity to make clear my junior position on the team."[2] The book certainly "sounds like" Steely, for it contains the major emphases, interpretations, and themes found in Steely's articles, most of which were published subsequent to the book. One such theme is that of diversity and freedom in Baptist life.

Clearly, diversity and freedom was Steely's starting point in painting the Baptist profile. He did not begin with theological distinctives such as believer's baptism, a regenerate church, democratic church government, or the like. He began with the more overarching principle of diversity created out of the Baptist emphasis on freedom. The opening line of the preface of *The Baptist Way of Life* reads, "The most casual student of Baptists and their way of life will be impressed by the great diversity existing within this family called by a common name."[3] To outsiders, said the authors, this

---

[2]Brooks Hays and John E. Steely, *The Baptist Way of Life*, The Way of Life series (Englewood Cliffs NJ.: Prentice-Hall, Inc., 1963) v; 2nd and rev. ed. (Macon GA: Mercer University Press, 1981) vii. (For the 1981 2nd ed. Steely added a chapter on "Authority." Pagination varies in the two editions. Subsequent references below are to the first edition.)

[3]Hays and Steely, *The Baptist Way of Life*, xiii.

diversity is "a source of bewilderment." To insiders, this "richly varied heritage" is both "delight and despair" as they reflect upon it and seek to explain it to others.

But for Steely, diversity was far more than a description of something within the denominational family. It was, more importantly, a cardinal feature of the denominational family. Explaining the Southern Baptist doctrine of the church to a Roman Catholic audience in 1981, he began by acknowledging that people outside the Baptist community doubtless grow weary of being told that "no one can speak for all Baptists." "Nevertheless," said the professor, "it is true, and it is significant."[4] That declaration, he continued, is a disclaimer of definitive authority for any aspiring Baptist pope as well as a confession of the many differences among Baptists. When Steely reflected upon Baptists' resources for meeting the challenges of a new century, he isolated their diversity and the tradition of freedom, among others. Diversity, he insisted, had many benefits for Baptists. One benefit is "a manifestation and a safeguard of that soul-liberty which has been a precious part of Baptist heritage for centuries, and thus a rejection of any enforced uniformity."[5]

What are the roots of Baptist freedom which issue into this rich diversity, so prized by Steely? Never addressing the question in a systematic fashion or in a single article, Steely does not, however, leave us without his answers. For example, he points to the Baptist understanding of personal religious experience as the foundation of all authentic Christian spirituality. This emphasis on the personal in religion "may be the most apt single portrayal of our Baptist way of apprehending the Christian vocation,"[6] he wrote.

Closely related to this matter of personal religious experience is the Baptist emphasis on the right of private judgment in all matters religious. In 1973 Steely delivered a paper to an ecumenical gathering of Roman Catholics and Baptists on the subject of the formation of doctrine in Christian history. Unmistakably, he recognized the role of tradition, so dear

---

[4]John E. Steely, "Church and Ministry in Baptist Perspective," *One in Christ* 17/3 (1981): 231. See also John E. Steely, "A Southern Baptist Reflection," *Ecumenical Trends* 15/9 (1986): 152.

[5]John E. Steely, "Baptist Church Life and Ministry," *Towards A.D. 2000: Emerging Directions in Christian Ministry*, Southeastern Studies 1, ed. John I Durham (Wake Forest NC: Faculty of Southeastern Baptist Theological Seminary, 1977; dist. by Mercer University Press) 139.

[6]Hays and Steely, *The Baptist Way of Life*, 37, 38.

to Roman Catholics, in shaping doctrine. But he closed by affirming that private judgment, so dear to Baptists, affirms that the church's tradition can err. Speaking candidly, though always charitably, Steely said to his Catholic friends, "And it is equally obvious that on precisely this point—the point at which the church's judgment and private conscience come into conflict—one finds a major division between and among ourselves in the present gathering."[7]

While making no attempt to offer a denominational defense of the right of private judgment, Steely identified the roots of this important Baptist emphasis in three sources. One was the doctrine of the priesthood of all believers, which he characterized in a later article as the "conviction that underlies the other distinctives of Baptists."[8] The second was the Baptist understanding of faith as both active and passive, demanding personal choice *and* divine action. And third, Steely said that the emphasis on personal choice and responsibility had been nurtured among Baptists "by the circumstances and conditions of the frontier,"[9] the geographical environment in which Baptists have prospered. Although Steely may have overworked the frontier theme in Baptist history,[10] he was absolutely correct in noting that Baptist individualism, church government, lay leadership and free forms of worship, all sources of freedom and diversity in the denomination, made Baptists more adaptable to the frontier culture.[11]

What did freedom and diversity mean for Baptists? How did these themes manifest themselves in the life of the denomination and in their discipleship as they applied their understanding of the gospel to the society around them? According to Steely, freedom and diversity meant the ongoing presence of controversy in denominational life.[12] Without a

---

[7]John E. Steely, " The Formation of Doctrine," *Catholics and Baptists in Ecumenical Dialogue*, J. William Angell, ed. (Winston-Salem NC: Wake Forest University Ecumenical Institute, 1973) 66.

[8]John E. Steely, " Current Issues in the Southern Baptist Convention in Historical Perspective," *Faith and Mission* 1/2 (Spring 1984): 14.

[9]Steely, "The Formation of Doctrine," 66, 67.

[10]Although he never quotes William Warren Sweet, Steely virtually accepted without qualifications Sweet's frontier determinism in his interpretation of Baptist history. Some of this emphasis may have come from Steely's rural Arkansas background, also. For this idea in Steely's writings see *The Baptist Way of Life*, 15-33, and "The Formation of Doctrine," 67.

[11]Hays and Steely, *The Baptist Way of Life*, 21.

[12]Hays and Steely, *The Baptist Way of Life*, 172.

magisterium or a binding theological creed or an infallible interpretation of the Bible or Christian history, Baptists were burdened by their enlivening freedom to a life of continuing debate and search for truth. Freedom and diversity meant, of course, differences of opinion on biblical and theological interpretation within the denomination.

More than anything else, however, diversity and freedom in Baptist life, according to Steely, meant the absence of any enforced uniformity. Steely was a restrained, careful, and cautious scholar. His writings come close to passion on only a few issues. These were his advocacy of ecumenism, racial equality, women in ministry, and his fear of coerced conformity. But this last, the demon of enforced uniformity, may have constituted his major concern because it was so basic and fundamental to all the rest.

In 1984, only two years before his death, Steely wrote one of his best articles in which he identified what he considered to be six major issues facing Southern Baptists. The six were biblical inerrancy, women issues, church-state issues, charismatic issues, creedalism, and the assimilation of blacks into Southern Baptist life. The "overarching" issue of these six, according to Steely, was as clear as it was dangerous. Creedalism! Affirming that creedalism is "a major departure from the traditional practices of Baptists," he wondered out loud "whether the Southern Baptist Convention would survive that kind of alteration in any recognizable form."

His conclusion to the 1984 article is even better than the body of his remarks. Indirect, interrogatory, and noncombative, it was typically Steely. He concluded with three questions, all of which related to his fundamental concern of enforced uniformity. First question: Who will decide and enforce the outcome to these six issues? Second question: What will happen to the priesthood of all believers and the matter of individual responsibility in Baptist life? Third question: What is the nature of unity in the Baptist community; are Baptists held together by theological sameness?[13] No one could mistake Steely's profound concerns in these questions nor would they be confused about his answers.

Steely's concern about an encroaching creedalism in the SBC was not simply a knee-jerk reaction to the inerrancy controversy of the 1980s. He sounded the creedal alarm in the early part of the 1970s, insightfully pointing out that Southern Baptists already had an unofficial and unregulated doctrinal restrictionism at work among them. Covert creedalism, he hinted, may be even more disastrous than overt creedalism,

---

[13]Hays and Steely, *The Baptist Way of Life*, 13-14.

but he had no affection for either.[14] They both smacked of enforced uniformity, the exact opposite of "freedom and diversity" in Baptist life.

Being Baptist also meant for John Steely that Baptists could not hoard freedom for themselves. Proud to point to the Baptist tradition of full religious liberty, Steely urged his denomination, now in possession of that liberty in the United States, not to relax their vigilance or become indifferent to those still living under oppression. The legacy of freedom should remind contemporary Baptists that liberty is indivisible. So long as anyone is oppressed, no one is free.[15]

Being Baptist . . . The Church

Writing in their book about seventeenth-century Baptists, Hays and Steely said, "It is to the credit of these early Baptists that they managed to remain true to their basic convictions without cutting themselves off from the body of Christendom."[16] Although in documentation Hays gets as much credit for this quote as Steely, surely this is a Steely line. In fact, it may be as close to autobiography as John E. Steely ever came! If not autobiography, it most definitely is a biography of the man. For while he was an unapologetic Baptist with warm emotional ties to the denomination that birthed him, John E. Steely worked and wrote as hard for ecumenism as almost any Southern Baptist of his generation.

---

[14]John E. Steely, "Where Are We as Southern Baptists? From a Historian's Point of View," *Baptist History and Heritage* 7/4 (October 1972): 202, 203. In their description of Baptist worship, Steely and Hays, as early as 1963, made the point that Baptists are an anticreedal people because creeds have been used to enforce a uniformity of doctrine. See *The Baptist Way of Life*, 52, 53, and 158, 159. Ironically, this vigorous anticreedal affirmation by Hays and Steely was published in the very year that Southern Baptists adopted "A Statement of the Baptist Faith and Message," a confessional document that assumed creedal characteristics by the time of Steely's death in 1986.

[15]Steely, "Baptist Church Life and Ministry," 140. See also chapter 15 of *The Baptist Way of Life*, esp. p. 198, and Steely's article, "Where Are We as Southern Baptists? From a Historian's Point of View," 199. Among others, these references demonstrate Steely's strong ethical concerns. By 1984 Steely correctly saw that Southern Baptists were weakening their historic tradition on some issues related to religious liberty and church-state concerns. See his "Current Issues in the Southern Baptist Convention in Historical Perspective," 10.

[16]Hays and Steely, *The Baptist Way of Life*, 16.

His first published article was a mild (Steely's writings like his person were always gentle) repudiation of Landmarkism, one of the major roots of sectarianism among Southern Baptists.[17] His last published article, a little piece in *Ecumenical Trends*, came out after his sudden death on 28 March 1986, and urged some Roman Catholic and Southern Baptist scholars with whom he had been working to focus on what united rather than what divided them. An editorial comment said that this appeal from Steely could be considered "his testament."[18] Indeed! Between those first and last articles Steely's writings urged Southern Baptists to embrace the concept of the universal church. He appealed to outsiders not to be misled by a distorted view of Baptist ecclesiology which emphasized only the local church.

He based his argument, correctly so, on the Baptist tradition itself. Acknowledging that some Baptists had developed a "lone ranger" ecclesiology and disdained cooperative endeavors with others, Steely insisted that such approach did "not negate the stronger and healthier tradition that dates back to the early days of English Baptist history, a tradition that stressed the interdependence of Christians and the fellowship in Christ that scorns the limits of time and space."[19] Steely documented this "stronger and healthier" tradition by pointing to the First London Confession, the Second London Confession, the Philadelphia Confession, and "A Statement of the Baptist Faith and Message" adopted by the Southern Baptist Convention in 1963. The latter document included a sentence which Steely relished. That sentence reads "The New Testament speaks also of the church as the body of Christ which includes all of the redeemed of all ages." Even though Steely saw the sentence as a "grudging concession," "almost an afterthought" on the part of the authors, he, nonetheless, recognized it to be a giant step forward from the localism of Landmarkism.[20] In this instance, he would take what he could get, even when it was far from what he wanted.

---

[17]John E. Steely, "The Landmark Movement in the Southern Baptist Convention," *What Is the Church?*, ed. Duke K. McCall (Nashville: Broadman Press, 1958) 134-47.

[18]John E. Steely, "A Southern Baptist Reflection," *Ecumenical Trends* 15/9 (October 1986): 152-54.

[19]Hays and Steely, *The Baptist Way of Life*, 110.

[20]"Church and Ministry in Baptist Perspective," 232-35.

Steely wanted an active involvement by Southern Baptists in the ecumenical movement, but he knew well the reasons for the isolationism.[21] Those reasons were (1) the general cultural isolation of Southern Baptists, (2) their stress on congregational polity, an excuse as well as a reason, (3) the insistence upon doctrinal agreement as a basis of fellowship, and (4) the vestiges of Landmarkism. But he also knew that all Southern Baptists were not isolationists. Numbered among those, he expressed the hope that all Christians would see that they belonged to each other.

In an intriguing article, published in 1968, Steely dealt with two of his major concerns, ecumenism and racism, in a most creative way. This was the period in the Civil Rights Movement when Black Power had emerged and was issuing into black separatism. Steely interpreted this phenomenon as the creation of a distinctiveness born of oppression. If any group should identify with an emerging distinctiveness born in the crucible of painful oppression, said Steely, it should be the Baptists. After all, that was the Baptist story, too. But, he went on to argue, racial separatism is as counterproductive for blacks in American society as denominational separatism is for Baptists in the world Christian communion. In essence, Steely used the article to contend for the integration of blacks into American society as well as for Baptists into the ecumenical movement. His closing sentences reflect what he considered the seriousness of the issues. He said, "In one instance, the future of a denomination is at stake and the welfare of the Christian world is involved. In the other instance, the future of a racial group is at stake and the welfare of the nation, indeed of the world, is involved."[22] Being Baptist for Steely meant an ecumenical view of the church.

But it also meant that the church was a local fellowship of believers. Committed to an ecumenical understanding of church, Steely also knew that when a Baptist speaks of "the church," the allusion was usually to a specific local congregation. That local congregation is perceived in Baptist minds as a "fellowship," a "community," a "family," in which "brothers and sisters are concerned for the others who share their faith and their calling."

---

[21]See *The Baptist Way of Life*, 123-24; and "The Landmark Movement in the Southern Baptist Convention."

[22]John E. Steely, "Baptists Face Decision," *Biblical Recorder* 134/33 (August 24 1968): 12-13.

The church as fellowship means a strong sense of participation by the people in the government and decisions of the church. But it also means that worship is not a solitary experience. Worship, as church government, has, for Baptists, a democratic element in it. All are expected to participate, which explains the enthusiastic hymn singing often accompanying Baptist worship services. Above all, the church as a local fellowship meant, according to Steely, "the engagement of life with life and the bearing of one another's burdens." Personal acquaintances, face-to-face encounters, familiar faces and "the greetings of those whose daily lives were intertwined with one's own," was uppermost in the Baptist interpretation of the local church as "fellowship." "It is no exaggeration," said Steely, "to say that Baptists can more easily dispense with the organizational and formal aspects of church—structure, office, liturgy, succession, constitution and bylaws, and physical facilities, for example—than with the face-to-face encounter with fellow believers and the sense of belonging to the company of Christian sisters and brothers."[23] This erudite and ecumenical scholar drilled beyond the usual technical and ecclesiological descriptions of the meaning of church and lifted out the obvious, the heart of what being church means for most Baptists. One of Steely's strengths as a historian is that he saw the obvious while others looked for the unusual, and he described the obvious with simplicity and clarity.[24]

To say that the church was a "fellowship" meant for Steely that the church was not primarily an institution. "The great misconception of the church," he said, "appearing in almost every generation of Christian history from the first, is the institutional one."[25] Institutionalism is a structural misconception of the church, manifesting itself in Baptist life through Landmarkism and in Roman Catholicism through the hierarchy. The church

---

[23]"Church and Ministry in Baptist Perspective," 239-41.

[24]While I do not have space to develop the idea, it is interesting to note that Steely gave considerable attention to what I would call the "common people" motif in the Baptist tradition of church. Because the church was a fellowship, according to Steely, and therefore centered on people, and because Baptists had, throughout most of their history, been of common stock, Steely often pointed to the "common people" heritage of Baptists. Some of this emphasis may have come from his own humble origins. Some of it, however, simply comes from an accurate reading of the Baptist tradition. See *The Baptist Way of Life*, 5, 156; and "Baptists Face Decision," 12-13, for some evidence of this in Steely.

[25]John E. Steely, "Historical Misconceptions of the Church," *Baptist Student* 40/6 (March 1961): 13.

does not invite people to come to the shelter of a saving institution or to the truth mediated through an authoritative clergy but "to unite in Christ with the witnessing community, the fellowship of those who have been and are being redeemed.[26]

His reading of Christian history made Steely apprehensive about any moves toward an institutional view of the church. He, therefore, often warned Southern Baptists that size, growth, and numerical increase were not certain signs of the blessings of God. Size and denominational strength was always for Steely a stewardship issue, an opportunity to minister in the name of Christ. A preoccupation with quantity rather than quality smacked of a nascent institutionalism. Burgeoning denominational bureacracy bothered Steely and he often wondered out loud where all of this would end for Southern Baptists.[27] He feared that the church as "fellowship," at least within denominational structures, was being overtaken by the church as institutuional machine. Steely was as uncomfortable with the impersonal nature of churchly institutionalism as he was with the isolationism of religious sectarianism.

Being Baptist . . . The Ministry

John E. Steely was the son of a Baptist minister, a teacher of Baptist ministers, and a Baptist minister himself. And many of his writings concern the ministry, especially as understood in the Baptist heritage. A Baptist traditionalist in his theology of the ministry, Steely emphasized the nonsacerdotal character of the ministry and refused to make pastors an ecclesiastical caste system with any kind of authority over the congregation of believers. He would have, had he lived to see it, been very much discouraged by the liberal interpretation adopted by the Southern Baptist Convention in 1988 which elevated pastoral authority and denigrated the priesthood of all believers.[28]

In their book, Hays and Steely enunciated seven principles of Baptist polity. Several of these, on one way or another, relate to the Baptist concept of the ministry. The first principle they list is that of the primacy of local

---

[26]"Historical Misconceptions of the Church," 14.

[27]For Steely's comments on institutionalism see "Where Are We as Southern Baptists? From a Historian's Point of View," 204; "Baptist Church Life and Ministry," 138-39; and "Current Issues in the Southern Baptist Convention in Historical Perspective," 12.

[28]*SBC Annual 1988*, 68-69.

congregational government. Local church "autonomy" does not mean an unchecked or unlimited freedom, however. The ultimate authority of a local Baptist church is the will of God, not the wishes of the people. "Theonomy" is therefore a better description of Baptist church life than is "autonomy." The will of God is discerned, however, in a Baptist church in and through the local congregation, not through a larger ecclesiastical body or through any particular individual, including the minister.[29]

Another principle of Baptist polity, according to Hays and Steely, is that of responsible membership. Because Baptist church members are people who have made free, voluntary, and responsible commitments to Jesus Christ as Lord, they also are responsible for the management and ordering of the local congregation. Democratic church government denies the rule of an aristocracy or hierarchy of any type. In fact, "no special insight," according to the Baptist tradition, has been given to the clergy concerning the will of God.[30]

John Steely elaborated upon this theme in his analysis of the 1963 SBC confessional statement. The confession's emphasis on "scriptural officers," said Steely, is, of course, a polite way of rejecting the hierarchy familiar to other Christian communions and an intended safeguard against the possibilities of *clerical domination*.[31] Continuing, he also insisted, in the language of the confession, that Baptist churches are "always operating through democratic processes." This democracy means that the leadership of the Lord is more reliably discerned when the responsibility for finding

---

[29]Hays and Steely, *The Baptist Way of Life*, 91.

[30]Hays and Steely, *The Baptist Way of Life*, 93.

[31]Steely, "Church and Ministry in Baptist Perspective," 235; underlining mine, for emphasis. Steely was obviously concerned about ministerial hegemony, especially in the structures of the Southern Baptist Convention. In "What the Southern Baptist Convention Can't Do," *Baptist Faculty Paper* 10/2 (Spring 1967): 4, Steely charged that the SBC could not be truly representative because of the disproportionate number of ordained ministers on denominational boards. So exercised over this issue by 1972, he called for a complete examination of the principles upon which the denomination was based and suggested that a synodical or presbyterian structure might be demanded! Speaking of any new structure, he said, "I should insist, also, that it provide a way for bringing the present disproportionate role played by pastors in denominational matters under some reasonable limitation. It appears to me that, unless this is done, any other changes will be only window dressing." See Steely, "Where Are We as Southern Baptists? From a Historian's Point of View," 201.

and implementing it is placed upon the entire community rather than in the hands of a few. Baptists would add, said Steely, "particularly when those few are the clergy." He was confident that there was "an anticlerical element" in the historic Baptist affirmation of democratic processes![32]

Steely's primary perception of the Baptist ministry was rooted in what he called "the traditional Baptist belief" of the priesthood of all believers. Simply stated, the priesthood of all believers means that "if any Christian is a priest, all Christians are priests." Further, if a priest is one who has access to God and speaks for God, all Christians are priests, not by any mysterious powers of ordination, but by the inward dwelling fo the Spirit of God in the life of the believer.[33]

Baptists historically have asserted that the church has no priesthood apart from that which belongs to all believers in Christ. What does this mean for the role of the pastor in a Baptist church? It means that ordination is a recognition of spiritual gifts and divine calling, not an acknowledgment of authority over other Christians. Pastors are not endued with a special character or elitist status in Baptist life. Steely never tired of saying that the distinctions between clergy and laity are essentially inappropriate in the Baptist understanding of the ministry. While the civil government may provide special recognition to the clergy for certain rituals such as marriage, the church is free to call upon any of its members to perform pastoral functions generally considered to be the work of the pastor.[34]

Steely believed that the Baptist concept of the ministry as the priesthood of all believers was one of the denomination's major resources for entering the twentieth century with creativity and skill. Calling on his broad knowledge of Christian history, he enumerated some of the various "models" of ministry which had been used to identify the status and function of the ministry. Ministers had been interpreted as medicine men, persons who held secrets and possessed power, and also as ecclesiastical rulers, hired hands, or skilled specialists. Baptists had a different heritage, however, one that emphasized that the minister was not essentially different from other church members, but singled out for specific responsibilities. This view believes that it is the ministry of the whole church that is

---

[32]Steely, "Church and Ministry in Baptist Perspective," 239.

[33]Steely, "Historical Misconceptions of the Church," 14.

[34]For documentation for this paragraph, see Steely's *The Baptist Way of Life*, 94-95, 100-101; "Baptist Church Life and Ministry," 141; and "Church and Ministry in Baptist Perspective," 242.

performed in the ordinances, preaching, and pastoral care, even when that ministry is committed to the hands of one person.[35]

Perceptively, Steely saw that one's understanding of the mission and nature of the church impacts the understanding of ministry. If the church is viewed institutionally, the pastor becomes the custodian of truth, knower of divine secrets and dispenser of grace. If, on the other hand, the church is seen as a "fellowship," the pastor becomes a minister of the Lord and of the congregation and a preacher of the Word of life. "A danger arises," Steely prophetically wrote in 1961, "that one will hold to the latter view in theory and yet conduct oneself on the assumptions of the former."[36] When we *say* the church is a "fellowship" but *act* as though it were the "ark of salvation," and when we *say* that the ministry is "a priesthood of believers" but *act* as though it were a religious caste system, we have, thought John Steely, deviated from historic Baptist positions.

The Baptist view of the pastor as one with the people is manifest, Steely pointed out, in the selection of persons to whom it is entrusted. A brilliantly educated man himself who committed his entire life to theological education, Steely nonetheless knew that Baptists have not insisted historically that formal education is the primary requisite for a valid and effective ministry. Steely had a deep appreciation for the sincere, deeply committed, and informally educated frontier Baptist preacher.[37] While this appreciation was rooted in a number of sources, including Steely's compassionate personality, surely one source was his understanding of the Baptist meaning of ministry.

This same understanding of the Baptist concept of ministry caused Steely to be one of the Southern Baptists' major advocates of women in ministry in the years prior to his death. In fact, as early as 1963 Steely and Hays trumpeted the role of women in the Baptist denomination, recognizing that most Baptists did not at that time ordain women to the ministry.[38] One of the challenges facing Baptists in the year 2000, argued Steely, was the "liberty" issue. And one expression of the liberty issue was "heard in the voices of women in the churches today, in their increasing attempts to gain acceptance as ministers." He believed "that the doors to equal opportunity

---

[35]Steely, "Baptist Church Life and Ministry," 141.

[36]Steely, "Historical Misconceptions of the Church," 14.

[37]See Steely, "Baptist Church Life and Ministry," 141-42; and Hays and Steely, *The Baptist Way of Life*, 94.

[38]Hays and Steely, *The Baptist Way of Life*, 95.

and acceptance ought to be opened, not grudgingly but gladly." Because he believed that women-in-ministry was a liberty issue, he did not see it as a challenge that *could* be reversed.[39] Because he believed that women-in-ministry grew out of the historic Baptist understanding of ministry in general, he did not see it as a development that *should* be reversed.

Being Baptist . . . The Bible

Throughout his writing career, John E. Steely was consistent in claiming that the ultimate authority for Baptists was the will of God.[40] He also was aware that such an affirmation did not resolve the knottier theological question of "How does one know that will?" Baptists discern that divine will, he said, through different channels. Chief among them were the Bible, personal experience, and the influence of other Christians. In practice, Steely believed, Baptists had other channels of divine authority. In particular he mentioned tradition, confessions of faith, officers of local churches, and the denomination.[41]

Despite his claims, which were certainly correct, concerning the ultimate authority of the will of God, Steely knew the critically important role which the Bible played in Baptist life. And so he said, "Central to almost all Baptist statements on authority is the affirmation that the Bible communicates the divine will and is the only definitive and sufficient rule for faith and practice."[42] He put it more succinctly and colloquially in *The Baptist Way of Life*: "Baptists are a people of the Book."[43] As such, they use the Bible in personal devotion, in the quest for church order, and in the search for theological orthodoxy.[44] Other evidences that Baptists are "Bible

---

[39]For the quotations in this paragraph, see Steely, "Baptist Church Life and Ministry," 144. For other Steely comments on women in ministry, see Steely's "Ministerial Certification in Southern Baptist History: Ordination," *Baptist History and Heritage* 15/1 (January 1980): 29, 61; "Church and Ministry in Baptist Perspective," 242; and "Current Issues in the Southern Baptist Convention in Historical Perspective," 9, 13-14.

[40]He made this point in the 1963 book and again in a 1982 article. See Hays and Steely, *The Baptist Way of Life*, 91; and John E. Steely, "Authority in Southern Baptist Thought, Sources of," *Encyclopedia of Southern Baptists*, Lynn Edward May, Jr., ed. (Nashville: Broadman, 1982) 4:2095.

[41]Steely, "Authority in Southern Baptist Thought, Sources of," 2096.

[42]Steely, "Authority in Southern Baptist Thought, Sources of," 2096.

[43]Hays and Steely, *The Baptist Way of Life*, 2.

[44]John E. Steely, "Biblical Authority and Baptists in Historical Perspective,"

people" are (1) the copious scriptural citations in Baptists' confessional documents, (2) the valuable emphasis placed upon the teaching of the Bible in local church education programs, and (3) the historic role of the Bible in Baptist preaching, a tradition Steely thought had faded in recent years.[45]

Steely probably had reservations about some Baptists' overdrawn rhetoric regarding the Bible's role in Baptist life. The relationship between denominational practices and the New Testament's teaching often was more assumed than demonstrated. An example of this, for Steely at least, was the Baptist practice of ordination.[46] Moreover, because we read the Bible through "spectacles provided for us by earlier interpreters," we do not always carefully distinguish between tradition and scripture.[47] Steely cautioned that "glowing or exalted language" about the Bible did not necessarily translate into an elevated view of the Bible. Nor can the biblical character of a lecture or sermon be measured by the repetitious citation of scripture. Steely hinted that Baptists may brag more about the Bible than they actually read it, especially in public worship services.[48]

The so-called "inerrancy controversy" which rocked the SBC in the decade of the 1980s did not claim much of Steely's writing energy. However, he confronted the conflict directly in one of his articles[49] and indirectly in two others.[50] Treating the controversy with amazing objectivity, Steely's position on the inerrancy movement in the denomination was, nevertheless, transparent. Inerrancy and its advocates, Steely suggested, had all the possibilities of cutting the ground out from under some historic Baptist emphases.

He defined the inerrantist approach to the Bible as "the view that the original autographs . . . were without error of any kind, not only in religious matters but also on historical and scientific subjects." Continuing, Steely

---

Baptist History and Heritage 19/3 (July 1984): 7.

[45]See Steely, "Biblical Authority and Baptists in Historical Perspective," 10-11; "Baptist Church Life and Ministry," 142-43; "Church and Ministry in Baptist Perspective," 234.

[46]Steely, "Ministerial Certification in Southern Baptist History: Ordination," 24.

[47]Steely, "The Formation of Doctrine," 64.

[48]Steely, "Biblical Authority and Baptists in Historical Perspective," 10-11.

[49]Steely, "Current Issues in the Southern Baptist Convention in Historical Perspective."

[50]Steely, "Biblical Authority and Baptists in Historical Perspective," and "Authority in Southern Baptist Thought, Sources of."

described the attitude behind inerrancy as suggesting that anyone who does not share this conviction thereby denies the authority of the Bible even in matters of faith and of the disclosure of God's will for the human family. But inerrancy is complicated by the fact that no autographs of scripture exist. Thus, said Steely with a bit of sarcastic surprise, the individual Christian is asked to make a faith affirmation about an unavailable document.[51]

In his analysis of inerrancy, Steely isolated three issues which he thought primarily important. These issues can be framed as questions. One, is the Bible, as inerrantists claim, scientifically and historically without error? Two, is inerrancy essential for the Bible to have its rightful authority for the believer and the church? Three, should inerrancy be used as a test of fellowship in Baptist life? Steely would have answered all three with an emphatic "No."[52]

What appeared to disturb Steely about inerrancy the most was not the theological argument concerning the *nature* of scripture. He certainly would not have accepted the inerrancy claims. But the implications and attitudes behind those claims were what threatened the historic emphases of freedom and diversity. He saw within the inerrancy movement of the SBC the ominous cloud of enforced uniformity. Inerrancy is one among many *interpretations* of the Bible, but Baptists have no inerrant interpretation. He saw that inerrancy was confusing an interpretation of Baptists' authority with the authority itself. Inerrancy's itch for an absolute and final word came too close to creedalism and authoritarianism for Steely. And it violated the prized distinctive of the priesthood of all believers.[53]

Summary and Conclusion

Historians are "hemmed in" when doing their work; they operate with lots of limitations. One such limitation is that the historian can only analyze what remains. Historical sources dictate, to some degree, what one can say about the past. For an interpretation of John E. Steely this means one must

---

[51]Steely, "Current Issues in the Southern Baptist Convention in Historical Perspective," 8-9.

[52]Steely, "Current Issues in the Southern Baptist Convention in Historical Perspective," 8-9; and "Authority in Southern Baptist Thought, Sources of," 2096.

[53]See Steely, "Authority in Southern Baptist Thought, Sources of," 2096-97; "Biblical Authority and Baptists in Historical Perspective," 9; "Current Issues in the Southern Baptist Convention in Historical Perspective," 13-14.

write about him based on what he himself wrote. But because so many writers write what is assigned or requested, one is left to ask, "Is this what he would have written had he been left to his own instincts or would he have written on different subjects and left a different literary deposit?" In other words, do his writings reflect his major concerns? And based on these writings, can we, in Steely's case, get a good, sure picture of what he thought was the meaning of being Baptist? With few exceptions, Steely seems to have written about his concerns, and one can get a good idea of what being a Baptist meant to him.

Being Baptist meant for John E. Steely that he was conservative on the historic Baptist distinctives. Personal Christian experience, the authority of the Bible for faith and practice, the centrality of the local congregation within the context of the universal Body of Christ, the ministry as the priesthood of all believers, religious liberty for all—these were the foundation stones of Baptist life. Undergirding all of this, however, was the Baptist emphasis on freedom which issued in a perplexing and challenging diversity.

Being Baptist meant for John E. Steely that he was progressive on the human issues. Much of this, it seems, came from his Baptist concern for freedom. He wanted blacks to be free to participate as equals in American society. He wanted women to be free to serve Christ in the church. He wanted his denomination to be free to interact with other Christian denominations. He wanted the church to be free from institutionalism so that it could focus on the people for whom Christ died.

Being Baptist meant for John E. Steely that he find "fellowship" in a local Baptist congregation. Steely was an academician, but his understanding of what it meant to be a Baptist was anything but "academic." Being Baptist meant, for Professor Steely, being a "church-man."

C. Penrose St. Amant:
Interpreter of the Baptist Vision[1]

Since being a first-year seminary student in the late 1950s, I have been a "St. Amant watcher" and a "St. Amant reader." Although I never had a formal academic course with him, I have watched him preach, lecture, and speak on special occasions numerous times. Incidentally, St. Amant, as Frank Stagg suggested, is one of those people you need to see and hear speak before you read. Once you have seen and heard him speak you cannot possibly read him without envisioning how he would have spoken it.

For the last thirty years I have also been an avid St. Amant reader. What he thinks on any subject, including something as mundane as Denny Crum's Louisville Cardinals basketball team, matters to me. His book reviews, for example, have always been of particular interest.

St. Amant has balance without blandness. And that, as much as anything else, is why I and many others have watched and read him for three to four decades. My image of St. Amant is that of a tightrope artist who "leans," but only very, very slightly, to the left, always maintaining his balance. In fact, about the time you think he is "leaning" left, he slightly and carefully shifts to the right, never for safety but for comprehensiveness. St. Amant balance is part personality but it is also part recognition that ambiguities exceed simplistic explanations.

A casual reading of the essays written in honor of St. Amant reflects what I am calling the "St. Amant balance." Stagg interpreted St. Amant's vocational move toward administration in light of "gifts for bringing people together, respecting their diversities and maximizing their commonalities."[2]

---

[1]This essay was in a volume in honor of Professor Penrose St. Amant that I edited for the National Association of Baptist Professors of Religion (NABPR). The volume appeared in the NABPR's journal Festschriften series as *Perspectives in Religious Studies* 16/4 (Winter 1989). The casebound presentation and library edition appeared at the same time: *Perspectives on Theological Education: Essays in Honor of C. Penrose St. Amant*, ed. Walter B. Shurden (Macon GA: Mercer University Press, 1989). While pagination of the body of the text is the same for the journal and the library edition, the casebound library edition is cited here as *Perspectives on Theological Education*.

[2]Frank Stagg, "C. Penrose St. Amant: An Interpretation of the Man," in *Perspectives on Theological Education*, 22.

Reflecting on St. Amant's successful ten-year deanship at Southern Seminary, Glenn Hinson said:

> St. Amant manifested "throughout his administration a remarkable feeling for *the right balance* of concerns: the denomination and the world of theological education, professional and graduate education, faculty and administration, students and faculty, church and society."[3]

Keith Parker, writing about St. Amant as president of Rűschlikon, echoed the same theme: "Penrose St. Amant . . . was a 'bridging' president, one whose gifts and unique leadership actually bridged the past, present, and future, as well as the multiple cultures and tasks the seminary faced."[4] More succinctly, Parker said of St. Amant that he was "always seeking a balance or healthy tension between inevitable opposites."[5]

But underscore this—in red, if necessary! In St. Amant, balance never meant blandness. Nothing could be further from Penrose St. Amant than the historian who hides behind the security of uninterpreted data. St. Amant has a point of view. The fact that it is expressed almost always calmly and in a dialectic neither washes out nor waters down perspective.

Nowhere does St. Amant's dialectical approach manifest itself more clearly than in his description of the Baptist identity. His interpretation of the Baptist vision is far more than an academic exercise in historical research; it is a life commitment based on a historical movement, but it is almost always expressed in polarities. Based upon his published articles, the following is what I see as his primary emphases in profiling the Baptist identity.

An Open Bible and an Open Mind

"An open Bible and an open mind" is Penrose St. Amant's succinct summary for what being a Baptist means. Indeed, his essential vision of the Baptist way is wrapped up in this phrase, so repetitious in his writings. He used the line in almost every article he wrote concerning the Baptist heritage.[6]

---

[3]E. Glenn Hinson, "C. Penrose St. Amant: Dean at Southern, 1959–1969," in *Perspectives on Theological Education*, 50.

[4]G. Keith Parker, "C. Penrose St. Amant: President at Rűschlikon," in *Perspectives in Theological Education*, 53.

[5]Parker, "C. Penrose St. Amant: President at Rűschlikon," 61.

[6]See, for example, the following articles by St. Amant: "Our Baptist Heritage,"

Why is he so fond of the phrase and what does he mean by it? He utilized the phrase because he believes that at the heart of the Baptist vision is a dynamic tension, a taut dialectic which is not subject to a singular and simplistic reductionism. The dialectic St. Amant addresses with the phrase is, of course, that of authority and freedom within the Baptist tradition. Synonyms for the St. Amant slogan pour from the professor's pen. They look like this:

Open Bible	Open Mind
Authority	Freedom
Lordship of Christ	Soul Competency
Unity	University
Loyalty	Liberty
Conviction	Tolerance
Biblical Faith	Believer's Freedom
Core	Periphery
Continuity	Change
Certainty	Mystery

In my judgment, St. Amant's most mature, thorough, and philosophical statement of the Baptist tradition is found in "Baptist Pluralism and Unity," an appropriately titled essay for St. Amant. He began the article by referring to the motto on the Great Seal of the United States—*E Pluribus Unum*. Throughout the article St. Amant hammered away at the idea that the motto enunciated an important element in the Baptist heritage. He concluded the article with the following paragraph:

> *E Pluribus Unum* (out of many, one) is not a static goal toward which we strive but a dynamic process that goes on and on. This motto does not pose a problem we hope one day to solve. For Baptists, it is a way of life.[7]

The Quarterly Review 10/3 (July-August-September 1950): 19; "Other Baptist Bodies," *Baptist Advance*, ed. Davis Collier Woolley (Nashville: Broadman Press, 1964) 368; "Our Baptist Heritage and the Church." *Baptist History and Heritage* 2/2 (July 1967): 88; "Southern Baptists: Unity in Diversity," *Search* 1/3 (Spring 1971): 13; "Baptist Pluralism and Unity," *Baptists and the American Experience*, ed. James E. Wood. Jr. (Valley Forge PA: Judson Press, 1976) 353; "Perspectives in Our Baptist Heritage," *Discovering Our Baptist Heritage*, ed. William H. Brackney (Valley Forge PA: American Baptist Historical Society, 1985) 11.

[7]Penrose St. Amant, "Baptist Pluralism and Unity," 359.

For St. Amant, being Baptist means "a creative balance between con-
servation and change." Two basic tendencies mark the Baptist heritage, he
said. They are "the unity that flows from our belief that God has spoken
and speaks in his Word and the diversity that flows from our freedom to
listen, to read, and to implement what we hear."[8]

With somewhat different language, St. Amant echoed the open Bible-
open mind, unity-in-diversity theme in his most recent statement of the
Baptist identity. St. Amant wrote of "the two foci that stand at the center
of the Baptist witness" and identified these as "Christ's lordship and the
individual's conscience under God."[9] Later in the same article he referred
to the polarity within the Baptist heritage as "the Biblical faith" and "the
believer's freedom."[10]

An open Bible! That is crucial to St. Amant, partly because of his
personal spiritual history, a history he later critiqued but never amputated.
"The thing I remember most vividly about the small Baptist community in
which I grew up in South Louisiana," he said, "is the ubiquity of Bibles
which people not only displayed but read."[11] And St. Amant's mother, a
Roman Catholic when she married, became a Baptist by reading the New
Testament, an event St. Amant describes with warm appreciation.[12]

Personally, therefore, St. Amant is anchored to Holy Scripture.
Unapologetically and straightforwardly he declares, "The Bible is the
written Word of God."[13] This affirmation of religious authority is for St.
Amant denominationally as well as personally rooted. "Baptists believe,"
he told the Baptist World Alliance, that "there is a sure Word from God
which illuminates the meaning of our human pilgrimage and provides
power and direction for the journey."[14] Biblical faith, he continued, cannot
be contrived by people to suit themselves because it "comes to us out of the

---

[8]St. Amant, "Baptist Pluralism and Unity," 353.

[9]Penrose St. Amant, "Perspectives in our Baptist Heritage," 11.

[10]St. Amant, "Perspectives in our Baptist Heritage," 13.

[11]St. Amant, "Perspectives in our Baptist Heritage," 14.

[12]Penrose St. Amant, "The Teaching Church and Our Baptist Witness," *The
Truth That Makes Men Free: Official Report of the Eleventh Congress of the
Baptist World Alliance, Miami Beach, Florida. June 25-30, 1965*, ed. Josef
Nordenhaug (Nashville: Broadman Press, 1986) 350.

[13]"Southern Baptist Theology Today: An Interview with C. Penrose St.
Amant," *The Theological Educator* 12/2 (Spring 1982): 17.

[14]"The Teaching Church and Our Baptist Witness," 346.

mighty events in Scripture, which bears a divine revelation." The substance and sustaining power of the Baptist witness is this "emphasis on the Bible as the norm of faith and practice."[15]

St. Amant's contention for "the open Bible" in Baptist life also has a serious philosophical and theological dimension to it. He fears the exclusivistic claims of fundamentalists based upon narrow and dogmatic assertions, but he also winces at the inclusivistic claims of liberals based upon theological relativism.[16] Here, again, is the taut dialectic.

St. Amant points out that serious consequences flow from a purely relativistic view of the world. Relativism breeds skepticism! And skepticism creates a philosophical vacuum from which new absolutist claims emerge. "The contemporary world, therefore," he said in 1982, "is ripe for the proliferation of cults, the resurgence of fundamentalism, and a renewed liberalism, all of which offer simplistic solutions to the complicated problems of today's world."[17] Pluralism, while always a revered virtue by St. Amant, can be pushed, he argued toward atomism. The result is not a creative diversity but a brokenness, isolationism, and alienation. This disintegration of authority is often accompanied by the cultivation of naked power. Baptists, therefore, must have and have had, according to St. Amant, a center and core. The Baptist center is the open Bible.

Penrose St. Amant is not personally, theologically, or denominationally capable, however, of speaking of the open Bible as the unity of Baptist life without simultaneously affirming the open mind as the source of diversity among Baptists. Just as the biblical faith creates Baptist loyalty, believer's freedom promotes Baptist liberty. In one of his earliest articles on the Baptist identity, St. Amant suggested that while the open Bible had saved Baptists from a superficial secularism, the open mind had saved them from a narrow sectarianism.[18] Of course, St. Amant recognized that Baptists had at times indeed been entrapped by both secularism and sectarianism. Within the Baptist genius, however, were antidotes to these twin demons.

The open mind! Why has St. Amant insisted upon it as integral to the Baptist identity? Because of his incurable penchant for balance? Yes, that is part of the answer. Because of his belief that today's unchecked authority

---

[15]"The Teaching Church and Our Baptist Witness," 350.

[16]"Baptist Pluralism and Unity," 355.

[17]"Southern Baptist Theology Today: An Interview with C. Penrose St. Amant," 7.

[18]"Our Baptist Heritage," 19.

becomes tomorrow's insufferable tyranny? Yes, that is another part of it. In addition to these more obvious and generic reasons for coupling freedom with authority and liberty with loyalty, St. Amant, I think, saw at least three other origins of diversity among Baptists.

One is biblical. An "open mind" is made necessary by the clear biblical teaching of diversity of gifts.[19] Primarily because he is historically and theologically oriented by academic training, St. Amant did not use this biblical argument as often or as thoroughly as he used others. In his last major description of the Baptist identity, however, he wrote explicitly of the one *charisma* (Rom 6:23) and the variety of *charismata* (1 Cor 12:1 and Rom 12:3ff.), the latter to be used for the common good of the Body of Christ. The variety of gifts must find free expression among Baptists and that occurs only where openness to diversity and individual conscience is honored.

According to St. Amant, the "open mind" is also made mandatory for a theological reason, and that is human selfishness. Baptists, he avers, have emphasized both "the sanctity and the sinfulness" of all people, including Baptists. And then he adds in Niebuhrian fashion, "Our philosophy of diversity, rooted in a basic respect for the individual conscience and in the recognition of the taint of self-interest in our judgments of what is just and true, is one of the threads that paradoxically binds us together."[20] Precisely because our vision of what is true and right is human and incredibly tainted by self-interest, we need "the corrective of competing visions."[21] An "open mind" is mandated by human sin.

A third reason for an "open mind" is cultural. The diversity in Baptist life and thought is merely a reflection of the "particular histories, races, nationalities, background, sections, and cultural and educational levels" expressed within and by the numerous Baptist groups in the United States and around the world.[22] It is a "mistake" to promote a Baptist melting pot where diversities are neutralized. Even if it were possible, said St Amant, the cancellation of Baptist differences in the hope of an abstract model of

---

[19]"Perspectives in Our Baptist Heritage," 12; "Southern Baptists: Unity in Diversity," 7.

[20]"Baptist Pluralism and Unity," 352.

[21]"Baptist Pluralism and Unity," 358; see also "Southern Baptists: Unity in Diversity," 8.

[22]"Perspectives in Our Baptist Heritage," 14.

unity would be undesirable.[23] The preacher in the historian is unrestrained as he describes Baptist diversity in music (from Fanny Crosby to Beethoven), in preaching (from George W. Truett to Harold Cooke Phillips), and in worship (from New Zion Baptist Church in rural Mississippi to the colorful liturgy of Myers Park Baptist Church in Charlotte, North Carolina).

What specifically does the "open mind" half of St. Amant's Baptist dialectic mean? His applications of the phrase to Baptist life are varied and numerous. He applies it, for example, to the study of the Bible, calling Baptists to embrace fearlessly biblical criticism.[24] One of his most repeated applications, however, of the "open mind" is to the *interpretation* of the Bible. It is in this connection that he is reminiscent of E. Y. Mullins's affirmation that "soul competency" is the centerpiece of Baptist theology. Writing in the midst of the Broadman controversy when fundamentalist Southern Baptists were seeking to impose their peculiar interpretation of the Bible on others, St. Amant called on Baptists to be Baptists:

> The final arbiter of what the Bible means for Baptists is not the biblical scholar, nor the pastor, nor the editor of this or that, nor a consensus of the Southern Baptist Convention, nor the so-called liberal or conservative or moderate by whatever definitions. We do not believe in the authority of popes or synods or conventions or associations or churches or pastors or professors over the individual conscience. *Either we take seriously the competency of the individual in this matter or we do not. And if we do not, we repudiate in one fell swoop an essential element in our Baptist heritage.* Diversity among us is the result of what has been called soul competency.[25]

In another place, St. Amant related soul competency to the Baptist doctrine of the priesthood of believers which carries with it the "right of Christians to read, study, and interpret the Bible and the responsibility to observe what it teaches."[26]

---

[23]"Baptist Pluralism and Unity," 354.

[24]"Southern Baptist Theology Today: An Interview with C. Penrose St. Amant," 16, 17.

[25]"Southern Baptists: Unity in Diversity," 6; the underlining is mine for emphasis.

[26]Penrose St. Amant, "Some Resources for Reconciliation in Our Baptist Heritage," *Baptist Heritage Update* 2/1 (Spring 1986): 5.

So the "open mind" means for St. Amant the legitimation of a serious scholarly study of the Bible and the necessity of the individual to be free to interpret the Bible. And because creedalism ends up with an imposed uniformity and operates on the basis of a "closed mind," St. Amant often applied his "open mind" category to a vigorous anticreedalism. As a historian of the Christian church, St. Amant knows that creedalism is both divisive and ineffective; theological unity cannot come from prescribed faith which is then imposed. Being biblical rather than creedal, St. Amant said, "Baptists have no leader who cannot be challenged in the name of truth and have no confession of faith that cannot be challenged on the basis of the Bible."[27] Speaking in the midst of the inerrancy controversy, when fundamentalists again were seeking to creedalize uniformity through the Baptist Faith and Message, St. Amant reminded Southern Baptists, "We have never been a creedal people and we had better not start now."[28] For St. Amant, an "open mind" said "Yes" to biblical authority but "No" to creedalism.

An "open mind," as St. Amant developed it, has two pastoral dimensions. One, open-mindedness is related to charitable attitudes. St. Amant quoted often an 1802 "circular letter" distributed by a Kentucky association. The "Dear Brethren" to whom the letter was addressed were warned "to watch against a spirit of dogmatical Arrogance and Bigotry."[29]

St. Amant also pointed out that Baptist freedom meant we should major on majors, not on minors. He enjoyed telling of the boat pilot who regularly plied the Mississippi River. Asked if he knew where the sandbars were, the pilot replied, "No, but I know where the channel is." St. Amant believed that the "open mind" would not dissipate its energies on bypaths and negations. It would focus on "majors" which unite, not "minors" which divide.[30]

Like John Clifford, E. Y. Mullins, George W. Truett, and other Baptist leaders before him, St. Amant is totally aware of the dangers of freedom and the "open mind." "Freedom can be a cloak for license and subversion,"

---

[27]"Southern Baptist Theology Today: An Interview with C. Penrose St. Amant," 29.

[28]"Southern Baptist Theology Today: An Interview with C. Penrose St. Amant," 27.

[29]"Perspectives in Our Baptist Heritage," 18; "Baptist Pluralism and Unity," 352; "Southern Baptists: Unity in Diversity," 13.

[30]"Southern Baptists: Unity in Diversity," 12; see also "Our Baptist Heritage," 19.

he confessed. But then he quickly added, "but the glory . . . of the Baptists is that we believe the dangers of freedom are much less than the dangers of tyranny."[31]

A Personal Faith and a Public Witness

It has now long since become a shibboleth to assert the need for a personal and a public faith. The fact of the matter, however, as Martin Marty has demonstrated, is that American Christianity has been in a tug-of-war for years over which is the more important. So have Baptists. Penrose St. Amant, through his preaching, lecturing and writing has called Baptists to both commitments. He believes it necessary, if Baptists are to be faithful to what it means to be Baptist, that they refuse to choose one or the other but affirm both at the same time. Unfortunately, St. Amant's single best treatment of this subject remains unpublished,[32] but many of his published writings address the subject. Concerning this dialectic of personal versus social faith, let us begin with a description of the "St. Amant balance" again!

> We are on a two-way street. If we start with the gospel for society, we run into the need for better people who alone can create and sustain a creative social order; and, therefore, we face the personal gospel. If we start with the personal gospel, we run into social structures which thwart personal creativity; and, therefore, we face the gospel for society. There is really only one gospel. This gospel promises forgiveness of sins, but also enjoins our responsibility for the welfare of the neighbors.[33]

Several years ago W. R. White wrote a book entitled *Baptist Distinctives*, including a chapter on "The Primacy of the Individual." Before White, E. Y. Mullins wrote in *The Axioms of Religion* of "the principle of individualism in religion." Before Mullins, John Clifford spoke of "sanctified individualism" as a major attribute of the Baptists. St. Amant

---

[31]C. Penrose St. Amant, "Baptist Heritage and Religious Liberty," *The Quarterly Review* 23/2 (April-May-June 1963): 20.

[32]Penrose St. Amant, "A Historical View of Baptist Involvement in Citizenship," an unpublished address presented to the Christian Citizenship Seminar in Washington, D.C., sponsored by the Christian Life Commission of the Southern Baptist Convention, 23 March 1964.

[33]Penrose St. Amant, "Baptists in a Revolutionary Age," *Baptist History and Heritage* 7/3 (July 1972): 147.

follows in their train. Without ignoring the community of the church, he, nevertheless, highlights the individual and the personal aspects of faith.

In his most systematic statement of the corporate demands of the gospel, St. Amant began, significantly, with a section on "Christian Conversion," because "the starting point of the Christian life is when God invades human life redemptively in Jesus Christ."[34] In an inspiring sermon before the 1975 Baptist World Congress, he quoted H. G. Wells who, after cataloging human achievements, concluded by saying that humans continue to behave like quarrelsome apes. Wells's simplistic remedy was "stop being an ape." To which St. Amant responded soteriologically:

> Well, more than this is required. What is required is not a pat on the back, a shot in the arm, a bit of eyewash to make the world look better. What is required is a drastic human transformation, a new birth, a new creation. . . .[35]

His soteriology, underlying the necessity of the personal appropriation of divine grace for human "apeness," is related also to St. Amant's Baptist understanding of epistemology, ecclesiology, and missiology. At the close of an interview on contemporary Southern Baptist theology, St. Amant said, "Throughout our conversation, I have stressed the personal dimension of our pilgrimage, as Christians who have embraced the Baptist way." And then after elaborating upon Martin Buber's thesis in *I and Thou*, a very important book for St. Amant, he added, "A certain depth of understanding is available in no way other than through personal encounter."[36] His concept of how one knows (personal encounter) is a philosophical corollary to the theological question of how one becomes a Christian (personal faith). Here is the primacy of the personal, so basic to the Baptist identity.

Baptist ecclesiology, erected upon the concept of a believer's church, cannot be understood apart from the vibrant personal faith of individuals, said St. Amant.[37] Likewise, the expansion and growth of the Baptist witness

---

[34]"A Historical View of Baptist Involvement in Citizenship," 1.

[35]Penrose St. Amant, "Are Christians Really New People?" *New People for a New World—Through Christ: Official Report of the Thirteenth Congress, Baptist World Alliance, Stockholm, Sweden, July 8-13, 1975*, ed. Cyril E. Bryant (Nashville: Broadman Press, 1976) 52.

[36]"Southern Baptist Theology Today: An Interview with C. Penrose St. Amant," 30.

[37]"Perspectives in Our Baptist Heritage," 12.

was due to "the emphasis placed upon Christian experience." Baptist Christianity, with its emphasis on personal experience, is always on the verge of asking, "If it be not light to me, what care I how light it be?"[38] Experientialism has been historically basic to the Baptist profile; it is also fundamental for Penrose St. Amant.

But just as Christ is Saviour in an intensely experiential and personal way, he is also Lord in a profoundly social and public way. The Baptist vision of Christianity, says St. Amant, pulls its adherents inexorably into the corporate realm. The theological foundation on which the public witness rests for Baptists is the Lordship of Christ.

How does the Lordship of Christ, "a theme familiar to Baptists," impact our public witness? St. Amant's writings suggest three ways. First, the Lordship of Christ challenges all idolatries. In St. Amant's language, "it offers a counterpoise to the tendency of man to sacralize his own words." Because "we have no Lord but Christ . . . no one else and nothing else can command the final allegiance of our lives."[39] Such a theological conviction may in one instance breed revolution when confronted by the idolatry of status quo. But in another instance it rejects revolution that seeks to usurp the rule of Christ in the life of the individual and church. The Christian and the church are obligated to desacralize contemporary gods, placing them under the Lordship of Christ.

Second, the Lordship of Christ challenges the passivity and inactivity of Christians. St. Amant has no time for the gnosticism which denies history or the pietism which ignores history. To establish a dichotomy between the secular and the sacred "has no basis either in the New Testament or in Baptist history."[40] The Baptist conscience, political freedom, the plight of the common person, and the democratic process have all acted to drive Baptists, however reluctantly, into the world with their word of witness.

Third, the Lordship of Christ also challenges human despair. Fatalism is heresy for disciples of Christ. "We can't do anything about it," is simply not a proper response for people who view the pain and injustice of the world through the eyes of the Nazarene. Although potent, the principalities

---

[38]"Our Baptist Heritage," 19.
[39]"Baptists in a Revolutionary Age," 146.
[40]"A Historical View of Baptist Involvement in Citizenship," 1.

and powers of the world are not omnipotent. Public witness, therefore, is a requirement of discipleship according to St. Amant.[41]

When interpreting the Baptist way, St. Amant often addressed specific social issues such as race,[42] international disarmament,[43] and support for public education.[44] More often than not, however, St. Amant utilized the Baptist heritage to confront "secularism" and "Culture Christianity." The terms, which could be treated separately, are often used interchangeably by the professor.

In one of his most provocative and persuasive articles,[45] St. Amant confronted the burgeoning secularism in American life with a stubborn insistence on the Baptist ideal of voluntarism. Published in 1963, St. Amant's article came out shortly after *Engel v. Vitale* (1962) and about the time of *Abington School District v. Schempp* (1963). In the first decision the Supreme Court prohibited, under the "no establishment" clause of the First Amendment, a prayer drafted by the New York Board of Regents. In the second decision, the Court forbade the devotional reading of the Bible in tax-supported schools.

These rulings, so symbolic of secularism, caused consternation among many of the religious in America. Some were so frightened that they began to question the effectiveness of the voluntary principle in American life. Indeed, some Protestant churchmen began to use the traditional Roman Catholic argument that the villain was the honored doctrine of the separation of church and state. The steeple was ringing for help from the courthouse!

St. Amant recognized the reality of a growing secularism, but he refused to believe "that we must repudiate the great tradition of the American churches,"[46] or the cardinal Baptist affirmation of the separation of church and state. Reminding Baptists of their past commitment to the separation of church and state, St. Amant warned of the future, "We must

---

[41]"Baptists in a Revolutionary Age," 146.

[42]"A Historical View of Baptist Involvement in Citizenship," 9; see also "Southern Baptists and Southern Culture," *Review and Expositor* 67/2 (Spring 1970): 150.

[43]Penrose St. Amant, "Communicating the Gospel in the Eighties," *The Quarterly Review* 41/3 (April-May-June 1981): 70, 71.

[44]Penrose St. Amant, "Baptists and Public Education: A Historical Perspective," *The Quarterly Review* 44/2 (January-February-March 1984): 66-78.

[45]"Baptist Heritage and Religious Liberty," 16-21.

[46]"Baptist Heritage and Religious Liberty," 17.

be vigilant, not only must we oppose encroachments upon this principle, we must prove to the world that the voluntary principle in religion . . . can produce a radiant and powerful faith.[47]

The demise of the wall of separation, St. Amant screamed, would mean not simply the secularization of American culture but more importantly secularization of American churches! What government supports, government regulates! The solution to secularism was not for weak churches to seek help from the muscles of government, but to strengthen homes and churches, the citadels of faith, and to affirm and accept the "grave responsibilities" of religious liberty.

Just as St. Amant used the Baptist principle of voluntarism against a pervasive secularism, so did he draw from the Baptist heritage to combat what he called "culture Christianity." A lover of art, music, and literature, Penrose St. Amant was certainly not deprecating "culture" in that sense of the word. "Culture Christianity" was for him faith shorn of the prophetic. "Culture Christianity" could escape the prophetic dimensions of the Christian faith by retreating into private virtues or by equating public Christian responsibility with specific political, economic, or ideological reform movements. Baptists, St. Amant believed, had not always avoided "Culture Christianity," but they had resources in the Baptist arsenal to steer them away from it. These resources, he said,

> involve a strong evangelical emphasis upon conversion with an equally strong stress upon Christian ethics, both in an individual and a corporate sense. They involve an awareness of the subtlety and pervasiveness of sin and the wondrous depths of grace. They involve regenerate lives which issue in disciplined and disciplining communities that have the audacity to seek to revolutionize human history. Our heritage brings together a certain biblical realism, a passionate concern for Christian experience, a sensitivity to the moral and spiritual dimensions of civilization, a suspicion of too much power in the hands of too few people, a fierce dedication to freedom, and a profound sense of destiny under God.[48]

After analyzing St. Amant's published statements on the general subject of the Baptist heritage and social responsibility one discovers St. Amant speaking in various roles. St. Amant the historian described what Baptists have and have not done and why. With his emphasis on the lord-

---

[47]"Baptist Heritage and Religious Liberty," 18.
[48]"Baptists in a Revolutionary Age," 153.

ship of Christ, St. Amant the theologian provided biblical foundation for action. St. Amant the prophet predicted consequences for failure to act. But St. Amant the preacher called for Baptists to care, to move through life compassionately, to participate in the meaning of the cross. He enjoyed quoting Baron Friedrich von Hugel's dying words, "Caring is everything; nothing matters but caring."[49]

Denominational Roots and Ecumenical Commitments

In Walker Percy's *The Second Coming*, Will Barrett left his native South in order to get away "from the ancient hatred and allegiances" of his father. He even tried to believe in the Christian God because his father did not. Will exclaimed, "Imagine having to leave the South to find God!" Penrose St. Amant has refused to believe that God could not be found in the South or among Southern Baptists. On the other hand, he never perceived of God as a Southern Baptist monopoly. His religious roots run deeply and affectionately into Southern Baptist soil, but geography and denomination do not by any means exhaust his understanding of the universal Church of Jesus Christ. St. Amant is denominationally rooted and ecumenically committed.

In a moving, autobiographical statement, St. Amant told of his appreciation for the church of his past.

> My earliest memory of the church is a small congregation worshipping in a modest frame building in a predominantly Roman Catholic village in south Louisiana. The wooden, cushionless benches were always hard, the sermons often long, and my mother's lap inviting. Often I went to sleep shortly after the sermon started and was usually awakened by the singing of a rousing gospel song. And yet what happened there was so meaningful that at the age of seven I made a public profession of faith in Christ, was baptized, and began to participate in the life of the church, a community of folk for whom Jesus Christ was Saviour and Lord. Upon its deepest level, whatever else the church means, it still means this to me.

And then he added:

---

[49]"Our Baptist Heritage and the Church," 89, 90, 113. See also Penrose St. Amant, "Is History Made by Heroes?" *Baptist History and Heritage* 1/1 (August 1965): 55.

The New Testament and our Baptist heritage have tended to confirm my childhood memories. It seems to me that the church is essentially a simpler fact than many church historians have made it. Is it not true that the gathering together of a local congregation of believers, the breaking of bread, prayers, and the worship of Jesus Christ, the Lord, is the oldest ecclesiastical fact in Christendom?[50]

"That little church in which I was nurtured," St. Amant believed, is also the "little church that lies at the heart of our Baptist heritage."[51] And at the heart of "that little church" were "plain people." St. Amant was fond of historian Robert Torbet's appraisal of Baptists in America. Torbet said that in the century following the Great Awakening Baptists were characterized by "a strong appeal to the plain people of the agrarian areas."[52]

One of St. Amant's strengths as an interpreter of the Baptist vision is that, despite his background of some privilege, he knew and appreciated the fact that Baptists were "plain people." "The Baptist movement," he said, "has always remained close to the common people,"[53] and that fact accounts for the remarkable growth of Baptists in America. St. Amant's respect for "plain people" and his emphasis on the priesthood of all believers served to reinforce each other, especially in the area of biblical interpretation. As a theological professor, dean, and president, St. Amant certainly never discounted or minimized the crucial role of the professional scholar in biblical interpretation, but neither did his life of scholarly pursuits ever blur his denominational vision that "a cardinal Baptist teaching is that the Bible should *not* be left to the experts alone but should be put into the hands of the people."[54] In the same vein, St. Amant lobbied for "a closer relationship between our theological seminaries and the people in the churches who make the seminaries possible by their support."[55]

Even in the light of his world travels—his education in Scotland and France and his seminary presidency in Switzerland—St. Amant, in one

---

[50]"Our Baptist Heritage and the Church," 83.

[51]"Perspectives in Our Baptist Heritage," 14.

[52]"For examples of St. Amant's use of this phrase, see "A Historical View of Baptist Involvement in Citizenship," 10; "Southern Baptists and Southern Culture," 151; "Baptists in a Revolutionary Age," 153.

[53]"Our Baptist Heritage," 18.

[54]"Perspectives in Our Baptist Heritage," 14.

[55]"Southern Baptist Theology Today: An Interview with C. Penrose St. Amant," 29.

sense, never left home. While never militantly defensive he could get testy over accusations, misinterpretations, and distortions of both his native South and his Southern Baptist heritage.[56] He placed in suspect, for example, the notion that Southern Baptists were simply a religious expression of Southern culture. His education and broad experience certainly set St. Amant free from the restrictive parochialisms of his past, but he was never set adrift on a sea of ingratitude.

But he had been set free! If he "never left home" in one sense, in a paradoxical sense he refused to stay home. He, for example, like most Southern Baptist scholars of his generation, had been liberated from the haughty Landmarkism in Southern Baptist life which insisted that the local church is the only church. "The genius of our heritage," he confessed, "is that the church at its best is both the body of Christ and the gathered community at the same time."[57].

St. Amant saw clearly a dangerous sectarianism in Southern Baptist life. He saw it in the unnecessary separation from the mainstream of Protestantism, in the reluctance to enter the ecumenical dialogue,[58] in our distorted emphasis on the local church,[59], in our biblical primitivism which ignores church history in general,[60] and in our defensive denominational historiography which tells our story as though it occurred in a cultural vacuum.[61]

Concerning the Baptist heritage and the larger Christian heritage, Penrose St. Amant called, characteristically, for balance, what he described as "a certain dialectical attitude." He wrote:

> To escape the posture of claiming too much for ourselves as Baptists, we do not need to abandon our heritage. We do not need to give up our roots and embrace the unreality of Christianity in general to deal with our sectarianism. We do need a discriminating reappraisal of our heritage now so that it becomes not a bastion to be defended but an instrument which carries our vision of the gospel in company with Christian comrades

---

[56]See for example, "Southern Baptists and Southern Culture," 144; and C. Penrose St. Amant, "Our Task," *Baptist History and Heritage* 1/2 (July 1966): 5.

[57]"Our Baptist Heritage and the Church," 85.

[58]"Baptists in a Revolutionary Age," 151.

[59]"Southern Baptist Theology Today: An Interview," 27.

[60]"Perspectives in Our Baptist Heritage," 16.

[61]"Southern Baptists and Southern Culture," 144-46.

shaped by other histories. We have much to give and much to learn. Let's do both.[62]

Conclusion

If space had permitted, I would have developed one other dialectic, not so much about St. Amant's interpretation of the Baptist vision (though certainly related) as about St. Amant himself. It would have been designated "Historical Consciousness and Contemporary Hope." He wrote often and passionately about Baptists' need to discuss and know their history. Within that history of voluntarism, freedom, religious liberty, "open Bibles," "open minds," and "plain people" were resources for guiding, inspiring and strengthening.

Although a student and lover of the past, Penrose St. Amant is essentially and fundamentally a forward looking person, optimistic and hopeful. In the broadest sense, his hope is based on the gospel, the good news of the life, death and resurrection of the Nazarene carpenter. In reading St. Amant, however, one comes away with the conviction that his hope is not unrelated to his Baptist heritage. The individualism of Baptist theology shapes St. Amant's hopefulness. He believes that one lonely soul can make a difference.[63] And maybe it was his "plain people" understanding of Baptist history that caused him to say that one does not have to do spectacular things to effect creative change.[64] Even in the face of secularism and the octopus-like arms of culture, squeezing the church at every point of its life, he continues to believe that life-transforming events occur in the" little church that lies at the heart of the Baptist heritage." Through most of his writing breathes the whisper, "the gates of hell shall not prevail."

Penrose St. Amant, as other articles about St. Amant happily demonstrate,[65] is no longer a mere interpreter of the Baptist heritage; he is now a part of that heritage. He has proved his maxim, rooted in his Baptist background, that one person can make a difference.

---

[62]"Baptists in a Revolutionary Age," 151.
[63]"Our Task," 6.
[64]"Baptists in a Revolutionary Age," 142.
[65]I refer especially to those articles in *Perspectives on Theological Education*.

Baptists
and Southern Baptist Convention History

■ ■ ■

A Historical Overview
of the Southern Baptist Convention[1]

Baptists of the Southern states organized the Southern Baptist Convention (SBC) during the days of 8-12 May 1845 in Augusta, Georgia. Geographically restricted to the Confederate states, the SBC began with a total membership of 351,951 in 4,126 local Baptist churches. By 2000 the SBC had churches in every state of the United States and had become the largest Protestant denomination in the country with a total membership of nearly sixteen million members in 40,000 local churches.

Baptists of the South, 1680–1845

Though the SBC was not formed until 1845, Baptists had been in the South since the last two decades of the seventeenth century. Much of what later could be described as the Southern Baptist identity took shape during the period from 1680 to 1845. Four factors were of particular importance.

The first of these was the synthesizing of diverse Baptist traditions, especially the Particular Baptists and the Separate Baptist traditions. Calvinistic in theology, the Particular Baptists developed out of English and American Puritanism and planted the first Baptist churches in the South near Charleston, South Carolina. Characterized by pietistic Puritanism, Calvinistic confessionalism, denominational connectionalism, and concern for ministerial education, this group left an important mark on Baptists of the South. Richard Furman, pastor of the First Baptist Church, Charleston, South Carolina, from 1787 to 1825, personalized this early Baptist tradition in the region.

Separate Baptists, on the other hand, emerged out of revivalistic New England Congregationalism and migrated to North Carolina in 1755. Led by Shubal Stearns, the Separate Baptists primarily bequeathed a legacy of religious freedom, revivalism, anticreedalim, suspicion of ministerial education, and independence in ecclesiology. In the 1780s the Separate

---

[1]This article first appeared in a slightly different form as, simply, "Southern Baptist Convention" in the *Encyclopedia of Religion in the South*, ed. Samuel S. Hill (Macon GA: Mercer University Press, 1984) 720-24. A second version of the article was prepared in 2000 for the revised edition of *Encyclopedia of Religion in the South* (due in 2005); the second version is the basis of this article.

Baptists and the Particular Baptists began consolidating, and by the end of the first decade of the nineteenth century they had virtually completed that process. Both the evangelistic emphases of the Separates and the more churchly emphases of the Particulars shaped the Baptists of the South.

The westward migration constituted a second factor that shaped the denomination prior to the formation of the SBC. Following the American Revolution, numerous Baptists joined the trek away from the Atlantic seaboard onto the newly opened trans-Appalachian frontier. The frontier became fertile soil for Baptist growth, intensifying Baptist individualism in ethics, congregationalism in church life, revivalism in ministry style, and simplicity in worship patterns. Moreover, the frontier further identified Baptists in the South as an agrarian people related primarily to the common people.

Thirdly, the modern missionary movement molded Baptists in the South prior to 1845. Under the leadership of Luther Rice, Baptists in the United States organized the Triennial Convention in 1814. The first national Baptist organization in America, the Triennial Convention promoted one cause, foreign missions. By 1832 Baptists founded the American Baptist Home Mission Society (ABHMS). Before 1845 Baptists of the South, ardent advocates of foreign and home missions, played a prominent role in the Triennial Convention and the ABHMS. When Southerners organized the SBC in 1845, they structured the new convention around two mission boards, one foreign and one domestic.

Finally, slavery and race exerted an enormous influence on the Baptists of the South. Before the invention of the cotton gin in 1793, a few Baptists in the South had condemned slavery. Most, however, had viewed slavery as a biblically sanctioned institution. During the heated abolition conflict of the 1830s, this latter attitude intensified and hardened.

The Southern Baptist Convention, 1845–1900

Baptists of the South separated from the Triennial Convention and the ABHMS in 1845 in defense of mid-nineteenth-century culture, primarily expressed in slavery. With the growing abolition sentiment of the 1830s and 1840s, both national Baptist mission societies confronted the question of appointing slaveholders as missionaries. In the early 1840s the mission societies affirmed and reaffirmed positions of neutrality on slavery. Baptists of the South questioned, and with good reason, the genuineness of that neutrality. They feared, among other things, being perceived as second-rate Christians because of their pro-slavery posture.

Baptists in Alabama forced the issue on 25 November 1844 when they addressed a fateful letter to the board of managers of the Triennial Convention. The Alabama Baptists resolved

> that our duty at this crisis requires us to demand from the proper authorities in all those bodies to whose funds we have contributed, or with whom we have in any way been connected, the distinct, explicit, avowal that slaveholders are eligible, and entitled, equally with nonslaveholders, to all the privileges and immunities of their several unions; and especially to receive any agency, mission, or other appointment, which may run within the scope of their operation or duties.

The board of managers of the Triennial Convention issued a frank and stinging reply. "If," they said, "any one should offer himself as a missionary, having slaves, and should insist on retaining them as his property, we could not appoint him." To avoid ambiguity the board said, "One thing is certain: we can never be a party to any arrangement which would imply approbation of slavery."

In response to this clear repudiation of slavery, 293 "delegates" representing diverse Baptist bodies such as local churches, state conventions, educational institutions, and missionary societies met at Augusta during 8-12 May 1845 and organized the SBC. W. B. Johnson, prominent South Carolina pastor, became the first president, and, in some ways, "father" of the SBC. Primarily responsible for drafting the "Constitution" of the SBC, Johnson probably also played a major part in composing an "Address to the Public," a document explaining why Southerners formed the SBC.

These two central founding SBC documents contained several important emphases. First, they stressed that the "extent of this disunion" involved only the Foreign and Home Mission enterprises. Southern Baptists did not separate from the American Baptist Publication Society, for example. Nor was the denominational divorce rooted in theological differences or differences regarding basic Baptist principles.

Second, Southern Baptists formed a new kind of denominational structure, one that was more centralized, more connectional, and more cooperative than any heretofore known among Baptists anywhere, in Europe or America. They forsook the decentralized, societal approach of the North and formed one convention with two boards, home and foreign.

Third, the SBC forged its unity in functional missionary endeavors and not in doctrinal or theological creedalism. "We have constructed for our basis no new creed; acting in this matter upon a Baptist aversion for all creeds but the Bible," they said. The SBC cemented the new denomination, not around doctrinal uniformity, but by "organizing a plan for eliciting, combining, and directing the energies of the whole denomination in one sacred effort, for the propagation of the gospel."

Within the "Address to the Public" one can identify three reasons for the formation of the SBC. One was constitutional, the second was historical, and the third was missional. First, and most importantly, Southern Baptists believed that the new convention was necessary because Northern Baptists violated the constitutions of the Baptist mission societies by refusing to appoint slaveholders as missionaries. For W. B. Johnson and the Baptists at Augusta, Southern Baptists organized the SBC because of constitutional usurpation by extreme antislavery advocates, not because of slavery.

Second, Southern Baptists argued that they formed the SBC because some Northern Baptists, by their recent antislavery actions, had ignored Baptist history. From 1814 till 1844 slaveholders, said Southern Baptists, had worked side by side with nonslaveholders in the Triennial Convention and with "no breath of discord between them."

Third, Southerners organized the SBC because Northerners "would forbid us to speak unto the Gentiles." They meant that they formed the SBC in order to fulfill their missionary responsibility, interpreting the antislavery actions of the Baptist mission societies as laying "a kind of Romish interdict upon us in the discharge of an imperative duty." In summary, Southern Baptists in 1845 claimed that they organized the SBC, not because of slavery, but because Northerners violated the constitutions of the two mission agencies, ignored the cooperative missionary history of Baptists in America, and denied Baptists of the South a means through which to fulfill their missionary responsibility.

Following the organization of the SBC, a denominationalizing process began among Southern Baptists that continued throughout the nineteenth century. At least three factors contributed to this sharpening of Southern Baptist identity. The first of these was cultural/political. Initiated by slavery and race, the "Southernness" of Southern Baptist life compounded under Southern Baptist attitudes toward secession, the Confederacy, the Civil War, and Reconstruction. When the SBC met 10-13 May 1861 in Savannah, Georgia, the delegates clearly identified with secessionism and everything Southern. They defended the right of secession, pledged themselves to the Confederacy, and substituted "Southern States of North America" for "United States" in the SBC constitution. In the nineteenth century Baptists *of* the South became *Southern* Baptists. The region, and especially the issue of race, impressed a discernible cultural identity on the SBC.

A second factor increasing the Southern Baptist consciousness in the nineteenth century was Landmarkism, essentially an ecclesiology fathered by James R. Graves in Nashville, Tennessee. With a view of history that stressed local Baptist church successionism back to the New Testament, Landmarkism claimed exclusive validity for Baptist churches, Baptist ministers, and Baptist ordinances. In essence this movement said that Baptist churches were the only true New Testament churches, Baptist ministers were the only true Christian clergy, and Baptist ordinances were the only true Christian ordinances. Landmarkism gave Southern Baptists an identity and left a legacy of anti-ecumenism, sectarianism, and authoritarianism in its churches. In doing so, it stamped the Southern Baptists of the nineteenth century with a distinct ecclesiological identity.

Institutional developments constituted the third factor that intensified the denominationalizing process among Southern Baptists in the nineteenth century. When the Baptist schism occurred in 1845, it involved only the two mission societies. By 1891, however, the SBC had organized the Baptist Sunday School Board (BSSB), which eventually displaced the older American Baptist Publication Society. Other new agencies monopolized Southern Baptist loyalty and drove a decisive wedge between the two major white Baptist denominations in America. In addition to the formation of the BSSB, Southern Baptists strengthened the Foreign and Home Mission Boards, founded Baptist colleges, organized the Southern Baptist Theological Seminary (1859), and created Woman's Missionary Union (1888). In the late nineteenth century Southern Baptists shunned overtures from Northern Baptists for reunification. By the turn of the twentieth century few significant points of contact remained between them.

The Southern Baptist Convention, 1900–1950

Southern Baptists have known phenomenal growth in the twentieth century. In 1900 they reported a total membership of 1,657,996 in 19,558 churches. By 1950 those figures had increased to 7,079,889 members and 27,788 churches.

SBC institutions also mushroomed in the first half of the century. In 1900 the SBC had only three boards (Foreign Missions, 1845; Home Missions, 1845; Sunday School, 1891) and one theological seminary (Southern Baptist Theological Seminary, 1859). By 1951 the convention had added one board (Annuity, 1918), four theological seminaries (Southwestern, 1908; New Orleans, 1917; Golden Gate, 1950; Southeastern, 1951), and six commissions (Brotherhood, 1907; Christian Life, 1913; Education, 1916; American Baptist Theological Seminary Commission, 1924; Radio and Television, 1946; Historical, 1951). After 1951 the SBC organized only one new seminary (Midwestern, 1957) and one new commission (Stewardship, 1960). Thus most of the SBC institutional development came in the first half of the twentieth century.

Three internal developments emerged as pivotal points in the denomination's history in the 1920s. Together, they began a centralizing process that continued throughout the century. One development was organizational, the second was financial, and the third theological. In 1927 the SBC created the Executive Committee of the SBC, recognizing that the SBC needed a coordinating body to act for the Convention between annual sessions. Reflecting American culture's preoccupation with business efficiency and the corporation model, the SBC made the Executive Committee the fiscal agent of the denomination. Over the years the committee has accumulated significant power in the SBC.

In 1925 the SBC launched the Cooperative Program, a financial arrangement between state conventions and the SBC that undergirded the entire denominational mission. The program evolved into the economic lifeline of the SBC. The SBC suffered several severe financial setbacks in the first half of the century. Indeed, Southern Baptists created the Cooperative Program as a result of one of those financial adversities, and it helped them to overcome later difficulties. The Cooperative Program further intensified the Southern Baptist identity, helping to forge an incredible loyalty by Southern Baptists to SBC programs and ministries.

Also in 1925, the SBC adopted their first doctrinal statement. Initially Southern Baptists intended the statement, known as the Baptist Faith and Message (BFM), as a consensus of theological affirmation and not as a binding creed on individuals, churches, and convention institutions. If J. Frank Norris and his extreme fundamentalist movement had not attacked Southern Baptists in the decade of the 1920s, the SBC may never have adopted a theological confession of any kind. When they organized in 1845, Southern Baptists claimed to have "a Baptist aversion for all creeds but the Bible," and for eighty years they made no effort to uniform theology. During the twentieth century, however, the BFM, along with other theological documents, has assumed an almost creedal character for the denomination.

Throughout the first half of the twentieth century the SBC was an aggressive evangelistic and missionary denomination, characterized by strong pulpit preaching. In fact, evangelism/missions, coupled with the tragic legacy of race, continued to be powerful shaping factors within SBC life.

Given the congregationalism of its local churches, the SBC achieved a stunning unity and denominational cohesion by 1950. Much of that "Southern Baptistness" had been molded and shaped by the Sunday School Board of the SBC. With its Sunday school literature, study course books, and numerous services to the churches, the Sunday School Board contributed enormously to the growing Southern Baptist identity.

A part of the identity of the SBC by mid-century consisted of being the "problem child" of American Protestant ecumenism. Without question, the SBC refused to participate in the major manifestations of the ecumenical movement. However, a close reading of SBC history from 1900 to 1950, while revealing more than enough denominational self-sufficiency and arrogance, demonstrated a surprising openness to Christian ecumenism on the part of some Southern Baptists. That openness increased in the 1960s and 1970s, only to revert to a rather narrow sectarianism in the latter part of the century.

The Southern Baptist Convention, 1950–2000

During the last half of the twentieth century the SBC continued its emphases on personal evangelism and church growth. Statistics document the amazing result. By the year 2000 the SBC consisted of almost sixteen million members in more than 40,000 local churches, clearly the largest Protestant body in North America. The SBC growth had been geographical as well as numerical. The SBC, beginning as a regional religious institution, became a national entity. While things looked good statistically by the year 2000, however, all had not been well in the Southern Baptist Zion for the previous fifty years.

In an official sesquicentennial history published in 1995, Jesse C. Fletcher described the SBC as an "uneasy consensus" in the decades of the 60s and 70s. This uneasy consensus may easily be pushed back into the 50s. While a number of issues exerted tension on the "uneasy consensus," the issues of racial justice, the role of women, and theological interpretations loomed large in SBC life.

Storming into this "uneasy consensus" in 1979, politically savvy and ideologically committed SBC fundamentalist leaders set out to capture the SBC and transform the denomination, saving it, as they claimed, from liberalism and institutionalism. By the year 2000 they had been incredibly successful, remaking a basically conservative denomination into one where independent fundamentalist Jerry Falwell eventually would feel at home.

Fundamentalists achieved their goal by electing SBC presidents for eleven years (1979–1990) consecutively. The fundamentalist presidents in turn utilized the appointive powers of the office to stack the trustees of all SBC agencies with people of narrow theological leanings. Met by stiff resistance from SBC moderates, the outcome of the controversy was uncertain for several years. Finally, in 1990, moderates gave up the political fight and formed the Cooperative Baptist Fellowship (CBF) as an alternative organization to the SBC.

Known as "The Inerrancy Controversy" because of the fundamentalist contention of the inerrancy of the Bible, this conflict proved to be the most devastating internal struggle in the SBC's 150-year history. Rather than negotiate an amicable Christian divorce, the fundamentalists and moderates followed a "winner-takes-all" strategy. When the dust settled in 1990, the fundamentalists owned the largest Baptist denomination in the world. They quickly used the last decade of the century to continue the process of transforming the SBC theological seminaries, Sunday School Board, mission boards, and other agencies into a Baptist denomination that looked far more conservative than the SBC of the past.

Because of the controversy, two concurrent forces dominated the SBC in the last two decades of the twentieth century. Ironically, these two forces both fragmented and centralized the SBC. These currents of change separated and yet consolidated, pulled outward and yet inward.

The loyalty to SBC institutions and agencies, built up over more than a hundred years, meant that fundamentalists retained most of Southern Baptist life. Doubtless it would have worked the same way had moderates won. However, centrifugal forces, while certainly not unraveling the SBC center, changed the inner character of the SBC.

With the exodus of moderate leadership from the SBC and the formation of the Cooperative Baptist Fellowship and the much smaller Baptist Alliance, some splintering of SBC denominationalism has occurred. Educationally, this splintering is easy to see. Moderates have created at least seven new theological institutions.

Moderates also created a new Baptist publishing company, a new ethics agency, a new historical society, a new Baptist press, and a new Baptist newspaper. Moreover, they have financially "adopted" the Baptist Joint Committee on Public Affairs, the religious liberty agency in Washington, D.C., which the fundamentalist SBC defunded. The Cooperative Baptist

Fellowship claims not to be a new denomination, but it has all the marks of one.

Although only a few SBC churches officially severed all ties with the SBC, many churches are now dividing their financial contributions between the SBC and the CBF. Two state conventions, Virginia and Texas, have resisted the fundamentalist takeover of the national convention, and they have distanced themselves from the new SBC. How big the "splinter," as the fundamentalists call the moderate defection, becomes is yet to be seen, but the splintering is in process.

In contrast to the splintering, the new SBC fundamentalist leadership has been consolidating its gains. Some Southern Baptists thought that fundamentalists, once they gained power, would mellow and share their newfound influence with all factions in the SBC. The exact opposite has happened. A constriction has occurred within the new SBC, and the major centripetal force, as one would expect, is theological. The SBC seminaries, once conservative but diverse, are now fundamentalist and exclusive. The best example, however, of the narrowing of SBC theology came in the 2000 annual meeting of the SBC where the Baptist Faith and Message was rewritten from a fundamentalist point of view. Beginning in 1845 with "an aversion to all creeds but the Bible," the SBC opened the door on the twenty-first century with a creedal look to it. Fundamentalist SBC leaders interpret this theological narrowing as a "conservative resurgence" that restores biblical orthodoxy and the historical roots of the SBC.

Nowhere has the constrictionism in theology expressed itself more than in the attitude toward the role of women. Arguing for the submission of wives to their husbands, the revised BFM of 2000 also excludes any possibility of women serving in pastoral leadership. Other changed emphases within the SBC are the minimizing of the priesthood of all believers and the separation of church and state, while maximizing the authority of the pastor. While moving closer to fundamentalist groups, the denomination has also become less open in its relationship to other mainline Christians and religious groups.

As the fundamentalist leadership of the SBC redefined the denomination in the last two decades of the century, they defunded agencies, dismissed personnel, restructured and renamed SBC agencies, refused to receive financial contributions coming through CBF, and narrowed the theological guidelines. From the perspective of the new SBC leadership, biblical truth has been restored to the SBC. From the perspective of the defeated moderates, the SBC has lost its Baptist way.

Bibliography

Robert A. Baker, *A Baptist Source Book, with Particular Reference to Southern Baptists*; idem, *The First Southern Baptists*; idem, *Relations between Northern and Southern Baptists*; idem, "Southern Baptist Convention," in *Baptist Advance*, ed. Davis C. Woolley; idem, *The Southern Baptist Convention and Its People (1607–1972)*; *Baptist History and Heritage* 16 (April 1981); William Wright Barnes, *The Southern Baptist Convention, 1845–1953*; E. Luther Copeland, *The Southern Baptist Convention and the Judgement of History: The Taint of an Original Sin*; John Lee Eighmy, *Churches in Cultural Captivity: A History of the Social Attitudes of Southern Baptists*; *Encyclopedia of Southern Baptists*, 4 vols.; Jesse C. Fletcher, *The Southern Baptist Convention*; Brooks Hays and John E. Steely, *The Baptist Way of Life*; Fisher Humphreys, *The Way We Were: How Southern Baptist Theology has Changed and What it Means to Us All*; Bill J. Leonard, *God's Last and Only Hope*; H. Leon McBeth, *The Baptist Heritage*; Walter B. Shurden, *Not a Silent People*; idem, *Controversies That Have Shaped Southern Baptists*; idem, *The Struggle for the Soul of the SBC*; Walter B. Shurden and Randy Shepley, *Going for the Jugular: A Documentary History of the SBC Holy War*; *Southern Baptist Convention Annual*, 1845 to the present; Rufus B. Spain, *At Ease in Zion: A Social History of Southern Baptists*; Jerry Sutton, *The Baptist Reformation: The Conservative Resurgence in the Southern Baptist Convention*; Robert G. Torbet, *A History of the Baptists*; G. Hugh Wamble, "Baptists of the South," in *Baptists and the American Experience*, ed. James E. Wood, Jr.

The Origins of the Southern Baptist Convention: A Historiographical Study[1]

The purpose of this paper is to describe how white Baptist church historians of the South have interpreted the founding of the Southern Baptist Convention since 1845. It is, therefore, an exercise in historiography. Most non-Southern Baptist church historians would doubtless ask, "Is it not obvious that slavery was the decisive factor in the formation of the SBC?" The answer: "No, it has not been obvious to white Southern Baptist church historians that slavery was the primary issue in the formation of the SBC." Indeed not until the last quarter of the twentieth century have these Baptist historians said without qualification that slavery was the fundamental cause of the SBC.

This investigation is limited to white Baptist church historians of the South in order to demonstrate changing patterns of interpretation by this group since 1845. One could easily broaden this research, and with great profit, by adding the interpretations of African American Baptist church historians, white Baptist church historians of the North, and secular historians of all kinds. But that is a more extensive and comprehensive work, waiting probably on the careful and diligent hand of some energetic Ph.D. student in search of an excellent dissertation topic.

We have taken a "somewhat strict" chronological approach, though the reader will see, and for obvious reasons we hope, some elasticity in the chronology. For the 155-year history of the SBC three patterns of interpretation emerged, each relating generally to a fifty-year period. During the first period of 1845–1900, white Baptist denominational historians of the South wrote defensively about the formation of the SBC, ignoring slavery as the causative factor in the formation of the Southern Baptist Convention. Indeed, they rarely mentioned the word *slavery*, much less pointed to it as the primary cause of the SBC. From 1900 to 1950 historians clearly identified slavery as a factor in the formation of the SBC, but some tended to obscure its impact by pointing to, sometimes even highlighting, other factors. In the last half of the twentieth century,

[1]This article was originally published in *Baptist History and Heritage* 37/1 (Winter 2002): 71-96, with Lori Redwine as coauthor. It is reprinted by permission of the Baptist History and Heritage Society, Brentwood TN.

1950–2000, Southern Baptist church historians have been more blunt in identifying slavery as the causative factor in the formation of the SBC.

The facts of the division between Baptists north and south is an oft-told story and need not be repeated here. While the facts are generally undisputed, the interpretation of those facts, as this paper demonstrates, have been greatly debated. Under the leadership of Luther Rice, Baptists organized their foreign mission society in 1814, and it was known as the Triennial Convention. In 1832 the denomination formed the home mission society, called the American Baptist Home Mission Society. In an effort to avoid division, the societies adopted in the 1840s resolutions of neutrality regarding the slavery issue. Partisan sentiments on such a momentous issue, however, simply could not be suppressed. The schism occurred among Baptists, therefore, in the mid-nineteenth century in their national mission societies. As Robert A. Baker said, "The pertinent question in each case was, will the Society appoint a slaveholder as missionary?"[2] By 1845 Baptists of the South believed, and with good reason, that the answer to that question was "No." They, therefore, assembled at Augusta, Georgia, in May 1845, to form a new convention, not, according to them, because of slavery but because their "rights" had been violated.

Slavery: An Ignored Factor, 1845–1900

Four major historical interpretations of the origins of the SBC appeared during the first fifty years of the convention. These documents came from William B. Johnson in 1845, William Williams in 1871, Lansing Burrows in 1881, and William H. Whitsitt in 1895. These four essays, as shall be readily seen, contained several common features. The most important of the documents, in terms of Southern Baptist origins, was Johnson's.

William B. Johnson . . . 1845. White Baptists of the South gave their earliest and most official statement of the reasons for the formation of the SBC at the organizational meeting of the SBC in 1845. This document, awkwardly titled as "The Southern Baptist Convention, to the Brethren in the United States; to the congregations connected with the respective Churches; and to all candid men," is, thankfully, referred to as the "Address

---

[2]Robert Andrew Baker, *Relations between Northern and Southern Baptists* (Fort Worth TX: published by the author, 1948) 81. Baker noted the differences in the circumstances of the Home Mission Society and the Triennial Convention, but the result was the same: slaveholders would not be appointed missionaries.

to the Public."[3] While the SBC charged a committee with the responsibility of writing the document, most historians have assumed that W. B. Johnson had a major hand in the document. His name was attached to the document in the 1845 SBC *Annual*. If not the most influential Baptist of the South in the mid-nineteenth century, W. B. Johnson was surely one of the two or three most significant Southern Baptist statesmen of the era. Elected as the first SBC president and author of the convention's most important founding documents, Johnson also served as president of the South Carolina Baptist Convention in 1845. Moreover, he was the only person at the 1845 SBC meeting also present at the formation of the Triennial Convention in 1814. He had served on the committee to draw up the constitution of the Triennial Convention, and he had served as president of the Triennial Convention from 1841 to 1844. Johnson declined to serve as president of the Triennial Convention in 1844 at the apex of the slavery controversy, allegedly for "health" reasons.[4] He was not too sick the next year to take the leadership of the SBC, however.

The opening sentence of the "Address to the Public" described both the deep trauma and the limited scope of the denominational schism: "A painful division has taken place in the missionary operations of the American Baptists."[5] The separation hurt, but it related only to foreign and home missions. Johnson, concerned with maintaining as many Northern Baptist ties as possible, underscored that "the extent of this disunion" should not be exaggerated. Anticipating correctly that the schism could become more extensive in the future, he nonetheless said that "*at the present time*" it involves only the foreign and domestic missions of the denomination.

---

[3]See *SBC Annual 1845*, 17-20. A copy of the document is printed in Robert A. Baker, *A Baptist Source Book, with Particular Reference to Southern Baptists* (Nashville: Broadman Press, 1966) 118-22.

[4]James M. Morton, Jr. has questioned Johnson's authorship, providing some evidence for his view. Regardless of who wrote it, however, Southern Baptists printed the statement in the *Annual* of the 1845 SBC "By order of the convention." It served clearly as a formal explanation of the organization of the SBC. For Morton's point of view, see James M. Morton, Jr., "Leadership of W. B. Johnson in the Formation of the Southern Baptist Convention," *Baptist History and Heritage* 5/1 (January 1970): 11-12. See also Robert G. Gardner, *A Decade of Debate and Division: Georgia Baptists and the Formation of the Southern Baptist Convention* (Macon GA: Mercer University Press, 1995) 43.

[5]*SBC Annual 1845*, 17.

A popular but erroneous interpretation among some Southern Baptists in the twentieth century has been that Baptists divided in 1845 over theological issues. The usual version of this interpretation argued that the split occurred because Northern Baptists were theological "liberals," while Southern Baptists were theological "conservatives." In his public explanation Johnson stated unequivocally that this was not the case. Said Johnson:

> Northern and southern Baptists are still brethren. They differ in no article of the faith. They are guided by the same principles of gospel order. . . . We do not regard the rupture as extending to foundation principles, nor can we think that the great body of our Northern brethren will so regard it.[6]

While the denominational divorce was rooted neither in theological differences nor in differences regarding basic Baptist principles, the separation had proceeded, said Johnson "deplorably far."

So how did Johnson, the first president of the SBC, interpret the division between Baptists north and south? He began by insisting that the "entire *origin*" of the division "is with others."[7] Authority had been "usurped," a covenant of trust had been breached, an "autocratical interdict" had been imposed, and all of this had come from the Baptists of the North. Southern Baptists wanted the public to know that while Baptists of the South had created a new convention they had done so only in response to the actions of others. The initiative and the cause of the division lay with "others," namely, Northern Baptists.

Within the "Address" one can identify three reasons for the formation of the SBC. One was constitutional, the second was historical, and the third was missional. First, and most importantly, Johnson believed the new convention was necessary because Northern Baptists violated the constitutions of the Baptist mission societies. For Johnson and the Baptists at Augusta, Southern Baptists organized the SBC because of constitutional

---

[6]*SBC Annual 1845*, 17. David Benedict, writing fifteen years later, confirmed Johnson's statement. Speaking of the Baptist division, Benedict said: "This separation was very quietly effected, and up to this time I have not heard of any collisions between the two wings of the denomination, *which agree in all matters*, except the lawfulness of Southern slavery." See David Benedict, *Fifty Years among the Baptists* (Boston: Sheldon & Company, 1860; repr.: Little Rock AR: Seminary Publications, May 1977) 217; italics for emphasis.

[7]*SBC Annual 1845*, 17.

usurpation by extreme antislavery advocates, not because of slavery. From the beginning of the Triennial Convention in 1814, said Johnson, its constitution had known "no difference between slaveholders and nonslaveholders."[8] In this historical observation, Johnson and the Southerners were correct, as Northerners themselves acknowledged.[9] "But an evil hour arrived," according to Johnson. This "evil hour," however, was not the practice and defense of slavery, but an hour when passionate voices injected the issue of slavery as a moral issue into the deliberations of Baptists missionary operations. Johnson insisted that the constitutions of the mission societies never, ever forbade the appointment of slaveholders as missionaries. According to Baptists in the South, therefore, the constitutional issue of refusing to appoint slaveholders led to the formation of the SBC, not slavery.

Secondly, Johnson argued that Baptists of the South formed the SBC because some Northern Baptists, by their recent antislavery actions, had ignored Baptist history. From 1814 till 1844 slaveholders, said Johnson, had worked side by side with nonslaveholders in the Triennial Convention and with "no breath of discord between them."[10] Additionally, Johnson asserted, and again correctly, that the mission societies of Baptists had adopted explicit resolutions of neutrality on the slavery issue, affirming that their sole purpose was the propagation of the gospel.[11] In forming the SBC, therefore, Southern Baptists were practicing what Baptists in America had always practiced; they were following "the old paths." With the organization of the SBC, Baptists of the South proposed "to do the Lord's work in the way [their] fathers did it,"[12] by refusing to admit slavery as an issue into the Baptist missionary enterprise.

---

[8]*SBC Annual 1845*, 17.

[9]See the report of the committee chaired by Francis Wayland at the 1845 meeting of the Triennial Convention in Providence RI, in A. H. Newman, *A History of the Baptist Churches in the United States* (New York: Charles Scribner's Sons, 1894) 448; see also the resolution introduced to the April 1845 meeting of the Home Mission Society as cited in William Williams, "Historical Sketch Contained in the Annual Sermon, in *SBC Annual 1872*, appendix D, 3-4.

[10]*SBC Annual 1845*, 17.

[11]Johnson quoted the resolution of neutrality adopted by the 1844 Triennial Convention. See *SBC Annual 1845*, 18. For the resolution adopted by the Home Mission Society in 1844, see Robert A. Baker, *A Baptist Source Book*, 97.

[12]*SBC Annual 1845*, 19.

Thirdly, Johnson said Southerners organized the SBC because Northerners "would forbid us to speak unto the Gentiles." He meant that he and others formed the SBC in order to fulfill their missionary responsibility. Johnson interpreted the antislavery actions of the Baptist mission societies as laying "a kind of Romish interdict upon us in the discharge of an imperative duty." By excluding slaveholders as missionary appointees, Northerners had monopolized the gospel, said Johnson. Such an "Autocratical Interdict of the North would first drive us from our beloved colored people . . . and from the much-wronged Aborigines of the country . . . and cut us off from the whitening fields of the heathen harvest-labor." Therefore, the purpose for the SBC was "the extension of the Messiah's kingdom, and the glory of our God." Disunion with the North was not the design. Nor was "the upholding of any form of human policy or civil rights" the purpose of the new convention. The SBC was formed "for the profit of these poor, perishing, and precious souls."[13] In summary, Southern Baptists organized the SBC, according to Johnson, because Northerners violated the constitutions of the two mission agencies, ignored the cooperative missionary history of Baptists in America, even repudiating official actions of neutrality, and denied Baptists of the South a means through which to fulfill their missionary responsibility.[14]

William Williams . . . 1871. William Williams, a church historian and the least known of the first four[15] faculty members of the Southern Baptist Theological Seminary in Greenville, South Carolina, preached the annual sermon in 1871 at the Southern Baptist Convention in St. Louis. By request of the SBC, the sermon appeared as "Appendix D" in the 1872 SBC *Annual.* Whether by Williams or the editors of the *Annual,* someone uncreatively titled the sermon "Historical Sketch, Contained in the Annual Sermon." Very much as Johnson's "Address," Williams's "Historical Sketch" served as an apologia for the organization of the SBC in 1845. In addition, however, Williams utilized their past to exhort Southern Baptists

---

[13]*SBC Annual 1845,* 18-19.

[14]In making his case for the formation of the SBC, Johnson followed the arguments of the circular letter of the Virginia Baptist Foreign Mission Society. J. B. Jeter probably wrote the Virginia document. For a complete copy of the Virginia document, see Baker, *A Baptist Source Book,* 109-13.

[15]The others were James P. Boyce, John A. Broadus, and Basil Manly, Jr. For a brief biographical sketch on Williams, see *Encyclopedia of Southern Baptists* (Nashville: Broadman Press, 1958) 2:1503.

of the 1870s to rally in support of their own weakened denominational institutions.[16]

In his annual sermon Williams, while using different language, underscored the three major points Johnson stressed thirty years earlier. As had Johnson, Williams came down hardest on the constitutional issue, claiming that the Northern Baptists forced the separation by the "infringement" of Southern rights. In one sentence he combined Johnson's constitutional and historical arguments: "The constitution of the Triennial Convention, as well as the history of its proceedings from the beginning, conferred *on all the members of the Baptist denomination in good standing*, whether at the North or the South, eligibility to all appointments emanating from the Convention or the Board."[17] Williams was making the point, so crucial to the Southern rationale, that neither constitutional statute nor historical practice had precluded slaveholders from serving in the missionary societies prior to 1844. Williams also echoed Johnson's missional point. Southerners created the SBC because the Triennial Convention had "cut off Southern ministers from the privilege of spreading the Gospel to the heathen."[18]

While following closely Johnson's explanations for the SBC, Williams introduced emphases of his own. In addition to the constitutional, historical, and missional reasons for the SBC, Williams injected what he saw as a moral reason for Southerners to create the SBC. Ironically, it was an argument of equality! Northerners, by excluding slaveholders, had denied the moral equality of Southern Baptists. The Home Mission Society by its anti-slavery actions, said Williams, had declared "an unwillingness to work together with them [slaveholders] upon terms of Christian equality."[19]

---

[16]During the period 1864–1888 some Baptists, especially Northerners, made efforts to reunify Baptists North and South. See Baker, *Relations between Northern and Southern Baptists*, 154. In his annual SBC sermon, Williams, like many Southern Baptists, argued for a more distinct identity on the part of Southern Baptists, not reunification with Baptists of the North. Said Williams: "Only our own organization can enlist to any considerable extent the cooperation and energies of the great mass of our people. A divided sympathy and support will only therefore cause our Convention to languish, and will bring discord into our own counsels, paralyze our own resources, and injure in the end the Lord's work, without accomplishing probably the end which it may have had in view." See *SBC Annual 1872*, appendix D, 8.

[17]*SBC Annual 1872*, appendix D, 1; italics for emphasis.

[18]*SBC Annual 1872*, appendix D, 4.

[19]*SBC Annual 1872*, appendix D, 2-4.

Williams's moral argument certainly must be Exhibit A of the blinding force of culture on conscience! Miffed at having equality snatched from him, he, as most Americans of his time, never thought of equality as an issue between the races.

Besides his moral argument, Williams made at least three other points. One, he spoke of the inevitability of the schism, a point made often by Baptists north and south during the 1840s. Two, Williams gladly quoted at length from a Northern Baptist newspaper of April 1845, which argued that the division would aid the cause of missions by causing both groups to double their efforts. Many seized upon this argument to justify the slavery schism. Three, while the biblical sanction of slavery played only a small part in the rationale and defense of the formation of the SBC, it is certainly present in the nineteenth-century documents. After the Home Mission Society voted to appoint only slaveholders, Williams said, "Of course, therefore, only those can consistently work with it and under its appointment, who recognize the Scriptural propriety of such a restriction."[20]

J. Lansing Burrows . . . 1885. The SBC celebrated its fortieth anniversary in 1885 by returning to the First Baptist Church of Augusta Georgia, the place of its birth. J. Lansing Burrows,[21] easily confused with his son Lansing Burrows, presented a "Historical Sketch of the Southern Baptist Convention, 1845–1885." Burrows referred to Johnson's "Address to the Public," two articles published in *Christian Review* magazine in 1845 and 1846,[22] and William Williams's 1871 convention address as documents presenting "the essential facts relating to the causes and principles involved in the [1845] division, and must ever be the principal documents upon which these events are to be woven into the history of the denomination."[23]

Because Burroughs thought the historical issues which led to the formation of the SBC had been adequately treated, he made only a passing comment regarding the origins of the denomination. As a result, he devoted his "Historical Sketch" to a brief history of the missionary work of the SBC. Burroughs's passing comment regarding SBC origins, however,

---

[20]*SBC Annual 1872*, appendix D, 2-4.

[21]For a brief biographical sketch, see *Encyclopedia of Southern Baptists* 1:210.

[22]The Boston board of the Triennial Convention issued a formal reply to Johnson's "Address" in the December 1845 issue of the magazine. In May 1846, Burroughs said, "an able rejoinder" to the Boston article was published.

[23]*SBC Annual 1885*, 38.

though brief, was significant. It added a bit more balance to the subject than had been presented by either Johnson or Williams.

Burroughs spoke of how Northern Baptists and Southern Baptists viewed each other as "sinners" during the days of division. "Some of the Northern brethren," he said, "moved by the then recent agitation of the slavery question, gained new light as to the essential sinfulness of slavery, came to regard Southern Baptists as sinners in countenancing that institution, and concluded that the original terms of fellowship in missionary operations could not be consistently perpetuated." On the other hand, "Southern Baptists came to regard Northern Baptists as sinners because of the repudiation of the compact of the Constitution, under whose provisions they had worked together for more than a quarter of a century."[24]

While Burroughs makes the point that each side considered the other as sinful, he clearly leans toward the "constitutional" argument so treasured by Southern Baptists. Not once but three times within a very brief space he noted that the two groups had worked together harmoniously under the Constitution of the Triennial Convention for thirty years. Not only so, but he repeated the theme so important to Johnson and Williams that the SBC constitution was "essentially the same" as that under which Baptists had previously united.

The fact that Burroughs embraced the Southern rationale should come as no surprise, for he had served historic Southern Baptist pulpits for more than thirty-five years. Those churches included First Baptist Church in Richmond, Virginia, Broadway Baptist Church in Louisville, Kentucky, and Freemason Street Baptist Church in Norfolk, Virginia. Yet, Burroughs was a Northerner! Born in Albany, New York, educated at Andover Seminary, ordained in Poughkeepsie, New York, he served as pastor of significant Baptist churches in Pennsylvania before going south. His long stint of ministerial service in the South had "Southernized" Burroughs, but his Northern roots may have caused him to want to spread the "sin" to both regions when he wrote his brief account of the origins of the SBC.

W. H. Whitsitt . . . 1895. In 1895 W. H. Whitsitt, the newly elected president of the Southern Baptist Theological Seminary, delivered a historical address at the jubilee meeting of the SBC in Washington, D.C. Entitled "Historical Discourse on the Fiftieth Anniversary of the Southern Baptist Convention," the address gave all the evidence of the hand of a well-trained church historian. Superbly organized and extremely well

---

[24]*SBC Annual 1885*, 37.

written, the address, however, did not deal explicitly with the origins of the SBC. Whitsitt was obviously more interested in providing a comprehensive overview of the SBC from 1845 to 1895 than in depicting origins.

One senses in Whitsitt, also, both the healing of time and hesitancy to fan past fires of hostility by resurrecting the knotty and emotional issues of history. While he certainly did not feel obliged to confess the sins of slavery of his Southern ancestors, neither did he want to excoriate Northern Baptists for alleged constitutional violations. Consequently, he avoided a rehash of negative historical interpretations, seeking instead to reconstrue SBC beginnings in as positive a manner as possible.

Whitsitt's positive interpretation was fourfold. First, echoing one of Johnson's emphases, he declared that the separation "was happily circumscribed in extent." Whitsitt reminded his 1895 Southern Baptist audience that the schism "related exclusively to the missionary operations." Quoting Johnson's "Address to the Public," he said that "the fathers of that day were solicitous that this point should be clearly understood."

Second, while limited in scope, the division, said Whitsitt, as Williams before him, was "unavoidable." "The best and wisest men in the North consented to a division because they regarded it as being . . . a necessary evil," said Whitsitt, while "the wisest and best men in the South accepted the division as being imperatively required."

Third, Whitsitt, continuing with his positive spins, said that "in many respects the separation has also been of signal advantage." For one thing the SBC exodus promoted peace and union between abolitionists of the North and those Northern Baptists who had remained neutral on the slavery issue. Moreover, the division intensified Southern Baptist missionary activity. He demonstrated with the increased financial giving records of Southern Baptists to home missions. For Whitsitt, this increased missionary zeal among Southern Baptists "was worth all the pain and sacrifice that we had to endure in breaking up the relations . . . with our Northern brethren." In making this point Whitsitt had a noble purpose, but the highlighting of missions in Southern Baptist history, ironically, has caused some of its historians to obscure the tragic legacy of racial prejudice.

Fourth, Whitsitt rejoiced that the 1845 rupture "was for the most part a peaceable one." Acknowledging the presence of unavoidable friction, "public negotiations on either side were marked by the dignity and moderation that become Christian brethren."[25]

---

[25]All quotations in the previous paragraphs are from the *SBC Annual 1895*, 78-

Slavery: A Muted Factor, 1900–1950

During the period from 1900 to 1950 white Southern Baptist historians began producing some major books on Baptist history. A. H. Newman of McMaster University in Canada, John T. Christian of New Orleans Seminary, Robert A. Baker and W. W. Barnes of Southwestern Seminary each wrote Baptist histories. Baker and Barnes are especially significant for this study because they focused their research on Southern Baptist history. No single pattern of SBC origins emerged from the four historians, but Barnes/Baker tended to follow a line of interpretation which, while identifying the centrality of slavery, abridged to some degree the impact of slavery on SBC history.

A. H. Newman . . . 1894. Toward the end of the nineteenth century one Baptist church historian of the South in the person of A. H. Newman demonstrated a growing absence of defensiveness regarding the slavery issue. Unlike Johnson, Williams, Burroughs, and Whitsitt, Newman neither remained silent nor ignored the crucial role of slavery in the formation of the SBC. Way ahead of his time, Newman's historiography, however, would not become dominant or more fully expressed until the last half of the twentieth century. In his *A History of the Baptist Churches in the United States* (1894) Newman clearly suggested that slavery was the major issue in the formation of the SBC.[26] He did so, however, without the slightest trace of moral denunciation of Southern Baptists and with the deft hand of a historian employing noninflammatory language.

Writing of the formation of the SBC and especially of the slavery issue, Newman said, "The Baptists of the South had, as a body, identified themselves with the institution, and were prepared not only to practice it, but to defend it with pen and sword."[27] In the next sentence one senses something of the historian's own posture as he described the Northern Baptist position. "The sentiment against domestic slavery grew rapidly at the North,"

79.

[26]Although Newman published his history in 1894, even a year before Whitsitt's Jubilee Address, we have listed Newman with the historians of the 1900–1950 period because his point of view was so markedly different from that of other historians who wrote in the nineteenth century. Moreover, Newman did not die until 1933, having taught in several major Baptist institutions until 1929.

[27]A. H. Newman, *A History of the Baptist Churches in the United States* (New York: Charles Scribner's Sons, 1894) 443.

he said, "and many Baptists were coming to feel that duty required them not only to protest against the enslavement of their fellowmen and brethren in Christ, but to use every practicable means for the overthrow of an institution which they looked upon as un-Christian and immoral."[28]

This fierce difference over slavery, not constitutional violations, appeared to be the essence of the issue for Newman. Indeed, Newman characterized W. B. Johnson's constitutional argument employed in the "Address to the Public" as "*the charge* of departure from the original principles of the Convention."[29] While one may view Newman's language of "the charge" as simply that of an objective historian, one may also see it as a means of minimizing the constitutional argument. As had Whitsitt, Newman also claimed the division of 1845 was unavoidable in nature, advantageous to missions, and peaceable in tone.[30]

A couple of significant points should be noted about Newman and his historiography. With deep roots in the South, he was theologically educated at the Rochester Baptist Theological Seminary in the North. Moreover, he was long associated with Canadian and British Baptists, having taught for twenty years at McMaster University, a Canadian Baptist school. Indeed, he was teaching at McMaster when he wrote his history of Baptists in the United States. Also, his history was published by Charles Scribner's Sons; it was not an address presented before the SBC! Nor was it published by a denominational publishing house.[31] From *where* a historian speaks or writes may impact historiography as much as *when* one speaks.

John T. Christian . . . 1926. John T. Christian, professor of Christian History at the Baptist Bible Institute in New Orleans, published a two-volume history of the Baptists in the 1920s. Devoting the second volume to Baptists in America, he called it *A History of the Baptists in the United States: From the First Settlement of the Country to the Year 1845.* However, he uttered not a word in the text itself regarding the 1845 division, nor of the factors which led to that tragic split. Indeed, the word "slavery" does not appear in the index of the book. Since he concluded his history at 1845, one can possibly understand the total lack of reference to

---

[28]Newman, *A History of the Baptist Churches in the United States,* 443.

[29]Newman, *A History of the Baptist Churches in the United States,* 451; ialics for emphasis.

[30]Newman, *A History of the Baptist Churches in the United States,* 449.

[31]For a biographical sketch of Newman, see *Encyclopedia of Southern Baptists* 2:977.

the formation of the SBC in 1845. What one cannot understand is how he avoided describing the turbulent circumstances which led to 1845. The only reference in the entire volume to the factors which led to the rupture of Baptists in America is found in the preface where, after alluding to the Anti-Missions and Campbellite conflicts, he said:

> There were other factors at work which were equally serious. About the year 1835 began those political debates and animosities which were to occasion the Civil War. These factional differences were manifested in religious affairs. They ultimately led to the division of the Baptists of the North from those of the South.[32]

Christian's historiography is a blatant example of how the historian's work shapes history by what the historian fails to say. One cannot imagine a history of the South without race, in one way or another, dominating the story. Neither can one understand the story of Southern Baptists apart from that theme.

W. W. Barnes . . . 1954. Professor of Church History at Southwestern Baptist Theological Seminary for forty years, William Wright Barnes wrote the official centennial history of the SBC. Published by the denominational press in 1954, the book was called simply *The Southern Baptist Convention, 1845–1953.* Beyond question Barnes assessed slavery to be the central cause of the formation of the SBC, so much so, in fact, that one SBC official writing in the *Encyclopedia of Southern Baptists* thought he overstated the case.[33]

In the chapter where Barnes discussed the formation of the SBC, he opened with an obvious but innocent sentence the SBC official wanted to modify: "The formation of the Southern Baptist Convention grew out of the division in the Home Mission Society and in the general Convention (foreign missions) over the question of slavery."[34] The issue of why Southern Baptists organized the SBC seemed closed in light of Barnes's directness.

---

[32]John T. Christian, *A History of the Baptists of the United States: From the First Settlement of the Country to the Year 1845* (Nashville: Sunday School Board of the SBC, 1926) 6.

[33]See J. W. Storer's article "Southern Baptist Convention, The" in *Encyclopedia of Southern Baptists* 2:1244.

[34]William Wright Barnes, *The Southern Baptist Convention, 1845–1953* (Nashville: Broadman Press, 1954) 12.

But while Barnes pinpointed slavery as central, he also muffled the racial factor by pointing to other issues. He followed the bluntness of his emphasis on slavery with an important "but." "But," he said in the very next sentence, "the tendency to division in American Baptist life was in evidence before slavery became an issue."[35] Barnes's slight equivocation regarding slavery appeared in the very first sentence of the book. Said Barnes, "From colonial times there were rivalries and jealousies between the Northern and Southern colonies."[36] He then added that the same conditions that hindered unity in secular life impacted Baptist groups in various geographical areas. In addition to the secular impact on Baptists, Barnes observed that Baptists themselves had imported varying emphases in theology and church polity from Europe to America. Then he concluded, "Some of these differences entered into the separation between Baptists of the South and the North in 1845."[37]

Interestingly, with one exception, Barnes failed to unpack "these differences" which he thought "entered into the separation." The exception was the issue of home missions. He described at length how prior to 1845 "pastors and editors in the South, and some state conventions, protested that the Home Mission Society was neglecting the Southern area and called for new organizations to meet the need."[38] But Barnes noted that these complaints, honestly made by Southerners, were unjustified. His point, however, was that division was in the air apart from the slavery issue. So while he was clear about the centrality of slavery in the schism, he muffled that issue slightly by other comments.[39]

Robert A. Baker . . . 1948/1974. Barnes's mantle as the "Dean of Southern Baptist Church Historians" fell on Robert A. Baker, Barnes's student who was a far more prolific writer than Barnes. Like his teacher, Baker taught church history for decades at Southwestern Seminary, focusing most of his scholarly research and writing on aspects of the history of the SBC. Baker produced the second book-length history of the SBC in 1974 with his statistically oriented study titled *The Southern Baptist*

---

[35]Barnes, *The Southern Baptist Convention*, 12.

[36]Barnes, *The Southern Baptist Convention*, 1.

[37]Barnes, *The Southern Baptist Convention*, 1.

[38]Barnes, *The Southern Baptist Convention*, 12.

[39]Professor Barnes probably correctly observed that if slavery had not divided Baptists North and South, the issue of home missions may have divided them East and West. See Barnes, *The Southern Baptist Convention*, 18.

Convention and Its People, 1607–1972. If his book was published in 1974, why, one may ask, include Baker with the historians from 1900 to 1950? For two reasons. One, Baker published in 1948 his Yale dissertation, dedicating it to "William Wright Barnes, my friend and teacher." Known as *Relations between Northern and Southern Baptists*, this book contained Baker's basic historiography regarding the founding of the SBC. He said very little on the subject in his 1974 SBC history which one cannot find in his 1948 *Relations*. Two, Baker's historiographical approach fits more closely with that of Barnes than with those church historians who wrote after 1950.

So what was Baker's approach? Very similar to Barnes, he interpreted slavery, without question, as the catalyst for the SBC.[40] For some reason, however, Baker's writings tended to diminish the role of slavery and race by calling attention to other factors, surely secondary in importance in the organization of the SBC. In a chapter on "Divisive Controversies" in the SBC, for example, Baker treated the three subjects of Campbellism, Antimissionism, and Sectionalism. One would think, given the magnitude of the subject for SBC history, that slavery would have merited a self-contained section of its own. However, Baker treated slavery under "Sectionalism," along with regional disagreements regarding home missions.[41]

Baker's preeminent theme in describing the beginning of the SBC in 1845 was not slavery but the ecclesiological structure Southern Baptists devised for the new convention. He appeared far more interested in interpreting the differences in the "societal" versus the "convention" approach to Baptist organization than pointing out slavery's power in the Baptist churches of the South. To be sure, he presented well the facts of the slavery debate. But his personal interpretations of the founding of the SBC centered far more on the ecclesiological differences which he thought existed between Northern and Southern Baptists.[42]

One further example of Baker's approach must suffice. Keenly aware of how Southerners in the mid-nineteenth century rationalized the founding of the SBC on the basis of constitutional, missional, and other factors,

---

[40]Baker, *Relations between Northern and Southern Baptists*, 81.

[41]Robert A. Baker, *The Southern Baptist Convention and Its People* (Nashville: Broadman Press, 1974) 153-59.

[42]See how this theme dominated in Baker, *The Southern Baptist Convention and Its People*, 161-77.

Baker recognized that underlying all of "these arguments for separation, of course, was the involvement of the South with the 'peculiar institution.' "[43] Almost in the next breath, however, Baker stated that "there were other strong considerations for a separate Southern body" other than slavery.[44] So, like Barnes, his professor, Baker was clear about the centrality of slavery in the formation of the SBC, but he tended to minimize its impact by pointing to less important issues.[45]

Slavery: The Primary Factor, 1950–2000

The last half of the twentieth century, and especially the last quarter of the century, has witnessed a significant change in interpreting Southern Baptist beginnings among white Baptist church historians in the South. Walter B. Shurden, Leon H. McBeth, Jesse C. Fletcher, and E. Luther Copeland, among others, have written in this vein.

Walter B. Shurden . . . 1972. In 1972 Broadman Press published *Not a Silent People: Controversies That Have Shaped Southern Baptists* by Walter B. Shurden.[46] One chapter entitled "The 'What about the Blacks?' Controversy or Baptists Argue over Slavery and Segregation" began by asking what caused the controversial fire of 1845. Shurden, following generally an interpretation of his professor Claude L. Howe, Jr., answered by saying that differences in theology, ecclesiology (denominational structure), or home missions did not cause the schism of 1845.[47] Obviously Shurden was addressing the interpretations of twentieth-century popular culture and Southern Baptist church historians rather than evaluating the judgments of nineteenth-century Baptists, though he gave slight attention to the latter.

---

[43]Baker, *The Southern Baptist Convention and Its People*, 171.

[44]Baker, *The Southern Baptist Convention and Its People*, 172.

[45]What we would call the Barnes/Baker interpretation of SBC origins was circulated widely by study course books in the 1950s and 1960s. See Hugh Wamble, *Through Trial to Triumph* (Nashville: Convention Press, 1958) 55-67; Pope A. Duncan, *Our Baptist Story* (Nashville: Convention Press, 1958) 40-47; Norman W. Cox, *We Southern Baptists* (Nashville: Convention Press, 1961) 28-31.

[46]Smyth & Helwys published an updated and slightly revised edition in 1995. See Walter B. Shurden, *Not a Silent People: Controversies That Have Shaped Southern Baptists* (Macon GA: Smyth & Helwys Publishing Inc., 1995).

[47]To see this verified on a state level see Gardner, *A Decade of Debate and Division*, 4, 5.

In asking, "What was the issue, the major issue and the immediate issue, in the organization of the Southern Baptist Convention?" Shurden answered:

> It was slavery, the same issue that tore the innarrds out of the nation a few years later. A cultural earthquake struck this young nation during the years 1830–1865; but before the quake created a political chasm between North and South, it had sliced the churches down their Mason-Dixon Line. The Southern Baptist Convention was organized in defense of the mid-nineteenth-century Southern culture.[48]

The date and context of Shurden's book should not be overlooked. 1972 was a comfortable distance from 1845 or even the racial turbulence of the late 1950s and 1960s. On the other hand, race was still very much a live issue for Southern Baptists in the 1970s. In the face of that fact, however, the denominational publishing house was open enough to risk an interpretation of the origins of the denomination that did not minimize the role of race.

H. Leon McBeth . . . 1987. A student of Robert A. Baker at Southwestern Seminary and now Distinguished Professor of Church History at Southwestern, Leon McBeth, by virtue of his mammoth and influential *The Baptist Heritage*, has become the leading interpreter of Baptist history in the last quarter of this century. While *The Baptist Heritage* is a comprehensive survey of Baptist history in general, it contains an excellent section on the formation of the Southern Baptist Convention.

McBeth's interpretation of SBC beginnings reflected slightly some of the emphases of the Barnes/Baker tradition, especially the role of ecclesiology and home missions. However, McBeth isolated and elevated slavery as the causative factor in a way uncharacteristic of either Barnes or Baker. Describing the formation of the SBC, McBeth said, "At least three factors led to that fateful schism: disagreements on methods of organization, problems in home mission work, and the slavery controversy."[49] But then the Southwestern historian hurriedly added, "While each of these played an important role, they were not of equal weight; slavery was the final and

---

[48]Gardner, *A Decade of Debate and Division*, 31.
[49]H. Leon McBeth, *The Baptist Heritage* (Nashville: Broadman Press, 1987) 381.

most decisive factor which led Southern Baptists to form their own convention."[50]

As if he thought it necessary to underscore slavery's centrality, McBeth wrote: "Slavery was the main issue that led to the 1845 schism; that is a blunt historical fact. Other issues raised barriers and, in time, might have led to division, if not North-South, possibly East-West. However, slavery *did* lead to division."[51] Moreover, it was clear that McBeth did not swallow the explanations of nineteenth-century Southerners as to why they founded the SBC. In part of his analysis of the 1845 "Address to the Public," McBeth said:

> Third, the purpose of the new body, the public address continued, was not the defense of slavery or "the upholding of any form of human policy," but simply "the extension of Messiah's kingdom." That statement reflects Southern sensitivity to the fact that some would view them as a "slave convention."[52]

One can understandably speak of the Barnes/Baker/McBeth tradition of church history at Southwestern Baptist Seminary. Together their three careers have virtually spanned the twentieth century at that one institution. But McBeth's historiography of the SBC, while building on the tradition of his teachers, also clarified that tradition. Near the end of the nineteenth century, W. H. Whitsitt, an excellent Southern Baptist church historian, could not bring himself to tell Southern Baptists the truth about their origins. One hundred years later, near the end of the twentieth century, Leon McBeth, did not shrink from telling them that truth.

Jesse C. Fletcher . . . 1995. Another student of Robert A. Baker, Jesse C. Fletcher, wrote a 463-page sesquicentennial history of the SBC in 1994. Published by Broadman & Holman, this was the third and best major history of the SBC. It was the best written, best organized, and best interpreted. Fletcher, chancellor of Hardin-Simmons University at the time of the writing, related creatively the SBC history to the history of national and world events, such as the depression, world wars, and the civil rights struggle. Mirroring the storytelling and artistry Fletcher demonstrated in *Bill Wallace of China*, his history sparkles with people stories. One of the

---

[50]McBeth, *The Baptist Heritage*, 381.
[51]McBeth, *The Baptist Heritage*, 382.
[52]McBeth, *The Baptist Heritage*, 390.

bright parts of the book is the way he corrected the "maleness" of Baptist history.[53]

Upon first reading Fletcher's artistic treatment of the founding of the SBC, however, one may conclude that Fletcher's history belongs more to the Barnes/Baker than the McBeth approach. At points he, too, appeared to lessen the slavery issue by pointing to other issues. For example, he said that the meeting in Augusta in 1845 was "because of discriminating procedures imposed by northern abolitionists."[54] While certainly true, that statement tends to cloud the real reason why those Baptists met in Augusta. Also, when Fletcher identified the three "intertwining historical roots" of the SBC, he placed slavery after denominational identity and missions. He summarized the reasons for the 1845 Augusta meeting this way: "Thus, though the story's crucial event took place in Augusta, Georgia, in 1845, that event constituted the interaction of a growing Baptist confessional and connectional consciousness, a passionate missionary conviction, and a visceral sectional spirit"[55]. Placing these three factors together as the precipitating causes of the organization of the Southern Baptist Convention skewed rather than clarified the crucial role of slavery.

A more careful reading of Fletcher presents another picture, however, one that places slavery at the very center of Southern Baptist beginnings. Early in his history Fletcher isolated slavery as a shaping factor in the SBC. He said:

> Baptists located in the Southern states developed a strong sensitivity for their region with its predominantly agrarian economy and, unfortunately, the institution of slavery. Though a product of New England commercialism, this cruel tradition found fertile ground in the South's agricultural base and soon became the undergirding reality of Southern culture. As Baptists grew in the South they became increasingly identified with their culture.[56]

Describing the 293 delegates who gathered in Augusta in May 1845, Fletcher said they were motivated by "deeply held religious convictions but they also were subject to a sectional and social bias that soon engulfed the

---

[53]Jesse C. Fletcher, *The Southern Baptist Convention: A Sesquicentennial History* (Nashville: Broadman & Holman, 1994) 16, 23, 31, 35, 85-87, 163, 173, 181, 225.

[54]Fletcher, *The Southern Baptist Convention*, 10.

[55]Fletcher, *The Southern Baptist Convention*, 13.

[56]Fletcher, *The Southern Baptist Convention*, 2.

region they represented in the bloodiest of all civil wars."[57] When Fletcher analyzed the original 293 delegates to the first SBC, he pointed both to the issues of race and gender as identifying factors in the formation and, by implication, legacy of the SBC. Writing historically but also prophetically of the Augusta gathering, Fletcher said:

> Who was there as well as who was not there reflected the cultural identification peculiar to Southern Baptist life. That cultural union would mark the Baptist Convention for decades to come. It was to be all but inseparable from a white male-dominated culture dependent upon agriculture, especially cotton. It was a culture marked at that time by slavery and for years following by its demeaning aftermath.[58]

While at times misting up the picture, Fletcher nonetheless objectively described the founding of the Southern Baptist Convention as accurately as any historian up to his time. Published by the denominational press, his book presented quite a contrast to the nineteenth-century interpreters of Southern Baptist beginnings.

E. Luther Copeland . . . 1995. In a stellar contribution to Southern Baptist historiography, E. Luther Copeland, former Southern Baptist missionary to Japan and former professor of Missions and World Religions at Southeastern Baptist Theological Seminary, wrote with prophetic courage and historical accuracy in *The Southern Baptist Convention and the Judgment of History: The Taint of Original Sin.* Published by University Press of America in 1995 and revised in 2002, Copeland's book must be reckoned, without question, as one of the most valuable interpretations of Southern Baptist history ever written.

Some white Baptist historians of the South ignored and others clouded the role of race in Southern Baptist history. Copeland, on the other hand, exposed the captivity of Southern Baptists to their culture. In the first paragraph of the first chapter of his scorching ethical history, Copeland rooted Southern Baptist history in slavery and chided Southern Baptist historians for diminishing its role. Copeland wrote:

> The SBC had its origin on the wrong side of the slavery question. It is true that there were other issues which have somewhat confused the matter, issues of regionalism, denominational organization, and the following of established procedures in spite of conscientious scruples. Southern Baptist

---

[57]Fletcher, *The Southern Baptist Convention,* 10.
[58]Fletcher, *The Southern Baptist Convention,* 11.

mythology has relegated the defense of slavery to the position of a secondary factor in producing the SBC in 1845, though outsiders are baffled by this "myth" and see it as an evasion of the truth. Even Southern Baptist historians have tended to set slavery in the context of other issues which had the potential to cause schism but did not. Thus they diminish the importance of the slavery issue.[59]

"It is a strange irony," bemoaned Copeland, "that a denomination which was born because of its support of slavery nevertheless seems to have thought of itself as 'God's last and only hope' for world evangelization."[60]

Copeland viewed the climate of intolerance as reflected in the Southern Baptist defense of slavery as the hermeneutical principle for understanding the entire history of the SBC. The SBC defense of slavery, he argued, "infected the major aspects of Southern Baptist life."[61] The SBC not only defended slavery in its beginning history, it has in its subsequent history, argued Copeland, sanctioned secession, affirmed white supremacy, practiced missionary imperialism, denigrated American Baptists and other Christians, demeaned women, and enforced a rigid theological orthodoxy, all because it had imbibed the intolerance of Southern culture, an intolerance born of the defense of the slavery system.[62]

It goes without saying that no SBC denominational press placed its imprimatur on Copeland's book. And neither SBC fundamentalists, moderates, nor liberals can find a hiding place from Copeland's indicting interpretation of SBC history. Whereas some church historians identified with the 1979 fundamentalist takeover viewed the so-called "conservative resurgence" as evidence of the providential movement of God, Copeland suggested a very different interpretation as he asked, "Is the present predicament of the SBC the judgment of God upon us for our sins?"[63] For those SBC moderates who believe that the SBC world went haywire only in 1979, Copeland uttered unflattering words in his conclusion:

---

[59]E. Luther Copeland, *The Southern Baptist Convention and the Judgment of History: The Taint of Original Sin*, rev. ed. (Lanham MD: University Press of America, 2002) 7.

[60]Copeland, *The Southern Baptist Convention and the Judgment of History*, 3.

[61]Copeland, *The Southern Baptist Convention and the Judgment of History*, xiii.

[62]Copeland, *The Southern Baptist Convention and the Judgment of History*, 129.

[63]Copeland, *The Southern Baptist Convention and the Judgment of History*, 2, 130.

This book has sought to delineate the influence of what I believe to be an original sin of the SBC, namely, the defense of the slavery system, upon the major aberrations of the SBC's life. Most of what I think is wrong with the denomination happened long before rightists captured the SBC. It occurred under moderate or relatively moderate leadership. The present predicament of the denomination is deeply rooted in its past and may be traced all the way back to our beginnings on the wrong side of the slavery issue. I am suggesting that the problems of the SBC did not begin in 1979 but in 1845.[64]

Summary

Baptist historiography is the telling of the Baptist story. And Baptist historiography, as Jesse Fletcher said, is both shaped by factors at the time of the telling, while also shaping the future of the Baptist identity.[65] Three factors in particular have shaped the telling of the story of how the SBC came into being. One, when the story was told. While not always the case in writing history, proximity, in this instance, obscured rather than clarified. The closer white Baptist church historians were to the 1845 event, the more silent they became about the issue of slavery as the causative issue or the more they confused the origins by pointing to factors other than slavery. Conversely, the further from 1845, the more historians zeroed in on slavery as the major cause. W. W. Adams, a creative and insightful New Testament professor, once facetiously said that he became a prophet when he started drawing his Social Security check. Likewise, white Baptist historians became prophets the further they were removed from the explosive emotional issue of slavery.

Two, where the story was told also impacted the telling of the story. Content related to context. To tell the story before an audience of the annual Southern Baptist Convention as did William H. Whitsitt in 1895 resulted in a very different story from the one told by E. Luther Copeland and published by the University Press of America in 1995. Three, how the story was told, of course, was very important. The writing of history is both science and art. But it is also a moral exercise. Courage and ruthless honesty are indispensable ingredients in historiography of any kind.

---

[64]Copeland, *The Southern Baptist Convention and the Judgment of History*, 129.

[65]Fletcher, *The Southern Baptist Convention*, 6.

The Pastor as Denominational Theologian in Southern Baptist History[1]

In a little book entitled *Baptists: The Passionate People* published in 1973, C. Burtt Potter, Jr., asked "fifty contemporary knowledgeable Baptists" the following question: "Who were the ten men with the greatest impact on Southern Baptists?"[2] Admittedly, the question is chauvinistic, and the answers are circumscribed by both the persons chosen to respond and the criteria used for determining "the greatest impact." All of that to one side, however, the responses were interesting.

The order of the men judged to have the greatest impact was as follows: (1) George W. Truett; (2) E. Y. Mullins; (3) John A. Broadus; (4) W. O. Carver; (5) A. T. Robertson; (6) Theron Rankin; (7) Isaac T. Tichenor and J. M. Frost [numbers 7 and 8 were tied]; (9) John A. Sampey; and (10) J. B. Gambrell, W. B. Johnson, James P. Boyce, and B. H. Carroll.

One of the most interesting features of this list is the absence of men who achieved acclaim in Southern Baptist life exclusively as pastors of Baptist churches. In fact, of the thirteen persons mentioned, only one is remembered exclusively as a pastor. And that was the first one, George W. Truett, whom Albert McClellan has correctly described as "one of the spiritual architects of the denomination."[3] Several of those listed served as pastor, but they are remembered primarily in conjunction with other activities. This would be true of J. M. Frost, founder of the Sunday School Board, W. B. Johnson, founder of the Southern Baptist Convention, and B. H. Carroll, founder of Southwestern Seminary, and others.

Doubtless, a much different list would emerge if the question was, "What ten people have most shaped the theology of Southern Baptists?" More pastors would probably appear on the list and should be on it.

---

[1]I presented this address at the annual meeting of the Historical Commission, SBC, and the Southern Baptist Historical Society in Louisville KY in April 1980. The Historical Society published the address in *Baptist History and Heritage* 15/3 (July 1980): 15-22. It is reprinted by permission of the Baptist History and Heritage Society, Brentwood TN.

[2]C. Burtt Potter, Jr., *Baptists: The Passionate People* (Nashville: Broadman Press, 1973) 121.

[3]Albert McClellan, *Meet Southern Baptists* (Nashville: Broadman Press, 1978) 38.

The purpose of this paper is to discuss the role of the pastor in Southern Baptist history as a denominational theologian. My thesis is that the rise and fall of the pastor as denominational theologian in Southern Baptist life is inextricably related to the rise and fall of the Southern Baptist theological professor as denominational theologian. The pastor, as denominational theologian, has undergone a historical evolution in Southern Baptist history.

Phase one of this evolution is the period prior to 1859 and the formation of any Southern Baptist theological institution. In this era, pastors were the primary denominational theologians. Phase two of the evolution begins with the founding of the Southern Baptist Theological Seminary in 1859 and the burgeoning role of theological professors in Southern Baptist history. This second period, which ended around 1960, witnessed the recession of the pastor as denominational theologian. Phase three of the evolution, from 1960 to the present, has seen the resurgence of the pastor as denominational theologian and the corresponding decline of the professor as theological interpreter.

The Dominance of the Pastor as Denominational Theologian, 1700–1859

Early Baptists in America, like their English counterparts, had no theologians in the sense that the word is used today. For more often than not, the word "theologian" is unfortunately restricted to professors in theological institutions. Southern Baptists did not organize their first theological institution until 1859, so there were no prominent teaching-theologians among Southern Baptists prior to that date. Because of the absence of teaching theologians, however, one should not conclude that Baptists were without theologians.

John Gill (1697–1771) and Andrew Fuller (1754–1815), prominent English Baptists, were both pastors, but they are rightfully remembered as Baptist theologians. Prior to 1859, Baptists of the South were so busy reading Gill and Fuller that they failed to produce anyone to compare with them. Again, however, lack of *prominent* theologians does not mean the total absence of theologians, a point which should be kept in focus about Baptists of the past and present. In the South the pastors, whether educated or illiterate, urbane or rustic, redneck or city slicker, were the only theologians the denomination possessed. They were the ones interpreting the Christian faith *to* the denomination, defending the faith *for* the denomination, and arguing for the specific faith *of* the denomination. In that sense, pastors were the denominational theologians.

With some error, the Baptist ministry in the Old South has been over-whelmingly stereotyped as the Baptist farmer-preacher. This image of the Baptist pastor, popularized by W. W. Sweet in his study of frontier Baptist life, is certainly present in Baptist history.[4] Indeed, in terms of sheer numbers, this was doubtless the prevailing pattern.

Originating primarily out of the Separate Baptist tradition in the South, the Baptist farmer-preacher embodied the religious sentiments of the common folk. Distinguished more by ardor than order, this type of Baptist pastor was often not only uneducated but unlearned. Moreover, some considerable pride was vested in his lack of educational status by both the preacher and his hearers. The Baptist farmer-preacher, as the name would suggest, was rural in orientation.[5]

Preachers such as Shubal Stearns, Daniel Marshall, and John Taylor were representative of this Baptist pastor.[6] Primarily by their popular and effective preaching, they helped shape Baptist life in the South. The theo-logical reductionism inherent in their revivalistic preaching both indi-vidualized and emotionalized the Southern Baptist understanding of faith. Their commitment to voluntarism in religious matters was a crucial factor in the fall of the religious establishments in the South. Separate Baptist preachers would probably never have perceived themselves as denomi-national theologians. But by action and word, through preaching and protest, they were in fact the Baptist folk theologians of their time.

They were not, however, the only Baptist model of the pastor-theo-logian. E. Brooks Holifield has made an unusually significant contribution to the understanding of American theology in Southern culture. A major part of his thesis is that two conflicting images of the Southern clergy existed during the antebellum period. One, represented in Baptist life by the farmer-preacher, was the folk preacher. The other was what Holifield dubbed "the gentleman preacher" or, as his book title has it, "the gentleman

---

[4]See William Warren Sweet, *Religion on the American Frontier. The Baptists: 1783–1830* (New York: Cooper Square Publishers, 1964) 36ff.

[5]The best discussions of the Separate Baptist ministry is in William L. Lumpkin, *Baptist Foundations in the South* (Nashville: Broadman Press, 1961) and James Owen Renault, "The Development of Separate Baptist Ecclesiology in the South" (Ph.D. diss., Southern Baptist Theological Seminary, Louisville, 1978).

[6]For sketches of these and other early Baptist preachers, see James B. Taylor, *Lives of Virginia Baptist Ministers* (Richmond: Zale and Wyatt, 1838).

theologians."[7] Characterized by learning, sometimes erudition, the gentleman preacher was urbane, gentile, often a man of means, and thoroughly professional. Sociologically, this model of Baptist ministry evolved in conjunction with the rise of the Southern city, and primarily out of the Regular Baptist tradition. Said Holifield, "One function of religion in the Southern towns was to reassure men and women that they were reasonable people living in a reasonable world; the elite clergy were charged with the duty of both symbolizing and conceptualizing that vision."[8] Holifield also demonstrates that these clergymen were not merely regional or Southern theologians; they were also denominational theologians.

Twenty-three of the one hundred "gentlemen theologians" examined by Holifield were Baptists. Among them were John Armstrong (1798–1844), the little-known graduate of Columbian College who spent two years studying in France and Germany before assuming the pastorate of the First Baptist Church of Columbus, Mississippi. Others who are better known and whose influence fits into the time frame prior to 1859 were W. T. Brantley, Sr. (1787–1845), A. W. Clopton (1784–1833), Richard Furman (1755–1825), Henry Holcombe (1762–1824), R. B. C. Howell (1801–1868), John Kerr (1782–1842), Basil Manly, Sr. (1798–1868), Jonathan Maxcy (1768–1820), and R. B. Semple (1769–1831). One rural Baptist pastor, and maybe for that reason unlisted by Holifield, who surely deserves a central place on any list of gentlemen preachers was Andrew Broaddus (1770–1848).[9]

The Baptist pastor, whether of the farmer-preacher or gentleman-preacher variety, functioned as denominational theologian in several ways. Primary among these was preaching. The role of preaching as a theologically formative factor among Southern Baptists has probably never been adequately appraised. Southern Baptists have always been more subject to charisma than to catechisms, more pulpit-performance oriented than classroom-content oriented. We prefer to hear the Word than to read or study the Word. Probably one of the reasons preaching has not been considered as a shaping factor on the Southern Baptist mind is the difficulty in

---

[7]E. Brooks Holifield, *The Gentlemen Theologians: American Theology in Southern Culture, 1795–1860* (Durham NC: Duke University Press, 1978). See esp. chaps. 1 and 2.

[8]Holifield, *The Gentlemen Theologians*, 28.

[9]Holifield discusses Broaddus at certain points in the book, but he does not list him among the Baptist elite. For the list, see Holifield, *The Gentlemen Theologians*, 218.

verifying it. The influence of written materials, unlike oral presentation, can be documented. One would overlook the importance of Stearns and Separate Baptist preaching if written documents were the only measure of significance, however. They wrote little. That fact does not minimize their role as denominational theologians who helped form the belief system of Southern Baptists.

A second way these early pastors mediated their theology was through hymnody, especially hymnbooks. John Boles, among many, has noted the close relationship between Baptist revivalism and singing. Writing about the Second Great Awakening and the origins of the Southern evangelical mind, Boles said, "The hymns contained in the contemporary Methodist, Baptist, and Presbyterian pocket-hymnals were arranged almost in the form of correspondence courses in theology."[10] A succession of hymnbooks published by prominent Southern Baptist clergymen were extensively used in Baptist worship. Among them were Jesse Mercer's *The Cluster of Spiritual Songs* (1817), Andrew Broaddus's *Dover Selection* (1828), compiled at the request of the Dover Association in Virginia, Richard Fuller's and J. B. Jeter's Southern supplement to *The Psalmist* (1847), and the Manlys' *Baptist Psalmody* (1850).[11] For many ordinary Baptists these hymnbooks were the only theology books they ever held. No way exists to calculate the impact of these books on Southern Baptist theology. Baptist pastors capitalized on the media of song and poetry.

Baptist pastors also theologized on behalf of and in defense of their denomination and the Christian faith by their apologetic writings. Theological controversies generated immense doctrinal formulations by Baptist pastors. For example, Thomas Paine's *Age of Reason* published in two parts in 1794 and 1795 was a deistic attack on biblical revelation. "No single literary event disturbed the orthodox more . . . ,"[12] said Holifield. One of the first Southerners to pen a finely wrought response to Paine was a young rural Virginia Baptist preacher named Andrew Broaddus. Broaddus went after Alexander Campbell with the same gentle and rational spirit with which he refuted Paine, Though much of his writing was polemical, Broaddus was, according to his biographer, "candid, fair and

---

[10]John B. Boles, *The Great Revival, 1787–1805: The Origins of the Southern Evangelical Mind* (Lexington: University Press of Kentucky, 1972) 122.

[11]See Walter Hines Sims, "Hymnals, Baptist," *Encyclopedia of Southern Baptists* (1958) 1:662-64.

[12]Holifield, *The Gentlemen Theologians*, 52.

honorable."[13] "Melancthon himself did not excel him in kindness, courtesy, and dignity,"[14] said Jeter of Broaddus.

If Broaddus was the Baptist pastor-theologian who took on the theological heavyweights, R. B. C. Howell, exalted pastor of First Baptist Church, Nashville, Tennessee, was one of the most popular theologians of Baptist distinctives. While repudiating Landmarkism on the one hand, Howell also defined Baptist thought over against pedobaptists. His *Terms of Communion at the Lord's Table* (1846), *The Evils of Infant Baptism* (1851), and other writings made him the Herschel Hobbs of the mid-nineteenth century.[15]

Preaching, hymnody, and apologetics were only three means by which Southern Baptist pastors reflected and shaped Southern Baptist thought, Other avenues, too numerous to mention, were also utilized. In them all Baptist pastors functioned as theologians of the church body to which they belonged.

The Decline of the Pastor as Denominational Theologian, 1859–1960

If the question were asked, "What five persons fulfilled the role of denominational theologian from 1859 to 1959 in Southern Baptist life?" how would you answer? Surely J. R. Graves, the Tennessee editor, would make the list. His colleague, J. M. Pendleton, would probably be mentioned, as would J. L. Dagg, the Mercer president and professor. Sooner or later, however, the names of John A. Broaddus, James P. Boyce, B. H. Carroll, E. Y. Mullins, A. T. Robertson, W. O. Carver, and W. T. Conner would surface. With this last series of names, a clear trend emerges. They were all seminary professors.

As the new trend emerges, an old tradition fades. Pastoral theologians were replaced in much of denominational leadership by the teaching theologians. Neither the dates nor the argument proposed can be pressed absolutely. After all, George W. Truett lived during this era. So did George

---

[13]J. B. Jeter, *The Sermons and Other Writings of the Rev. Andrew Broaddus with a Memoir of His Life* (New York: Lewis Colby, 1852) 26.

[14]Jeter, *The Sermons and Other Writings of the Rev. Andrew Broaddus*, 26.

[15]For Howell, see Linwood Tyler Horne, "A Study of the Life and Work of R. B. C. Howell" (Th.D. diss., Southern Baptist Theological Seminary, Louisville, 1958) and Joe W. Burton, *Road to Augusta* (Nashville: Broadman Press, 1976).

McDaniel, M. E. Dodd, J. Clyde Turner, and R. G. Lee, all of whom surely functioned as popular theologians of the denomination.

If, however, one were forced to choose *one* person who embodied Southern Baptist theology during the century 1859–1959, would it not be E. Y. Mullins? He was in many respects *the* Southern Baptist theologian of that period. Mullins personified a Southern Baptist pride, a pride in denominational theological education.

Accompanying this pride was the denominational recognition of theological professors. If the farmer-preacher and the gentlemen theologians were the prevailing images of the Baptist ministry in the previous era, the teaching theologian is a predominant model in the period 1859–1960. How and why did this model of ministry develop? How did the teachers replace the pastors as denominational theologians?

For one thing, some of the most impressive Southern Baptist pulpiteers were men who taught. John A. Broadus was the only Southern Baptist of this period to deliver the prestigious Beecher Lectures on Preaching at Yale University. He was nationally acclaimed as one of the great preachers of his age. He was "Mr. Southern Baptist" of the last quarter of the nineteenth century.

In his brief jubilee history of the Southern Baptist Convention in 1895, W. H. Whitsitt extolled his old friend and colleague. "For thirty years," said Whitsitt of Broadus, "he was the leading force in our counsels and history." Whitsitt concluded his history to the Southern Baptist Convention audience in Washington, D.C., with pathos and praise: "The foremost leader of our history, great in the might of his gentleness, has passed away from us, but his fame and usefulness shall go and grow throughout the years and ages. When you who sit here shall be aged and feeble men and women, little children will gather about your knees with reverence and delight, to look upon one who has seen and heard and spoken with John A. Broadus."[16]

Discounting the grief of Whitsitt which carried him to the precipice of hagiography, he nonetheless spoke a truth. Broadus, the only person for whom the Southern Baptist Convention has ever had a memorial service, embodied and interpreted Southern Baptists to themselves and their world. Much of his popularity and power came from his preaching. But he was not alone as a great preacher among the teaching theologians. B. H. Carroll and E. Y. Mullins were both known as outstanding preachers. Their preaching prowess gave them credibility in Southern Baptist life.

---

[16]*SBC Annual 1895*, 90.

The stars of the teaching theologians rose in Southern Baptist life, also, because of their denominational statesmanship. Where, for example, did Broadman Press get its name and why? From John A. Broadus and Basil Manly, Jr., because of their initiative in founding the first Sunday School Board. Who was a prime mover in the formation of the Baptist World Alliance? A Greek scholar by the name of A. T. Robertson. Who drafted Southern Baptists' first confession of faith and steered them through the evolution crisis? E. Y. Mullins, a Southern Baptist seminary president. Who spearheaded the Seventy-five Million Campaign which resulted in the Cooperative Program? L. R. Scarborough, the Yale Phi Beta Kappa who was president of Southwestern Seminary. Where was the first office of the Christian Life Commission? It was no office at all but a desk in the corner of the faculty office of J. B. Weatherspoon at Southern Seminary. And who was the founding father of the Historical Commission of the Southern Baptist Convention? W. O. Carver, the same as in Dargan-Carver Library and the W. O. Carver School of Missions and Social Work.

These teaching theologians were not ivory-towerists, disengaged from the institutional machinations of denominational life. They saturated denominational life with their ideas by incarnating those ideas into denominational structures; hence their prominence as denominational theologians. In the period from 1872 to 1942, a seminary president or a previously seminary-related professor served as president of the Southern Baptist Convention for twenty-four of those seventy years. No seminary- or ex-seminary-related person has served in that capacity since 1942.

Certainly another factor which catapulted the teaching theologians into the spotlight as *the* denominational theologians was their writing. But it was a specific kind of writing, more popular than scholarly, more denominationally directed than world-scholarship directed, and more homiletical and inspirational in tone than argumentative and rational. This was certainly true of B. H. Carroll. And while E. Y. Mullins wrote several scholarly works, he will probably be remembered longer for his second book, *The Axioms of Religion* (1908), a work in which he sought a new interpretation of the Baptist faith,[17] Mullins's third book, published in 1912, was his ninety-six page *Baptist Beliefs*. still quite popular as an exposition of Baptist theology. These two books, in addition to the 1925 Statement of

---

[17]For interesting background information on how this book developed, see Isla May Mullins, *Edgar Young Mullins: An Intimate Biography* (Nashville: Sunday School Board of the SBC, 1929) 138-39.

the Baptist Faith and Message, were largely responsible for Mullins's image among Southern Baptists as "their" theologian.

No Southern Baptist pastor of Mullins's day could compete with the beloved seminary president for the title of "denominational theologian." As previously mentioned, Mullins earned that unofficial title partially by virtue of his love and gift for preaching. The annual E. Y. Mullins Lectures on Preaching at Southern Seminary have stood over the years as a tribute to his commitment to the preaching task of the minister.

Moreover, Mullins personified the best of denominational statesman-ship, and this thrust him forth as the major interpreter of the direction the denomination should take. Denominational politics was something he loved and the art of compromise something in which he excelled. One does not have to read much of Southern Baptist history of the twentieth century to know why Southern Seminary instituted the E. Y. Mullins Denominational Service Award.

His preaching and denominational service were reinforced by his popu-lar writings. They would serve for a quarter of a century or more after his death as the preeminent Southern Baptist interpretation. Louie D. Newton, famous Georgia pastor for almost three decades after Mullins's death, and one often dubbed "Mr. Baptist" himself, found his hero and theological mentor in E. Y. Mullins. Said Newton of Mullins in 1934, "The more I study the man and his message, the greater he looms in my thought. I have read and reread his books, finding in them the clearest statements of the Christian interpretation of life."[18] Newton has indicated that *The Axioms of Religion* has remained his favorite book since Mullins presented him with an autographed copy in 1909.

Mullins's vocational context must be remembered. He was the presi-dent and professor of theology at a Baptist seminary. For most Southern Baptists, it was Mullins's seminary context which gave credibility to what he said and did and wrote. In other words, the seminary, not the pastorate, legitimized him as *the* denominational theologian.

---

[18]As cited in Robin Winston Smith, "Louie D. Newton: A Baptist Statesman of the Twentieth Century" (Ph.D. diss., Southern Baptist Theological Seminary, Louisville, 1979) 32.

The Reemergence of the Pastor
as Denominational Theologian, 1960–Present

The Axioms of Religion served as a kind of popularized Southern Baptist *Summa Theologica*. Seventy years after the publication of the book, Broadman Press released a revised edition in 1978. When Broadman sought a revision and updating of this statement of the Baptist faith, they turned to a popular ex-pastor rather than a seminary professor. That decision is highly symbolic and not altogether coincidental. Herschel H. Hobbs, pastor emeritus of the First Baptist Church, Oklahoma City, and for twenty years the preacher of the Baptist Hour Radio Program, and a former president of the Southern Baptist Convention, edited the new edition.

Herschel H. Hobbs served Southern Baptists as "the E. Y. Mullins" of the 1960s and 1970s. Similarities between the two men are striking. First, though he never studied directly under Mullins, Hobbs was supremely influenced by him. In a 1976 interview with the editor of *The Theological Educator*, Hobbs said, "Over the years there have been two books I've lived with. They are the Bible and E. Y. Mullins's *The Christian Religion in Its Doctrinal Expression*. I memorized Mullins's book while I was in seminary."[19] In the same interview Hobbs extolled "the competency of the soul in religion" as the basic Baptist distinctive. He was also quick to point out that this idea constituted the major thesis of Mullins's *The Axioms of Religion*.[20]

A second similarity between the two men is that both served as denominational statesmen, steering the denominational ship through turbulent waters. Mullins was president of the Convention during the Evolution Controversy, while Hobbs led the Convention in the Elliott Controversy. Thirdly, and closely related to the second, each man was the principal writer of a major Southern Baptist confession of faith. Mullins's hand was behind the 1925 "Statement of the Baptist Faith and Message." Hobbs guided the committee which drafted the 1963 revised version of that

---

[19]"Southern Baptist Theology Today: An Interview with Herschel H. Hobbs," *The Theological Educator* 6/22 (Spring 1976): 22.

[20]"An Interview with Herschel H. Hobbs," 21.

Confession.[21] Fourthly, both were popular pulpit personalities. And finally, both Hobbs and Mullins directed their writings to Baptist audiences.

Hobbs, the pastor, replaced Mullins, the professor, as Southern Baptists' major spokesman and denominational theologian. This shift is symptomatic of a larger trend in Southern Baptist life which witnesses the reemergence of pastors and the decline of professors as denominational theologians. Surely, the argument, as the dates, cannot be pressed in an absolutist fashion. But the trend is present, and it cuts across theological lines. If Herschel H. Hobbs has represented "the middle of the road" in Southern Baptist life, has W. A. Criswell not been on the right side of the road? And has John Claypool not been to the left of Hobbs, and Carlyle Marney to the left of Claypool? All were or are pastors. Each has had profound influence on various segments of the denominational life. Claypool, for example, may have had more influence on seminarians in Louisville in the 1960s than any theological professor at Southern Seminary. Why the shift? Here are only four suggestions; others could be listed.

One, theological controversies for the last two decades have rocked the denominational ship. These controversies usually have been focused on theological seminaries. The result is that theological education in general, and seminary personnel specifically, have been placed under suspicion.

Two, pastors of large churches, as exemplified in the presidency of the Convention, have become dominant leaders in Southern Baptist denominational life. Seminary personnel, as well as other denominational workers, are not as visible in the denominational process as they once were. Clyde Fant, Jr., former seminary professor, now pastor of the First Baptist Church of Richardson, Texas, made this point in a recent article in *The Baptist Program*. Fant said, "And while denominational workers are not entirely shut out of participating in the denominational process in general, they largely are."[22] He added, "This is a mistake that needs immediate remedy. We need more seminary professors and other denominational workers

---

[21]For a more extensive analysis of the part these two men played in these confessions, see Walter B. Shurden, "Southern Baptist Responses to Their Confessional Statements," in this volume and also in *Review and Expositor* 76/1 (Winter 1979): 69-84.

[22]Clyde Fant, Jr., "I Returned to the Pastorate," *The Baptist Program* (January 1980): 8.

involved with the larger life of the convention."[23] He referred specifically to state denominational and Southern Baptist Convention committees.

Three, the reemergence of the pastor as theological interpreter of denominational life is also related to the role of the media in Baptist life. For example, the Baptist Hour Radio Program has featured prominent Baptist pastors, specifically Herschel Hobbs. Also, the telecast of Sunday morning worship services has tended to project the influence of pastors of prominent churches over a much wider geographical area. Moreover, Broadman Press, the book publishing arm of the Convention, has often called on the pastors for an inspirational and homiletical approach to theology.

Four, and closely related to the point just made, pastors have popularized while seminary personnel have grown increasingly specialized. Though the point is debatable, seminary professors may not have published as much for the average Southern Baptist in recent years as did Mullins and his colleagues of a former day. Related to the popularization-specialization issue is the centrality of preaching in Southern Baptist life. In the third volume of the *Encyclopedia of Southern Baptists*, H. C. Brown, Jr., wrote an article on Baptist sermons. He placed representative Southern Baptist preachers for the years 1958–1970 into five categories: (1) Baptist Statesmen, (2) Pastor-Preachers, (3) Educators and Denominational Leaders, (4) Evangelists, and (5) Civil Rights Leaders.

Concerning category three, educators and denominational leaders, Brown said, "Professors, administrators, and other denominational leaders generally have allowed their pulpit skills to atrophy while attending to other responsibilities, but a number of them are strong preachers."[24] Brown's analysis contains both an accusation and a commendation, but it is the accusation which is germane to this discussion. Preaching has been a major channel for theologizing in Southern Baptist life. If indeed pulpit skills have atrophied among professors and denominational workers, one can find here an explanation for the rise of the pastor as denominational theologian.

Conclusion

The people whom Southern Baptists unofficially select to be their denominational theologians reflect what they value in ministry. At different periods in Southern Baptist history and in different social contexts,

---

[23]Fant, Jr., "I Returned to the Pastorate," 8.

[24]H. C. Brown, Jr. "Sermons, Baptist," *Encyclopedia of Southern Baptists* (1971) 3:1952-55.

Southern Baptists have valued different kinds of ministry. Prior to 1859 the farmer-preacher served as theologian to the rural areas while the gentlemen preachers served as theologians in the growing towns. From 1859 to 1960, during which period Southern Baptists formed six theological seminaries, a developing pride in ministerial education helped Baptists to select the teaching theologian as the denominational theologian. Since 1960, and the date may be pushed back to the 1940s, doctrinal, social, and ecclesiastical developments have caused Southern Baptists to revere the voices of the pastors of the large pulpits.

Southern Baptist Responses
to Their Confessional Statements[1]

"We have constructed for our basis no new creed; acting in this matter upon a Baptist aversion for all creeds but the Bible"[2] was the word Southern Baptists sent out when they formed the Southern Baptist Convention in 1845. That Southern Baptists inherited a rather sound prejudice against creedalism is beyond serious dispute. That this was a heritage which had modified a broader proconfessional Baptist heritage is also a question beyond serious dispute.

One may see an intriguing contrast between Southern Baptists and American Baptists regarding the attitude toward confessionalism. If Englerth is correct, American Baptists have experienced a radical shift in the use of confessional statements. Once, Englerth argues, American Baptists used confessional statements; now they scorn them.[3] The Southern Baptist story, on the other hand, appears quite the reverse. By 1845 Baptists in the South manifested little interest in public declarations of faith. That spirit maintained itself throughout the first quarter of the twentieth century. In recent years, however, while American Baptists have studiously avoided creedalism, Southern Baptists have steadily, if unconsciously, moved in that direction. The purpose of this paper is to chart the responses of Southern Baptists to confessionalism during three periods: 1845 to 1925, 1925 to 1963, 1963 to the present.

---

[1]This article first appeared in *Review and Expositor* 76/1 (Winter 1979): 69-85, and is reprinted here with the permission of the *Review and Expositor*. Published in the year that the Fundamentalist-Moderate Controversy began among Southern Baptists, the article desperately needs updating. The trend depicted in this article of a creeping creedalism within the SBC developed fully into a rigid creedalism by century's end. At the beginning of the twentieth century, the SBC had no doctrinal statement. By the end of the century, the seminaries, agencies, and boards of the SBC were strapped with a binding creed. Creedalism also accelerated among both state conventions and associations under fundamentalist leaders in the SBC.

[2]*SBC Annual 1845*, 19.

[3]See Gilbert Rimel Englerth, "American Baptists and Their Confessions of Faith" (Ph. D. diss., Temple University, Philadelphia, 1969) 350-68. This study was restricted to white Baptists of New England and the Middle Colonies. Englerth's thesis, which has much to offer, is not without need of some modification.

Southern Baptists and Confessionalism, 1845–1925

From 1845 to 1925 the SBC had an anticonfessional disposition. What were the forces that helped solidify that attitude? One can point to at least five factors: Separate Baptist revivalism, Campbellite criticism, Landmark ecclesiology, the nature of the Southern Baptist Convention, and the Southern and frontier culture.

Much that is distinctive in Southern Baptist life can be traced directly to the Separate Baptist heritage.[4] Coming out of New England revivalism and settling in North Carolina in 1755, these fiery frontiersmen were characterized by individualism, congregationalism, biblicism, and egalitarianism. Separate Baptists released a devotion to freedom which is without parallel in Baptist history. Because they wanted religious freedom they rejected any infringement of the state in matters of faith. Because they wanted ecclesiastical freedom for the local church, they tended to be suspicious of associational authority.[5] Because they wanted theological freedom for the local church and the individual conscience, they were apprehensive of confessions of faith.

No Separate Baptist illustrates this anticonfessional attitude better than Elder John Leland (1754–1841). Speaking derisively of confessions of faith, he asked, "Why this Virgin Mary between the souls of men and the scriptures?" He went on, "Confessions of faith often check any further pursuit after truth, confine the mind into a particular way of reasoning and give rise to frequent separation." And finally, "It is sometimes said that heretics are always averse to confessions of faith. I wish I could say as much of tyrants."[6]

For more than two decades after they came to the South, Separate Baptists refused to merge with the older Regular Baptists. One of the chief barriers to union was the Philadelphia Confession of Faith. The Regular Baptists had, over the years, adopted the Confession, and they wanted that

---

[4]See William L. Lumpkin, *Baptist Foundations in the South* (Nashville: Broadman Press, 1961) and James Owen Renault, "The Development of Separate Baptist Ecclesiology in the South, 1755–1976" (Ph, D. diss., Southern Baptist Theological Seminary, Louisville, 1978).

[5]See Walter B. Shurden, *Associationalism among Baptists in America, 1707–1814* (New York: Arno Press, 1980) 25-30.

[6]See *The Writings of the Late Elder John Leland*, ed. L. F. Greene (New York: G. W. Wood, 1845) 114.

document to be the basis of union with the Separates. The Separate Baptists finally agreed, but only after the nature and authority of the Confession was clearly delimited and virtually defanged.[7] When merger came in 1777, 1787, and 1801, Separate Baptists had modified the impact of confessionalism in the South.

The rise and spread of the Campbellites exacerbated the anticonfessional legacy bequeathed by Separate Baptists to Southern Baptists. The followers of Alexander Campbell became Southern Baptists' bitterest denominational enemies. In the first third of the nineteenth century, Campbell's disciples multiplied throughout the trans-Appalachian frontier. Their theme was "Where the Scriptures speak, we speak; where the Scriptures are silent, we are silent." Restorationist in character, the movement sought to recover first-century Christianity on the basis of the Bible alone.

The biblicism of the Campbellites compelled them to decry all human theological documents. Confessions of faith and creedal affirmations were not only useless, said Campbell, they obstructed the search for a biblical faith. Baptists and Campbellites became locked in denominational battle on the Kentucky-Tennessee frontier. They sought to "out-Bible" each other. In the face of the Campbellite criticism of Baptist confessions of faith, Baptists de-emphasized confessionalism. This is an interesting development when compared to those Southern Baptists today who most favor enforcing a strict subscription to confessions. In the early nineteenth century Baptists *rejected* confessions for the sake of the Bible. Today some want to *use* confessions for the sake of the Bible.

Landmarkism constituted a third factor reinforcing anticonfessionalism among Southern Baptists. Because of its rigid and doctrinaire ecclesiology, Landmarkism may be suspected of being one historical source of contemporary creedalism among Southern Baptists. Indeed, later Landmark Baptist denominations adopted stringent creeds.[8] J. M. Pendleton and J. R. Graves, however, because of their emphasis on local church autonomy, opposed creedalism. Their atomistic view of the church made confessional statements for general Baptist conventions unnecessary.[9]

---

[7]Robert B. Semple, *A History of the Rise and Progress of the Baptists in Virginia* (Richmond: published by the Author, 1810) 74-75.

[8]William L. Lumpkin, *Baptist Confessions of Faith*, rev. ed. (Valley Forge PA: Judson Press, 1969) 377-81.

[9]See Englerth, "American Baptists and Their Confessions of Faith," 93-96, 291-97, for a good discussion of Pendleton; for Graves, see Harold S. Smith, "The Life and Work of J. R. Graves, 1820–1893," *Baptist History and Heritage* 10/1

The nature and purpose of the Southern Baptist Convention was a fourth factor that discouraged that body from adopting theological confessions. Some have continued throughout Southern Baptist history to point to the purpose of the SBC as a forceful reason for avoiding confessions.[10] When Southern Baptists gathered in Augusta, Georgia, in May 1845, they wanted only to establish an organization with missionary objectives. Constructing an ecclesiastical body that would have theological supervision was not what they had in mind. Baptists in Augusta did not establish *The Southern Baptist Church.* They established a *convention* of churches for the purpose of "organizing a plan for eliciting, combining, and directing the energies of the whole denomination in one sacred effort, for the propagation of the Gospel."[11] The argument of the nonecclesiastical nature of the SBC was utilized in 1932 and 1937 when the convention twice declined to appoint delegates to the World Conference on Faith and Order. Both replies were identical and said that "the Southern Baptist Convention has no authority in such matters, being only a convention organized for missionary, educational, and benevolent purposes with no ecclesiastical functions."[12] Of course, adopting a creed is usually considered an ecclesiastical function.

A fifth factor militating against confessionalism in the SBC was cultural: the spirit of individualism nurtured on the frontier and, to some degree, within Southern culture in general. While impossible to document and obviously more indirect than other factors I have mentioned, the milieu in which Southern Baptists prospered cannot be totally disregarded. One does not have to agree totally with W. W. Sweet's famous interpretation of American religion in order to see some validity in his argument.[13]

While maintaining that anticonfessional forces influenced the SBC between 1845 and 1925, one must also recognize the presence of a confessional heritage in Southern Baptist life. That heritage is seen particularly in what may be called the Charleston Tradition. Founded in 1751 as the first Baptist association in the South, the Charleston (SC) Baptist Associa-

(January 1975): 26.

[10]See John E. White, "Another View," *Biblical Recorder*, 9 August 1922, 3; and John Hurt, "Should Southern Baptists Have a Creed/Confessions?" *Review and Expositor* 76/1 (Winter 1979).

[11]*SBC Annual 1845*, 3.

[12]See *SBC Annual 1932*, 71; *SBC Annual 1937*, 39-40.

[13]See William Warren Sweet, *Religion on the American Frontier: The Baptists, 1783–1830* (New York: Cooper Square Publishers, 1964).

tion adopted the Philadelphia Confession of Faith in 1767. Other associations in the South followed the Charleston example.[14]

The Charleston Tradition reappeared in 1859 in James P. Boyce, a South Carolinian, and the founder of the Southern Baptist Theological Seminary. Boyce insisted that a confessional document, known as the "Abstract of Principles," be signed by every professor to teach at the seminary.[15] Subsequently, Southern Baptists organized five other seminaries. Each followed the pattern of requiring a statement of subscription by the faculty.

Also in the South the New Hampshire Confession of Faith exerted considerable influence in the nineteenth century. It became the confessional document of a number of associations in the South. Actions of associations and theological seminaries are not the same as the action of the SBC, however. Neither the Charleston Tradition nor the New Hampshire Confession altered, in the nineteenth century, the Convention's policy of refusing formal adoption of confessions of faith.

Cracks in the anticonfessional structure of the Convention did not begin appearing until the decade prior to 1925.[16] Precipitated by the Ecumenical Movement, the first two SBC statements came in 1914 and 1919.[17] Neither of these, however, constituted a comprehensive confession of faith. They elicited little response from Southern Baptists, although these documents helped wedge the door open for later and more complete statements.

In 1920 the Foreign Mission Board adopted a doctrinal statement to which new appointees of the Board were to subscribe.[18] Missionaries already under appointment were also asked to sign the statement, and one report indicated that they were enthusiastic.[19] However, J. F. Love, corre-

---

[14]Lumpkin, *Baptist Confessions of Faith*, 352.

[15]See Boyce's 1856 inaugural address at Furman University as cited in Robert A. Baker, *A Baptist Source Book* (Nashville: Broadman Press, 1966) 135. For conflict surrounding the "Abstract" see 139-40.

[16]See James E. Carter, "The Southern Baptist Convention and Confessions of Faith, 1845–1925" (Th.D. diss., Southwestern Baptist Theological Seminary, Ft. Worth, Texas, 1964) for an exhaustive and excellent treatment of confessionalism among Southern Baptists to 1945.

[17]1914: See Carter, "The Southern Baptist Convention and Confessions of Faith, 1845–1925" 78-88, and *SBC Annual 1914* 73-78. 1919: See Carter, 88-102, and *SBC Annual 1919*, 75, 106, 113.

[18]*SBC Annual 1920*, 196-99.

[19]See *Biblical Recorder*, 21 July 1920, 5.

sponding secretary of the Board, appeared defensive about having such a statement.[20]

Evolution, Modernism, and biblical inspiration became explosive issues for Southern Baptists by 1921. Professors Hall and Dow of Baylor, Staten of William Jewell, Sampey of Southern Seminary, and President Poteat of Wake Forest came under the editorial gun of C. P. Stealey, fundamentalist editor of the Oklahoma Baptist Newspaper. Stealey became the single most important advocate of creedalism within the Southern Baptist Convention.[21] He carried that spirit into the SBC during the troublesome years, 1923–1926.

The year 1922 was a crucial year for Southern Baptists and the confessional question. Though the debate over whether the SBC should adopt a confession existed prior to 1922, it had not stirred the convention as in that year. The 1922 situation was stimulated by "the Stephens Conference." Representatives from the Northern Baptist Convention (NBC) and the SBC met in January 1922 at Stephens College in Columbia, Missouri. One of the recommendations of that conference was that the presidents of the Northern and Southern conventions carry resolutions to their respective conventions calling for the establishment of a joint committee to draw up "a statement of Baptist doctrine and polity." At the 1922 SBC meeting a committee was appointed to study the Stephens Conference request. The committee, chaired by John E. White of South Carolina, an important name in the developing confessional battle among Southern Baptists, recommended and the SBC adopted a report which turned down the Stephens request.[22]

This action by the SBC and subsequent similar action by the NBC precipitated a discussion of confessionalism.[23] John E. White became the chief anticonfessional voice in the SBC. He explained why his committee gave their negative report at the 1922 SBC meeting. Among other things, he said, "We did not believe the Constitution of the Southern Baptist Convention would stand for the Convention's assumacy of creed-making authority."[24]

---

[20]See *Baptist Messenger*, 21 July 1920, 5.

[21]J. Frank Norris is usually accorded the Fundamentalist leadership role among Southern Baptists. Certainly, Norris was the most colorful and bombastic, but he alienated himself from the SBC. Stealey did not. He remained within the Convention, a loyalist in denominational affairs, a fundamentalist in theological matters, and a creedalist in the confessional controversy.

[22]*SBC Annual 1922*, 20, 66.

[23]See *Biblical Recorder*, 7 June 1922, 6; 19 July 1922, 6; 26 July 1922, 6.

[24]*Biblical Recorder*, 9 August 1922, 3.

By the time the SBC met in Kansas City in 1923, the antievolution issue had gained in intensity. Southern Baptists, therefore, adopted President E. Y. Mullins's statement on "Science and Religion."[25] C. P. Stealey had planned to present an antievolutionary statement but did not do so because of the Mullins action. Concerning the Mullins statement, Stealey said, "His statement is not couched in the positive language that we should have preferred, but it is, nevertheless, airtight."[26] Eventually, however, Stealey changed his mind about the "airtightness" of the Mullins statement.

By 1924 and the Atlanta meeting of the SBC, Stealey was pressuring the Convention to adopt a binding doctrinal statement. Both he and R. K. Madien of Missouri submitted doctrinal statements to the Convention in 1924. While both efforts were rejected, a special committee was appointed "to consider the advisability of issuing another statement of the Baptist faith and message and to report at the next convention."[27] E. Y. Mullins chaired the committee. Other members were L. R. Scarborough, C. P. Stealey, W. J. McGlothlin, S. M. Brown, E. C. Dargan, and R. H. Pitt.

Southern Baptist Responses to the 1925 Confession

Some of the debate prior to the 1925 Memphis Convention centered on the duties of the Mullins Committee. Was it simply to consider the "advisability" of issuing another statement or was it *definitely* to issue a statement? The committee itself was divided on the question. Mullins did not think it necessary to issue a statement in light of the 1919 and 1923 Convention pronouncements. Pitt, Dargan, and McGlothlin agreed. Stealey, however, was certain Southern Baptists wanted the SBC to issue a confession. Scarborough and Brown also favored issuing one.

E. Y. Mullins wrote George W. McDaniel, SBC president, for his interpretation of the committee's duties. Mullins explained McDaniel's ruling in a letter to committee member W. J. McGlothlin: "Dr. McDaniel rules that the committee was appointed to report on the advisability of issuing a new doctrinal statement, but he also rules that there was a clear implication that the committee might prepare a doctrinal statement and have it in readiness in case of a favorable report by the committee as to issuing such a statement. He thinks this is part of the duty of the committee."[28] The com

---

[25]*SBC Annual 1923*, 19-20.
[26]See *Baptist Messenger*, 23 May 1923, 8-7.
[27]*SBC Annual 1924*, 95.
[28]Letter from E. Y. Mullins to W. J. McGlothlin, 25 October 1924, E. Y.

mittee made its report in Memphis in 1925.[29] In adopting that report, the Convention released its first thorough confessional statement. Controversy preceded the statement, accompanied both the work on the statement and its adoption at Memphis, and immediately followed its approval.

What were the various Southern Baptist responses to the 1925 Statement of the Baptist Faith and Message?[30] Basically, Southern Baptists responded in four ways. The responses came immediately, dominated Southern Baptist life for almost two years, and were generally predictable.

The first and most vocal response came from those whom E. Y. Mullins labeled the "big F Fundamentalists."[31] For the purposes of this article they shall be called "strict confessionalists." They may also be viewed as "creedalists." Led by C. P. Stealey and J. Frank Norris, they were dissatisfied because the confession was not rigidly and explicitly anti-evolutionary. Immediately after Mullins presented the report in Memphis, Stealey gained the convention floor and attempted to amend article 3 which dealt with the creation of man.[32] His motion lost 2,013 to 950. The next day, however, M. A. Phillips of Louisiana presented the following resolution which was adopted.

> Whereas, the action of the Convention yesterday upon the statement of the Baptist Faith and Message is being interpreted by some as an endorsement of evolution: therefore, be it resolved:
> (1) That such an interpretation is a misinterpretation.
> (2) That no paragraph, sentence, or word in our statement of Faith and Message can truly be cited as an endorsement of evolution.[33]

One might think that the Phillips Resolution had removed all ambiguity from article 3. C. P. Stealey did not think so. He used the pages of the *Baptist Messenger* for the next year to call for a more stringent statement

---

Mullins Correspondence, the Southern Baptist Theological Seminary, Louisville.

[29]*SBC Annual 1925*, 70-76.

[30]George W. McDaniel, president of the SBC, 1924–1926, suggested the name for the Confession in a letter to Mullins. He said that the title, "A Statement of the Baptist Faith and Message," is "far preferable to using the word 'creed' and is preferable to 'Articles of Faith.' " See letter dated 1 May 1925 in E. Y. Mullins Correspondence.

[31]See letter from E. Y. Mullins to George W. McDaniel, 24 July 1925, E. Y. Mullins Correspondence.

[32]*SBC Annual 1925*, 76.

[33]*SBC Annual 1925*, 87.

on creation and also to call in question the veracity of E. Y. Mullins. The 1925 Confession not only failed to solve the issue which gave it its rise—evolution—it had created bitterness in the denominational household. Conflict continued through the next convention.

Southern Baptists met in Houston in 1926 with George W. McDaniel as president. He concluded his presidential address with these words: "This Convention accepts Genesis as teaching that man was the special creation of God, and rejects every theory, evolution or other, which teaches that man originated in, or came by way of, a lower animal ancestry."[34] The messengers immediately adopted the McDaniel Statement as the sentiment of the Convention. If any possibility remained for an evolutionary interpretation of article 3 after the Phillips Resolution of 1925, the McDaniel Statement surely removed it.

The "strict confessionalists" were not finished, however. On the fourth day of the Convention, S. E. Tull, a messenger from Arkansas and an ally of Stealey, presented a resolution "that this convention request all its institutions and boards and their missionary representatives"[35] to sign the McDaniel Statement. Following Houston, the issue became "the signing-up question." Historian W. W. Barnes said, "The members of most of the Boards and institutions declined to sign the statement."[36]

Note the growing restrictions which the Stealey-led faction wanted to impose. First, in the early 1920s, they issued calls for orthodoxy. Second, they issued calls for a confessional statement to guard the orthodoxy. Third, they issued calls for a revision of the confession to guarantee the orthodoxy. Fourth, they called for the imposition of their revision of the Confession to make binding the orthodoxy. Such an evolutionary conception of confessionalism is what caused E. Y. Mullins to write, "Personally I feel that intellectual and spiritual health among us calls for a vigorous stand for a genuine Baptist position of breadth and tolerance."[37]

A second response to the 1925 Confession came from the "anticonfessionalists." These were Southern Baptists who did not want a confession of any kind or for any reason. The most outspoken of these was John E.

---

[34]*SBC Annual 1926*, 18.

[35]*SBC Annual 1926*, 98.

[36]William Wright Barnes, *The Southern Baptist Convention, 1845–1953* (Nashville: Broadman Press, 1954) 258.

[37]Letter from E. Y. Mullins to R. H. Pitt, 30 July 1925, E. Y. Mullins Correspondence.

White, president of Anderson College, Anderson, South Carolina. Allied with White were, among others, E. Hilton Jackson, a prominent Washington attorney, M. Ashby Jones, an Atlanta pastor, and R. H. Pitt, editor of the *Religious Herald* of Virginia.

This group was more vocal prior to the convention, attempting to prevent the adoption of the 1925 Confession, than they were after the Confession was finally adopted. One of the major arguments against the Confession focused on the nature and authority of the Southern Baptist Convention. Referring to the upcoming SBC in Memphis in 1925, John White wrote, "If it adopts and promulgates a formal, written, official Convention creed, let it be understood that it is a realized departure from the former and long-established conception of its functions and of its traditional attitude toward creedal authority."[38]

The anticonfessionalists also argued that doctrinal controversy could not be settled by the adoption of a creed. "If 'history repeats itself' in this matter," wrote the editor of the *Biblical Recorder*, "so far from preserving our unity these continuous declarations of faith will cause division."[39] After the 1925 Convention he pointed out that, because of the diversity of Southern Baptists, no single doctrinal statement could satisfy all Southern Baptists. This group proved to be politically ineffective at the 1925 Convention. According to E. Y. Mullins, the anticonfessionalists were in the minority. He later wrote, "They could not have carried their point in the Convention."[40] "When the vote was taken," concluded James E. Carter, "the anticonfessionalists were not really involved in the discussions."[41]

Another group at the 1925 Convention, however, did prove to be politically astute. While not agreed on the necessity for a confession in the first place, they were willing to have a confession as long as its authority was carefully limited and its scope restricted to religious matters. They won at Memphis. Led by E. Y. Mullins, these may be identified as the "mainstream denominationalists" or "confessionalists." Somewhat apprehensive, prior to the Memphis Convention, about the adoption of the statement, they

---

[38]John White, "A Baptist Aversion to All Creeds but the Bible," *Biblical Recorder*, 11 March 1925, 1.

[39]*Biblical Recorder*, 15 April 1925, 6.

[40]Letter from E. Y. Mullins to J. N. Mitchell, 23 February 1926, 3, E. Y. Mullins Correspondence.

[41]Carter, "The Southern Baptist Convention and Confessions of Faith," 128; see also *Biblical Recorder*, 20 May 1925, 10.

extolled the virtues of the Confession after Memphis. Interestingly enough, they had to defend the Confession against both those who had not wanted a confession at all and those who wanted a more fundamentalist statement.

R. H. Pitt had been appointed a member of the committee to draft the Confession of 1925. In the end, however, he did not sign his name to the committee's report. Following the 1925 Convention, Pitt bemoaned both the fact of the Confession and the division it had produced. Mullins wrote him a personal letter suggesting that things could be worse: "If the land-mark element had been in charge of the committee we would have had a much worse 'kettle of fish' than we have."[42]

The most intense criticism of Mullins and the 1925 Confession came from those on the right. C. P. Stealey protested that the Confession allowed for theistic evolution.[43] Mullins replied that it made no such allowance and claimed that the rest of the committee agreed with him.[44] Later Mullins sought to reinforce a conservative interpretation of the 1925 Confession, however, by pointing to the opinion of Dr. J. M. Gray of Moody Bible Institute. Gray wrote Mullins and described the Confession as a "magnificent deliverance." Mullins added, "certainly our Memphis Doctrinal Statement has met with the enthusiastic endorsement of every Fundamentalist who has retained his balance and poise."[45]

So the position of the "mainstream denominationalists" was a perplexing one. Their response to the Confession following Memphis, however, was a positive one. They saw the statement as a tool of denominational unity which did not coerce theological uniformity. They defended the Confession from anticonfessionalists by predicting that things could have been worse. They defended the Confession from the strict confessionalists by arguing that it was theologically adequate.

A fourth response to the 1925 Confession was that of wholesale neglect. This appeared to be the response of the majority of Southern Baptists and we dub them "nonconfessionalists." Writing nine years after the adoption of the 1925 Confession, W. W. Barnes, noted Southern Baptist church historian, wrote, "The convention adopted the statement by a large

---

[42]Letter from E. Y. Mullins to R. H. Pitt, 30 July 1925, E. Y. Mullins Correspondence.

[43]See *Baptist Messenger*, 20 May 1925, 1.

[44]*Baptist Messenger*, 10 June 1925, 1.

[45]See Letter from E. Y. Mullins to S. M. Brown, 15 March 1925, E. Y. Mullins Correspondence.

majority of the messengers present, but it has been received by Southern Baptist churches generally with a tremendous outburst of silence."[46]

James E. Carter meticulously examined the uses and influence of the Baptist Faith and Message to 1945. He reported that though it was widely distributed, included in church manuals, and adopted by Southwestern Baptist Theological Seminary, it was never used by state conventions up to 1945, and remained comparatively unused by associations and churches.

Reasons for limited use of the Confession, says Carter, were (1) Southern Baptists' reluctance concerning doctrinal centralization, (2) the popularity of the older New Hampshire Confession among Southern Baptists, and (3) the agitation and debate which followed the 1925 statement.

John H. Leith said of the 1925 Southern Baptist Confession, "it is widely used and exercises a very great influence."[47] To the contrary and more accurately, Carter says, "it has been rarely used and has exercised very little influence." He concluded, "The confession of faith that represented the Southern Baptist Convention's first venture in issuing a complete confession of faith was not very influential and not well accepted."[48]

Southern Baptist Responses to the 1963 Confession

The SBC adopted its second major Confession in 1963.[49] The Elliott controversy constituted the background of this particular doctrinal statement.[50] Without imposing artificial constructs, one may utilize the same four basic responses to the 1963 Confession as were used for the 1925 Confession. Some significant differences as well as obvious similarities

---

[46]William Wright Barnes, *The Southern Baptist Convention: A Study in the Development of Ecclesiology* (Seminary Hill TX: published by the author, 1934) 8.

[47]John H. Leith, *Creeds of the Churches*, rev. ed. (Atlanta: John Knox Press, 1973) 344.

[48]Carter, *The Southern Baptist Convention and Confessions of Faith*, 171.

[49]The SBC issued statements between 1925 and 1963 but none of them constitute a major pronouncement. The closest to a confession of faith was issued in 1946 as a "Statement of Principles." See *SBC Annual 1946*, 37-39.

[50]For a brief discussion of the Elliott Controversy, see Walter B. Shurden, "The Problem of Authority in the Southern Baptist Convention," *Review and Expositor* 75/2 (Spring 1978): 220-22.

exist, however. One difference, which sets the context for the following discussion, is chronological in nature. Following the 1926 meeting of the SBC in Houston, little was heard of the 1925 Confession. Likewise, subsequent to the Kansas City Convention in 1963, little was made of the 1963 Confession. In fact, it lay dormant from 1964 to 1969. With 1969 and the beginning of the Broadman controversy, the confessional question reappeared among Southern Baptists in its most vigorous form. More will be said about this resurgence later.

How have the "mainstream denominationalists" responded to the 1963 Confession? First, this Confession, unlike the 1925 Confession, did not originate with the extreme Fundamentalist wing of the Convention. Rather, it began with the "mainstreamers" of the 1960s, particularly Herschel H. Hobbs, Porter Routh, and Albert McClellan.[51] Herschel H. Hobbs, pastor of the First Baptist Church, Oklahoma City, Oklahoma, and president of the SBC in 1962–1963, served as chairman of the committee which drew up the 1963 Confession adopted in Kansas City. In some ways, Herschel H. Hobbs was the E. Y. Mullins of the 1960s. His hand was the prominent one in writing the 1963 Confession, and his voice has been the most outspoken in defending the statement.

Hobbs has constantly reminded Baptists of his day, as did Mullins a generation before, of the purpose and authority of all Baptist confessions. The confessional, rather than the binding creedal nature of the 1963 Confession has been insisted upon by Hobbs and other mainstreamers. In fact, Hobbs has repeatedly said that the statement would never have been adopted apart from the preamble which carefully limited the authority of the Confession itself. Because of the militant resurgence of "strict confessionalists" in the late 1960s and throughout the 1970s, Hobbs has had to make this point more often and with more conviction than Mullins ever did. This constant effort at defending the Confession, however, has helped give it a prominence the 1925 Confession never achieved.

The relationship of the "strict confessionalists" to the Kansas City Confession is an interesting one. As noted above, they were not the prime movers in asking for this Confession. Their interests in 1962–1963 were originally far more specific. They wanted to rid Southern Baptist semi-

---

[51]See Herschel H. Hobbs, "Baptist Faith and Message—Anchored but Free," *Baptist History and Heritage* 13/3 (July 1978): 34; see also Herschel H. Hobbs, "Southern Baptists and Confessionalism," *Review and Expositor* 76/1 (Winter 1979): 55-68.

naries of theologians like Ralph Elliott. Their strategy did not appear to include doctrinal statements as a means for accomplishing their goals. Except for the year following the adoption of the 1963 Confession, the "strict confessionalists" were relatively quiet about the statement. Indeed, the entire SBC somewhat shelved the Confession for five years. With 1969 and the eruption of the Broadman Controversy, the silence became shock waves. One result has been that the 1970s has provided the loudest and longest debate over confessionalism in Southern Baptist history. Another consequence has been the growing prominence and authority of the 1963 Confession.[52]

At the New Orleans meeting of the SBC in 1969, "strict confessionalists" began using the Kansas City Confession as a tool to try to insure orthodoxy, uniform theological beliefs, and eventually to ban commentaries published by the Sunday School Board.[53] The Broadman Controversy did not actually erupt in 1969 until after the New Orleans meeting; other, more general issues were present there which concerned the emerging "strict confessionalists." By 1973 they had organized, calling themselves the Baptist Faith and Message Fellowship (BFMF). This group, led by William A. Powell, M. O. Owens, and others, began publishing a newspaper. The paper has constantly called for strict adherence to its interpretation of the 1963 Confession, particularly in reference to article 1, on the Bible. While the BFMF has not completely succeeded in imposing their interpretation of the Confession on Southern Baptist Convention agencies and institutions, they have certainly sensitized some of the denominational leadership to the presence of the Confession. As shown below, SBC agencies and institutions have increasingly given attention to the document.

At this point an interesting development in the use and purpose of the convention's two major confessions should be noted. When the Mullins committee presented the 1925 Confession, they included an introductory statement concerning "the historic Baptist conception of the nature and function of confessions of faith in our religious and denominational life." The first part of that particular statement said that confessions were *"for the General instruction and guidance of our own people* and others concerning

---

[52]For this development, see Shurden, "The Problem of Authority in the Southern Baptist Convention," *Review and Expositor* 75/2 (Spring 1978): 229-31.

[53]See *SBC Annual 1969*, 58-59; *SBC Annual 1970*, 63, 66, 74, 77, 78; *SBC Annual 1971*, 71; *SBC Annual 1972*, 55.

those articles of the Christian faith which are most surely held among us.[54] That statement was also included in the 1963 Confession. However, the resolution calling for the 1963 Confession asked that a doctrinal statement be drafted "which shall serve as information to the churches, and which *may* serve as *guidelines to the various agencies* of the Southern Baptist Convention."[55] The "guidance of our own people" of 1925 was far more general than the "*may serve as guidelines to the various agencies*" of 1963. In the 1970s the BFMF wanted to transform the "may" into a "must." From the "must" of a single theological document, the next step would be the "must" of a single interpretation of that document. "Strict confessionalists" apparently would be happy with that development, for their basic response has been to try to fasten Southern Baptists rigidly to that interpretation of the 1963 Confession.

"Anticonfessionalists" have also persisted in Southern Baptist ranks during the 1960s and 1970s. Their numbers, however, appear to have diminished and their voices have been increasingly muted in denominational life. An anticonfessional sentiment was evident at the 1963 convention in an attempt to amend the Hobbs report by striking out all of the Confession except the Scripture references. The motion failed, as did another effort to have the Hobbs report received merely as information.[56]

The spirit of anticonfessionalism was also present in two short-lived organizations of the 1960s and 1970s. A group calling themselves "Baptists for Freedom" (BFF) organized at the time of the Elliott controversy. While this group was tangentially concerned with creedalism, particularly the adoption of the 1963 Confession, they were primarily a pro-Elliott group. The BFF sponsored a fellowship dinner during the 1963 SBC meeting in Kansas City. G. Avery Lee, minister of the St. Charles Avenue Baptist Church, New Orleans, Louisiana, spoke to the group. He said of the impending action at the Convention:

> We [SBC] will adopt a new statement of Faith. . . . So long as we follow the preamble in the strict spirit of the preamble—remembering that this statement is a *consensus of opinion*, not a binding creed, nor a complete agreement—we will remain in a strong fellowship of difference. But if we ever start making this statement of faith mandatory, using it to clobber individuals and institutions, if we "instruct" each of our seminaries to

---

[54]*SBC Annual 1925*, 71; italics for emphasis.
[55]*SBC Annual 1962*, 64; italics for emphasis.
[56]See *SBC Annual 1963*, 63.

adopt this statement, . . . if we ever use this statement as a test of fellowship of faith . . . then we will have sold our birthright for pottage and lost
our heritage of freedom and individual expression.[57]

A second organization came into existence just prior to the New
Orleans convention of 1969. It was "The E. Y. Mullins Fellowship." This
organization, like the BFF, did not emerge primarily to fight confessionalism, but the spirit of the anticonfessionalists was clearly present.[58] The
organization dissolved by 1971.

Thus, as in 1925, the anticonfessionalist attitude proved politically
ineffective—almost nonexistent—at the 1963 Convention. It has remained
relatively silent in subsequent years and would appear to represent a very
small minority among Southern Baptists. Numbers and noise can be
deceiving, however. Many who probably prefer this position ideologically
have moved into the camp of the "mainstream denominationalists" in order
to resist what they perceive as an encroaching creedalism from the right.

Finally, has there been a "nonconfessionalist" response to the 1963
Confession? The answer is a mixed "yes" and "no." "Yes," because average
Southern Baptist Church members probably do not have the slightest idea
that the 1963 statement of the Baptist Faith and Message exists. If they
knew, they probably would not care. "No," because the 1963 Confession
has not been disregarded or neglected as was the 1925 Confession. Though
precise information is not available on exactly how individuals, local
churches, and associations have responded and used the 1963 Confession,
other developments suggest a growing acceptance and use of it.

I recently sent five questions to executive-secretaries of thirty-three
Southern Baptist sate conventions. I received thirty-one responses. The five
questions were:

1. Has your state convention officially adopted the 1963 Baptist Faith
and Message? Yes____ No____

2. If the answer to question one is "yes," can you give me the date the
1963 statement was adopted by your convention? Date_____.

3. Is subscription to the 1963 statement mandatory for churches to send
messengers to your convention? Yes____ No____

---

[57]G. Avery Lee, "Areas of Tension between Freedom and Responsibility," 10;
writer's personal copy.

[58]See Robinson B. James, "The Beginnings of the E. Y. Mullins Fellowship";
writer's personal copy.

4. Are employees of your convention required to sign the 1963 statement? Yes___ No___

5. Are employees of your convention urged to sign the 1963 statement? Yes___ No___

Seven of the thirty-one states responding have officially adopted the 1963 Confession. These states are Arkansas, Georgia, Hawaii, Illinois, Ohio, Pennsylvania-South Jersey, and West Virginia. Significantly, five of these adopted the Confession since 1969. Only Arkansas answered "yes" to number four. Several states gave an answer that bordered on "almost yes" to question number five. While the information was not specifically requested, Colorado and Maryland indicated that most of the newly constituted churches in their states adopt the 1963 Confession. In light of the geographical locations (West vs. Southeast) and the age of the respective conventions (Colorado—1956; Maryland—1836), this is interesting.

With the exception of question 3 and modifications where necessary, I sent four of the questions listed above (questions 1, 2, 4, 5) to nineteen of the boards, agencies, and commissions of the Southern Baptist Convention. All nineteen responded. Of the four SBC boards (Annuity, Foreign, Home, Sunday School), only the Home Mission Board has officially adopted the 1963 Confession. Adopting the statement in 1976, the Home Mission Board does not, however, require employees to sign the document. The Annuity Board receives the Confession as "guidelines" and requires no signing. The Foreign Mission Board has "a sense of agreement and support for the statement as adopted" by the SBC. The FMB also asks candidates for foreign mission service the following two questions: "Are you familiar with the content of the Baptist Faith and Message? Are you in agreement with this statement?" The Sunday School Board requires employees "in certain designated positions" to sign the Confession.

All six Southern Baptist seminaries require faculty members to subscribe to some confessional statement. While these statements have been diverse in the past, there is definitely a growing sensitivity to the 1963 Confession. Golden Gate and Southwestern presidents indicated that their schools have officially adopted the Confession, Golden Gate in 1977 and Southwestern in 1964.[59] Midwestern Seminary has "updated" the 1925 statement with the 1963, and faculty members now sign the later document. In July 1978, the executive committee of the board of trustees at New Orleans Seminary voted to recommend to the full Board in March 1979 that

---

[59]The exact date of adoption is not given.

they adopt the 1963 Confession as a "corollary" to the existing "Articles of Religious Belief." Faculty members apparently will be expected to sign both statements, though final action was not settled at this writing. Southeastern Seminary has not officially adopted the 1963 statement, but the 1978–1979 seminary catalog says the seminary is "guided by the action of the Convention messengers in Kansas City, Missouri, 1963, wherein they adopted the Southern Baptist Convention statement of Faith and Message as a guideline for all convention agencies." Southern Seminary continues to subscribe to the "Abstract of Principles," used at the institution since 1859.

The SBC has six commissions. They are the Brotherhood, Christian Life, Education, Historical, Radio and Television, and Stewardship Commissions. Not one of the six has officially adopted the 1963 Confession, nor do they require subscription to it by their employees. The same is true for the Southern Baptist Foundation and the Woman's Missionary Union. The Seminary Extension Department officially adopted the statement in 1975 but does not require subscription.

Some conclusions are obvious from the responses. One, the boards and seminaries have given considerably more attention to the 1963 Confession than have the other SBC agencies. Two, most of the attention has come since 1969 and the reawakening of strict confessionalism among Southern Baptists. Out of the nineteen organizations surveyed, five have, in some sense, officially adopted the 1963 statement on the Baptist Faith and Message. Southwestern and Midwestern seminaries apparently acted around 1964. No agency of the SBC adopted the Confession for another ten years. The Seminary Extension Department acted in 1975, the Home Mission Board in 1976, and Golden Gate Seminary in 1977. New Orleans Seminary, as indicated above, is to act in 1979. Three, by the end of 1979 four seminaries will require subscription to the statement, while the Sunday School Board requires subscription by "certain designated employees."

James E. Carter was again on target when he said, "It is clear that the Baptist Faith and Message of 1963 has been used more extensively than the older statement. It has also been used in ways that the 1925 statement was not used."[60] The question is why? I offer five reasons, listed in order of their importance.

One, the 1960s were turbulent years for Southern Baptists as for all of American religion. In addition to the major Elliott and Broadman controversies, constant minor theological and ethical conflict surrounded most of the SBC seminaries and the Sunday School Board. The Christian Life Commission and the Home Mission Board had to counter charges of liberalism, also. The 1970s, marked by a generally conservative mood in American Religion and the SBC, have accented polarization.

Two, the aggressiveness and noisemaking of the strict confessionalists of the 1970s is without parallel in Southern Baptist life. They have created an atmosphere of fear, and they appear to have intimidated some in positions of denominational leadership.

Three, the "confessionalists" or "mainstream denominationalists" have unwittingly given prominence to the Confession by indirectly using it as a call for denominational unity. They have also been placed in the position of having constantly to clarify its purpose. Defending the statement has elevated the statement.

Four, anticonfessional voices have declined, or they have been absorbed into the middle. They have certainly been quieted. One suspects that many are now skittish of publicly subjecting the *idea* of confessions to scrutiny and are downright fearful of questioning the 1963 statement. This constitutes a virtual reversal of nineteenth-century Southern Baptist history.

Five, inevitable centralization occurs as a denomination grows older and bigger. W. W. Barnes predicted and warned Southern Baptists of this in 1934 in his privately printed *The Southern Baptist Convention: A Study in the Development of Ecclesiology*. Southern Baptists might do well to study that little book again.

---

[60]James E. Carter, "American Baptist Confessions of Faith: A Review of Confessions of Faith Adopted by Major Baptist Bodies in the United States," in *The Lord's Free People in a Free Land*, ed. William R, Estep (Fort Worth TX: Faculty of the School of Theology, Southwestern Baptist Theological Seminary, 1976) 71.

The Southern Baptist Synthesis: Is It Cracking?[1]

It was not a Baptist but a Roman Catholic whom I paraphrase: "There is no hope for the future if the past remains unreceived and unconfessed and unforgiven."[2] I would add only one word: "There is no hope for the future if the past remains unreceived and unconfessed and unforgiven and *unknown*." I am not plugging my discipline or engaging in historical histrionics when I say to you with all the conviction of my soul: "No hope . . . for the future . . . if the past remains unknown."

I have been a member of a Southern Baptist church now for twenty-five years—all of my adult life. And because of my call from God to minister, because of my professional commitment as a Baptist historian, because I am an unapologetic lover of things Southern Baptist, I have attempted to be more than a casual observer of Southern Baptist life. And never in the last twenty-five years have I felt so deeply the urgency of history for the life of our denomination. Knowing our heritage is no longer a plaything; it has become an imperative thing. Forces and factors are loose in our denomination and our society which make awareness of heritage a necessity, not a luxury. To put it bluntly, we are facing the erosion of a rich denominational heritage which cannot be preserved by ignoring our

---

[1]I first presented this address as lecture 1 in the Carver-Barnes Lectures at Southeastern Baptist Theological Seminary, Wake Forest, North Carolina, 4-5 November 1980, only a little more than a year after the Fundamentalist-Moderate controversy began in June 1979. In reading this article, keep in mind the date, 1980. The material was published in *Outlook* (March-April 1981) and later in *Baptist History and Heritage* 16/2 (April 1981): 2-11. It is reprinted by permission of the Baptist History and Heritage Society, Brentwood TN. As do many others, often when I speak, I fail to document carefully with footnotes because I do not have publishing in mind. That was the case with this lecture. The only alteration I have made from the initial material, therefore, has been the addition of footnotes where I could provide them. To remain as close to the original presentations as possible, I have left untouched my signals for emphasis in the oral presentation, such things as under linings, bold, and italics. I have also retained the oral nature of the sentences.

[2]A paraphrase of a line from Henri J. M. Nouwen, *Reaching Out: The Three Movements of the Spiritual Life* (Garden City NY: Doubleday, 1975) 68. To be precise, Nouwen said, "[T]here will be no hope for the future when the past remains unconfessed, unreceived, and misunderstood."

heritage. We must receive it all. We must confess and forgive much of it. But, above all, we must know it.

My topic is "The Southern Baptist Synthesis: Is It Cracking?" One of the common interpretations of the Protestant Reformation has to do with the dissolution of the Medieval Synthesis. It goes roughly like this: During the period from Charlemagne to the Renaissance, there developed a synthesis in Western Europe. That synthesis was constructed around the Roman Catholic Church. All of human life and experience—music, art, economics, education, politics, and philosophical perceptions of reality—all of those were brought together, synthesized, in the Roman Catholic Church. Life was a neat and stabile unit. Then in the fourteenth century cracks began to appear in this synthesis. The cracking came from many sources. A rising nationalism cracked the political unity. Then there were mysticism, humanism, and nominalism. And finally "a wild boar" entered the vineyard of the Lord, wrecking and ruining. The medieval Humpty-Dumpty had a great fall. And then the Enlightenment stamped irreverently on the remaining pieces. The synthesis was shattered. Life was never to be the same again in the West.

By no stretch of the imagination do I want to press the analogy. I simply want to use the metaphor. What I do want to suggest is that a Southern Baptist synthesis was shaped in the eighteenth, nineteenth, and first half of the twentieth centuries. I then want to point to some significant stresses placed on that synthesis since World War II. Finally, I want to make a closing observation on living in a synthesis under stress.

The Southern Baptist Synthesis: Its Shape

I am being only three-fourths facetious when I say that the extent of the knowledge of some Southern Baptists of their denominational heritage reaches all the way back to the last meeting of the Southern Baptist Convention that they attended! These are the rootless among us. On the other hand, some others think we emerged from the waters of Jordan with a full-blown denominational structure. Baptist principles are certainly rooted in biblical convictions, but the shape of the denominational synthesis emerged in a later period. Let me now try to identify some of the components of that synthesis.

The Eighteenth and Nineteenth Centuries

During the eighteenth and nineteenth centuries at least four distinct traditions among Baptists of the South helped shape the Southern Baptist synthesis.

The Charleston Tradition. The first of these is the Baptist tradition which emerged out of Charleston, South Carolina. In the eighteenth century Charleston was to the Baptists of the Southern Colonies what Philadelphia was to Baptists of the Middle Colonies—the hub of Baptist activity. Organized in the late seventeenth century, the First Baptist Church of Charleston was not only the first church in the South, it was for a number of years the most influential church. From its influence in 1751 came the Charleston Association—the first Baptist association of the South. William Screven (d. 1713) *planted* the Charleston Tradition; Oliver Hart (1723–1795), a later pastor of First Church, *spread* the tradition when he founded the association; but the Reverend Richard Furman (1755–1825), pastor at Charleston for thirty-eight years *perfected* the tradition.

The tradition had roots. It was rooted in the Particular Baptists of England, who in turn were rooted in English Calvinistic Puritanism. The Charleston Tradition is one of the major reasons why E. Brooks Holifield of Emory could say, "The Southern Baptists held fast to the old Puritan ideal of a pure Church filled with regenerate saints."[3] Puritanism is still difficult for scholars to define. But at the heart of it were two central affirmations which were bequeathed to Charleston. One was the centrality of religious experience; the second was the sole authority of Holy Scripture.

The Charleston Tradition, personified in Richard Furman, may be summarized in one word, and that word is ORDER. Charleston provided *theological order*. In 1767 the Charleston Association adapted and adopted *The Philadelphia Confession of Faith*. Naturally, it became known as *The Charleston Confession*. Calvinistic in character, that confession became a consensus of Baptist theology in the South. While it was a confession which expressed a Baptist consensus, it was never intended as a creed to bind a Baptist conscience. That part of our heritage, it appears, will have to be relearned.

---

[3]E. Brooks Holifield, *The Gentlemen Theologians: American Theology in Southern Culture, 1795–1860* (Durham NC: Duke University Press, 1978) 175.

Charleston also provided *ecclesiological order*. "A Summary of Church Discipline" was adopted by the Charleston Association.[4] This early church manual insisted upon the independence of the local churches. But it avoided "lone rangerism" in church life by balancing the demand for local church independency with a call for cooperation in associational life. Southern Baptist connectionalism in denominational polity comes from Furman through W. B. Johnson. Cooperation was a key.

And then there was *liturgical order*. It represented a style in public worship that was ordered and stately, though pulsating with evangelical warmth. The ordinances were more important to those eighteenth-century Baptists than to many of their successors. Worship appeared to be neither spontaneously charismatic nor primarily revivalistic. It was directed toward heaven, not earth. The object was to praise God, not entertain people.

Finally, the Charleston Tradition emphasized *ministerial order*. The very first educational fund promoted and supported by a group of Baptists in America was initiated by the Charleston Association in 1755. Charleston never demanded education as a prerequisite to ministry, but neither did they demean it. Neither did they make the mistake of later generations by equating education with graduation. Richard Furman never graduated, but he was thoroughly educated. And he insisted that a preacher's sermon should, as he put it, "smell of the lamp."

From this proeducational, nonanti-intellectual Charleston sentiment were born Baptist colleges: Furman, Georgetown, Richmond, Wake Forest, and Mississippi College. And the roots of Southern Baptists' first theological seminary are clearly traced to the Charleston Tradition. James P. Boyce, an aristocratic and educated South Carolinian, founded Southern Baptist Theological Seminary in 1859 in Greenville, South Carolina. In 1877 the seminary moved to Louisville, Kentucky, so it could survive in the penniless days of the post-Civil War.

In brief, the Charleston Tradition consisted of pietistic Puritanism, Calvinistic confessionalism, quasiconnectionalism, churchly liturgics, and a commitment to an educated ministry. Permit me a generalization and I

---

[4]Here again Charleston followed the Philadelphia pattern of Baptist life. When the Philadelphia Association published their confession of faith in 1743, they attached to it a document known as "A Short Treatise of Church Discipline." For a copy of the Charleston Discipline, see James Leo Garrett, Jr., *Baptist Church Discipline* (Nashville, Broadman Press, 1962.

would dub these folk "semipresbyterians." The word for Charleston is ORDER.

The Sandy Creek Tradition. The second word in the Southern Baptist synthesis is ARDOR.[5] That word came out of the Sandy Creek Tradition. These were the Separate Baptists. Much that is distinctive in Southern Baptist life can be traced directly to the Separate Baptist heritage. Coming out of New England revivalism during the era of the Great Awakening, these fiery frontier folk migrated to the South and settled in Sandy Creek, North Carolina, in 1755. They were a people possessed by ardor. And that ardor expressed itself in individualism, congregationalism, biblicism, and egalitarianism. They released a devotion to freedom which is without parallel in Baptist history. Because they wanted religious freedom to evangelize every soul who crossed their path, they rejected any infringement from the state in matters of faith. The result? The walls of the Southern establishment in matters of church-state came tumbling down. Because they wanted ecclesiastical freedom for the local church, they tended to be suspicious of associational authority. Because they wanted theological freedom for the individual conscience, they were reluctant to pledge themselves to confessions of faith.

And their leaders? Shubal Stearns was their patriarch and pastor at Sandy Creek. Daniel Marshall, Stearns's brother-in-law, began a Baptist church wherever he could gain two converts, a motion, and a second to the motion. And he did that in North Carolina, South Carolina, Virginia, and Georgia. Samuel Harris was a sheriff turned evangelist who outran the church growth movement by 200 years. And elder John Leland, a Baptist freedom lover if ever there was one, is probably groaning in his grave over the tightening vise of creedalism in Southern Baptist life. He was so turned off by Baptist confessions of faith that he called them "a Virgin Mary between the souls of men and the scriptures." Confessions of faith, he said, "often check any further pursuit after truth, confine the mind into a particular way of reasoning and give rise to frequent separation." And finally he spoke to the subject by saying, "It is sometimes said that heretics

---

[5]Claude L. Howe, Jr, my major Church History professor at the New Orleans Baptist Theological Seminary introduced me to the designations of "Order" and "Ardor" for the Charleston and Sandy Creek Traditions in Baptist life. Any praise for these descriptions of Baptist life should go to Professor Howe, not me. On the other hand, Professor Howe is not responsible for the way I characterize these traditions.

are always averse to confessions of faith. I wish I could say as much of tyrants."[6] He wrote, as James L. Sullivan would say, with carbolic acid on asbestos paper!

Quickly, now, let me identify four characteristics of Separate Baptist ardor. First, their worship was *revivalistic*. Stearns and company were a highly emotional, deeply *pietistic* kind of people. They had one value: winning people to Jesus Christ and to an emotionally identifiable experience. Faith was feeling and every Sunday was a camp meeting. Their praise of God was not vertical but horizontal. Unlike the city slickers at Charleston, they did not praise God by praising God; they praised God by reaching women and men. They had a mourner's bench and they expected public groaning, not polite amens. They were ardent revivalists.

Second, their ministry was *charismatic*. The call of God to preach, like the conversion which preceded it, was internal and experiential, never a professional choice. Ministerial education was not encouraged but discouraged. Their preachers were not out to educate but to alarm. And their preaching was marked by "a holy whine." Proclamation was immersed in tearful pathos and with a singsong pattern to it that many Southern Baptists since have found effective for discovering the holy in life. Of Shubal Stearns it was said: "His voice was musical and strong, which he managed in such a manner as, one while, to make soft impressions on the heart, and fetch tears from the eyes in a mechanical way; and anon, to shake the very nerves, and to throw the animal system into tumults and perturbations."[7] They were ardent preachers!

Third, their ecclesiology was ruggedly *independent*. They formed associations, their first being the Sandy Creek in 1758. But unlike the Charleston Tradition, the Sandy Creek Tradition did not spend as much time defining associational authority as they did declaring local church autonomy. The Separate Baptist concept of connectionalism did not contribute to a later Southern Baptist centralized denominational structure. Rather, you find here some roots of later Landmarkism.

---

[6]See these quotes in *The Writings of the Late Elder John Leland*, ed. L. F. Greene (New York: G. W. Wood, 1845) 114.

[7]Morgan Edwards, "Materials towards a History of the Baptists in the Province of North Carolina," in Morgan Edwards, *Materials towards a History of the Baptists*, prepared for publication by Eve B. Weeks and Mary B. Warren (Danielsville GA: Heritage Papers, 1984) 93.

Their worship was revivalistic; their ministry was charismatic; and their ecclesiology was independent. Fourth, their theological approach was *biblicistic*. With a highly literalistic approach to scripture, they found not two but nine Christian rites in the Bible. Their biblicism is what made them so ardently opposed to confessions of faith. Their background was New England congregationalism where nonbinding confessions had evolved into binding creeds. And they had watched the creeds become substitutes for the authority of the Word of God. They would have none of that. For years, therefore, different postures toward confessional statements kept the Charleston and Sandy Creek Traditions from merging.

Then what about their theology? Were they Calvinists or moderate Calvinists or just outright Arminians? You get different answers from different Baptist historians. John Leland is probably to be trusted as a guide at this point. Leland said, "It is a matter of fact that the preaching that has been most blessed of God, and most profitable to men, is the doctrine of sovereign grace in the salvation of souls, mixed with a little of what is called Arminianism."[8] In fact, the Separate Baptists were not systematic theologians. They were heralds of the sovereign grace of God and they directed it to the free wills of all who would lend an ear.

In brief, the Sandy Creek Tradition consisted of revivalistic experientialism, anticonfessionalism, exaggerated localism, fierce libertarianism, and a commitment to personal evangelism. Permit me another generalization, and I would dub these people "semipentecostals." And now a suggestion: if you marry a semipresbyterian from Charleston to a semipentecostal from Sandy Creek, you will get a whole host of Southern Baptists spreading all over the Southland. That is what happened. Beginning in 1777 in North Carolina and continuing until 1801 in Kentucky, the Charlestonians and the Sandy Creekers began coming together. Together they formed the Southern Baptist Convention and the blending helped shape the Southern Baptist synthesis.

The Georgia Tradition. The third tradition contributing to the Southern Baptist synthesis may be called the Georgia Tradition. This tradition is understood by pointing to two locales, not one. The two are Augusta and Atlanta. And there are two Baptist leaders who personify this tradition. They are W. B. Johnson, first president of the Southern Baptist Convention, and I. T. Tichenor, the leader of the Home Mission Board who helped to forge a Southern Baptist consciousness in the despairing denominational

---

[8]Cited in Greene, ed., *The Writings of the Late Elder John Leland*, 172.

days of the post-Civil War. And the "words" to describe this tradition? The words for the Georgia Tradition are "local color."

Arriving in Augusta on May 8, 1845, W. B. Johnson had in his pocket a proposed constitution for the about-to-be-formed Southern Baptist Convention. After the convention convened, a "Public Address" was drafted to explain why the Southern Baptist Convention was being organized. Johnson wrote the address. Two ideas dominated those two documents. The ideas were denominationalism and sectionalism. These ideas have provided for Southern Baptists much of their local color throughout the history of the Convention.

First, sectionalism. We Southern Baptists have not always spoken with candor on why the Convention was formed. We have often smoke-screened this part of our heritage. Theological differences between Baptists North and South had nothing to do with the denominational division. And Baptists at Augusta clearly said so: "Let not the extent of this disunion be exaggerated . . . , " they said, "Northern and Southern Baptists are still brethren. They differ in no article of faith."[9] Nor did ecclesiology or missionary neglect of the South by the North contribute significantly.

The issue was *slavery* which was a part of the larger issue of a *growing sectionalism* in the country. Following the invention of the cotton gin, Baptists of the South became Southern Baptists, a people who for years to come would defend the Southern way of life. But, that defense would begin cracking in the 1950s. Here is a part of our heritage which we must receive and confess and forgive.

Slavery gave local color to nineteenth-century Southern Baptists just as it did to every other major Southern denomination. Bigotry was not a Baptist monopoly. But my main point here is that the slavery issue fueled the sectionalism of Baptists in the South. No pun intended, it "colored" the Southern Baptist Convention. It colored it not only in terms of race, but more generally in terms of *region*. Again, Baptists *in* the South became *Southern* Baptists, a *regional* people. But that would begin cracking in the 1940s.

The organization of the Southern Baptist Convention was also colored by cooperative denominationalism. As often pointed out by historians, Southern Baptists formed in 1845 a new kind of denominational structure, one that was more connectional, more centralized, and more cooperative than any heretofore known among Baptists. They forsook the decentralized,

[9]*SBC Annual 1845*, 17.

societal approach of the North and formed one Convention with two boards, the Domestic and Foreign Mission Boards, which were accountable to the one Convention.

What would cement this new denominationalism? What would hold it together? Would it be theological and creedal? And the answer was given: "We have constructed for our basis no new creed; acting in this manner upon a Baptist aversion for all creeds but the Bible."[10] Southern Baptists waited eighty years to adopt their first confession, and then only reluctantly and under pressure. When they adopted the confession of 1925, however, a crack appeared in the anticonfessional posture of the Convention.

If the new denomination was not to be united by theological uniformity, then by what? Article 2 of the Constitution answered forthrightly: "It shall be the design of this Convention to promote Foreign and Domestic Missions, and other important objects connected with the Redeemer's kingdom." They were organizing a plan, as the preamble to the Constitution states, "for eliciting, combining, and directing the energies of the whole denomination in one sacred effort, for the propagation of the gospel."[11] *Cooperation* was the *method*. *Missions* "and other important objects connected with the Redeemer's kingdom" was the *motive*. That was what happened at Augusta.

The ideas of sectionalism and denominationalism were intensified by I. T. Tichenor in 1882. In that year he became the executive secretary of a crippled Home Mission Board, and moved it from Marion, Alabama, to Atlanta, Georgia. In order to save the board from an imminent death, Tichenor had to do two things. He had to guarantee Southern Baptists' allegiance to the *Southern* board by breaking their support for the Home Mission Society of Baptists in the North which was more influential and affluent. He did so by appealing to Southerners' *sectionalism*. Also, he had to persuade Southern Baptists to work through a central denominational mission board rather than through the increasingly powerful state convention boards. He did so by pointing to the value of a *cooperative* denominationalism. He was successful in both cases.

So the Georgia Tradition colored the Southern Baptist Convention with an intense sectionalism and a devout cooperative denominationalism. For years the sectionalism restricted us in both our relationship with blacks and our outreach beyond the Confederacy. Our denominationalism, however,

---

[10]*SBC Annual 1845*, 19.
[11]*SBC Annual 1845*, 3.

provided a cooperation between churches and the Convention which should explain part of the genius of the Convention.

The Tennessee Tradition. The fourth tradition that went into the shaping of the synthesis came out of Tennessee. J. R. Graves was the central figure. Landmarkism was the movement. And Nashville and Memphis, the respective homes of Graves, were the places. To describe this tradition, so powerful in its impact on the synthesis, let us use the words "questionable honor." I will forego an enumeration of the Landmark distinctives, knowing that you are aware of them. But let me make the crucial point. Landmarkism, with its emphasis on local church succession-ism and the exclusive validity of Baptist churches, Baptist ministers, and Baptist ordinances, gave to Southern Baptists a claim to fame as being the only ones God had. Over against the restorationism of the Campbellites and the pedobaptism of the Methodists and Presbyterians, Landmarkism gave to Southern Baptists a "trail of blood" which said the oldest is the best. The assumption was that longevity validates truth.

Many Southern Baptists, however, believed the nonhistorical assump-tion and felt much better about who they were. Much of our antiecumenism and almost all of our sectarianism may be traced to the Tennessee Tradition. In other words, Landmarkism gave us an identity based on a fallacious history. By the turn of the twentieth century, Southern Baptists were being told it was not so. Cracks in the Landmark structure continued in the twentieth century and even to this day create something of an identity crisis for some Southern Baptists.

Now a word of summary concerning these four traditions. By 1900 this Southern Baptist goulash had been mixed and stirred and looked something like this. The Charleston Tradition had poured into the bowl *order*, which provided denominational connectionalism, a theological consensus, and, while never neglecting evangelism, facilitated ministerial education as an important object of the Redeemer's Kingdom. Charleston provided leader-ship and stability for an emerging denomination. It gave us a *churchly* identity.

The Sandy Creek Tradition contributed *ardor*, which provided revivalistic momentum, an adventuresome spirit and a love for liberty. It gave us an *evangelistic* identity.

The "Southernness" of the Georgia Tradition gave us a *cultural* identity. Just as important, however, it intensified the denominational identity of a close-knit organizational connectionalism which was present at Charleston. It gave us a method and a motive for cooperation.

The Tennessee Tradition yielded an *ecclesiological* identity resulting in a narrow sectarianism. In doing so, however, it overlooked the older and continuing Charleston ecclesiology, which affirmed the universal church. However, the Tennessee Tradition gave a sense of pride to nineteenth-century Southern Baptists.

The First Half of the Twentieth Century

A process of denominationalizing had begun among Southern Baptists before the dawn of the twentieth century. A "Southern Baptist spirit" was developing around distinctly Southern Baptist institutions. The synthesis solidified around several institutions and movements m the twentieth century.

Institutions and the Denominationalizing Process. First, the nature and organizational plan of the 1845 Southern Baptist Convention strengthened the synthesis. A comprehensive denominational structure, based on cooperation, encouraged *devotion* to and *financial responsibility for* diverse types of Christian ministry. The synthesis of the Convention was missionary, not doctrinal, in nature.

Second, the Foreign and Home Mission Boards *symbolized* the synthesis. Both were begun in 1845. Both elicited support from Baptists all over the South and Southwest. Both became a bond of denominational loyalty.

Third, Baptist colleges, though formed under state conventions rather than the Southern Baptist Convention, nevertheless helped to create a Southern Baptist consciousness.

Fourth, the Southern Baptist Theological Seminary, while organized outside the Southern Baptist Convention, was widely and correctly perceived as a Southern Baptist institution. It, and the five other Southern Baptist seminaries which followed in the twentieth century, afforded Southern Baptists a theological educational enterprise which has to make Furman and Boyce and Carroll and Dement and Stealey grin all over heaven. Rooted in the Word of God and made possible by Southern Baptist cooperation, these six schools, which contain twenty percent of all theological students in the United States and Canada, have provided Southern Baptists with justifiable denominational pride.

Fifth, the Woman's Missionary Union, organized in 1888, underscored missions as the one sacred effort of the Convention. Women became denominationalists by giving their money, encouraging the local churches to give theirs, and by educating the children, young people, and the men in missionary education.

Sixth, by 1891 the Southern Baptist Convention had its own Sunday School Board. No institution has done more to denominationalize and synthesize Southern Baptists. It lassoed every interdenominational movement that came down the churchly pike in the latter nineteenth and early twentieth centuries and promptly "Southern Baptistized" it. This was true of the interdenominational Baptist Young People's Union, the interdenominational Baracca Sunday Schools, and the interdenominational student movement. The Sunday School Board has provided a common literature, challenged our educational programs to set common standards of excellence, stressed the common task of evangelism, and produced and published in 1940 the first "Southern Baptist Book of Common Prayer"— the *Broadman*, and later, *Baptist Hymnal*. It has united us with everything from Vacation Bible School to the January Bible Study, common Christian stock in most Southern Baptist churches. While unifying us, it has not uniformed us; no organization can or should do that. The denominational unity created by the board has not only respected Southern Baptist diversity; it has, when not under critics' attacks, encouraged it.

Other Developments. All of the other agencies and commissions of the Convention have made signal contributions to the Southern Baptist synthesis. But time precludes their mention. I would, however, call your attention to three other developments in the twentieth century which must not be overlooked. They are the Executive Committee, the 1925 confession of faith, and the 1925 Cooperative Program.

Formed in 1917, the Executive Committee has become the administrative and organizational linchpin of the Convention. It has been of enormous value in coordinating a mushrooming denomination.

The Baptist Faith and Message of 1925 was a kind of Southern Baptist Elizabethan settlement, a theological statement broad enough to include all Southern Baptists and narrow enough to affirm the Christian fundamentals. This part of the Southern Baptist synthesis has come under attack in recent years. It is now accused by some critics of being too broad and not strict enough.

The Cooperative Program became the financial synthesis of Southern Baptists. It is the lifeline of the Southern Baptist way for doing the gospel. Without its development in 1925, the Southern Baptist Convention would today be a different people. If Southern Baptists fail to increase their support for the Cooperative Program, the Convention will be different in the future.

The Southern Baptist Synthesis: Its Stresses

Since World War II, and particularly in the last two decades [1960s and 1970s], phenomenal stress has been placed on the Southern Baptist synthesis. Let me identify some of the stress points.

There has been a *cultural* stress. This has been partially due to the geographical expansion of Southern Baptists. Until World War II, the geographical base of the Convention remained fairly constant, centered in the Southeast, South, and Southwest. Between 1845 and 1942 only six additional states were added to the original fourteen state conventions affiliated with the Convention. Today [1980] we have thrity-four state conventions and we have churches in all fifty states.

Two forces, *migration* and a *continuing emphasis on evangelism*, have created this new geographical distribution. But the expansion has placed pressure on the "Southernness" of Southern Baptist life. Geographical expansion has inevitably produced a growing cultural pluralism in the Convention. While still a predominantly regional, white, middle-class denomination, the synthesis is beginning to be challenged by cultural diversity.

For example, approximately thirty percent of the churches in the Southern Baptist General Convention of California are predominantly ethnic minority. And an estimated ninety percent of Southern Baptist churches in California have multiethnic memberships. And the trend, for which we thank God, is that more ethnic minorities are coming into our churches every year. While thanksgiving is in order for the increasing cosmopolitanism of Southern Baptist life and our evangelistic successes, we must face the need to orient new people to a denominational heritage they have inherited but do not know and many do not understand. In addition to some Bold Going, Bold Growing, and Bold Giving, we must have some Bold *Knowing* of what holds this Convention together. And we can do this without resorting to an indoctrination of our past regionalism and Landmarkism.

Cultural diversity has come at Southern Baptists from another direction. The civil rights struggle of the 1960s with a focus on blacks and the human rights struggles of the 1970s with a focus on women have both also stressed the synthesis. And until we update our Baptist freedom, so central to our heritage, and make our Convention and churches genuinely open to all Southern Baptists, the stress will continue.

A second stress point is *denominational loyalty*. Southern Baptists stayed a country mile away from the organized ecumenical movement of the early part of this century. And yet some Southern Baptists who would have been the sharpest critics of that kind of ecumenism are right in the middle of a new fundamentalist ecumenism. Encouraged by the boom of the electronic church, and stimulated by the activity of parachurch groups such as the Moral Majority, this new nondenominationalism has made unbelievable inroads into Southern Baptist life. Several months back, Bill Pinson had a little article in Baptist Press entitled, "Can Southern Baptists Survive the Evangelicals?" His point was—and it is a good one—that Southern Baptist life could be eroded by the pervasive presence of the new fundamentalist ecumenism. The ecumenical threat to Southern Baptist denominational loyalty does not come from the left; it comes from the right. Some Southern Baptists have more loyalty to non-Southern Baptist seminaries, non-Southern Baptist agencies, and non-Southern Baptist movements than they do to the denominational enterprise.

And this allegiance manifests another stress point, and that is *financial*. Statistics on the Cooperative Program have continued to look good. What these statistics do not demonstrate, however, is how much Southern Baptist money is being siphoned off from the Cooperative Program and channeled to nondenominational causes. Said one associate of the PTL ministries: "We don't keep statistics on denominational preferences because that goes against what Jim [Bakker] meant for us to be—interdenominational. But a good per cent of our supporters are Baptists, I expect."[12] And Pat Robertson's Christian Broadcast Network indicates that Baptists, the network's largest denominational contributor, give about thirty percent of what funnels in. It would be interesting and disconcerting to compare the total receipts of the Convention's Radio and Television Commission to the total amount given by Southern Baptists to the nondenominational electronic church. And do you imagine that the Christian Life Commission will get as much Southern Baptist money this year as Jerry Falwell's Moral Majority?

A leading critic of the Southern Baptist agencies is reported recently to have told some churches in Virginia to "give at least enough" to the Cooperative Program "to have the maximum number of messengers" at the Southern Baptist Convention so as to control the Convention. No wonder that some among us would resist a revision of the Convention's

---

[12]As I went back to reconstruct the documentation for this originally oral presentation, I could not find the source of this quotation. However, one who remembers the circumstances of ministries such as PTL can hardly doubt the affirmation that many supporters of this charismatic ministry were Baptists.

Constitution which would call for a more liberal financial contribution in order to participate in the denominational process. Such a revision would impact churches on either end of the theological spectrum.

There are at least two other stress points which are integrally related. And they are *creedal* and *theological* in nature. But they shall be discussed in the next lecture.[13]

The Southern Baptist Synthesis: Its Future

Well, is the synthesis breaking up? No, not breaking up; cracking, yes. But maybe better, it is reshaping. Some of the elements in the synthesis needed to be cracked. Our regionalism and our racism had to go if Southern Baptists were to be true to the gospel they proclaimed. And our Landmarkism simply could not withstand our devotion to the study of scripture or our heritage which came from Charleston, or our presence in a new world. We had another ecclesiology, both biblical and historical, which had to emerge. Martin Marty recently referred to the Southern Baptist Convention as the Catholic Church of the South. He meant, I guess, that we are big and powerful and semiestablished. He knows us well enough, however, to have meant that there is a kind of "protestant catholicity" among Southern Baptists. We have always been a diverse people. The statement is not made simply as a plea for tolerance, though that in itself would justify it. It is made as a historical fact.

We came from sophisticated cities like Charleston and from rustic crossroads like Sandy Creek. We came educated and uneducated. We came with evangelism and we came with educational institutions. We came with the local church and the universal church. We came with Calvinistic theology, Arminian theology, and no theology. We came applauding confessional statements, and we came deploring confessional statements. We came affirming culture and rebuking culture. But mostly, I think, we just came together. That togetherness is a marvel to those of us on the inside and a mystery to those on the outside. And it is the togetherness, the diversity, the synthesis, which we must receive and confess and forgive. Above all, we must know it. Or there will be no hope for the denomination's future.

---

[13]See the next chapter in this volume.

The Inerrancy Debate:
A Comparative Study
of Southern Baptist Controversies[1]

Southern Baptists are presently in their fourth major debate in the twentieth century. The first came in the mid-1920s and is generally known as the Fundamentalist Controversy. The second came in the early 1960s and is known as the Elliott Controversy. The third began in 1969 and lasted through the early 1970s and is known as the Broadman Controversy. And now the fourth, the Inerrancy Debate, began in the late 1970s and the end is not in sight.

My purpose is to compare the contemporary conflict with the three which preceded it. I will try to provide as much of the relevant pieces of each story so that you can see clearly the contrasts and similarities, though there are obvious limitations in an address of this length.

The Historical Context of the Debates

One should begin with the historical contexts of the debates. And contexts are both national and denominational. The spirit of the times will not necessarily determine debates within Christian denominations, but they certainly contribute. They can fuel the fire or they can dampen it. They can prolong it or they can abbreviate it. They can focus it or they can distract it.

Without question, the social matrix of the current controversy is more inflammatory than any of the other three Southern Baptists have known.

---

[1] I presented this address as lecture 2 in the Carver-Barnes Lectures at Southeastern Baptist Theological Seminary, Wake Forest, North Carolina, 4-5 November 1980. In reading this article, keep in mind the date, 1980. The material was published in *Outlook* (March-April 1981) and later in *Baptist History and Heritage* 16/2 (April 1981): 12ff. It is reprinted by permission of the Baptist History and Heritage Society, Brentwood TN. As do many others, often when I speak, I fail to document carefully with footnotes because I do not have publishing in mind. That was the case with this lecture. The only alteration I have made from the initial material, therefore, has been the addition of footnotes where I could provide them. To remain as close to the original presentations as possible, I have left untouched my signals for emphasis in the oral presentation, such things as under linings, bold, and italics. I have also retained the oral nature of the sentences.

Politically and religiously, it is a time of "hit lists." The Southern Baptist inerrantists appear to be a part of both the new religious and political right wing. "The world is not moving toward toleration but away from it," said Martin E. Marty.[2] And most, I think, would judge that Marty is correct in his observation.

Moving away from toleration—that was *partially true* of the 1920s and the first Fundamentalist attack on the Southern Baptist Convention. *Only* partially true, however. Because while the twenties were characterized by an impulse to use coercion to preserve the past, as expressed in the aggressiveness of the Ku Klux Klan and the introduction of legislation to prevent the teaching of evolution in public schools, they were also "the roaring twenties." It was an age of flappers and speakeasies, of frolicking and gaiety. Dual moods existed then and now, but it seems that the eighties have begun as a more serious and far more conservative time. Clothing is now dark gray!

If the national turn to the right was partially true of the twenties, it was not true at all of the early sixties. The criticism of Ralph Elliott and his book, *The Message of Genesis* was not buoyed by culture. For the sixties (not even the early sixties) were not dominated by repression but by an emerging permissiveness and liberation. Nor was it true of the days of the Broadman Controversy in the early seventies, though slightly more so than the sixties.

Thus, the right-wing movement in the denomination today has a stronger ally in the culture than have previous movements among Southern Baptists. This decade may be a time of trying men's souls, but it may also become a time for coercing men's souls. The Norrisite attack on the Southern Baptist Convention was a problem within the Convention for about five years. The real heat was between 1921 and 1926. The Elliott Controversy lasted almost three years (1961–1963), as did the Broadman debate (1969–1972). We have already had two years of the present conflict, and according to the Pressler-Patterson plan, it will last as long as it takes to gain control of Convention agencies.[3] They have announced a ten-year plan, and there is no good reason not to believe them. They have promised

---

[2]While I could not retrieve the documentation for Marty's statement, I imagine it came from an issue of *Context*.

[3]From the year 2003, the date of this writing, one can look back and know precisely how long the national controversy lasted. It began in 1979 and ended in 1990.

persistence. Again, the general atmosphere of the age may help sustain the movement.

But what about the denominational context of the controversies? In the 1920s the Southern Baptist Convention was not as vulnerable to critics as it is today. A stronger sense of denominational loyalty existed. Leaders within the Convention knew each other better. In addition, in the first half of the decade (1919–1924) Southern Baptists were engaged in their first massive financial campaign, an effort to raise seventy-five million dollars. That campaign failed, incidentally. It raised fifty-nine million, and the Convention agencies were left with heavy debts. Part of the reason for that failure was the Fundamentalist undercutting of denominational allegiance.

So dollars dominated the 1920s for Southern Baptists. These dollars were in the form of the Seventy-Five Million Campaign and the national depression. Surviving as a strong denomination was more important to most Southern Baptists than hearing what Frank Norris and C. P. Stealey had to say. One other thing should be noted. In the 1920s Southern Baptists had not experienced any serious previous denominational squabbles. Residuals of former tensions were not as present then as today.

In the Elliott Controversy, Southern Baptists had just emerged from the secure cocoon of "the religious 50s." The Convention was expanding in every way. A strong denominational consciousness had gotten stronger. And the Elliott Controversy was thirty-five years removed from the Fundamentalist fire of the 1920s. There were no smoldering ashes to fan into a blaze.

From the Elliott Controversy of the early 1960s to the present debate, however, there were ashes. And they have flared again and again. The sense of victory in the removal of Ralph Elliott from his teaching post at Midwestern Baptist Theological Seminary fueled a militancy which became more and more assertive.

By the time of the Broadman Controversy, beginning in 1969, religious America had gone through what Sydney Ahlstrom called "the tumultuous 60s." Southern Baptists were acquainted with the phrase. In addition to the Elliott Controversy at Midwestern, New Orleans Seminary and Southeastern Seminary had theological rumblings, as well as did Southern Seminary. Also, throughout the decade, the prophetic posture of the Christian Life Commission on the issue of civil rights caused consternation. Not once, but three times motions were presented on the floor of the Convention to abolish the commission. Walker Knight, editor of *Home Missions* magazine, was also in the fray. A minor theological fuss developed in 1969 when Broadman Press published Convention president

W. A. Criswell's book entitled *Why I Preach that the Bible Is Literally True*. And four months before the release of volume 1 of *The Broadman Bible Commentary*, a motion was presented at the New Orleans Convention "that the Convention urge the Sunday School Board to have all writers to sign a statement with each manuscript of belief in the infallibility of the entire Bible, and that the seminaries secure from professors a like statement annually."[4] The motion failed, but served as a prelude to the Broadman Controversy.

From 1969 to 1973, every one of the twelve volumes of *The Broadman Bible Commentary* was criticized. By Convention action, volume 1 had to be withdrawn and rewritten. Following the Broadman conflict, the issues in it and the Elliott Controversy were kept alive by three institutions, none of which are Southern Baptist-related agencies. One is the Mid-America Baptist Theological Seminary, located in Memphis, Tennessee. Advertising that all professors subscribe to the plenary verbal inspiration of scripture, the school receives much—maybe most—of its funding from Southern Baptist churches which apparently prefer to support it on an independent basis than to support the six Southern Baptist seminaries. The school has maintained a low profile in Convention politics. The mere presence of the school, however, has nurtured controversy in Southern Baptist circles.

A second organization has not been quiet. Begun in March 1973, at the First Baptist Church of Atlanta, Georgia, "The Baptist Faith and Message Fellowship" has agitated for a strict adherence to the confessional statement adopted in 1963 during the Elliott Controversy. The Fellowship has consistently attacked what it perceives as doctrinal impurity among Southern Baptists through its newspaper, *The Southern Baptist Journal*.

Finally, but most significantly, *Christianity Today*, an interdenominational journal edited by Harold Lindsell, became a major tool for "channeling all theological issues into the inerrancy debate."[5] Lindsell, a Southern Baptist church member whose ministry has been interdenominational in context, also wrote two books, *The Battle for the Bible* (1976) and *The Bible in the Balance* (1979), which were very critical of Southern Baptists. In 1978 Lindsell was elected president of the Baptist Faith and Message Fellowship.

By the spring of 1979, when Paige Patterson and Paul Pressler announced plans to elect a Convention president committed to inerrancy

---

[4]*SBC Annual 1969*, 58.
[5]*The Christian Century* 97/35 (5 November 1980): 1061.

and to end an alleged drift toward "liberalism" in the Convention, the fires had been stoked. They were stoked by twenty years of denominational tension. Patterson himself said that the present move was brought on "as much as anything else by the unwillingness of certain groups to really deal with the Broadman Commentary issue." The fires were stoked also by the erosion of denominational loyalty as represented in the Baptist Faith and Message Fellowship, by Mid-America Seminary, and by the Criswell Bible Institute where Patterson is president. And the fires were stoked, thirdly, by Harold Lindsell's writings.

The cumulative effect of all these movements, plus the cultural matrix, freight the denomination with a weight it has not had to bear in past controversies. It makes the present conflict, therefore, far more serious.

One other factor, often overlooked, is that Southern Baptists have been in a "generational crease" for the last five to seven years. We have had a changing of the guard in almost every agency and institution as well as in some of the larger pulpits in Southern Baptist life. Denominational leadership has not been able to solidify around an E. Y. Mullins or a Herschel H. Hobbs. People do not know each other well. The result is a very low trust level in the denomination. Polarization is more acute than it has ever been in our denomination's history. And that is the context of the inerrancy debate, nationally and denominationally.

The Issues of the Debates

Now, let us turn to a second area of comparison: the issues of the debates. All four of the controversies have had the Bible as a focal point of the rhetoric surrounding the controversies. The issues, however, cannot be limited to "the Battle for the Bible." That is to generalize to the point of distortion. Southern Baptists have never had a problem with the sole authority of scripture. In fact, it is that very Baptist principle which has made us reluctant to absolutize any human words, any confession of faith, or any creed for the Bible.

Our souls, like Luther's, have always been captive to the Word of God. Southern Baptists have affirmed that the Bible, not natural revelation, not churchly tradition, not bishops—Baptist or otherwise, not creedal documents, is our only authority for belief and behavior. So to keep the record clear, the question is not the authoritative nature of scripture. But the question has been one of *interpretation* and *approach* to our common authority. Diversity of interpretation *about* the Bible is not the same as *denial of* the Bible. And that is exactly why Baptists have had as one of their basic convictions the concept of soul freedom. Running through all four of the debates, therefore, are two themes: (1) the affirmation that the Bible is the Word of God, (2) the fact that Baptists have differences of opinion among themselves concerning the interpretation of scripture.

There was a specific issue in the Fundamentalist movement of the 1920s. It was the issue of evolution. In 1923 J. Frank Norris said, "I intend to start a fight on evolution and on the denomination and I never expect to stop it until it is extracted, root and branch, and if the denomination is split, it will split over the question of evolution." The one phrase which C. P. Stealey, a Norris ally, wanted in article 3 of the 1925 Confession was the phrase "And not by Evolution."[6] Any interpretation of the Bible which said that God used the evolutionary process in creation was portrayed as denying the Bible.

Another issue in the 1920s was J. Frank Norris's vitriolic attacks on denominational leaders and institutions. L. R. Scarborough, president of Southwestern Seminary during the controversy, wrote a little tract entitled "The Fruits of Norrisism." He called Norrisism "an old cult under a new name" which "gives nothing to associational, state, or home missions and only enough to foreign missions to get representation in the convention."[7] Norris's hobby, it was said, was "tending to the convention." He and C. P. Stealey focused the issue on professors in Southern Baptist colleges and seminaries. Professors Hall and Dow of Baylor, Staten of William Jewell, Poteat of Wake Forest University, and Sampey of Southern Seminary all came under the editorial gun of C. P. Stealey.

In both the Elliott and Broadman Controversies the central word was not "evolution" but "infallibility." Specifically, divergent interpretations of the book of Genesis constituted the center of the conflicts. In the Elliott Controversy the spotlight shone most brightly on Genesis 1–11. Opponents of Elliott claimed that to refuse to take these chapters literally was to deny the Bible. His supporters claimed that the important thing about the Bible was its message, not its literary nature. Genesis 22 and the proposed sacrifice of Isaac by Abraham was the pivotal, but certainly not the only, passage of interpretation under debate in the Broadman Controversy.

---

[6]For the Norris and Stealey quotations, see my *Not a Silent People: Controversies That Have Shaped Southern Baptists*, rev. ed. (Macon GA: Smyth & Helwys Publishing, 1995) 59, 64.

[7]As cited in Robert A. Baker, *A Baptist Source Book: With Particular Reference to Southern Baptists* (Nashville: Broadman Press, 1966) 196-97.

A spirit of antidenominationalism, so prevalent in J. Frank Norris, did not dominate these two controversies. What was under criticism in the Elliott Controversy was a Southern Baptist seminary professor, the institution he taught in, the book he wrote, and Broadman Press which published it. Because Henton Davies, the writer of the Genesis commentary in *The Broadman Bible Commentary*, was not a Southern Baptist professor, the criticism was directed at the book itself and primarily at Broadman Press for publishing it.

From "evolution" to "infallibility," the code word of the present controversy is "inerrancy." While there is no indication that it will remain so, the inerrancy advocates are far more general in their accusations than critics in past controversies. Baylor University has undergone some scrutiny recently but with no major consequence. And the names of six or seven seminary professors were listed as unorthodox last spring by Paige Patterson, but no charges, to my knowledge, have been filed with their respective boards of trustees.

At this stage of the debate the issue does not appear primarily to be biblical or theological. The issue appears to be—and has been for two years—political. The very first action of the inerrancy advocates was to construct political organizations to see that an "inerrancy" president was elected at the Convention. After organizing meetings in several states, they supported Adrian Rogers in 1979 for president, and he was elected on the first ballot. Following that, the politicizing has intensified. When Rogers declined to serve a second term, this group threw their support behind and helped elect Bailey Smith. The political issue was clarified almost two months ago when Paul Pressler announced: "We are going for the jugular." He exegeted that to mean that his political caucus was out to control Southern Baptist institutions. And Pressler is aware that "the jugular" of these institutions is the trustees. He said, "We are going for having knowledgeable, Bible-centered, Christ-honoring trustees of all our institutions, who are not going to sit there like a bunch of dummies and rubber stamp everything that's presented to them."[8] So the primary issue at present is political.

No single person or institution or book is the object. And in this the inerrancy controversy differs from the Broadman, the Elliott, and, to some

---

[8]As cited in Walter B. Shurden and Randy Shepley, *Going for the Jugular: A Documentary History of the SBC Holy War* (Macon GA: Mercer University Press, 1996) 56.

degree, the 1920s debate. Inerrancy advocates think the problem is systemic to the denomination, not isolated to specific cases. *The result is that they are going after the machinery of the denomination as well as the minds of Southern Baptists*. But that leads us to a third area of comparison and that is methods used in the controversies.

The Methods of the Debates

When Norris and Stealey went after the issue of evolution in the 1920s, the attack was fourfold. First, the leadership, especially Norris, was *charismatic*. Norris was a spellbinding preacher by anybody's standards. His language was concrete and crusading, intimidating and unambiguous. He once described the mayor of Fort Worth and his associates as a "two-by-four, simian-headed, sawdust-brained, bunch of grafters." He accused them of "tampering with the wires" of his radio station and declared that "some of you low-down devils that monkey around this property, arrange for your undertaker before you come around here."[9] The audience cheered. Norris was more like Urban II at Claremont, whipping up the troops for a crusade, than he was Eisenhower, staying in the general's quarters and mapping out strategy. Norris had no plan; he had a pulpit.

Second, the approach was *journalistic*. Norris had *The Searchlight* and Stealey had *The Baptist Messenger*, the Oklahoma state paper.

Third, Stealey led the fight for a creedal statement. He was on the committee, chaired by E. Y. Mullins, to draw up Southern Baptists' first confessional statement. But in the end, it was not binding enough for Stealey. That was 1925. One year later the Convention adopted the McDaniel Statement, a strong antievolution statement that satisfied Stealey. But he and his associates were not through. Three days after the McDaniel Statement was adopted, a resolution was presented, saying "that this convention request all its institutions and boards and their missionary representatives" to sign the McDaniel Statement.[10] Stealey then engineered his home-state convention to withhold undesignated funds of the Cooperative Program from Southern Baptist seminaries whose faculties refused to sign the statement. The funds were released in two years even though two of the three faculties did not sign the statement.

---

[9] See Shurden, *Not a Silent People*, 58.

[10] Shurden, *Not a Silent People*, 64-65. See also David William Downs, "The McDaniel Statement: An Investigation of Creedalism in the Southern Baptist Convention" (Th.M. thesis, Southern Baptist Theological Seminary, Louisville, 1980).

In the Elliott Controversy there was no charismatic-led attack such as that of Norris. K. Owen White, pastor of First Church, Houston Texas, and president of the Convention in 1963, was one of the biggest pastoral names. Nor were there private papers involved. The state Baptist papers, however, were more widely divided than in the Norris controversy. Also, some critics of Elliott arranged pre-Convention planning conferences, but these were primarily designed to strategize for resolutions and motions on the floor of the Convention. No systematic effort was made to control the election of trustees for all Convention agencies, though there was some effort—and success—in determining the board of Midwestern Seminary. And interestingly enough, the confessional statement which came at this time was not the work of those opposed to Elliott but of the established leadership of the Convention. It was an establishment effort at peacekeeping.

Like the Elliott Controversy, the criticism of *The Broadman Bible Commentary* was noncharismatic in leadership, widely debated in the Baptist press (with more editors supporting Broadman than they had Elliott), and vigorously aired on the floor of the Convention. There were no independent papers and no ongoing political organization or refined orchestration to control the agencies. The effort was *singular* in purpose—to get the Sunday School Board by Convention action to withdraw volume 1 of the commentary. It was withdrawn and rewritten and while the confessional statement of 1963 was used, unsuccessfully, in 1972 to try and ban all twelve volumes, the statement did not play a major role in the strategy of the Broadman critics.

What about the inerrancy advocates of today? First, they have run up against a group of editors of state Baptist papers who have, I think, almost all editorialized against the movement. Not in the 1920s, 1960s, or 1970s have the Baptist papers been so solid in this opposition. In fact, in the other three controversies there was a division of editorial opinion. This does not appear to be the case today. However, two independent papers, *The Southern Baptist Journal* and *The Southern Baptist Advocate* serve as the media for inerrancy.

The Baptist Faith and Message of 1963 is being used in the current debate very much like the 1925 confession was used by Stealey, but more intensely. In fact, an obvious effort is being made to redefine the confession, particularly the article on Holy Scripture, into stricter words and a more restricted interpretation. Resolution 16 on "Doctrinal Integrity"[11] is

---

[11]*SBC Annual 1980*, 51.

the most recent attempt at revising the confession and transforming it into a creed. A "liberal," in the minds of the inerrancy advocates, is now one who believes in the Baptist Faith and Message as adopted by the Southern Baptist Convention in 1963.

Notice what has happened to Southern Baptists and creedalism. In 1845, the Convention said it had no creed but the Bible. In 1925, it adopted its first confession. W. W. Barnes, professor of Church History at Southwestern Seminary and one for whom this lecture series is named, said joyfully in 1934 that the confession was received by Southern Baptist churches generally with "a tremendous outburst of silence." Barnes went on, however, to make some ominous remarks about the Convention adopting doctrinal statements. Said Barnes:

> The reception that that creed has received, or perhaps one should say, has not received, seems to suggest that Southern Baptists are not yet ready for doctrinal centralization, but the first step has been taken. It may be another century, but if and when the doctrinal question again arises, succeeding generations can point to 1925 and say that the Southern Baptist Convention, having once adopted a creed, can do so again. Perhaps by that time other centralizing forces will have developed and the convention may have the means and the method of compelling congregations to take notice of the creed then adopted.[12]

Barnes's gloomy forecast was wrong on two counts. It did not take a century, it took only thirty-eight years. And to this point no effort has been made to force congregations to adopt it. But, Barnes saw the creedal trend clearly. First, there is a call for inerrancy. Second, the confessional statement is interpreted to guard inerrancy. Third, there are suggestions to revise the confession to guarantee inerrancy. Fourth, there is a call for the imposition of the revised confession to make binding the inerrancy. Creedalism is not creeping among us; it is galloping!

The unique thing about the inerrancy debate, however, is not creedalism. Nor is it the most dangerous thing. The unique thing and the most dangerous thing is that we now have for the first time in the Southern Baptist Convention a highly organized, apparently well-funded, partisan political party who are going not only for the minds of the Southern Baptist people but for the machinery of the Southern Baptist Convention.

---

[12]William Wright Barnes, *The Southern Baptist Convention: A Study in the Development of Ecclesiology* (Seminary Hill TX: published by the author, 1934) 60.

Their method is clear. First, they turn out the votes at the annual meeting of the Southern Baptist Convention even if they must bus people in. Second, they seek to elect a Convention president who they believe is committed to their goals. Third, their president appoints a Committee on Committees sensitive to their goals. Fourth, the Committee on Committees names a Committee on Boards sensitive to their goals. Fifth the Committee on Boards nominates to the Convention trustees who are sensitive to their goals. Sixth, you get the votes back out to the Convention to make sure the Committee on Boards's report is accepted. In no controversy in the history of the Southern Baptist Convention has the system been misused this way. Those who say that "this is just the same old thing" are unaware of our heritage.

The Consequences of the Controversies

Well, what have been the consequences of the four controversies? I have intimated this throughout the lecture. But let me summarize.

The consequences of the Norris-Stealey movement? (1) A confession of faith was adopted which was satisfactory to neither side but generally accepted by all. (2) Southern Baptists were unsuccessful in their $75 Million Campaign. (3) A specific antievolution statement was adopted and attempts made to impose it. (4) Norris was discredited, forced from the Convention, and successful in alienating a few ministers and churches from the Convention. (5) Stealey was eventually dismissed from his editorship.

The consequences of the Elliott Controversy? (1) Elliott was dismissed, not for heresy, but for insubordination. He was fired because he would not promise that he would voluntarily refrain from republishing his book. (2) The book was not banned by Convention action, but it was not republished by administrative decision of the Sunday School Board. (3) A young seminary was severely crippled. (4) A second Southern Baptist confession was adopted. (5) The trustees of Midwestern Seminary approved the historical method, but not necessarily the interpretations of *The Message of Genesis*. (6) Seminary professors and the Sunday School Board were placed under a cloud of suspicion.

Consequences of the Broadman Controversy? (1) A book was withdrawn by Convention action. (2) The 1963 Confession became increasingly more visible in the Baptist Faith and Message Fellowship. (3) The suspicion of denominational agencies intensified.

And what shall be the consequences of the Inerrancy Debate? One, of course, cannot be sure, but some things are clear. (1) Polarization is occurring, and there appears to be no arbitrator, no E. Y. Mullins or Herschel Hobbs on the scene. (2) The religion department of one college and the names of seminary professors have been accused of heterodoxy. There will, doubtless, be others. (3) The debate will continue and doubtless intensify. The inerrancy advocates are persistent. They have not been slowed down by all the state editors, nor by a 1979 Convention resolution rebuking their activities, nor by a mild rebuke by one of the most influentially conservative voices in the Convention, W. A. Criswell, nor by defeat at several state conventions. Some have begun to see the gravity of the problem and are countering with quasipolitical movements. (4) The debate could jeopardize Bold Missions in the same way that the Fundamentalist Debate of the 1920s helped wreck the $75 Million Campaign.[13]

Someone asked a French priest what he did during the revolution. He answered, "I survived." Let us hope and pray that the Southern Baptist synthesis, so rich in diversity, so flawed by the likes of us sinners, so used by God despite the flaws, shall be sustained.

---

[13][Editor's note. The "$75 Million Campaign" (begun in 1919 for mission outreach) ended in 1925 with $58.6 million, short of the goal but a significant sum for the time. The "Bold Missions Thrust" campaign was launched in 1978 as a concerted effort to reach the world with the Gospel by the year 2000.]

What "Being Baptist" Meant for Southern Baptists during World War II[1]

My purpose is to describe the Baptist identity from the perspective of Southern Baptists during the years from 1938 to 1946. In other words, I am concerned with a single question: What did *being Baptist* mean for Southern Baptists during those years? The focus, therefore, is not, as the title may suggest, on Southern Baptists' attitudes toward war or their commitment, or lack of it, to peacemaking during World War II.[2] Rather, the concern here is to depict Southern Baptists' understanding of the Baptist identity during the war years.

Moreover, I am not seeking to describe the major features of the Southern Baptist Convention itself during those years. Except as those issues may have impacted their perception of the Baptist identity, I will not address Southern Baptists' celebrated commitment to denominational evangelism and missions, their passion for Christian education at the seminary and college levels, their concern—indeed, almost fixation—for the denomination's financial solvency, their growth and expansion patterns, their social concerns or lack of them, their constitutional revisions and bylaw changes, the almost total lack of women in their deliberations, or other such factors characterizing the internal life of the denomination. While important—even crucial—issues for the denomination's history, these have been addressed in varying degrees in the three standard denominational histories by W. W. Barnes, Robert A. Baker, and Jesse C. Fletcher.[3] What these denominational histories failed to address clearly,

---

[1] I presented this paper at the annual meeting of the Baptist History and Heritage Society at Pensacola FL, in the spring of 2001. The paper was published in *Baptist History and Heritage* 36/3 (Summer/Fall 2001): 6-27. It is reprinted by permission of the Baptist History and Heritage Society, Brentwood TN.

[2] See *Baptist History and Heritage* 28/2 (April 1993) and Paul R. Dekar, *For the Healing of the Nations: Baptist Peacemakers* (Macon GA: Smyth & Helwys, 1993) for information on this general subject.

[3] The three book-length histories of the Southern Baptist Convention are William Wright Barnes, *The Southern Baptist Convention, 1845–1953* (Nashville: Broadman Press, 1954), Robert A. Baker, *The Southern Baptist Convention and Its People, 1607–1972* (Nashville: Broadman Press, 1974), and Jesse C. Fletcher, *The*

however, was how Southern Baptists understood the Baptist identity during the period of World War II.

World War II began in 1939, although the United States did not enter the fray until 1941. The war ended in 1945. So, the chronological parameters of this paper include one year prior to the war to one year after the war. To fudge on the dates just slightly, therefore, I have portrayed here the Southern Baptist perception of what it meant to be Baptist at the middle of the twentieth century.

Southern Baptist Documents Profiling the Baptist Identity

Where does one go to find answers to the question of what Southern Baptists considered to be the Baptist identity at mid-century? Baptists are not a creedal people—a point made abundantly clear in the sources for this paper—so, one lacks access to a Baptist *Book of Concord*, such as the Lutherans possess, or a *Book of Common Prayer*, such as the Episcopalians own, or even a *Westminster Confession*, such as the Presbyterians treasure.

One could analyze the 1925 Baptist Faith and Message[4] (BFM-25) in search of the Baptist identity, but that was ill-advised in this study for two reasons. One, the BFM-25 did not fit the chronological period under study. And two, even though still on the Southern Baptist books and unrevised at the beginning of the war, the BFM-25 never held much sway or achieved denominational prominence. Certainly it had not been creedalized as a kind of Baptist *Westminster* by the beginning of World War II.

W. W. Barnes, for forty years crusty professor of church history at Southwestern Baptist Theological Seminary, underscored the virtual irrelevance of the confession of faith in Southern Baptist life. In 1934, almost exactly a decade after the adoption of the BFM-25 and in one of the most prophetic books on Southern Baptist history I know anything about, Barnes teased about the denominational insignificance of the BFM-25. He wrote: "The convention adopted the statement by a large majority of the messengers present, but it has been received by Southern Baptist churches generally with a tremendous outburst of silence."[5] So, while the BFM-25 possessed—and possesses—valuable descriptions of the Baptist identity,

---

Southern Baptist Convention: A Sesquicentennial History (Nashville: Broadman & Holman Publishers, 1994).

[4]*SBC Annual 1925*, 71-76.

[5]William Wright Barnes, *The Southern Baptist Convention: A Study in the Development of Ecclesiology* (Fort Worth TX: published by the author, 1934) 8.

it had not shaped the Southern Baptist awareness of the Baptist identity in a powerful way by the beginning of World War II. Indeed, few, if any, references to the BFM-25 appeared in the research for this particular paper. Barnes hit the bull's-eye with his evaluation that the confession of faith had been received "with a tremendous outburst of silence." The lack of influence of the BFM-25 surely may be attributed to the pervasive and profound anticreedal attitude of most Southern Baptists during the first half of the twentieth century. That anticreedal attitude, of course, underwent a radical metamorphosis by the end of the century, as fundamentalists captured and creedalized the SBC.

While I did not utilize the BFM-25 to discover the Southern Baptist understanding of the Baptist identity during the second world war, two genre of sources proved especially valuable for this paper. These two categories were (1) official statements adopted and released by the Southern Baptist Convention and (2) personal statements by prominent Southern Baptists during this period. These sources appeared rather plentiful rather than scarce, as one might expect. More extensive research doubtless would uncover many more of the personal statements, the second category mentioned above. These twin statements of the Baptist identity—the official and the personal—were not only plentiful; they were also amazingly congruent. What the official documents affirmed, the personal statements mirrored and vice versa.

At least three factors explain Southern Baptists' interest in describing the Baptist identity during this era. First, the circumstances of the war itself gave rise to an emergency clarification of the Baptist identity. The evolving fascist nations and totalitarian governments in Germany, Italy, and Japan, caused Baptists, with their historic love of freedom, to underscore their distinctive principles on several different occasions. Second, in addition to the war, the prominence of the ecumenical movement during the decade of the 1940s elicited statements clarifying the Baptist identity. Third, and maybe most significantly, the emerging power of the Roman Catholic Church and its growing influence in America in the first half of the twentieth century awakened grave concern within Southern Baptist ranks. Their affirmation of the Baptist identity often stemmed from a fear of Roman Catholic power and corollary issues related to separation of church and state and religious liberty.

Before profiling the Baptist identity, as Southern Baptists identified it in the era of World War II, I am compelled to pause and say some brief words about the major sources for this study. I do this not because I am trying to follow the rather wooden "Review of the Sources" segment one finds in most doctoral dissertations but for other, more important reasons. The sources require comment for at least two reasons. First, a cursory reading of Southern Baptist history since the 1940s leads one to believe that these documents, especially those emanating from official SBC actions, remain relatively unknown, even among Southern Baptist historians. Second, several of these documents were uniquely and distinctly *Southern* Baptist documents. They were not sources from the broader Baptist heritage merely adapted for Southern Baptist purposes. For example, the Baptist Faith and Message of 1925 was a revision of *The New Hampshire Confession of Faith* of 1833. The BFM-25 was not, therefore, a specifically Southern Baptist document.

Out of the first category of sources, official SBC pronouncements, I focused on five strategic documents. They are the "Report on Interdenominational Relations" of 1938,[6] "A Pronouncement upon Religious Liberty" of 1939,[7] the "Reply to World Council of Churches" of 1940,[8] the very important but little known statement, "Southern Baptists and World Peace" of 1944,[9] and, most importantly, the relatively unknown "Statement of Principles,"[10] proposed in 1942, issued in 1945, and adopted in 1946.

Four personal statements of the Baptist identity comprise the second category of sources, admittedly not as important as the first. These four statements came from the hands of three of the most influential Southern Baptists of the period under study. John R. Sampey, president of the Southern Baptist Theological Seminary from 1929 to 1942 and president of the SBC for the three-year period of 1936–1938, wrote two of the statements. He entitled one "The Faith and Doctrine of Baptists"[11] and the other, his SBC presidential address of 1938, he called "Spiritual Equipment: The Need of the Times."[12]

While Sampey was a central spokesperson for Southern Baptists, the most significant of the personal statements recounting the Baptist identity

---

[6]*SBC Annual 1938*, 24-25.

[7]*SBC Annual 1939*, 114-16.

[8]*SBC Annual 1940*, 99.

[9]*SBC Annual 1944*, 149-50.

[10]*SBC Annual 1946*, 38-39. See also *SBC Annual 1942*, 94; and *SBC Annual 1945*, 59-60.

[11]John R. Sampey, "The Faith and Doctrine of Baptists," *The Christian Index* 119/12 (15 June 1939): 12.

[12]John R. Sampey, "Spiritual Equipment: The Need of the Times," *The Christian Index* 118/19 (12 May 1938): 3-4, 19.

came from George W. Truett, pastor of the First Baptist Church of Dallas, Texas. Truett reigned unchallenged as the single most important Southern Baptist leader during the World War II period until his death on 7 July 1944. In 1939 Truett delivered his presidential address before the Baptist World Alliance meeting in Atlanta. He called it "The Baptist Message and Mission for the World Today."[13] Ernest A. Payne, great British Baptist historian, writing after the BWA congress, hailed Truett's speech as "a masterly exposition of Baptist principles."[14] Indeed, it was a classic. J. B. Lawrence, the enormously influential executive secretary of the Home Mission Board from 1929 to 1954, published in 1945 a brief piece entitled "The People Called Baptists."[15] If J. R. Sampey, George W. Truett, and J. B. Lawrence are not reliable Southern Baptist sources of the Baptist identity during the era of World War II, one probably will search in vain for dependable sources.

How did these Southern Baptist documents and denominational leaders describe the Baptist identity? What issues claimed their attention as they elucidated the Baptist vision of Christianity? I want to address four components of the Baptist identity in order of the prominence Southern Baptists gave them during this period. I do not suggest that this ranking is the correct way for arranging the tiles which comprise the Baptist mosaic. The Baptist identity can be approached from many angles.[16] I am saying, however, that my reading of this period of Southern Baptist history causes me to rank them in the following order.

First, and quite surprisingly, Southern Baptists wrote often and preached repetitively of the centrality of the individual in matters of faith. Those who deplore and derisively dub Baptists as hyperindividualists will not be happy with this assessment. Or maybe they will, for it provides fodder for their point of view. One has to read only a few of the documents to encounter the recurring affirmation that the individual human being was central in describing the Baptist identity.

---

[13]George W. Truett, "The Baptist Message and Mission for the World Today," in *The Life of Baptists in the Life of the World*, ed. Walter B. Shurden (Nashville: Broadman Press, 1985) 108-27.

[14]As cited in Shurden, *The Life of Baptists in the Life of the World*, 107.

[15]J. B. Lawrence, "The People Called Baptists," *The Christian Index* 125/23 (7 June 1945): 3, 7.

[16]I have addressed this issue in "The Baptist Identity and the Baptist Manifesto" that is included in this volume and in *Perspectives in Religious Studies* 25/4 (Winter 1998): 321-24.

While a toss-up as to what should be listed in second place, the role of the state in religious matters gets the edge in my evaluation. Violations of separation of church and state and corollary issues related to religious liberty preoccupied the SBC during this time.

Third, Southern Baptists wrote often about their understanding of the church. This concern sprang from both their effort to differentiate themselves from Catholic ecclesiasticism and from the Southern Baptist imperative to respond to the ecumenical movement.

Fourth, Southern Baptists, like other Baptists before and after, could not speak of what it meant to be Baptist without addressing issues related to religious authority, issues such as the centrality of Holy Scripture, the preeminence of the New Testament, and the Lordship of Christ over both church and individual conscience.

The Baptist Identity
and the Prominence of the Individual Person

Surely, the closest thing during these years to a Baptist confession of faith was the "Statement of Principles." The SBC adopted it in 1946 as a kind of centennial confession of its beliefs. In his sesquicentennial history of the SBC, Jesse Fletcher pointed out correctly that neither Barnes, Baker, nor McBeth had mentioned this document in their histories.[17] This is most interesting since this centennial statement was, as stated previously, a distinctly *Southern* Baptist Confession of faith. Proposed initially by the Social Service Commission of the SBC in San Antonio in 1942 because, as they said, "the hour in which we live calls for a statement of the great Baptist principles,"[18] the statement was several years in the making. An authentically "blue ribbon" committee, broadly representative of Southern Baptists and chaired by Ellis Fuller, president of Southern Seminary, issued the statement in 1945. Because the convention did not meet that year due to the war, Southern Baptists adopted it the next year, in 1946.

Part of the reason why this document is so little known is the same as the insignificance of the BFM-25 before it: Southern Baptists simply were not fixated on the idea of confessional statements. Louie Newton, for example, the unrivaled Baptist leader of Georgia during these years,

---

[17]Fletcher, *The Southern Baptist Convention*, 177.
[18]*SBC Annual 1942*, 94.

editorialized in *The Christian Index* following the proposal of the statement in 1942, saying that there was no reason for it.[19]

Needed or not, Southern Baptists adopted it, printing it in both the 1945 and 1946 SBC annuals. Not quite two pages in length, the brief confession contained three headings, "Preamble," "Principles," and "Fields of Application." And the very first sentence, following the preamble, boldly affirmed the following: "Our distinctive belief is our Doctrine of Man in the personal order of life, that is, what God says concerning man."[20] The confession then spelled out this "distinctive belief" by asserting (1) the infinite value of the individual, (2) the soul competency of the individual, (3) the inalienable rights of the individual, and (4) the responsibility of the individual.

The "Statement of Principles" continued, "Out of this doctrine of the individual grows the Baptist conviction concerning all aspects of religious experience and life."[21] So what Baptist concepts derived from this allegedly "distinctive belief" about the individual? They listed five such concepts: (1) personal conversion, (2) a voluntary and democratic local church, (3) the authority of the New Testament, (4) the separation of church and state, and (5) religious liberty. The committee fused three of the five ideas directly to the centrality of the individual. The one regarding the New Testament probably intended to highlight the right of personal interpretation of scripture, but it did not clearly enunciate this fact. The statement on church and state is also somewhat obscure, but, again, the assumption would have been that such separation protects the individual conscience.

---

[19]Newton opposed the addition of the California churches into the SBC, and he said further, "Another action of the convention which seemed to me unnecessary was the creation of a committee to restate the Baptist position. I wonder how any group of Baptists can improve on the Baptist Bill of Rights, adopted in 1939, upon the statement of the Baptist position by Dr. George W. Truett in his presidential address at the Sixth Congress of the Baptist World Alliance, upon the numerous declarations of the convention in fairly recent years touching every phase and factor of the Baptist position." See Louie Newton, "The San Antonio Convention," *The Christian Index* 122/21 (28 May 1942): 9. Note that Newton failed to refer to the BFM-25, another indication of its unimportance at this stage of denominational history.

[20]*SBC Annual 1946*, 39.

[21]*SBC Annual 1946*, 39. Likewise, the first sentence in the section of the 1939 statement on religious liberty which laid out "the principles that animate the activities of the Baptists" was "the worth of the individual." See *SBC Annual 1939*, 115; and John R. Sampey, "The Faith and Doctrine of Baptists," 12.

After they identified their "Principles," Southern Baptists demonstrated how those fundamental Baptist tenets related to their contemporary world. In other words, the confession underscored the fact that the stress on the individual led not to hyperindividualism but contained vastly important social and ethical implications. This stress on the individual really was not "excessive individualism" run amuck. To the contrary, what you find in the last major section of the document is a Baptist protest against a pack mentality and totalitarian view of life which ran roughshod over the individual in the decade of the 1940s.

For example, these Baptists, in the face of the ecumenical movement, affirmed Christians' obligations to seek Christian unity. They protested, however, what they called "overlordship of the individually redeemed or their churches." In a very real sense, sectarianism, totalitarianism, imperialism, classism, racism, and "exploitation, manipulation, or neglect" are all condemned in this document. But here is the central point: this Baptist ethical protest, doubtless more elevated in rhetoric than implemented in reality, evolved out of a basic theological belief in the value, worth, and centrality of the individual person. This accent on the individual human being mandated that Christianity come down in the middle of human history, not retreat from it. Had Southern Baptists followed the theological logic in the 1946 confession, they probably would have been a far more socially involved people in subsequent years.

To utilize the 1946 statement as primary documentation for Southern Baptists' stated commitment to the centrality of the individual is no isolated historical prooftexting. Boredom would seize us, if time and space permitted fuller elaboration from other sources. Suffice it to say that of the nine documents which form the primary research for this paper, eight of them trumpeted, in one way or another, this "cardinal, bedrock principle," as Truett put it, from which "all our Baptist principles emerge."[22] The only document which failed to refer to it explicitly was the 1940 "Reply to the World Council of Churches." But if you count local church autonomy as a derivative of the idea, which the "Statement of Principles" certainly did, you will discover it in that document as well.

Again, what constituted the varied components of this "principle of individualism" which George Truett saw as the "supreme emphasis" of the New Testament? As Baptists described it during this period, it included the following: authentic personal/individual experience with the Holy, an

---

[22]Truett, "The Baptist Message and Mission for the World Today," 113.

egalitarian community of faith, the right of personal interpretation of scripture within the bounds of local church authority, a holy disdain of a superior clergy, believer's baptism, religious liberty, separation of church and state, protest against totalitarianism, the competency of the individual soul before God, and, in summary, the principle of voluntarism in all matters of religious faith.

You are doubtless aware that some Baptists—Southern and otherwise—today look with grave suspicion upon this undiminished and unvarnished affirmation of the individual. Some among us, including both historians and theologians, have interpreted this emphasis on the prominence of the individual and soul competency as a historical aberration in Baptist history and the fomenter of great evil among the Baptist people. Voices as divergent and different as Al Mohler, the *Manifesto*, and even some Reconstructionists, have railed against this Baptist affirmation of the individual person. On the other hand, while understanding the theological potholes involved, one may see this emphasis as baptistic, both historically and theologically, as "Amazing Grace." The role of the individual is not the only issue, and it is not the whole issue in describing the Baptist identity, not by any means. But if you extract what these mid-century Southern Baptists meant by "the principle of individualism" from the Baptist identity, you end up with something other than Baptists as they understood it. Clear continuity rather than radical discontinuity exists between this emphasis on the individual's worth, competency, and responsibility and the voices of people such as Thomas Helwys, John Murton, John Clarke, and Obadiah Holmes, all of whom worked and wrote in seventeenth-century Baptist life.[23]

---

[23]The following interpretations, vastly different in quality and significantly different in interpretations, fit loosely into this Baptist critique of Baptist individualism: *Baptist Concepts of the Church*, ed. Winthrop S. Hudson (Chicago: Judson Press, 1959) 11-29, 196-218; James B. Jordan, "Editor's Introduction," *The Failure of American Baptist Culture*, ed. James B. Jordan and Gary North, Christianity and Civilization no. 1 (Tyler TX: Geneva Divinity School, 1982) v-xv; Curtis W. Freeman, "Can Baptist Theology Be Revisioned," *Perspectives in Religious Studies* 24/3 (Fall 1997): 273-302; "Re-Envisioning Baptist Identity: A Manifesto for Baptist Communities in North America," *Perspectives in Religious Studies* 24/3 (Fall 1997): 303-10; Gregory A. Wills, *Democratic Religion: Freedom, Authority, and Church Discipline in the Baptist South, 1785–1900* (New York: Oxford University Press, 1997); and R. Albert Mohler, compiler, "Introduction," *E. Y. Mullins: The Axioms of Religion*, ed. Timothy George and Denise George

The Baptist Identity and the Role of the State

During the turbulence of a world war, one may expect to read religious expositions on the role of government in human affairs. In issuing "A Pronouncement upon Religious Liberty" in 1939, the SBC highlighted their rationale for speaking out:

> No issue in modern life is more urgent or more complicated than the relation of organized religion to organized society. The sudden rise of the European dictators to power has changed fundamentally the organic law of the governments through which they exercise sovereignty, and as a result, the institutions of religion are either suppressed or made subservient to the ambitious national programs of these new totalitarian states.[24]

Hitler, Mussolini, and others of their ilk, however, were not the only threats. "Every session of the Congress," said these Baptists, raised questions concerning the relation of the Federal Government to the agencies of faith. The SBC deplored mandatory social security for churches and religious institutions, repudiated state aid to sectarian schools, and rebuked the president of the United States for appointing an ambassador to the Vatican, among other church/state concerns.[25] Not surprisingly, these years of church/state struggles birthed one of the great American voices for religious liberty, the Baptist Joint Committee on Public Affairs.

Contending that the church should not be above, below, or alongside the state, Baptists argued for separation of church and state, a point of view "championed," they asserted, by "Baptists everywhere."[26] What powered this hardheaded Baptist advocacy for separation of church and state? It certainly was not a disdain for the state. Baptists acknowledged themselves to be citizens of two commonwealths, and they claimed the right to be good citizens of both.[27]

Not disdain for government, but a shrill call for freedom of individual conscience fueled the Baptist call for church-state separation. Arguing from what he unapologetically called this "principle of individualism," reflected in the New Testament and embraced by Baptists everywhere, George Truett

---

(Nashville: Broadman & Holman Publishers, 1997) 1-32.

[24]*SBC Annual 1939*, 114.
[25]*SBC Annual 1939*, 115.
[26]*SBC Annual 1939*, 114.
[27]*SBC Annual 1939*, 116.

logically concluded that every individual person had "the right to worship God according to the dictates of . . . conscience; and that no man, nor set of men, no government, religious or civil, has the right to dictate how a person may worship God, and to punish him if he does not worship that way." He followed those lines with two of his most quoted sentences about the Baptist vision of Christianity: "The right of private judgment is the crown jewel of humanity. And for any person or institution to dare to come between the soul and God is a blasphemous impertinence and a defamation of the crown rights of the Son of God."[28]

So the Baptist view of the state came from a radical demand for a free conscience. Whence comes the free conscience? It came from God, of course.[29] God, not people or people's governments, reigned sovereign over life.

Moreover, Baptists insisted that the very essence and meaning of "faith" mandated an unshackled soul. For Baptists, faith, to be genuine, had to be free. Word usage should be noted and heeded here. Baptists enlisted a number of words to make their point, but three illustrations must suffice: "voluntary,"[30] "personal conviction,"[31] and "spiritual."[32] Faith, to be valid, is "voluntary" obedience to God. The only conversion that counts is conversion by "conviction." "Spirituality," a huge word in American society today, meant for Baptists of the World War II era, "the free pursuit" of piety. "Forced faith," "coerced faith," "unchosen faith," "involuntary faith," "convictionless faith," "ritualistic faith," "sacramental faith"—all such theological construals would have been an oxymoron for these Baptists.

They called this soul freedom for which they stood passionately an "inherent right." It came, like one's genes, with creation itself. No govern-

---

[28]Truett, "The Baptist Message and Mission for the World Today," 114.

[29]"Statement of Principles," *SBC Annual 1946*, 38. "God gives to the individual man natural, inalienable rights and privileges which should be recognized in human society."

[30]See "A Pronouncement upon Religious Liberty," *SBC Annual 1939*, 115; and Truett, "The Baptist Message and Mission for the World Today," 116.

[31]See "Report on Interdenominational Relations," *SBC Annual 1938*, 24-25. This report was talking about church union rather than freedom of conscience, but the Baptist emphasis is exactly the same. The report said, "We believe that intelligent, personal conviction in religion is essential to strength in Christian character. . . ."

[32]See "A Pronouncement upon Religious Liberty," *SBC Annual 1939*, 115.

ment could "concede" it, for it was not the government's to distribute. They also called it an "inalienable right." The word simply means "nontransferable." This right could not be transferred to the state without casting government in the unenviable "function of God."[33] For this reason Baptists carefully distinguished between religious toleration and religious liberty.[34]

An "inherent" and "inalienable" right, absolute religious liberty was cheered also by Southern Baptists as a "universal" right. It was applicable to all persons in all places, Baptists, Christians, Jews, "and . . . everybody else." Baptists puffed freedom of conscience, said Truett, not merely for themselves but "for Protestants of all denominations, for Romanists, for Jews, for Quakers, for Turks, for Pagans, and for all men everywhere."[35] Clearly, these Baptists envisioned America pluralistically, a republic with moral foundations but with rooms for people of all faiths and those with no faith.

While the right *to* religious freedom meant the right *from* religion, it also meant freedom *for* religion. In the marketplace of ideas, Baptists envisioned an intellectual and spiritual free-for-all. Thus, faith of any kind possessed the right to worship, the right to evangelize, and the right to teach and propagate its ideas.[36] If you could persuade, said Baptists, you deserved to prevail.

Finally, Baptists recognized that freedom had a price tag on it. The kind of individualism which produced this passion for freedom was not a "every tub sits on its on bottom" caricature, insensitive to other bottomless tubs. Blessed with a bottom to sit on, these World War II Southern Baptists understood, in their heads at least, that they had work to do. Free people were responsible people. "Religious liberty is the nursing mother of all liberty,"[37] said the pastor from Dallas to the Baptists of the World in Atlanta. Some took him seriously and they wrote a few years later: "Believing that God has created all men free and equal and has given to them certain inalienable rights which must ever be respected, we assert the right of all nations, both great and small, to self-government, and the obli-

---

[33]"A Pronouncement upon Religious Liberty," *SBC Annual 1939*, 115.

[34]Truett, "The Baptist Message and Mission for the World Today," 115.

[35]See "A Pronouncement upon Religious Liberty, *SBC Annual 1939*, 116; Truett, "The Baptist Message and Mission for the World Today," 116; "Statement of Principles," *SBC Annual 1939*, 38.

[36]See "Southern Baptists and World Peace," *SBC Annual 1944*, 150; "Statement of Principles," *SBC Annual 1946*, 38.

[37]Truett, "The Baptist Message and Mission for the World Today," 115.

gation of the strong to protect the weak, whether small nations, racial minorities, or underprivileged peoples, in the exercise of their God-given freedom."[38]

The Baptist Identity and the Nature of the Church

An appropriate starting point to discuss Southern Baptists' understanding of the church during the war years is to state what they did not intend by "church." They certainly did not mean "*The* Southern Baptist Church." No such thing has ever existed among Baptists and should never exist. When the SBC declined the invitation to join the World Council of Churches in 1940, it gave ecclesiology as one of it reasons:

> Directly replying to your invitation, permit us to advise that the Southern Baptist Convention is a voluntary association of Baptists for the purpose of eliciting, combining, and directing the energies of our denomination in missionary activity at home and abroad, and in education and benevolent work throughout the world. Our Convention has no ecclesiological authority. *It is in no sense the Southern Baptist Church.* The thousands of churches to which our Convention looks for support of its missionary, benevolent, and educational program, cherish their independence and would disapprove of any attempted exercise of ecclesiastical authority over them.[39]

On scrutinizing their reasoning, of course, one wonders why ecclesiology would forbid the SBC from union with the World Council of Churches and yet permit that same type union with the Baptist World Alliance. In truth, the SBC could have and can and does join anything it wants, for it has its own independence and autonomy. In doing so, however, it does not commit any Baptist church, any Baptist association, or any

---

[38]"Southern Baptists and World Peace," *SBC Annual 1944*, 149.

[39]See *SBC Annual 1940*, 99. In his response to the welcome given by Governor Leon Phillips of Oklahoma at the 1939 meeting of the SBC, David M. Gardner of St. Petersburg, Florida, echoed the nonecclesial character of the SBC when he said: "Why are we here? We are here in the capacity of a Southern Baptist Convention, the freest people on earth. We are not here as a convention of churches, nor as a convention of boards, institutions, and agencies. We are not here as a convention of state groups. We are not delegates from churches, not even representatives of churches, but as a convention of individual Baptist messengers from churches meeting without ecclesiastical authority, quality, or functions." See *The Christian Index* 119/20 (25 May 1939): 3.

Baptist state convention to its actions, because it is not *The* Southern
Baptist Church.

The fact that the SBC denied explicitly that it was a church is significant for several reasons. One, during the last twenty years or so, that
phrase—"The Southern Baptist Church"—has appeared with increasing
regularity in letters to editors by Baptists who should know better and by
secular religion writers who seem not to have a clue about Baptist ecclesiology above the local church level. Two, the increasing centralization
within the SBC in the last twenty years makes some think that the SBC has
furtively and unofficially, through its resolutions and financial and confessional constrictionism, become *The* Southern Baptist Church, the very
thing that fundamentalist leadership allegedly deplored in the 1980s. Three,
at the very time that the SBC touted church independence and decentraliza-
tion as reasons for not aligning with the World Council of Churches, some
within the SBC accused it of a growing centralization. Indeed, any
objective analysis would conclude that centralization was occurring during
this period, some of it the inevitable result of a growing denomination.[40]

But if the SBC of the 1940s stated explicitly what the church was not,
did it say clearly what it was? Could it be positive as well as negative? The
SBC answered with an unambiguous "yes." Terminology and word usage
again were crucial. Baptists, because of their polity, preferred the word
"churches," but they used the word "church," in the singular, in at least
three ways. First, they used the word to depict an individual Baptist church.
Second, they used it to describe another denomination with a connectional
or episcopal system of church polity, such as "The Methodist Church" or
"The Presbyterian Church." Third, they used it to point to what the Bible
called "the Body of Christ," insisting that the Body of Christ "is not to be
identified with any denomination or church that seeks to exercise

---

[40]A brief editorial described a leader who complained of "Baptist organized
work." The man had "heard some rumblings of an effort to control a certain state
agency through one of the Southwide boards, and was protesting against it." Then
Gilbert went on to say: "Of recent years there has been entirely too much talk of
Southwide this and that to set well with the churches and pastors, especially the
churches and pastors that have a regard for cherished Baptist opinion. At this time
when the trend in public affairs points to a breakdown in democracy, Baptists
should not despise their independence nor forget their cherished views on soul
liberty." *The Christian Index* 118/19 (12 May 1938): 8.

ecclesiastical authority, but includes all the regenerated whoever and wherever they are, as these are led by the Holy Spirit."[41]

Like their understanding of the state, these Baptists understood their ecclesiology to be derivative of their anthropology. Their concept of church stemmed from their emphasis on the individual. Therefore, said the "Statement of Principles" of 1946, "the local church, a voluntary fellowship of baptized believers, is responsible directly and only to Christ, the Creator and Head of the church. It is a democratic body in which all the members are equally free and responsible participants. Its divinely called ministry is chosen by the church itself under the guidance of the Holy Spirit."[42] That definition required little ink, but within it the SBC asserted at least six decisive points for their relatively simple understanding of the church.

First, the churches are of God; they belong to Christ. Here we again bump into that cherished Baptist phrase—"the undelegated sovereignty" of Christ. Christ, not pope or priest or preacher, reigned as the "only head and sovereign of his churches."[43]

Second, the churches are local. In this case, localism usurped universalism, but it did not obliterate it. Churches, Baptists said, have names and addresses, like First Baptist Church, 1400 Main Street. But there is a church without address or zip code, and these Baptists gladly called it the Body of Christ.

Third, the churches' membership rests on the principle of voluntarism, only people of conviction are baptized, voluntarily. Compulsion and manipulation of any kind and of all kinds cannot create the churches of Christ.

Fourth, the churches are democratic in process where members are both "equally free and responsible participants." They politely rejected the offer to join the WCC because they were "sensible of the dangers of totalitarian trends which threaten the autonomy of all free churches."[44] Whether such totalitarianism actually existed in the WCC is another matter.

Fifth, the ministry is a divine calling, subject to the churches rather than the churches being subject to the ministry. The churches are never to "bend to a superior clergy."[45]

---

[41]"A Pronouncement upon Religious Liberty," *SBC Annual 1939*, 115.
[42]*SBC Annual 1946*, 38.
[43]*SBC Annual 1938*, 24.
[44]*SBC Annual 1940*, 99.
[45]*SBC Annual 1938*, 24.

Sixth, God's Spirit guides the churches; Baptist churches, while democratic in process, are theocratic in principle.[46] Baptists sought through the democratic process to implement the will of God.

The Baptist Identity and Religious Authority

Since Southern Baptists battled vigorously over the nature of the Bible and religious authority for the last twenty years of this century, a brief review of what mid-century Southern Baptists said regarding religious authority may be instructive. Clearly, Southern Baptists during the era of World War II held a lofty view of Holy Scripture. Interestingly, however, code words such as "inerrancy" and "infallibility" were rare in official SBC documents. They appeared in none of the official SBC documents used in this study.

Even the word "Bible" appeared less than the word "Scripture." What showed up more often than anything else, however, was an allusion to the *New* Testament—not simply the Bible—as the Baptist authority for faith and practice. In adopting "A Pronouncement upon Religious Liberty" in 1938, Southern Baptists enumerated the basic principles that animated Baptist life. They also referred to those basic teachings as principles which Southern Baptists believed "to be clearly taught in the New Testament."[47]

Eight years later when the SBC adopted the "Statement of Principles" in 1946, the Southern Baptist people said that "the one and only authority in faith and practice is the New Testament as the divinely inspired record and interpretation of the supreme revelation of God through Jesus Christ as Redeemer, Saviour, and Lord."[48] Note three aspects of this affirmation of religious authority. First, the "one and only authority in faith and practice is the New Testament." Second, the New Testament is the "divinely inspired record and interpretation." Third, the New Testament is the divinely inspired record and interpretation "of the supreme revelation of God through Jesus Christ as Redeemer, Saviour, and Lord."

In 1937 John R. Sampey, president of the Southern Baptist Theological Seminary and also president of the SBC, attended the Life and Work Conference in Oxford and the Faith and Order Conference in Edinburgh. He went as an official representative of Southern Baptists at the request of the Executive Committee of the SBC. In his presidential address before the

---

[46]*SBC Annual 1939*, 115.
[47]*SBC Annual 1939*, 115.
[48]*SBC Annual 1946*, 38.

Southern Baptist Convention the next year in Richmond, Sampey reflected on his ecumenical sojourn. Noting his personal reservations concerning organic church union, and then holding aloft the cardinal Baptist principle of soul competency, this revered Old Testament scholar said:

> An intelligent and convinced Baptist with the New Testament in his hand finds little to draw him toward a Church which denies the competence of the individual soul to do business with God through Christ Jesus as the sole Mediator. We cannot get the consent of our minds to surrender the freedom with which Christ Jesus has set us free, in order to unite with Roman Catholics, Anglo-Catholics or even evangelical Pedobaptists. We rejoice in spiritual fellowship with all who love our Lord Jesus; but we must stand for the faith and order of the New Testament as we understand it.[49]

Not once, but twice he referred to the New Testament as the bedrock of Baptist belief.

This same president of the Southern Baptist Theological Seminary only a few years earlier went even further, extolling Jesus as the ultimate religious authority for the Southern Baptist Theological Seminary. Speaking on the occasion of the Diamond Jubilee Anniversary of Southern Seminary in 1934 before the SBC, Sampey sought, as he said, "to interpret the soul of the Seminary." He spoke of the seminary's devotion to Holy Scriptures, its love affair with preaching, its commitment to personal evangelism and the cultivation of the shepherd's heart, its ecumenical and democratic temper, and the prominence of worship. But he reached the climax of his address in his final point, and he spoke powerfully of Christ as the ultimate religious authority for Southern Seminary. Said Sampey:

> The Lord Jesus has the first place in the heart of the seminary. In all things he must have the preeminence. Christ Jesus is our Lord. If he corrects Moses, and elevates his standards, we stand with Jesus rather than with Moses. Even the Bible cannot hold the place in our hearts that Jesus holds. He is King of Kings and Lord of Lords.[50]

---

[49]Sampey, "Spiritual Equipment: The Need of the Times," 3. For a similar account of Sampey's ecumenical experience, see John R. Sampey, *Memoirs of John R. Sampey* (Nashville: Broadman Press, 1947) 249-52.

[50]John R. Sampey, "Diamond Jubilee Address," 24; copy in the possession of the writer.

This emphasis on the Lordship of Christ over both churches and conscience was no isolated theme. The phrase "the undelegated sovereignty of Jesus Christ" appeared frequently. Often utilized to deflect Roman Catholic teachings, the phrase also suggested more: it meant that that the will of Christ was first and foremost in the believer's life. Again, hear the 1938 "Report on Interdenominational Relations" speaking on the Lordship of Christ:

> We here declare our unalterable belief in the universal, unchangeable, and undelegated sovereignty of Jesus Christ. We believe that he is the rightful and only head and sovereign of his churches; that his word and will, as revealed in the holy Scriptures, is the unchangeable and only law of his reign; that whatever is not found in the Scriptures, cannot be bound on the conscience of men; and that the supreme test of true Christian discipleship is obedience to the will of Christ, as revealed in the Bible.[51]

These Baptists, as most of their kinsfolk through the ages, had a Christocentric Bible.

Conclusion

If one compares the SBC at the mid-century years to the SBC at the end of the century, what stands out? First, at mid-century Southern Baptists trumpeted the individual and the individual's soul competency, but at the end of the century that conviction has not only been muted but transformed by Al Mohler, J. R. Sampey's successor at Southern Seminary. Individual soul competency is now viewed as the source of theological ambiguity among Southern Baptists.

Second, on church/state issues, you would probably find far more openness to such things as prayer in schools and faith-based charities among contemporary Southern Baptist leadership than one would have ever discovered at mid-century. The Southern Baptist leadership at mid-century appeared far more radical in their call for separation of church and state.

Third, in the ecumenical attitudes of the SBC leadership of the 1940s, one finds a crystal-clear opposition to organic church union, but along with that attitude one senses a somewhat gentle kinship with other Christians, expressed in the Southern Baptist stress on "spiritual union." Indeed, an outspoken liberal minority, composed of prominent pastors, opposed the

---

[51]*SBC Annual 1938*, 24.

SBC's rejection of membership in the World Council of Churches. On the other hand, the ecumenical spirit within the SBC today appears more to be an ecumenism of the right. It is open primarily to the right extreme of the theological spectrum; it, therefore, naturally embraces the theological viewpoint, for example, of Jerry Falwell.

Fourth, at mid-century, women appeared virtually invisible in leadership positions, and, at the end of the century, that situation has not only continued but hardened, with theological rationale to buttress it.

Fifth, while Southern Baptist leaders at the end of the century speak long and often of "biblical inerrancy," the mid-century leadership referred to the "authority of the New Testament." That New Testament clearly had Christ as the supreme and central revelation of God. Deleting that sentence—"the criterion by which the bible is to be interpreted is Jesus Christ,"—as Southern Baptists did in revising the 2000 revision of the Baptist Faith and Message doubtless would have had rough sledding in the late 1930s and the 1940s. After all, it was the president of the Southern Baptist Theological Seminary who was also a president of the SBC, who said, "Even the Bible cannot hold the place in our hearts that Jesus holds."

George W. Truett had towered, almost giant-like, over the entire SBC in the 30s and 40s. He died on 7 July 1944. L. R. Scarborough had towered over the western half of the SBC in the 30s and 40s. He died 10 April 1945. J. R. Sampey had towered over the eastern half of the SBC. He died 18 August 1946. Truett in 1944! Scarborough in 1945! Sampey in 1946! Within a brief span of twenty-five months, a SBC tradition could have passed quietly and heroically off the scene. That legacy fell, however, on very young but stout shoulders—shoulders keenly aware of a great Baptist tradition in the South. These young shoulders belonged to Duke K. McCall, Theron Rankin, Baker James Cauthen, James Sullivan, Porter Routh, and Albert McClellan. Eventually Grady Cothen, Foy Valentine, Darold Morgan, Randall Lolley, and Russell Dilday, among others, shouldered that tradition as well. By 2000 that Truett/Scarborough/Sampey legacy had been muffled within the SBC, only to emerge in new organizational structures. In the SBC a new and different and vigorous tradition had begun.

If you divided the twentieth century of the SBC into quarters— 1900–1925, 1925–1950, 1950–1975, 1975–1900—and then you tried to put the most influential Southern Baptist name with those years, whose pictures would fit into those four chronological frames? I suggest it would look like this:

1900–1925	E. Y. Mullins
1925–1950	George W. Truett
1950–1975	W. A. Criswell
1975–1900	Adrian Rogers

Within each half of the twentieth century one can see a distinct and contrasting vision of what it means to be Baptist. The differences in those visions are the differences in the SBC at mid-century and at the end of the century.

Baptists
and Cooperative Baptist Fellowship History

■ ■ ■

Reflections on the Baptist Consultation
of Moderates in Atlanta, 23-25 August 1990[1]

I'm bullish on Atlanta! However, I went to the meeting with minimal expectations. And for several reasons. One, I have recognized for several years the tension and diversity within the Moderate movement in the SBC. We Moderates have often been unified only in what we opposed, not in what we affirmed. Given the fact that we trumpet the theme and value of diversity, that's the way it should be. What that has meant, however, is that we have been united only in our opposition to the Fundamentalists; we've never flown under a single banner. The closest we came in twelve years to a slogan was the overweight, awkward, impersonal phrase of "denominational loyalty" and that became increasingly obsolete with each passing meeting of the annual SBC. So we have been without a code word such as "Inerrancy."

Nor have we had a single leader or a handful of the same leaders. The Fundamentalist Movement could be rightly called the Pressler-Patterson Party (Although I have always contended that the most important name in the Fundamentalist triumph was neither Pressler, Patterson, or Criswell, but Rogers. As a historian, I hope neither Fundamentalists nor Moderates overlook the fact that the Fundamentalist ship would have never left port without the charismatic man from Memphis.), but what name or names can we Moderates attach to our resistance movement? We have some, of course, and they are such good ones. But they look like an old Boston law firm: McCall, Sherman, Chafin, Cothen, Slatton, Moore, Vestal, Honeycutt,

---

[1]Originally published in *Baptists Today* 8/7 (October 1990): 4, this article, published here unaltered except for new explanatory footnotes, is my description and interpretation of the initial meeting of what came to be known as the Cooperative Baptist Fellowship. Billed as a "Consultation of Concerned Southern Baptists," the historic meeting occurred 23-25 August 1990 at the Inforum in Atlanta. The meeting marked the end, at the national denominational level, of the "SBC Holy War" that began in 1979. Daniel Vestal called the Consultation and Jimmy Allen presided. For more information on background factors to the Consultation, see Daniel Vestal, "The History of the Cooperative Baptist Fellowship," in *The Struggle for the Soul of the SBC: Moderate Responses to the Fundamentalist Movement*, ed. Walter B. Shurden (Macon GA: Mercer University Press, 1993) 253-74.

Lolley, Dilday, et al.[2] In fact, we have had no single leader, not even a duo or trio. Our quarterbacks have come to the line of scrimmage to bark out the signals at most only two years running. What we have had are truckloads of leaders. At the annual sessions of the SBC we have had more leaders than the Fundamentalists; they have had more followers. And that is a major difference.

Not only have we not had a single banner or slogan or a single leader, but neither have we had unified action on anything except voting against the Fundamentalists. Fundamentalists voted *for* their candidate. We voted *against* their candidate, but we Moderates did not always vote *for* our candidate. We could not agree even to that degree.

In Atlanta some things happened: we got, if not a slogan, some "words." Print up the buttons! Unfurl the banners! The first word is "solidarity." John Hewett, the gifted young word-merchant and pastor from First Church Asheville gave it to us. Slicing through some laborious questions about how the alternate funding mechanism would work, Hewett said that the funding process grants us "the gift of solidarity." Stirring us and challenging us to stop the nit-picking and foot-dragging, Hewett closed the briefest and most powerful speech of the meeting with, "Let's trust each other to do it right and do it well. Let's do it now!" And we came together with a standing, ear-busting, spine-tingling ovation. Something happened. We came together. And we came together on something other than our resistance to the Fundamentalists. We voted *for* something rather than *against* something. The word is "solidarity."

Jimmy Allen gave us a word: "The Fellowship." It is a word akin to "solidarity." It is a dynamic rather than static word. It is a personal rather than organizational word. "The Fellowship" refers to the movement, the momentum, the energy that is now swirling among Moderates. David Sapp gave us a third word: "A bucket." The "bucket" refers to the Baptist Cooperative Missions Program (BMCP), the funding mechanism that will serve as an alternate to the Fundamentalist controlled Cooperative Program.

Dan Vestal gave us a word: "renewal." It is a word we desperately need. This fight has sapped our spirituality. We now have something new to pray for and work for. No need to deny what has happened with us and

---

[2]The names refer to Duke McCall, Cecil Sherman, Kenneth Chafin, Grady Cothen, James Slatton, Winfred Moore, Daniel Vestal, Roy L. Honeycutt, Randall Lolley, and Russell Dilday. All played significant roles on the Moderate side of the SBC struggle.

the Fundamentalists. We don't trust them to respect our faith and they don't trust us to have faith. Tragically and sinfully, that will be the case for a long time to come. Moderates now have an opportunity to turn their back on "distrusting" and *renew* the art of trusting again. How our Fundamentalist sisters and brothers do that or if they do that is up to them. I hope they can; I hope we can; I hope I can. Trust is essential to a healthy spiritual life.

"The Fellowship" and the "bucket" and the spirit of "solidarity" give us a chance for spiritual "renewal." I hope we will renew our commitment to the Bible as the Word of God with the full recognition that such renewal does not and never has demanded the dogma of inerrancy. Inerrancy is a distorted way of attributing high praise to Holy Scripture. There are other, more legitimate and more honest, ways of thanking God for the Bible.

In Atlanta we got some words; we also got the nearest thing to unified leadership that we have ever had. Their names are Dan Vestal and Jimmy Allen. In my judgment, Vestal represents the conservative wing of "The Fellowship" while Allen represents the center of the movement. Randall Lolley embodies the progressive edge of the movement. All three are good and enormously respected individuals. All need to be heard from and we need to give them a platform. All three are essentially conservative Christians. Look at Dan Vestal! In his former pastorate he *led* the SBC in Cooperative Program giving for several years. No single individual in the Fundamentalist Movement represents old line Southern Baptist Orthodoxy as well as Dan Vestal. Only one thing separates him from the voting majority of the messengers at the Southern Baptist Convention for the last twelve years: he is inclusive and they are exclusive; he spells Baptist with a capital and they spell it with the lowercase; he lives under a massive canopy and they live in a pup tent.

Jimmy Allen is a former president of the SBC, a former pastor of one of the major Texas churches, and a former SBC agency head. Scratch him and he cries Southern Baptist piety. Impeccable! Credible! Believable! Any effort to categorize him as a radical or as a nonloyal Southern Baptist is, to borrow a phrase from George Will, "nonsense on stilts."

Randall Lolley, like Vestal and Allen, a Ph.D. graduate of South-western Seminary, has been since the controversy began the most popular and trusted Moderate Southern Baptist east of the Mississippi. And for good reasons. The former pastor of First Baptist Winston-Salem and of First Baptist Raleigh, he is presently the pastor of First Baptist, Greensboro, North Carolina. But he is primarily known for the twelve years he led the Southeastern Baptist Theological Seminary as president. "Randall"—that is all you have to say to Southern Baptists to suggest courage, integrity, and a down-home kind of authentic commitment to the gospel. He represents the best that Southern Baptists have produced in the last half of the twentieth century.

One of the overpowering realities of Atlanta was the people who were present. To gauge the credibility of any Southern Baptist meeting, the question needs to be asked, "Who was there?" The answer is that over 3,000 of Southern Baptists' best, brightest, and most committed. One of the most persuasive pieces of advertisement for "The Fellowship" would be a publication of the list of registrants. The Southern Baptist public needs and deserves to know the names. Print it up and spread it abroad!

I do the unthinkable and mention only some of those present. Some Southern Baptist giants: Grady Cothen, former president of the Baptist Sunday School Board and of New Orleans Baptist Theological Seminary; Albert McClellan, former associate executive secretary of the Executive Committee of the SBC; Foy Valentine, former executive director of the SBC Christian Life Commission; Darold Morgan, former president of the SBC Annuity Board; Carolyn Weatherford Crumpler, former executive of the WMU; Randall Lolley; and Duke K. McCall, former president of Southern and New Orleans seminaries and former executive secretary of the SBC, who though absent in body was one of the major guiding hands in the whole affair.

Some state convention presidents and past presidents: Neal Jones (Virginia), Leon Smith (North Carolina), Chess Smith, Floyd Roebuck, Bill Self (Georgia), Steve Tondera (Alabama), James Yates (Mississippi), and John Hughes (Missouri). Some pastors of flagship SBC churches: James Flamming, First Richmond, Virginia; Hardy Clemmons, First Greenville, South Carolina; Peter Rhea Jones, First Decatur, Georgia; Randall Lolley, First Greensboro, North Carolina; Doug Watterson, First Knoxville, Tennessee; Ken Chafin, Walnut Street, Louisville, Kentucky; Alan Walworth, First Huntsville, Alabama; Jon Stubblefield, First Shreveport, Louisiana; Raymond Lloyd, First Starkville, Mississippi; Lavonn Brown, First Norman, Oklahoma; Cecil Sherman, Broadway, Ft. Worth, Texas. Past and present WMU leadership of the SBC: Catherine Allen, Dorothy Sample, and Delanna O'Brien. Some Southern Baptist academicians: Herbert Reynolds, president of Baylor University; Kirby Godsey, president of Mercer University; John Newport, former vice president of Academic Affairs at Southwestern Baptist Theological Seminary; and Alan Neely, Glenn Hinson, Nancy Ammerman. Some younger ones to watch for in the future: John Hewett, First Asheville, North Carolina; Scott Walker, First

Charleston, South Carolina; Stephen Shoemaker, Crescent Hill, Louisville, Kentucky; Timothy Owings, First Augusta, Georgia.

One of the most important things to happen in Atlanta is who registered. My sense is that most of those who registered were doing more than accumulating information for the people back home. They were making a statement about who they think Baptists really are, what they ought to support and why.

One cannot address the question "Who was there?" without asking the question "Who was not there?" Among the hard-core Fundamentalists, only Lee Roberts was there. His purpose in being present one can only guess, but maybe he is writing an exposé, much as he did when he attended the first meeting of the Southern Baptist Alliance in Raleigh. Noticeably absent, except for some courageous faculty from Southeastern and Southern Seminaries, were SBC agency people. James Dunn, of course, was there. Keith Parks was there, though it was widely rumored that he had been told by some of his board members that he should not attend. And Delanna O'Brien of the WMU was present. Though others may have been present, Dunn, Parks, and O'Brien were the only three national agency heads I saw. Likewise, very few state denominational workers were present.

One cannot but ask why the absence of such people. Are they fearful of being seen with these people who have not only bought the gas but driven the denominational bus through much of the last half of the twentieth century? My guess is that many are. Such a guess is not a harsh judgment. It is only an acknowledgment that Fundamentalism uses the tactic of intimidation and fear, and that such tactics now tragically work within the denominational structures. Distancing themselves from the Fellowship will not save denominational workers in the future, however. A free future belongs to those, Fundamentalists and Moderates alike, who follow conscience fearlessly. For state workers to be ordered or even encouraged to stay away from Moderate or Fundamentalist meetings is to relegate state leaders to the backwaters of denominational leadership.

For me, Atlanta felt different from almost everything I've experienced in thirty-five years of Southern Baptist life. It certainly felt different from the last twelve years of the SBC. Had it not, most of us would have checked out on Friday morning, at the very latest. It was not only different by degree; it was night-and-day different. Microphones were not cut off; the parliamentarian, who was unnecessary, was a Southern Baptist; only one or two "points were not well taken" and that in good humor;[3] creative rather than destructive tension was present; we sang mostly from the front of the hymnbook; sermons aimed at both the head and the heart were thoroughly biblical though not overwhelmingly anecdotal or alliterative; women were more than tolerated tokens, though still less influential than necessary; democracy was at work in both the plenary and workgroup sessions.

If Atlanta did not feel like the last twelve years of the SBC, neither did it feel like the SBC before the last twelve years. It had more zest, more creative energy, more of a something's-getting-ready-to-happen attitude, more of a Free Church spirit than the prefundamentalist SBC. There were no institutions to defend or protect or gain power over. No bureaucracy cried for allegiance, though one would be naive to think this was a noninstitutional or anti-institutional gathering.

Atlanta did not feel like the Southern Baptist Alliance,[4] either. The Alliance, small though it is, was present, influential and respected by those who pulled this meeting together. But the Alliance was not dominant. The Alliance represents, in my judgment, something of a hope that the Fellowship will be more courageous and less bland than some might want it to be.

Atlanta did not feel like a Baptists Committed[5] meeting, either. This was basically not a political gathering; it did not and does not have a political agenda within the SBC. Many of those at Atlanta will continue to be a political presence within the SBC. No one should doubt that. But Atlanta was not about political power within the SBC; it was about some SBC people finding power to do something other than politics.

---

[3]During the annual SBC meetings from 1980 to 1990, Moderates often accused the Fundamentalists of manipulating the annual meetings by shutting off microphones when Moderates were speaking and by hiring a Church of Christ minister as parliamentarian who worked against Moderates and who often ruled against Moderates by saying, "The point is not well taken."

[4]The Southern Baptist Alliance, later called the Baptist Alliance, represented a smaller but more liberal wing of the SBC Moderate movement. For a brief history of the Alliance, see Allan Neely, "The History of the Alliance of Baptists," in *The Struggle for the Soul of the SBC.*

[5]Officially known as "Baptists Committed to the SBC," this organization, centered in Texas, represented a political counteroffensive against the Fundamentalist takeover of the SBC. See Jimmy Allen, "The History of Baptists Committed" in *The Struggle for the Soul of the SBC.*

I liked the feel of the size of Atlanta. Larger than any one of us would have anticipated, it was small enough to feel like family. And one of the deep, pervasive longings of most who met in Atlanta was a sense of belonging, a sense of "home." Home does not have to be big to be home. I predict, however, that the coming Spring Convocation will have far more than 3,000.

What about the future of "The Fellowship?" Part of the excitement is that no one knows exactly where we are going and how. But those who found a "home" in "The Fellowship" also, I am convinced, found some hope. The future depends on one factor: how many churches will use this new mechanism for serving up their stewardship of the gospel. The sooner churches sign on, the more solid the future of "The Fellowship." And there is no reason for any church in the SBC *not* to sign on.

One of the unique things about the new funding mechanism is that it provides for diversity in method without damaging existing Southern Baptist missionaries, professors, and agency workers. A church can continue its exact funding process and channel its funds through the BMCP [Baptist Cooperative Missions Program]. Those Moderates who have been hesitant to act because of fear of "hurting the missionaries" need fear no longer.

While the "bucket" provides for each church to maintain its present allocation to SBC agencies, it also makes possible for each church to alter its funding of SBC agencies. What is afforded to churches is also provided for individuals. Individuals can fund all, some, or none of the SBC programs, no matter what their local churches decide to do. What the Cooperative Program lacks in flexibility, the "bucket" creates. The bucket simply says that it is unconscionable to ask people to support what is theologically, ethically, and organizationally repugnant to them.

In addition to funding SBC agencies, "new ventures" will doubtless be born which many Southern Baptists will enthusiastically support. We can enter the next century shaping new ministries and supporting old ones. "Exciting" is not big enough or powerful enough to describe what is on the horizon.

Historically, what was created in Atlanta was the makings of a new Baptist animal. I call it a "conciety." It is a combination of the old society and convention methods of doing the gospel together. Prior to 1845 and the formation of the SBC, Baptists in America used the society method for carrying on their denominational enterprises. Societies had several characteristic features. One, each society had a single focus or purpose such as education, home missions, or foreign missions. Two, a society was composed of individuals, not churches. Three, membership was financially based, not church based.

Beginning in 1845 but incomplete until well into the twentieth century was the convention method of doing cooperative missions. Unlike a society, a convention embraced multiple causes, not just one. Also unlike societies, the convention method eventually developed an exclusively church-based membership.

What came out of Atlanta was a "conciety." Individuals, as well as churches, can contribute to the "bucket." And while the multiple causes of the SBC are available for support, new challenges and causes can be adopted. We have come together in a new and creative way for doing the old and taking on the new.

The future will be littered with questions which intend to halt, harass, and harness "The Fellowship." Most will come from without the movement and from some people and churches which have in the past tried to milk the denominational cow dry without being willing to buy the feed. To suggest that Dan Vestal, Jimmy Allen, Duke McCall, and the folks of the Atlanta consultation are "holding our missionaries hostage" is to walk very close to the edge of the irrational. To quote Carlyle Marney out of context, "Tell that to the Marines but don't try to take up a collection." While I am sure that "The Fellowship" must be careful to answer all questions which come to us, my heartfelt wish is that we shall not be held back or distracted by questions, allegations, and innuendo. The questions are not big enough, the allegations not true enough, and the innuendo simply doesn't matter.

Dan Yeary, preaching at the Atlanta meeting, called upon us to forget the language of "exile." I SECOND THE MOTION! Take the harps down! And also the bugles and banjoes and fiddles! Let's sing a new song! Pick up and strike out! Plow some new fields! Rebuild the walls! Let the grand old men, our fathers in the faith, men like Duke McCall, dream dreams! Let the young folk, our fathers and mothers of the future, folk like John Hewett and Carolyn Cole Bucy, see visions! God only knows what will and can happen.

I'm bullish on the "Bucket!" And I am genuinely excited about this infant we call "The Fellowship." Even though it was steaming hot in Atlanta 23-25 August 1990, it felt strangely similar to the season of Advent. Hope was being birthed.

An Address to the Public
from the Interim Steering Committee
of the Cooperative Baptist Fellowship
adopted 9 May 1991[1]

Introduction

Forming something as fragile as the Cooperative Baptist Fellowship is not
a move we make lightly. We are obligated to give some explanation for
why we are doing what we are doing. Our children will know what we have
done; they may not know why we have done what we have done. We have
reasons for our actions. They are:

Our Reasons Are Larger than Losing

For twelve years the Southern Baptist Convention in annual session has
voted to sustain the people who lead the fundamentalist wing of the SBC.
For twelve years the SBC in annual session has endorsed the arguments and
the rationale of the fundamentalists. What has happened is not a quirk or
a flash or an accident. It has been done again and again.

If inclined, one could conclude that the losers have tired of losing. But
the formation of the Cooperative Baptist Fellowship does not spring from
petty rivalry. If the old moderate wing of the SBC were represented in
making policy and were treated as welcomed representatives of competing
ideas in the Baptist mission task, then we would coexist, as we did for

---

[1]I presented this address to the Cooperative Baptist Fellowship (CBF) on 9
May 1991 in Atlanta. The CBF adopted the address that was designed primarily to
distinguish Moderate Southern Baptists from Fundamentalist Southern Baptists.
"An Address to the Public" represents one of CBF's earliest attempts at self-
definition. The document gives insight into what Moderate Southern Baptists
believe to be consistent with the Baptist tradition of freedom and responsibility.
After providing a cursory background to the Fundamentalist-Moderate Controversy,
the document lists some of the major issues in the conflict. It then commits
Moderates to the building of a new organization that will embody Baptist principles
and extend the missionary work of their people. For a brief history of the address
see the following document in this volume.

years, alongside fundamentalism and continue to argue our ideas before Southern Baptists.

But this is not the way things are. When fundamentalists won in 1979, they immediately began a policy of exclusion. Nonfundamentalists are not appointed to any denominational positions. Rarely are gentle fundamentalists appointed. Usually only doctrinaire fundamentalists, hostile to the purposes of the very institutions they control, are rewarded for service by appointment. Thus, the boards of SBC agencies are filled by only one kind of Baptist. And this is true whether the vote to elect was 60-40 or 52-48. It has been since 1979 a "winner take all." We have no voice.

In another day Pilgrims and Quakers and Baptists came to America for the same reason. As a minority, they had no way to get a hearing. They found a place where they would not be second-class citizens. All who attended the annual meeting of the SBC in New Orleans in June 1990 will have an enlarged understanding of why our ancestors left their homes and dear ones and all that was familiar. So forming the Cooperative Baptist Fellowship is not something we do lightly. Being Baptist should ensure that no one is ever excluded who confesses, "Jesus is Lord" (Philippians 2:11).

Our Understandings Are Different

Occasionally, someone accuses Baptists of being merely a contentious, controversial people. That may be. But the ideas that divide Baptists in the present "controversy" are the same ideas that have divided Presbyterians, Lutherans, and Episcopalians. These ideas are strong and central; these ideas will not be papered over. Here are some of these basic ideas.

1. *Bible*. Many of our differences come from a different understanding and interpretation of Holy Scripture. But the difference is not at the point of the inspiration or authority of the Bible. We interpret the Bible differently, as will be seen below in our treatment of the biblical understanding of women and pastors. We also, however, have a different understanding of the nature of the Bible. We want to be biblical—especially in our view of the Bible. That means that we dare not claim less for the Bible than the Bible claims for itself. The Bible neither claims nor reveals inerrancy as a Christian teaching. Bible claims must be based on the Bible, not on human interpretations of the Bible.

2. *Education*. What should happen in colleges and seminaries is a major bone of contention between fundamentalists and moderates. Fundamentalists educate by indoctrination. They have the truth and all the truth. As they see it, their job is to pass along the truth they have. They must not change

it. They are certain that their understandings of the truth are correct, complete, and to be adopted by others.

Moderates, too, are concerned with truth, but we do not claim a monopoly. We seek to enlarge and build upon such truth as we have. The task of education is to take the past and review it, even criticize it. We work to give our children a larger understanding of spiritual and physical reality. We know we will always live in faith; our understandings will not be complete until we get to heaven and are loosed from the limitations of our mortality and sin.

3. *Mission.* What ought to be the task of the missionary is another difference between us. We think the mission task is to reach people for faith in Jesus Christ by preaching, teaching, healing, and other ministries of mercy and justice. We believe this to be the model of Jesus in Galilee. That is the way he went about his mission task. Fundamentalists make the mission assignment narrower than Jesus did. They allow their emphasis on direct evangelism to undercut other biblical ministries of mercy and justice. This narrowed definition of what a missionary ought to be and do is a contention between us.

4. *Pastor.* What is the task of the pastor? They argue the pastor should be the ruler of a congregation. This smacks of the bishops's task in the Middle Ages. It also sounds much like the kind of church leadership Baptists revolted against in the seventeenth century.

Our understanding of the role of the pastor is to be a servant/shepherd. Respecting lay leadership is our assignment. Allowing the congregation to make real decisions is of the very nature of Baptist congregationalism. And using corporate business models to "get results" is building the church by the rules of a secular world rather than witnessing to the secular world by way of a servant church.

5. *Women.* The New Testament gives two signals about the role of women. A literal interpretation of Paul can build a case for making women submissive to men in the church. But another body of scripture points toward another place for women. In Galatians 3:27-28 Paul wrote, "As many of you as were baptized into Christ have clothed yourselves with Christ. There is no longer Jew or Greek, there is no longer slave or free, there is no longer male and female; for all of you are one in Christ Jesus" (NRSV).

We take Galatians as a clue to the way the church should be ordered. We interpret the reference to women the same way we interpret the reference to slaves. If we have submissive roles for women, we must also have a place for the slaves in the church.

In Galatians Paul follows the spirit of Jesus who courageously challenged the conventional wisdom of his day. It was a wisdom with rigid boundaries between men and women in religion and in public life. Jesus deliberately broke those barriers. He called women to follow him; he treated women as equally capable of dealing with sacred issues. Our model for the role of women in matters of faith is the Lord Jesus.

6. *Church.* An ecumenical and inclusive attitude is basic to our fellowship. The great ideas of theology are the common property of all the church. Baptists are only a part of that great and inclusive church. So, we are eager to have fellowship with our brothers and sisters in the faith and to recognize their work for our Savior. We do not try to make them conform to us; we try to include them in our design for mission. Mending the torn fabric of both Baptist and Christian fellowship is important to us. God willing, we will bind together the broken parts into a new company in preview of the great fellowship we shall have with each other in heaven.

It should be apparent that the points of difference are critical. They are the stuff around which a fellowship such as the Southern Baptist Convention is made. We are different. It is regrettable, but we are different. And perhaps we are most different at the point of spirit. At no place have we been able to negotiate about these differences. Were our fundamentalist brethren to negotiate, they would compromise. And that would be a sin by their understandings. So, we can either come to their position, or we can form a new fellowship.

We Are Called to Do More than Politic

Some people would have us continue as we have over the last twelve years, and continue to work within the SBC with a point of view to change the SBC. On the face of it this argument sounds reasonable. Acting it out is more difficult.

To change the SBC requires a majority vote. To effect a majority in annual session requires massive, expensive, contentious activity. We have done this, and we have done it repeatedly.

But we have never enjoyed doing it. Something is wrong with a religious body that spends such energy in overt political activity. Our time is unwisely invested in beating people or trying to beat people. We have to define the other side as bad and we are good. There is division. The existence of the Cooperative Baptist Fellowship is a simple confession of that division; it is not the cause of that division.

We can no longer devote our major energies to SBC politics. We would rejoice, however, to see the SBC return to its historic Baptist convictions. Our primary call is to be true to our understanding of the gospel. We are to advance the gospel in our time. When we get to heaven, God is not going to ask us, "Did *you* win in Atlanta in June of 1991?" If we understand the orders we are under, we will be asked larger questions. And to spend our time trying to reclaim a human institution (people made the SBC; it is not a scriptural entity) is to make more of that institution than we ought to make. A denomination is a missions-delivery system; it is not meant to be an idol. When we make more of the SBC than we ought, we risk falling into idolatry. Twelve years is too long to engage in political activity. We are called to higher purposes.

Conclusion

- That we may have a voice in our Baptist mission . . . for that is our Baptist birthright. . . .
- That we may work by ideas consistent with our understanding of the gospel rather than fund ideas than are not our gospel. . . .
- That we may give our energies to the advancement of the Kingdom of God rather than in divisive, destructive politics. . . .

For these reasons we form the Cooperative Baptist Fellowship. This does not require that we sever ties with the old Southern Baptist Convention. It does give us another mission delivery system, one more like our understanding of what it means to be Baptist and what it means to do gospel. Therefore, we create a new instrument to further the Kingdom and enlarge the Body of Christ.

A Brief History
of "An Address to the Public"[1]

I went to the first annual meeting of the Cooperative Baptist Fellowship on
Wednesday, 8 May 1991, and I had in my briefcase a document which I
called "The Preamble to the Constitution of the Baptist Fellowship." I had
been commissioned by the Interim Steering Committee of "The Fellowship" on which I served to come up with a draft of a preamble to the proposed constitution. Actually, a committee which I chaired was to come up
with the document, but the committee did not have a chance to meet before
the meeting of the Steering Committee on 8 May. I carried the document
to the Steering Committee, fully expecting that after discussion of the document by the plenary session of the Committee that it would be referred to
the subcommittee that I chaired. To my surprise, the Steering Committee
voted not to submit it to the subcommittee on "Purpose and Policy" and
endorsed the statement as was.

A word is in order about the history of that statement which eventually
was submitted to the 9 May Thursday-night session of "The Fellowship"
and entitled "An Address to the Public from the Interim Steering
Committee." The Interim Steering Committee previously had met in
Atlanta, on 7-9 March 1991 at the Airport Sheraton. I was cochair of the
subcommittee on "Purpose and Policy," and on Friday, 8 March 1991, I
submitted, on behalf of the committee, article 2 of the proposed constitution
which was a statement of purpose and read as follows: "The purpose of the
Baptist Fellowship is to enable the people of God to carry out the Great
Commission under the Lordship of Jesus Christ (Matthew 28:18-20), in a
fellowship where every member exercises God's gifts and calling."

After some very helpful and constructive debate, the Steering
Committee adopted a statement of purpose which read as follows: "The
purpose of the Baptist Fellowship is to enable the people of God to carry
out the Great Commission under the Lordship of Jesus Christ, in a
fellowship where every Christian exercises God's gifts and calling." As you
can see, there were two alterations. One, the scripture reference was
dropped. Two, "member" was changed to "Christian."

---

[1]I wrote this brief history on Sunday evening, 12 June 1991, three days after the
adoption of "An Address to the Public."

That statement of purpose was essentially proposed in the subcommittee by Duke K. McCall, former president of the Southern Baptist Theological Seminary in Louisville, Kentucky, and also the former president of the Baptist World Alliance. We debated many statements of purpose, some of them very long, before deciding to go with the brief but inclusive statement of Dr. McCall.

Upon adoption of the statement of purpose by the Steering Committee, Cecil Sherman, in my judgment the single most important member of the Steering Committee, moved that the subcommittee on "Purpose and Policy" submit at the next meeting of the Steering Committee a preamble to the Constitution which would state the historical context out of which the Fellowship had emerged. As chair of that committee, I was charged with that responsibility.

Before I left the Interim Steering Committee meeting, I asked several members of the committee to send me some suggestion regarding the preamble. Among those specifically requested were Charles Wade, pastor of the First Baptist Church in Arlington, Texas, and cochair of the subcommittee; Cecil Sherman, pastor of the Broadway Baptist Church in Fort Worth, Texas; Duke K. McCall; and Grady Cothen, former president of the Sunday School Board of the Southern Baptist Convention.

As time drew near for the next meeting of the Interim Steering Committee and the meeting of the Baptist Fellowship, I called three people and asked for input into the document. Those three were Duke K. McCall, Cecil Sherman, and Nancy Ammerman. Only Sherman sent a document, and it was a magnificent piece of work. However, I thought the document was too long for the purposes specified, so I set out to write one of my own. My document ended up being even longer and not nearly as good as the Sherman document. So, I set mine aside and began to work on editing his. I did the editing by calling on the phone several people and asking them to listen to the document and to make suggestions.

The first person I called was Kenneth Chafin, pastor of Walnut Street Baptist Church in Louisville, Kentucky. Chafin and Sherman were the most influential leaders within the workings of the Steering Committee. Chafin listened to several paragraphs of the document and asked, "Who wrote this . . . Cecil?" I responded, "Yes." Chafin said, "Walter, this could be Atlanta!" By which he meant that this could be the most historic occurrence at the meeting of the Fellowship 9-11 May in Atlanta. He was high in his praise of the document, saying that this is what people would remember about our meeting and that it would give the people something to take back to their churches. As I read through the document, Ken would interrupt, making suggestions. He was particularly insistent that I take out the "Breaking away" language in the document, encouraging me to use "Forming" language instead. This I did, and it was wise. This was Chafin's most important contribution to the document, though he made some other editorial suggestions.

I called Nancy Ammerman, planning to read the document to her, but she was teaching a course for Candler School of Theology at Marietta. I called Duke McCall and I missed him as well.

I then called my brother, Robert Shurden, chair of the Religion Department at Carson-Newman College and a New Testament scholar. He listened to the document, taking notes and not interrupting the reading. After finishing, he made several suggestions. His most important, however, was that there was no statement on the Bible in the document and he said that he did not know how we could issue a statement without tackling the central issue in the entire controversy: the Bible. I asked him what he would say. He talked and I took notes. What was included in the document on "Bible" was essentially his suggestions but put in my words. I felt it was a crucial addition to the document, vastly improving it and also making it the more controversial. I felt, however, that if we were going to say anything we had to confront the fundamentalists on the nature of the Bible. This is where they were most wrong, but they had used the emotional appeal of the Bible to beat us to death. Moderates had been too afraid to confront them on this issue.

I then called Hardy Clemons, pastor of the historic First Baptist Church, Greenville, South Carolina. He listened to the document read through completely and had nothing but high praise for it. I had but a very short time to talk with him. I did ask him what he thought about adding a statement on the Bible and he said he thought it would be appropriate and relevant.

The last person I called before editing the document in its final form was Leon McBeth, professor of Church History at Southwestern Baptist Theological Seminary in Fort Worth, Texas. I called Leon because he was a dear friend, a good historian who tended to be far more conservative than I in terms of our attitude toward the SBC, and because he had just finished publishing two books on Baptists, one of which was a book of documents. Because of the latter, I knew that he would know what I was up to. As I expected, Leon was the least enthusiastic of the people I talked with about the document.

Also, as I expected, McBeth made some very helpful suggestions. He was particularly concerned about the statement on personal evangelism, thinking that it gave fundamentalists too much of the good stuff. He also advised on making the last paragraph before the conclusion sound less like there was a total "giving up" on the SBC. Like too many in my estimation, he was still living with the myth that the SBC could be altered to reflect the historic and mainstream attitude of Southern Baptist people. I disagreed. But I thought his language softened the last paragraph, so I inserted what became the first and second sentences of the last paragraph before the conclusion. Those sentences begin and end with "We can no longer . . . in overt political activity."

After taking these suggestions from wise and insightful people, I also gave myself to the task of editing and doing some minor rewriting. Three other people read the document in full before I took it to Atlanta. They were my wife, Kay Wilson Shurden, my secretary, Ruth Cheves, and one of my colleagues at the Christianity Department at Mercer, Richard F. Wilson. All were helpful in suggesting editorial changes.

On Wednesday morning my secretary, with the assistance of Mrs. Jeannette Taylor of the president's office at Mercer, duplicated copies so that I could have them for the Steering Committee on Wednesday afternoon at our meeting at the Colony Square Hotel in Atlanta. Daniel Vestal and I had agreed that I would first read the statement to the Committee before passing it among them to read. He wanted them to "hear" the statement without comment, though he had no idea what was contained in the statement. After we distributed the document, several committee members raised questions and made suggestions. I had mentioned that the statement was in many ways more like the "Address to the Public" adopted by the SBC in 1845 than it was a "Preamble" to a constitution. Rudy Zachary, one of the youngest and a very helpful member of the Steering Committee suggested that it be received as an "Address to the Public" rather than a "Preamble." This was agreed by the group. A number of positive comments were made about the document. I think it is not too much to say that the committee was "moved" by the document.[2]

The only major content concerns that I recall came from Charles Wade of Arlington, Texas. He made the point regarding the section on women

---

[2]See Daniel Vestal's comment regarding the reading of the document to the Interim Steering Committee in his "The History of the Cooperative Baptist Fellowship," in *The Struggle for the Soul of the SBC: Moderate Responses to the Fundamentalist Movlement*, ed. Walter B. Shurden (Macon GA: Mercer University Press, 1993) 263.

that we ought as Christians stress the mutual submission of all Christians and not give the impression that Christians are not to be submissive people. Secondly, he wondered if it is enough to say "Being Baptist should ensure that no one is ever excluded who confesses 'Jesus is Lord.' " He wondered aloud if there should be some statement, for example, on believer's baptism. He got little support from the group, as I recall.

The discussion then focused on whether the document should be returned to committee or accepted as read. Kenneth Chafin and Jimmy Allen both encouraged the group to endorse the statement as it was and forego the committee work and wrangling over words. The vote was overwhelming in favor to do so. That night I gave Rudy Zachary, a computer whiz, my floppy disc and a hard copy with minor corrections, and he made me a copy which I read to the Fellowship on Thursday evening prior to the presentation of the Proposed Constitution. He also made a copy for distribution to the press.

On Thursday morning at the Steering Committee meeting, I approached Kenneth Chafin and said, "Ken, I really think that Cecil Sherman should read the 'Address to the Public' tonight. What do you think?" "I think you should read it," he said. Kenneth Chafin and Cecil Sherman had been the two most important Moderate leaders in the twelve-year resistance to the Fundamentalist takeover. In my judgment, Sherman had been the single most influential Moderate leader. In that leadership role Cecil Sherman had to speak out; when he did he spoke clearly, with more reference to the truth of the situation than to the politics of the situation, and he, therefore, was often accused, falsely in my judgment, of being abrasive. Because he was perceived by more of the Moderate public as more of a "firebrand" than I (though I never found myself in disagreement with Sherman in the twelve-year conflict with fundamentalists), and because I had the advantage of being heard as an objective historian—those are the reasons why Chafin thought I should read the statement. But it was precisely the historian in me that wanted Sherman to read the statement; I certainly did not want history to think that it was primarily my statement. And I knew it would be so perceived.

After talking with Sherman, and as an indication of the measure of the man, I honestly thought that he was far more interested in the statement being heard than he was in getting credit for the statement. As soon as I walked off the platform after reading the statement, Cecil Sherman walked up to me and said, "You did it right and you did it well." We sat down near the podium and commiserated on the importance of the meeting and the importance of the statement.

A Ten-Year Birthday Letter to *Baptists Today*[1]

Dear *Baptists Today* (BT),

It is a very strange thing to be wishing you a happy tenth birthday! I can still remember when they brought you home from the hospital, the day you first showed your fragile face. It was April 1983. You were dressed appropriately, in black and white.

Your existence, in one sense, marks time for all the rest of us. When you first came into the world, I was a forty-six-year-old professor on sabbatical leave who had just begun to realize that the sand was falling faster and faster and faster. Now, only ten years later, I am, gratefully, a four-time fifty-six-year-old grandfather who is still a bit taken aback by the deference shown me by numerous former students when I wind up at some Baptist watering hole.

Ten years from now, on your twentieth birthday party, I will be sixty-six and if there is still such a thing as social security I will more than likely be retired. When you are only thirty, I will, God willing, be seventy-six. By the way, if you folks at *BT* have any real influence and power, please reach up and stop the sun for awhile as did ole Joshua. Life is racing by me far too swiftly! Your birth marks not only your days, but ours.

BT, I do not know how to begin this birthday letter other than to say how much you have meant to all of us in the family. Our life as Baptists, especially the moderate Baptist family, would have been different—very, very different—without you. You may not have reflected very long on the fact that you really are the oldest child—the first "institution"—created by moderate Southern Baptists.

When your face first saw the light of history in April 1983, no other moderate child existed. The political network, created by the Gatlinburg

---

[1]*Baptists Today* is the unofficial national Baptist newspaper created by moderate Baptists of the South. I was invited to give an address on the tenth anniversary of *Baptists Today*. I delivered the address in the form of a "Birthday Letter" at a banquet on 16 April 1993 at the First Baptist Church, Decatur GA.

Gang[2] in September 1980, was in place, but no ongoing institutions had been created at that time.

It takes courage to be the first to wade into deep and troubled water. But you did. You remind me very much of the characteristically oldest child in the family. You know, the one all the others turn to, the one who sets the tone, the one with courage to act. In fact, you remind me very much of Walker Knight. You have led and you have nurtured and you have looked after all the rest of the moderate siblings that have come after you.

Just look at who followed you into the Baptist world! Southern Baptist Women in Ministry was born in June after you came in April. Next came the Forum in June 1984, the Southern Baptist Alliance in December 1986, Baptists Committed in December 1988, the Associated Baptist Press in July 1990, the Baptist Cooperative Missions Program and the Fellowship in August 1990, Smyth and Helwys in November 1990, the Baptist Center for Ethics in May 1991, the Baptist Theological Seminary in Richmond in September 1991, and the William H. Whitsitt Baptist Heritage Society in October 1992, and, apparently, more chillun' will follow.[3]

I honestly don't know what these younger brothers and sisters would have done without you. You became the clear and caring voice for announcing the birth of all these other children of Momma and Daddy Moderate. But you were far more than a mouthpiece for birth announcements; you were advocate, champion, encourager, and proponent.

As younger siblings, we knew you loved us and wanted us to survive and make a contribution to the family. To a great extent, you really helped to make life possible for us. One of the most important things you have done is to embrace us all. If you have a favorite among all the siblings, I honestly don't know which it is. You have been accused, so I've heard, of being partial to Women in Ministry, the Alliance, and I heard from someone that you were nothing more than a PR sheet for CBF and the

---

[2]This refers to a group of moderate Southern Baptist pastors who met in Gatlinburg TN in September 1980 and launched the resistance movement to the fundamentalist takeover of the SBC. Cecil Sherman, pastor of the First Baptist Church in Asheville NC, called the meeting. For his account of the meeting, see, Cecil E. Sherman, "An Overview of the Moderate Movement," in *The Struggle for the Soul of the SBC: Moderate Responses to the Fundamentalist Movement*, Walter B. Shurden, ed. (Macon GA: Mercer University Press, 1993) 15-23.

[3]You will find an account of the beginnings of these organizations in *The Struggle for the Soul of the SBC.*

second Sherman[4] of Atlanta. But it honestly appears to me that the family as a whole has been more important to you than any individual offspring. I'm glad you have included us all.

Well, other than express my knee-deep gratitude for what you have done for all of us, what do I most want to say to you on your tenth birthday? What, indeed, does one say to a ten-year-old, twice-monthly newspaper that describes itself as "a national, autonomous publication of news and opinion for Baptists in the U.S.A"?

As much as anything else on your tenth birthday, I want to wish you well with criticism, both the criticism which you dish out and that which is dished back at you. Don't ever forget that part of your business is to critique, to criticize, to share your judgment with the public. I would hate to be made to choose between what is most important in your self-description—"national," "autonomous," "news," "opinion," or "Baptists." But put a gun to my head and make me decide, and I just might say the word "opinion." If it is not the most crucial word, it is certainly the riskiest.

I read George Will, the columnist, for two reasons. One, he writes with amazing clarity. And anyone who communicates clearly in our muddled world deserves an audience. Second, I rarely agree with him, but he almost always challenges my thinking. He has a case he wants to make, and he makes it clearly. He has an opinion and he wants to bring me to it.

The thing that made *Home Missions* the best publication Southern Baptists had in the 60s and 70s is that it had a point of view, and it came from one who was not running for office of any kind in the Southern Baptist Convention. In fact, rather than being ambitious, many thought Walker Knight, the courageous editor, was suicidal. Likewise, the thing that made the *Christian Index* one of the two or three best state Baptist papers during the Jack Harwell years is that he had an angle on things. You might say it cost him his job.

The word "bias" has gotten an unnecessarily bad name in my judgment. Many people do not understand that you can be both objective and biased, all at the same time. The best example I know of that in Baptist history is Isaac Backus. He wrote his three-volume history of New England and everything he said was historically precise. He got his facts accurate. But he had a bias. It was a bias toward religious freedom for all people. It was a bias toward genuine separation of church and state. Backus was out to do

---

[4]The reference is to Cecil Sherman who became the first national coordinator of the Cooperative Baptist Fellowship that was located in Atlanta.

more than catalog facts and report names and dates and incidents. He was a partisan. He was out to change things in his society and the staid old commonwealth of Massachusetts. Baptists with good sense still read Backus. They do so because he had a point of view, an opinion on one of the most pressing issues of his day and ours.

So, *BT*, have an opinion. Get out in front of us. Stretch us. Pull us forward into the future. At the same time use your opinion to drag us back to our Baptist roots, which incidentally you have done superbly. My money says that not a Baptist newspaper anywhere has done a better job of teaching the Baptist heritage over any ten-year period than you from 1983 to 1993.

But back to this issue of criticism. Over these last ten years you have given out criticism aplenty. The fundamentalists think you have picked mostly on them, and most of us moderates have wanted you to pick mostly on "them" and probably you have. I personally hope that you do not forfeit this calling of criticizing fundamentalism. People of power ensconced in institutional leadership always need to have a public voice breathing down their necks, and fundamentalists are now in power in many places in America, especially the SBC. So keep the heat on them!

But, please! Don't get stuck there, *BT*. The Southern Baptist Convention Holy War is over. Fundamentalism doesn't deserve much of your attention, and the rest of us cannot afford any longer to waste our stewardship of time and energy and money in such a frivolous fashion as reading about it. So just remember: some letters simply do not deserve to be published or answered; there are more important things to do. Some stories do not need to be covered; they are not important.

In truth, for the future, your criticism, which is to say your discernment about things Baptist, will need to take aim at us moderates. We, of course, won't like it anymore than the fundamentalists, but we need it every bit as much as they. Too many of us moderates have been prophets too long to the fundamentalists. Somebody moderate needs now to be a prophet to us moderates. Or to say it another way, we moderates need spiritual direction. You can provide it, *BT*, by taking that word "opinion" seriously.

So, I wish you well on your tenth birthday in dispensing criticism. I also wish you well as you have criticism dished back at you. Your track record here is, so far as I know, very good. Neither Walker Knight nor Jack Harwell, your distinguished editors, have ice water running in their veins, but you folks have been remarkably nondefensive, while holding your ground.

But criticism of you, *BT*, will and should come. You probably would do well to get some voice mail like the synagogue I heard about. It goes like this: "Welcome to Temple Beth Shalom. If you're calling from a touch-tone phone and would like membership information, press 1. For our service schedule, press 2. To complain *to* the rabbi, press 3. To complain *about* the rabbi, press 4, 5, 6, or 7."

I am sure, *BT*, that you have to have more lines available for criticism of the paper than almost anything else. I urge you to keep those lines fully open.

But I also hope you will remember the sagacious comment made by the instructor at the baseball umpiring school down in Florida. The wise old umpire told the aspiring young umpires the following, "Just because they are yelling at you doesn't mean you are wrong!" I am convinced that Jesus lived his life out of that single sentence. "Just because they are yelling at you doesn't mean you are wrong."

Incidentally, *BT*, I played with that line during a Palm Sunday sermon once. You can turn it around in several ways. For example, try it this way: "Just because they are yelling for you doesn't mean they won't turn on you." Jesus knew that. I know that it is not an encouraging word for a ten year old, but I hope, *BT*, that you know it is truth. "Just because they are yelling for you doesn't mean they won't turn on you."

Here's another twist to the umpiring counsel: "Just because they are yelling for you doesn't mean you are right." Jesus knew that on Palm Sunday. Conviction must be based on something other than majority opinion. Your opinions must no more be rooted in the cheers of the moderates than they should be erased by the jeers of the fundamentalists. My guess is that Jesus was not reinforced by applause. Take that Palm Sunday crowd, for example. Even their genuinely sincere and spontaneous acts did not put steel into the spine of Jesus.[5] He simply was not what John Claypool once described as a "gallery person"; he did not play his life to the crowds, whether of the common people who heard him gladly or the religious establishment who plotted to do him in.

So, I could not let your birthday pass without wishing you well with criticism, your own of us and ours of you. But on your tenth birthday, I also wish you freedom. I know what your motto has been for years. "A Voice to Champion Freedom." You won't have a voice to champion freedom or

---

[5] I am honestly not sure, but I believe I have borrowed this umpiring story from Ernest T. Campbell.

anything else worthwhile among Baptists if you end up being owned by any group, groups, or individuals.

I hope you will never become "owned" by the CBF, the Alliance, Women in Ministry, Smyth and Helwys, the newly emerging seminaries (for which I am so grateful), or any of the rest of the many moderate organizations and movements which are developing. I hope that you are never owned financially, and I hope that you are never owned psychologically.

Our tendency will be the same as the fundamentalists: we'll want to "own" our own paper and for a very good reason. We want you to present the shiny side of our lives and our movement. We want good PR. We want you to oppose our adversaries as pompously and piously and proudly as we oppose them. I remember that committee of moderate leaders composed of Don Harbuck (God bless his memory), Bill Self, and Jim Strickland who paid you a visit in the fall of 1984 and urged you to take a stronger position against the SBC fundamentalists. If I had known they were making the trip, I would have been right along with them. For at times I have thought you timid, reserved, hiding behind your so-called journalistic objectivity. I sometimes have thought you were going for a fifteen-round decision or at most a TKO, and I wanted a first-round knockout. Don't be so sure, *BT*, that I won't yet pay you a visit, dishing out advice you didn't ask for but which I think you desperately need. Give me the privilege. I'm what you call a subscriber.

But don't be intimidated. Certainly don't be intimidated by me. But neither be intimidated by CBF or the Alliance or anybody else. Don't let happen to you what has happened to Baptist Press and to a growing number of the state Baptist papers: don't become a "house" organ.

I know that this will be frightening at times. You are caught in the rut of having to have subscriptions. I know the temptation will be for you as it was for Jesus right after his baptism: to take a shortcut and go for the money and the power and the acceptance. Follow his example: don't do it! I know and I am sure that you know the dangers of excessive individualism which becomes a depraved narcissism. It can happen to a newspaper just as it can happen to an individual or church or denomination. Even in the face of those dangers, however, I urge you to keep yourself as you say on your masthead, "autonomous."

I notice your masthead also says that you are "a national, autonomous publication." *BT*, now concerning that word, "national," I think you need to work on that for the next few years! You certainly made a giant step in the direction of that word by changing your name in 1990 from *SBC Today* to *Baptists Today*. Incidentally, my sense is that an adjective in front of

Baptists cheapens the word, very much like an adjective in front of gospel—"personal" gospel, "social" gospel—truncates the gospel. I'm glad you are now known today by *Baptists Today* or as I call you by your nickname, *BT*.

But would you let a friend make a suggestion to you on your birthday? Broaden your advisory board beyond moderate Southern Baptists. Include American Baptists, African-American Baptists, and others who would like to be represented and, more importantly, whose voices we need to hear and have represented. Other voices which reach deep into parts of the Baptist community which you have not had represented would make the title of the paper more accurate. You should not be named "Moderate Southern Baptists Today." You have the right name. Now live up to it! Because as you live up to that name you will be helping all the rest of us make contact with an unbelievably rich heritage which goes much further back than 1845.

One final thought on your birthday, *BT*. As much as any one of your single readers, I hope you know that I want you to remain a courageous voice for Baptist principles. But for the future, I honestly think you need to call us back not simply to our Baptist roots and what those roots mean today; I think you need to constantly call us back to where we all began. Where we began was not 1979 in Houston or 1845 in Augusta or 1611 in England. Where most of us began was with a simple promise, a promise to a serious following of a first-century Jew named Jesus of Nazareth.

Maybe if you kept this before us—a serious following of Jesus—maybe you would dish out criticism redemptively and receive it nondefensively. Maybe you would not only save yourself from being "owned" by your constituency, you would help save the rest of us from being owned by our octopus-like culture. Maybe if you kept before us the promise we made years ago, maybe you would not have to worry about being "national," and all the rest of us would not have to worry about being tribal because the Kingdom of God is neither. And the Kingdom of God is what Jesus took seriously.

I am not naive about this issue. I know that what it means to follow Jesus is at the heart of much of our denominational controversy for the last twelve years and, indeed, at the heart of most of the controversy of the Christian community since the first century. It is not an easy question to resolve—what it means to keep the promise, what it means to follow Jesus. But it seems to me, *BT*, that we can at least say that following Jesus means to take seriously what Jesus took seriously.

I know you have to spend a good bit of your time reading news releases from BP, ABP, AP, and RNS. What I am suggesting, *BT*, is that you spend a good portion of your time in the future reading Matthew, Mark, Luke, and John, trying to find out what Jesus took seriously. When you find out, tell us about it. God knows we need to hear it. We need it to find some wholeness for our own souls, and we need to hear it in order to have some healing to carry to this broken world all around us.

My guess, *BT*, is that you will outlive all of us who read you and support you and believe in you. We certainly hope so. I wish you a very happy birthday at ten, but I wish you many more decades of vibrant life and fruitful ministry. I hope that in the year 2083, when all of us in this room will be history, you will celebrate your centennial right here in the First Baptist Church of Decatur.

What I hope you will be celebrating is a hundred years of integrity and courage and inspiration, a hundred years of applying historic Baptist principles to contemporary life, a hundred years of helping readers to take Jesus of Nazareth very, very seriously.

Happy Birthday, BT! And many more.

A Birthday Letter
to Three-Year-Old Smyth & Helwys[1]

Dear Smyth & Helwys (SH),

Forgive my lack of creativity. But I do for you what I did for *Baptists Today* on its tenth birthday celebration last April. I have written you a birthday letter. While I know no other way to read it to you, I want to do what we used to say in Mississippi and "read it out loud."

So, now you are three years old! It really seems that you are much, much older than that to me. My, how you have grown! I can hardly believe my eyes when I see what you have become in only three short years. Look at this: as of 31 December 1993, you had twenty-one full-time employees, you had published thirty-eight books, and you had 1,300-plus churches in forty-six states using *Formations* Sunday school literature. With all your progress and sophistication, I hope you don't mind if I refer to you affectionately as SH.

Long before you were born, SH, I knew you would come into existence one day. One did not have to be a historian—certainly not a prophet—to see that someone such as you would simply have to be born. Like those first Baptists after whom you are named, you were born from the birth pains of freedom. In this regard, you are very much like all the other Moderate Baptist entities that have come into existence in the last ten or eleven years. All were born because the Baptist spirit and indeed the human spirit yearns to be free. Cecil Staton has written that the founders of SH were not Smyth and Helwys—not even Staton and Jackson and Nash and Pitts, but Pressler and Patterson.[2] He is, of course, correct. The Moderate Baptist Movement, like my sagacious friend Loulie Pettigrew says, is really the Baptist Resistance Movement. What it resisted is theological tyranny and denomi-

---

[1]I presented this address at the invitation of Smyth & Helwys Publishing on 13 January 1994 at the Woodruff House of Mercer University in Macon GA.

[2]The name "Smyth and Helwys" comes from the two earliest Baptist leaders, John Smyth and Thomas Helwys. Cecil Staton, Ron Jackson, Scott Nash, and Jim Pitts were the original founders of Smyth & Helwys. Paul Pressler and Paige Patterson led the fundamentalist movement that took over the SBC, including the Sunday School Board, the SBC publishing arm.

national uniformity and crass bossism. What it embraced was the Baptist spirit to be free from coercion and control.

My birthday letter to you, SH, consists of three admonitions. I suppose I spent too much time in Southern Baptist circles listening to preachers with their six to twelve alliterations in a single sermon. I am drawn to only three alliterations for you tonight, and as you will see even then, one of them is laboriously strained and warps the otherwise brilliant symmetry of my birthday greeting. All three points pertain to your future. These three, as I hope you would know, represent only a partial list of my hopes and concerns for you, SH.

Point One. BE BIBLICAL.

I fear that Moderate Baptists have let the Fundamentalists take the Bible from us. They have waved the Bible in our face for so long and they have intimidated us with their certitude about the Bible so much that some, I fear, cringe at the admonition "Be Biblical." SH, do not fear and do not cringe.

To "be biblical" is not the same as being Fundamentalist. Indeed, I think it is high time we began to identify Fundamentalism as the cultural, psychological. and nonbiblical phenomenon that it is.

To "be biblical," SH, is to point out the diversity and not simply the uniformity within the Bible itself. One cannot reconcile the view of suffering in Deuteronomy with that in Job. And why should we try? Suffering is a colossal mystery to our always-tiny minds and often-bruised spirits. We stand at the edge of suffering like a little boy at the edge of the ocean with his britches legs rolled up. We can only dip our toes into this mystery. Why not two views rather than one?

And one cannot reconcile the view of Christianity toward the state described in Romans 13 and that depicted in Revelation 13, and why should we try? Different times call for different texts. One day you resist mightily; another day calls for gratitude. It is part of the dangerous sojourn of the life of faith to know one from the other. Thank God we have more than one text!

To "be biblical" is to press us to take Jesus as seriously in Matthew and Mark and Luke as we take Paul in Romans. And I would even add, "more seriously."

To "be biblical" is to call us beyond that kind of Bible study that is simply the transmission of right knowledge to Bible study that is the alteration of our lives. Compassion is more legitimately the right end of a

Sunday school class than is orthodoxy, whether defined by liberals or fundamentalists.

So come to us—your constituency—SH, out of the Bible. Let it be your anchor and your point of beginning and your primary text. Help us to become a more, not less, biblical people. Give us some January Bible studies on Genesis 1–11 and let's give the glorious book of Hosea a rest for a few years.

Lest I be misinterpreted, I want to make it clear that I sense you have no intention of doing otherwise than to "Be Biblical." I simply want you to know that I think that is what we need from you now and in the future. Moderates, also, have a long way to go to reach biblical literacy. So BE BIBLICAL.

Point Two. BE BAPTIST.

I am delighted at your name—Smyth and Helwys. It begins at the beginning of the Baptist story and therefore has the opportunity to include the whole sweep of the Baptist heritage. Have you noticed that other Baptist publishing houses, both extinct and extant, have taken more provincial names? Carey Kingsgate, Judson, and Broadman. All of these are national or regional in character. The Baptist family has been too long divided into racial, national, cultural, and theological clans. I have no idea, SH, that you will remedy that problem by your existence. But you can help.

In fact, you have a chance to create an "ecumenically Baptist" publishing house. You have done a good job of publishing some of the work of British Baptists, Canadian Baptists, and others. Thanks! Those of us among Moderate Baptists in the South need to hear from these sisters and brothers in the faith.

Above I said "Be Biblical." I am not backing up on the primary admonition when I also say to you to "Be Baptist." I mean to urge you, SH, to keep your work close to the Baptist vision of spirituality, one which at its best has never needed an apology. I am one who believes that if we become a more historical people, aware of our Baptist, Protestant, and Christian heritage, we shall have a better chance of becoming a more biblical people. It was in a church history course, not a biblical or theological course, in seminary that I learned that the satisfaction theory of the death of Jesus is more historically conditioned that it is biblically mandated. I have been aware for the last fifteen years that the Baptists in my neighborhood who know the most about what it means to be Baptist are "older" Baptists, the kind who use to go to BTU³ where they had "to give parts" on what being Baptist was all about. My historical hunch is that the demise of BTU plays some minor role in the rise of the new kind of fundamentalism among Baptists. SH, just as if you help us to be biblical you will save us from fundamentalism, so if you help us to be Baptist you will save us from the twisted sectarianism of Landmarkism.

Point Three. BEWARE.

This last "be" helps you understand why I said the alliterative symmetry is strained. It is, however, the best I can do. So BEWARE. Of what?

Beware of power. I predict you will eventually have a good portion of it. Beware! It is harder for an institution to resist power than it is for an individual. What we would never do or say as individuals, we'll do when we get together in groups and we'll justify as institutions in the name of realism and survival.

Increasingly, the passage of scripture that I am returning to again and again for personal reflection is the temptation narrative of Jesus. Maybe you folks, like those of us in all institutions, ought to make it your institutional text. I predict you will have enormous power in Baptist life. Beware.

Beware of power. And "Beware of" possessions. We really do not live by bread alone, whether by "bread" one means the dough one eats or the dough one spends. I predict that in time you will be powerful. I predict that in time you will be profitable. I am sure that your investors and creditors will be glad to hear that optimistic word from such a financial wizard as I! I genuinely hope I am right. I wish you all good compensation and good measure from your employment at SH. With the hours you work, you deserve it.

But I remind you again that SH does not live by "bread" alone. SH lives by virtue of a cause and a commitment that gives meaning to life. My analysis of the people who founded SH and those of you who have come to work at SH is that you have come together because you thought you were coming to something worth working for. I still believe that people will respond to need when they will not respond to personal gain or prestige.

Do you remember that little obscure story over in the tenth chapter of the book of Numbers when Moses and the people were striking their tents

---

³This refers to "Baptist Training Union," a Sunday evening discipleship training program in Southern Baptist Churches that began dying in the 1960s. Part of the purpose of the program was to teach the Baptist heritage.

and making tracks for the Promised Land. Moses needed help. He did not know the desert sufficiently well. So he turned to a relative by the name of Hobab for help. But how do you motivate another person for such a dangerous mission? Moses took two approaches to encourage Hobab to help. First, he tried the "prosperity theme." It was an early take on the "Health and Wealth" gospel which we have heard so much of in recent years in this country. He took the approach that "getting beats giving." Said Moses to Hobab, "We are setting out for the place which the Lord has promised us; come with us and we will do you good." Come with us, said Moses, and we will cut you in on the grace and the gravy of life. And to all of this, to Moses's surprise, Hobab said, "Thanks, but no thanks."

Then Moses took a different tack. He took the approach that "giving beats getting." Said Moses the second time around, "Do not leave us, I pray you, for you know how we are to encamp in the wilderness, and you will be as eyes to us." Moses would need to know in his wilderness wandering which trail to take and which to avoid, which water was safe and which was not, which tribes were hostile and which were friendly. He was offering Hobab an opportunity to do something valid and significant for a cause that mattered.[4]

All of you people at SH—those who have invested in it, those who founded it, those who work at it every day to make a success out of it—I believe you have responded to a need rather than to personal prestige or personal gain. Beware of forgetting that, of forgetting how you began, of where you were in the desert when you struck out on this risky journey. I hope I am around to see your twenty-first birthday, SH. I predict one day a beautiful building with all the accouterments of "bread"—grand offices with large plate-glass windows and a good bit of desk overhang and fancy stationery. I do not begrudge you any piece of bread you get; you deserve it. Just BEWARE. Remember that you were born to serve, to serve the cause of freedom.

Beware of taking your calling for granted.

Beware of taking your work for granted.

A word or a chapter or a lesson has been known to redirect the life of a human being for good.

---

[4]I am indebted for the insights and some of the language I have used to a sermon by Ernest T. Campbell, "The Need to Be Needed." He preached this at Riverside Church, New York City, on 21 October 1973.

In his Cotton Patch Version of the New Testament, Clarence Jordan called the devil in the temptation story "The Confuser."[5] Beware of thinking that you cannot be confused about what it is you are up to and why you are doing what you are doing.

Did you hear about the airplane that took off from London's Heathrow airport? A metallic, computer-like voice came over the loudspeaker: "Ladies and gentlemen, Vista Airlines would like to welcome you to the first transatlantic flight that is being controlled completely by computer. The possibility of human error has been eliminated because there is no pilot and no crew on board. All of your needs will be taken care of by the very latest technology. Please, just relax and enjoy your flight. Every contingency has been prepared for, and nothing could possibly go wrong, . . . possibly go wrong, . . . possibly go wrong, . . . possibly go wrong. . . . "

SH, do not leave us. You shall be as eyes to us.

BE BIBLICAL. BE BAPTIST. BEWARE.

Happy third birthday.

13 January 1994   *Walter B. Shurden*

---

[5]Clarence Jordan, *The Cotton Patch Version of Matthew and John* (New York: Association Press, 1970) 20.

A Decade of Promise[1]

Somewhere about the year 409 BCE, Alaric and his Visigoths parked themselves at the gates of Rome. In his masterful retelling of that story in *How the Irish Saved Civilization*, Thomas Cahill described the Romans' arrogant and contemptuous attitude toward Alaric: "He might as well have been," said Cahill, "the king of the Fuzzy-Wuzzies, or any other of the inconsequential outlanders that civilized people have looked down their noses at throughout history." The Romans, supremely confident of handling this nuisance, dispatched a couple of diplomats to conduct the tiresome negotiations with Alaric and rid themselves of these smelly barbarians.

The Roman diplomats played poker with empty bluffs. They tried to intimidate. The "invincible strength" of Rome's warriors will doom any of your misguided attacks, warned the Romans. But Alaric the Barbarian, a humorous as well as a sharp man, responded gleefully, "The thicker the grass, the more easily scythed."

Recognizing now that they had no fool on their hands, the Romans asked finally, and in desperation, what was Alaric's price of departure. Alaric answered somewhat matter-of-factly: his men would sweep through the city of Rome, take all the gold, all the silver, and everything of value that could be moved. They would also take with them every barbarian slave in Rome's custody.

The Romans protested hysterically. But through their now anxiety-ridden laughter and feigned anger, the Romans asked Alaric, "But . . . what will that leave us?"

Alaric paused. "Your lives," he said.[2]

After eleven years of hand-to-hand combat with our fundamentalist sisters and brothers (mostly brothers!), we came to the Atlanta Inforum on a very hot 23rd of August in 1990 as the "Consultation of Concerned Southern Baptists."

We came to Atlanta, but, truth be told, we came *only with our lives*.

The denomination was in the process of being carted off by folks with an attitude, an attitude of intolerance and narrowness that had been standing

---

[1]This is a heretofore unpublished address that I gave at the tenth anniversary banquet of the Cooperative Baptist Fellowship in Atlanta on 27 June 2001.

[2]Thomas Cahill, *How the Irish Saved Civilization* (New York: Doubleday, 1995) 30-31.

at the gates of the SBC, not simply since 1979 but, as Luther Copeland said in one of the best Baptist books ever written, since 1845.[3] But it is true that when American culture began to change dramatically in the late 1970s, the attitude of intolerance began to strut triumphantly and somewhat haughtily over both culture and Caesar and Christ. The attitude swept in and took over the 150-year history of the Southern Baptist Convention.

And they walked off with all the gold and the silver, the six seminaries and the mission boards and the publishing agency and the Christian Life Commission and everything that was of value at the national denominational level. We got out . . . with our lives . . . and some good colleges and universities and some state conventions that would later go up for grabs. But mostly, we got out with our lives.

And some Baptist convictions. They forgot to take the heritage with them. Or else they did not want it. And here, my friends, is one of the two reasons I can think of for dubbing the first ten years of CBF history a decade of promise. It was a decade of promise because we got out with the broader and deeper and richer part of the Baptist tradition and the principles that had undergirded that tradition for 400 years.

So, as my late fourth-grade-educated daddy would have said, "We toted off some stuff, too." It was stuff they didn't want; it was the historic Baptist principles that cluster around freedom. And to your everlasting credit, most of you have never forgotten over this past decade of clumsy, stumbling beginnings, that the other side of Baptist freedom is Christian responsibility and Christian discipleship.

To speak of our Baptist freedom is not to talk of some New Age navel-gazing, unaware that we live under the Lordship of Christ or that we are to live out Kingdom of God values. To speak of our freedom is not to be fixated on ourselves. Real freedom always works for a broader good. You have worn your freedom over this past decade as a badge of stewardship for others. And that stewardship raised up new seminaries, sent out new as well as seasoned missionaries, called for new publication materials, espoused a more compassionate set of ethics, and affirmed both women and men, lay and clergy in the ministry of Christ.

We got out with the freedom to have both an open Bible and an open mind,

---

[3]E. Luther Copeland, *The Southern Baptist Convention and the Judgment of History: The Taint of an Original Sin*, rev. ed. (Lanham MD: University Press of America, 2002).

a concept of the church that is both ecumenical and congregational,
a view of religious freedom that thinks both of others as well as self,
a concept of ministry that included both laity as well as clergy,
an understanding of the church's mission that included both justice and
     mercy as well as evangelism and missions.

What many have said about our struggle is true. It was a power struggle. If, however, that somewhat crass interpretation is the only spin you put on the story, you miss the essence of the story. It was not only a struggle for the gold and the silver and the artifacts of imperial denominational power. It was also a struggle for principles. I have heard many calls in the last ten years admonishing us to forget the past, to stop fighting the fundamentalist-moderate war, to cease bashing the fundamentalists, and, believe me, I understand fully that call.

But my fear is that if we forget the struggle, we may forget the reasons for the struggle. The Passover and July 4 and Bastille Day are not observed annually in order to bash the Egyptians and the British and the royalty; they are days to recall the price people paid for the struggle for freedom. If it were only a struggle for buildings and offices and endowments, surely we must forget that. If all we were discussing was who was to be in charge—sure, that's petty and somewhat sinful stuff. UNLESS . . . unless who is in charge also has something to do with principles espoused. And I contend that it was a struggle for principles, and we will forget that at our peril.

One of those principles was gender equality. That was not simply a bid for power; it was then and it is now a moral issue. And in the words of James Carville, that wholly objective and nonpartisan political pundit, "We're right and they are wrong!" Mark my words. One day the Southern Baptist Convention will apologize to women. They will apologize to women for some of the same reasons that they and all the rest of us had to apologize to African Americans. They will apologize to women for the same reasons that some of us here tonight have had to apologize to women.

Another principle for which we contended was the equality of the laity. That was not simply a bid for power; it was a serious theological issue. In terms of the Baptist vision of Christianity, we're right and they are wrong. The Priesthood is universal; it belongs to all believers. Baptists never, ever intended to be clergy-dominated people. After working with some of the gifted laity of CBF for the last ten years, one understands why.

Another of the principles underlying much of the controversy was the nature and mission of the church of Jesus Christ. The Kingdom of God is not solely about handing out tracts or personal witnessing, but it is certainly about some of that; but the Kingdom of God also has to do with the struggle for justice and mercy and peacemaking as part of the mission of the church. And many of you came to CBF because you understood the mission of the church to include, not exclude, acts of mercy and justice.

Yet another principle in contention was the nature of biblical truth—its breadth and depth. We were saying, "Our little systems have their day, they have their day and cease to be, they are but mere broken lights of Thee, and Thou, O God, art more than they." They were saying, "We have the truth, the whole truth, and nothing but the truth." And we are right and they are wrong.

These principles, for which many of you in this room contended, made it a decade of promise for us. But we have our sins, too. And our sins—real sins not feigned sins, sins we have committed and sins we omitted—our sins do not permit smugness or arrogance on our part. Repentance toward God, not contempt toward others, is our needed response tonight. I really will not allow my opening illustration to be pushed beyond my use of it. I'm not calling others barbarians. I am calling on us to confront our own inward primitivism, our own thorny self-serving aspirations to control in however so subtle ways. You and I have not yet begun to live out the radical meaning of Baptist freedom under the Lordship of Christ as it relates to our individual lives, our local churches, or CBF. We yet have work to do.

As our great grandchildren look back on us from the vantage point of the year 2101, the cardinal question will not be, did CBF live and survive? The only important question is, did the principle endure? Will we live it out? Will we push it forward? Fighting for freedom is a heady and intoxicating thing. But squandering freedom appears to be an inevitable thing. The natural evolution of freedom in Christian history is that it gets crushed by the juggernauting forces of creedalism, sacerdotalism, and centralization, by people who speak glibly and cavalierly about knowing God's will. And then the fight for freedom breaks out all over again.

So we got out with our lives. But we also got out with treasured principles. If we had kept the gold and the silver and lost our heritage, we would have lost more than the battle; we would have lost the war. Baptists cannot live by bread alone or by brick and stone alone, either. Ideas matter. Fundamentalists and moderates have different ideas. And those ideas work themselves out in church life and denominational life in vastly different ways. If there really is no difference in the SBC and the CBF except who is in charge, we ought to close this thing down and go back and accept our role as submissive losers in a war over gold and silver. But there was something more at stake than gold and silver. Convictions were involved.

So, we got out with our lives. And we got out with the principles. But we also got out with each other, with other lives, good and decent and, in some cases, fearless, lives. *And that's the second reason it has been a decade of promise.* We didn't get out with the most people, and we didn't get out with all the good people, but we got out with *some very good people.* And that is of no small moment when you remember what lives we got out with: Duke McCall and Grady Cothen, Foy Valentine and Keith Parks, Carolyn Crumpler and James Dunn, Randall Lolley and Russell Dilday, Jimmy Allen and Roy Honeycutt. Most of our administrators came with us, though some of the best of those got tongue-tied and stumbled at places along the way.

And most of those who taught us came with us. In a sense they had no choice! We were doing and saying what they had taught us to do and say. So Frank Stagg and Glenn Hinson and Ken Chafin and Morris Ashcraft and Henlee Barnette and Alan Neely and Wayne Oates and the list could go on and on of our teachers who came with us.

But there were also pastor-types who rode the lead horses and performed valiantly in the trenches: Jim Slatton and Don Harbuck and Lavonn Brown and Bill Sherman and Bill Bruster and John Jeffers and Daniel Vestal and especially, especially Cecil Sherman. Maligned by some even on our side of the aisle as "too abrasive," Cecil Sherman was right more times on more issues in SBC life in the 1980s and 1990s than any other single person I know.

He was right to call the Gatlinburg Gang together to resist the attitude of control.

And he was right to quit the Peace Committee when others would not resist the attitude of control.

And he was right to accept the role as the first coordinator of the CBF to help create a future for freedom among moderate Baptists.

And he was right to say after he was installed: "In these days Baptist ideas are at risk. I go to the Fellowship to fly our flag. . . . Somewhere there needs to be something that is free. At the Fellowship I will try not to use freedom as an excuse to be irresponsible. But we will be free."[4]

Cecil Sherman and all the others whose names I have called lost the battle. They did not lose nearly as big as some would pretend, but they lost.

---

[4]As cited in *Fellowship: Newsletter of the Cooperative Baptist Fellowship,* September 2000, 10-11.

Most of us in this room tonight would rather lose a battle with those Baptist people than win triumphantly with any group of conquerors anywhere.

We got out with our lives, but we lost our titles, our professorships, our desk overhang, our fancy letterheads, and tons of brick and mortar. What we lost, as one said after his antique-laden home burned down, was "stuff." But we got out with some real good lives.

And then, lo and behold, good, new lives emerged. From that horrendous pain came wonderful and creative new life among us. Some of them we had hardly known. Others we had not heard of: Patsy Ayers, Oeita Bottorff, Ann Neil, Suzi Paynter, Reba Cobb, Nancy Ammerman, Cindy Johnson, Joy Steincross, Martha Smith, Molly Marshall, Sarah Frances Anders, and Donna Forrester, to name a few. The ugly attitude of exclusivity would have never given that list a leadership role in the new SBC or even the old SBC. The struggle freed us up to do things we could have never done before.

And then look at who else showed up for us: John Hewitt and John Tyler and Bill Owen and Jim Lacy and John Cothran and Steve Tondera and Patrick Anderson and Tommy Boland and Hardy Clemons. Here is a mixture of both laity and clergy whose astounding gifts would never have been accepted on the altar of the fundamentalist regime.

It will go down as a decade of promise because of the lives we got out with and the principles they stood for and struggled for. And now the trick for the future: how to hold on to the principles that gave us our life. How to hold on to the dangerous, ephemeral, somewhat clumsy and often nasty thing we call Baptist freedom? How do we balance the inebriating power of freedom with the sobriety of faithful discipleship? How do we remain free and faithful Baptists? How do we fortify ourselves so that freedom cannot be snatched from us in the future? And how do we inform ourselves so that we don't give freedom away? My reading of Baptist history convinces me that more freedom has been given away than has ever been taken away in Baptist life. Our own blissful passivity rather than the angry invasion of aggressors has done as much harm as anything.

Do not be surprised if, at some point in our future, another Paul Pressler or Paige Patterson will emerge even in our midst who will want to control and restrain and exercise authority over conscience and churches and tell you what to believe and how to believe and what is biblical and what is not. Let's promise each other here tonight that if we err, we will err together, and we will err together on the side of freedom so that we will at least have a chance to be faithful.

When Larry and Carolyn Dipboye asked me to speak tonight and I consented, I wrote them back and asked them to tell me what to say. Larry suggested, wanting brevity I think, that I give a Baptist Gettysburg Address. So with sincere apologies to President Lincoln, let me close.

One decade ago our sisters and brothers brought forth in this city a new Baptist group, conceived in liberty, and dedicated to the radical proposition that all Baptist Christians are equal. Now we shall be for the foreseeable future engaged in an effort to keep that proposition alive, testing whether any group of Baptists anywhere can long endure with freedom as their watchword. We have come here tonight to dedicate a few minutes and a few memories to those who for the past decade risked their careers and literally offered up their lives, their time, and their money that freedom, rather than control, might live among Baptists. We have come here to remember a "decade of promise." It is altogether fitting and proper that we should do this. But, in a larger sense, we cannot dedicate—we cannot consecrate—we cannot hallow this past decade with our words or even our memories. The brave women and men, mostly still living but a few now dead, who struggled here for the last ten years, consecrated the history of CBF far above our poor power to add or detract. The Baptist world will little note nor long remember what we say here, but it can never forget what they did here. It is for us to dedicate ourselves here in Atlanta, ten years later, to the unfinished work which they so nobly advanced. Let us resolve that they did not act in vain and that CBF shall have a new birth of freedom and that soul freedom, Bible freedom, church freedom, and civil freedom shall not perish from CBF or from the larger Baptist tradition.

Six Words for the First Ten Years of CBF[1]

At the closing session of the 1990 "Consultation of Concerned Southern Baptists" in Atlanta, Jimmy Allen, who had presided over the meeting, was speaking. Some of you will remember that he began to weep as he said, "This will be a day we will look back to and long remember." Most of us knew at the time that he was telling the truth. Those were electric days. Ten years after Jimmy Allen spoke those words the Baptist editors in 2000 chose the formation of CBF (Cooperative Baptist Fellowship) as the most important Baptist news story of the 90s.

What follows are personal reflections, not historically researched conclusions, on the past ten years of the Cooperative Baptist Fellowship. So that I will not get confused with Moses, I have only six, not ten reflections. So here are "Six Words for the First Ten Years of CBF Life."

1. *Beginnings*. The first word is *beginnings*. Let me begin by tweaking our ten-year celebration. CBF began in 1990, not 1991. Daniel Vestal was the first leader of CBF. That's not a minor matter for historians, it seems to me. I am aware, of course, that moderates did not actually organize CBF until 1991. But the specific CBF strand of history is a clear continuation from what began in 1990, not simply what happened in 1991. Historically, in terms of our continuous history, we are eleven years old, not ten.

The 1990 beginning meeting of what was to be CBF may have been the most exhilirating Baptist meeting I've ever attended. If not, the 1991 meeting in Atlanta certainly was. Nancy Ammerman brought us to our feet in 1991 when she said, "This is one free Baptist who had rather be in the desert with you than be back in Egypt making bricks." Her allusion to the desert indicated that we all knew we were going somewhere, but we did not yet know where or how. Some did not want to go. Leaving the SBC was too much for them. Some of us had already left. It was a genuine grief experience.

Shortly after the 1990 moderate meeting in Atlanta, I wrote a brief article for *Baptists Today* entitled "Reflections on The Baptist Consultation of Moderates In Atlanta."[2] In the closing sentences of that article, I said: "I

---

[1] I gave this address at the annual meeting of the William H. Whitsitt Baptist Heritage Society in Atlanta on 28 June 2001. It subsequently was published, essentially as is, in *The Whitsitt Journal* 8/2 (Fall 2001): 1, 3-5.

[2] See that article in this volume.

am genuinely excited about this infant we call 'The Fellowship.' Even though it was steaming hot in Atlanta 23-25 August 1990, it felt strangely similar to the season of Advent. Hope was being birthed." While certainly not a perfect place, CBF has been a very hopeful place for many ever since. For others, it has been the *only* place that felt like a Baptist denominational home.

An honest reflection, however, is that some of that early excitement has dissipated. I'm not sure why I say this. Maybe it is an autobiographical confession of good ole fashion Baptist backsliding. Maybe it is simply the inevitability of a movement becoming an organization. Maybe it is that the heady wine of volunteerism got professionalized over the last decade, something we all knew had to happen. Whatever it is, one of the things CBF would do well to ask itself constantly is: "How do we feed the fire of beginnings?" What causes the fire to die down in any religious movement, even go out? Is it too much to hope that the fire can be kept alive? I am grateful that so many are working so hard in CBF circles to try and make that happen.

2. *Diversuty*. The second word is *diversity*. The Interim Steering Committee of 1990/1991 consisted of some amazingly committed and talented people with big egos and different ideas. Daniel Vestal had a full-time job keeping us focused and on the same playing field. As a group, we would not be repressed or muzzled. I have been told that the same has been true of the coordinating councils for subsequent years, and I assume it is still true today. I hope so. It is little more than an expression of our diversity as moderate Baptists.

If we thought we had escaped controversy by leaving the SBC, we were wrong. Moderate Baptists have always had a left and a right and a middle or, to say it another way, a "high" church, a "low" church, and a "broad" church. At a retreat of East Tennessee moderates at Gatlinburg back in 1987, I spoke on the subject "Some Myths of Moderates." One of the myths, I suggested, with which moderates amused themselves was the one which said, "You watch what I am telling you, the fundamentalists will turn on each other and start fighting among themselves; they've got too many egotists among them." I noted at that time, and correctly I think, that fundamentalist Christians have no monopoly on egotism! A few of our differences in CBF have doubtless been a matter of swollen egos, but many of our differences were and are an honest contention for priorities.

What we had in common when we came together in 1990 was a bruising defeat. We also had a common concern to be free from fundamentalist domination. But from the very beginning we brought different agendas into the tent we call CBF. One agenda was missions. I am well aware that surveys have told us that this is the first priority of most CBFers. But the creation of a new missionary society was not the sole, even primary, reason why some of the most passionate among us became excited about the formation of CBF. Theological education done in a vigorous and nonindoctrinating manner was a priority for some. Baptist convictions regarding the autonomy of the local church, the priesthood of all believers, separation of church and state, and soul liberty were a draw for others. Still others came to CBF for freedom to engage in justice issues: gender equality, racial equality, peacemaking, hunger issues, and religious liberty for all. Doubtless, a few tall souls came for all those reasons.

There is little reason to think that this contention for priorities will cease. I doubt you can talk so freely about freedom the way we have in CBF and not have remarkable diversity. Thus far, we have been able to move on together even after the debates produced winners and losers. One hopes that we can move together into the future without too much uniformity.

I'm still fond of that line from Daniel Vestal after the 1991 meeting when some reporters asked him about the lengthy discussions surrounding the formation of CBF. Vestal said, "This is the first time in twelve years these people have been to a Baptist meeting where they can talk." Then he said, *"Viva la chaos."* Maybe we ought to be slow to tame the contention for priorities in CBF. Chaos, itself, has energy in it.

3. *Bible*. A third word is *Bible*. In the "Address to the Public" which the Interim Steering Committee delivered to the General Assembly in 1991 we tried to express some of the basic differences between the leadership of the SBC and CBF. Intentionally and deliberately, we listed the "Bible" as the first point of difference, a difference that was almost impossible to debate in a serious way during the conflict. Here is what we said in that "Address" in 1990:

> Many of our differences come from a different understanding and interpretation of Holy Scripture. But the difference is not at the point of the inspiration or authority of the Bible. We interpret the Bible differently, as will be seen below in our treatment of the biblical understanding of women and pastors. We also, however, have a different understanding of the nature of the Bible. We want to be biblical—especially in our view of the Bible. That means that we dare not claim less for the Bible than the Bible claims for itself. The Bible neither claims nor reveals inerrancy as a

Christian teaching. Bible claims must be based on the Bible, not on human interpretations of the Bible.[3]

Given that the Bible played such a central role in the controversy, should we not have given more attention over the last ten years to the issues surrounding the Bible? If we could somehow parlay the old "study course" approach, on which many of us cut our teeth, into a far more serious investigation of biblical issues—how we got the Bible, how culture impacted biblical writers, how culture impacts our own reading of the Bible—we will find, I believe, willing and devoted listeners in most of our churches.

Any college professor of first-year Bible courses anywhere in Baptist life can testify to the fact that kids coming from our churches simply do not know the Bible. We need in CBF a renewed emphasis on being a seriously biblical people. This is not a call to outdo the fundamentalists in bragging on the Bible. It is a call for a serious confrontation with those aspects of the Bible that challenge and correct our own commitments in life. It is a call to make our slogans about the Bible and the lordship of Christ more than mere rhetoric.

4. *Ecumenical.* A fourth word is *ecumenical.* In the "Address to the Public" we said the following about the church.

> An ecumenical and inclusive attitude is basic to our fellowship. The great ideas of theology are the common property of all the church. Baptists are only a part of that great and inclusive church. So, we are eager to have fellowship with our brothers and sisters in the faith and to recognize their work for our Savior. We do not try to make them conform to us; we try to include them in our design for mission. Mending the torn fabric of both Baptist and Christian fellowship is important to us. God willing, we will bind together the broken parts into a new company in preview of the great fellowship we shall have with each other in heaven.[4]

Candidly, I wish we had been much more deliberate over the last ten years in our ecumenical commitments, both with other Baptists and with other Christians. We had some good relations with European Baptists in the early years. We have done some few things with American Baptists. Significant inter-Baptist contacts, both personal and denominational, have been made, but we could have done so much more.

---

[3]See p. 267 of this volume for this quotation.
[4]See p. 269 of the present volume.

I wish that some of us had pushed harder for conversations with American Baptists and African American Baptist groups and Canadian Baptists who share something of our vision of what it means to be Baptist Christians. And it is not too late for this. Indeed the new Strategic Plan calls for some ecumenical commitments. But personally, I would like to see CBF go beyond Baptist ecumenism and engage in serious conversations with other Christians. Most of the CBF people I know are genuinely open Christians, essentially ecumenical in their attitude toward the broader Christian church. If that assessment is correct, we should find ways to act on it. It could be a point of spiritual renewal for us to link arms with other Christians.

From what I can see the National Council of Churches, among others, could do with some of our personal piety and passion for missions, and we could do with a whole lot of their commitment to social justice and understanding of the Kingdom of God. We can engage in ecumenical activities without making ecumenism the saving grace of all Christian virtues. I, for one, do not think ecumenism is *the* cardinal virtue of Christians. I do think, however, that we would be stretched in our Christian discipleship by such interaction. Beyond that, we need to assist our other Baptist friends who have carried the Baptist emphasis on voluntarism to the ecumenical table. We have sat on this bench far too long; it is time for us to act. We should not live in isolation from our other Christian brothers and sisters anymore than we should live in isolation from each other.

5. *Leadership*. A fifth word is *leadership*. Certainly a major development for CBF over the first decade was the selection of early CBF leadership, especially Cecil Sherman and Keith Parks. The Coordinating Council elected Sherman on 9 January 1992. By year's end, 19 November, Keith Parks was on board. Sherman brought passion for the issues in the SBC struggle, passion for the Baptist vision, and for Christian missions. Parks brought enormous credibility from SBC circles after years of missionary statesmanship. One does not have to agree with either Sherman or Parks on every issue of CBF life to affirm their crucial, even indispensable role in the formative stages of CBF.

With Sherman's retirement, CBF called Daniel Vestal to the front of CBF. An authentically conservative Baptist, Daniel Vestal has proven himself to be a sincere listener to CBF people. Like Sherman before him, he understands the diversity of the movement which he leads.

As one privileged to serve on both search committees to recommend the first two coordinators of CBF, I can tell you that both choices appeared obvious after a period of time. Both were honest and serious searches. Early in the process of each search, Sherman and then Vestal were widely rumored to be the shoo-in candidates. Certainly not one of the committee members on either search was unaware of the rumors. Those rumors, however, did not impede, distract, or disrupt an honest search.

Eventually other capable ministers were added to the Atlanta staff. In addition, we have had some unusually gifted moderators, women and men, lay and clergy. Moreover, hundreds of talented people have given their time in volunteer work on the coordinating council. Leadership has been extremely important to CBF in its first ten years.

6. *Identity.* The sixth word is *identity*. Many have mumbled throughout the decade that CBF is a Baptist group in search of identity. CBF has struggled, however, to define that elusive identity by the adoption of official documents, such as the constitution, mission statements, the Strategic Plan, and other such paper profiles. But we all know that paper rarely really defines a group.

As much as some have resisted it, CBF surely has been identified by its relationship to the SBC. Early on, we were identified by where we sent our money, partially to the SBC. The SBC turned around and defined CBF in 1994 when it refused our financial contributions in order, as the SBC said, "to maintain fidelity to the Convention" and "to avoid compromising the integrity of the Cooperative Program." The SBC did us a favor. They sharpened our identity by doing for us what some among us were reluctant to do: delineate SBC from CBF. The SBC also sharpened that differentiation in 2000 when it adopted the revised edition of the Baptist Faith and Message. By deleting the statement that affirmed that Christ is the criterion by which the Bible is interpreted and by excluding women from pastoral ministry the SBC differentiated itself even further from CBF.

We have self-identified ourselves as a "missions delivery system" and again as "a religious endorsing body." But we are more than either of those or both put together. We have been identified as a convention which will not call itself a denomination. There is more truth to that than some have wanted to admit. We have been identified as a "missions society." But we are not a full-fledged convention and we are not merely a missions society. In terms of Baptist polity we are a hybrid, a "conciety." In truth, such polity nomenclature does very little to identify CBF in a meaningful way.

While certainly not the only way, a good way to discover another's identity is simply to look at their check stubs. Where does their money go? How much do they give and to what?

Also, if you want to know who someone is, you ask them to tell you themselves. But if you are clever, you will not pay heed to all their press releases or take for granted all that they say about themselves.

Moreover, if you want to know who someone is, listen to their enemies. *But* you also have to know the identity of the enemies as well. It is a necessity that CBF not let their adversaries fully define them. If CBF does not speak up, its adversaries will have a field day with negative definition. That is why it remains crucial for CBFers to articulate how they differ from SBCers. We are still too close to the turbulence of birth to let distorted descriptions of CBF go unchallenged. That is why it was good for Daniel Vestal to contrast CBF with SBC in Orlando last year.

With all the huffing and puffing about CBF's ailing identity, with all the hall talk and all the effort expended in defining who we are, we do have some identifying marks, don't we?

We are Baptists.

We are *not* Southern Baptists.

We are Baptists with a rather vigorous missionary program. The vast proportion of our money goes to missions.

We are Baptists who have partnered in theological education with some eleven new programs and schools which are markedly different from the six seminaries of the SBC.

We are Baptists who have partnered with the Baptist Joint Committee, Smyth & Helwys, the Baptist Center for Ethics, Women in Ministry, Associated Baptist Press, Whitsitt Baptist Heritage Society, and *Baptists Today*, among others.

We are Baptists who have not only allowed but encouraged shared leadership, male and female, lay and clergy.

We are Baptists who have resisted thus far a tightly drawn doctrinal or ethical statement.

We are Baptists who want to honor the self-government of congregations by carrying lightly whatever denominational "authority" we may have.

With all the frustration surrounding CBF identity, we have nonetheless chiseled a rather discernible profile over the last decade. We would do well to resist the temptation of sharpening that profile excessively. A sharp and unmistakably delineated profile is precisely where the trouble began in 1979. In terms of identity, I say, "*Viva la chaos.*" If the chaos becomes too disorderly, we'll find an anchor somewhere.

These six words could easily be sixteen. Other words are important, but these six are the words that I think are important for our first ten years of CBF.

Whispered Blessings[1]

In recent years few things have gripped me more in Baptist worship than Baptist ordination services. Some of the most spiritually moving, unapologetically tearful, and authentically inspiring worship services I have been part of have been those services that I once considered tedious, obligatory, and even boring. I am not sure for all the reasons of change. Two aspects of these ordination services stand out for me, however.

One difference is *Who* is being ordained. The inclusion of women in the ministry has made lots of differences in lots of ways. To watch people who have been shut out finally get in is an emotional trip for a vulnerable conscience. It is a golden moment to watch enormous and well-suppressed gifts get liberated for Christ's church and cause.

Another thing that has made the difference in these ordination services is *Who* is doing the blessing, the ordaining. At Crescent Hill Baptist Church in Louisville and at First Baptist Church in Macon, the last two churches where Kay and I have been members, the entire congregation is invited to lay on hands. Not just the clergy or ordained deacons, but all God's people exercise the priesthood of blessing. To watch a granddaughter bless her grandmother is almost more than the heart can take. To watch a seven-year old reach down and hug his father, not really knowing why—why that will melt the hardest souls among us.

Like me, I am sure that you have stood in line waiting your turn to lay hands on these people and thinking of what you would say when your time came. I would bet that many of you also do what I do and wonder what all the other blessing people are saying to the blest.

What words were uttered from that devoted friend which caused such an uncontrollable eruption?

Was it simply the sound of the voice that caused the kneeling one to reach out blindly for hands to grasp and hold on to?

And what precipitated the abandonment of decorum and caused eyes to open and arms to reach up and hug and kiss and give thanks?

Tonight, in less emotional but in every bit as sincere a way, I want to wrap my hands around the ten-year-old head of the Baptist Center for

---

[1]I gave this speech at the tenth anniversary celebration banquet of the Baptist Center for Ethics in Atlanta on 28 June 2001.

Ethics and whisper two blessings into its ear. Of course, I hope you will whisper your own blessings, as well.

Whisper one. *"Bless you, Baptist Center for Ethics, for what you have already done"*:

for taking a risk and beginning the enterprise when so many were playing it safe;

for creating an alternative to all of the right-wing claptrap mouthed in our society by and among other Baptists;

for creating resources that are useable in local congregations. (My own Sunday school class used your series "The Practice of Living Faithfully" with great profit recently.)

Bless you, BCE, for designing and distributing one of the best, most usable electronic newsletters available to ministers and Christians in local settings. You need to know that I have recommended and forwarded it to my children, to my friends, and even to a few of my enemies.

Bless you for sponsoring conferences which challenge and inspire and which expose us to voices we would otherwise not hear.

Bless you for following those five guiding stars with which you began:

Star One: being proactive rather than reactive.

Star Two: recognizing the centrality of congregations and congregational leaders in the mission of character formation and social change.

Star Three: providing an educational and analytical approach rather than a pontifical and dogmatic approach.

Star Four: innovating the new ways rather than excavating the old ways.

Star Five: understanding that a "McNugget" ethics approach is needed in the Information age.

Whisper two. *"Bless you, BCE, for what you can do for all the rest of us in the future, in our individual lives, our congregational lives, and our CBF life."*

We Baptists, especially we CBF-kinds-of-Baptists, have experienced a social and economic comeuppance in our society which has cast us in a very different place from many of our ancestors. Help us, BCE, not to forget the "plain people," not to get tripped up by a spiritual or intellectual or theological elitism. Help us to remember that the symbols most associated with Jesus of Nazareth are a cross and a towel, not a Ph.D. degree or a well-stuffed portfolio.

Help us realize, BCE, that the challenge for us in the next century is to learn to take seriously what Jesus took seriously: God's rule over our lives, sharing in Jesus's name what we have and who we are, including the ex-

cluded, blessing the unblessed, learning to live on less so others can have
enough.

Help us also in this new century not to get embarrassed about "the
Spirit of the Lord" coming upon us. Remind us that Jesus said that the
"Spirit of the Lord is upon me because. . . . "

Teach us how to finish that sentence, how to tell when the Holy Spirit
has gripped our lives, invaded our souls, and housed itself in our bodies.

Keep reminding us that when the anointing comes,
   when the fire of heaven falls on our lives,
      when "The Spirit of the Lord is upon us"
         we will know it.
And it will not be because of individual ecstasy
   or devotion to sacred institutions
      or the power to attract a crowd.
It will be because we preach good news to the poor,
   proclaim release to the captives.
      recovering of sight to the blind,
         setting at liberty those who are oppressed,
            proclaiming the Jubilee year of the Lord.
Keep our feet to the fire about what really happens
   when we get filled with God's Spirit.
      The poor get good news!
         The captives get released!
            The blind get their eyes back!
               The oppressed are liberated!

Remind us that this poetry in Luke 4 is suggestive and imaginative, not
exhaustive or prescriptive. Save us from the unbending literalism that
misses the point of the ancient Jewish prophecy which was lived out by
Jesus of Nazareth.

Keep nagging at us about the point of the poetry, that when the Spirit
of the Lord comes upon us, *Compassion* happens to us.

In all that you do, BCE, make *Compassion* the controlling and central idea
   of your life and, therefore, of our lives.
      Move us to view life with a moral squint,
         sensitize our consciences,
            enlarge our sympathies,
               help us, in self-forgetfulness, to extend care,
                  and to work so that love
                     can find an outlet in a suffering world.

Keep before us that challenging definition of the church which says that "The church is all who love Christ in the service of all who suffer."

"The church is all who love Christ in the service of all who suffer." Don't let us get far from that definition when we are seeking to resolve budget questions or financial matters.

"The church is all who love Christ in the service of all who suffer." Don't let us get far from that definition when we spend hours in long-range planning.

"The church is all who love Christ in the service of all who suffer." Don't let us get far from that definition when we debate every policy issue that comes before us.

I hope you are still standing strong 100 years from now, BCE, and that you are still teaching us that we need the Spirit of God upon us, because we need compassion to be the controlling and central idea of our lives.

Bless you, BCE, for this first decade.

Bless you, BCE, for these coming years.

God bless you and God bless us through you.

Twenty Reflections after Twenty Years[1]

1. The most prophetic line of the Southern Baptist Convention Holy War: "We will have a great time here, if for no other reason than to elect Adrian Rogers our president." It came from W. A. Criswell at the SBC Pastors' Conference in Houston, Texas, in 1979. It brought the SBC house down with cheers and applause. More pessimistic observers would simply say that those words brought the SBC house down. But they didn't.

2. The saddest moment of the controversy: 22 October 1986, at Glorieta, New Mexico, when the SBC seminary presidents caved in before the fundamentalist juggernaut. Glorieta marked the end for the moderates. You do not compromise with truth-oriented fundamentalists who think that they have the truth, the whole truth, and nothing but the truth.

3. The reason for the outcome: Passion won, culture played a part; leadership was very important.

4. One of the biggest and often-heard myths during the controversy: "The fundamentalists will moderate once they get in power." I stand by what I said regarding the new SBC in my final chapter in the revised edition of *Not a Silent People*: "Theologically and ideologically the SBC has been *fundamentalized*; ecclesiologically the SBC has been *centralized*; culturally, in terms of gender issues, the SBC has been *chauvinized*; ecumenically the SBC has been *sectarianized*; denominationally the SBC has been *de-baptistified*."[2]

5. The greatest error history will make in interpreting the controversy: Thinking it was a lopsided victory. It was a much closer fight than history will reflect. But history will mark it up as a "win" for the fundamentalists and a "loss" for the moderates without paying attention to the very close percentages by which the fundamentalists won the presidency year after year.

6. A warning to all from the controversy: The Southern Baptist *Church* has replaced the Southern Baptist *Convention*. W. W. Barnes predicted this back in the 1930s. Baptists are congregationalists, not "presbygationalists"

---

[1]Along with others, I was invited by *Baptists Today* to give some reflections on the SBC controversy after twenty years. This little piece was published in *Baptists Today* 17/6 (June 1999): 6, 19.

[2]Walter B. Shurden, *Not a Silent People*, rev. ed. (Macon GA: Smyth & Helwys Publishing, 1995) 107-108.

or "episcopagationalists." Moderates must work at carrying their emerging connectionalism lightly. The "community" in Baptist life is primarily the local church. This is neither Landmarkism nor sectarianism. It is historic Baptist church polity.

7. The bad news coming out of the controversy: It was worth doing then. It will be worth doing again when Baptists have forsaken their Baptistness.

8. The biggest casualties of the war: Little girls born into SBC churches during the struggle who would grow up wanting to be part of the SBC ministry in the twenty-first century.

9. The most appropriate biblical text for the Holy War: Acts 19:32: "Meanwhile, some were shouting one thing, some another; for the assembly was in confusion, and most of them did not know why they had come together."

10. The most surprising outcome of the controversy: The belief, as Fisher Humphreys said, that the Bible alone as God's word was unaffected by the controversy. Moderates believe that as much as fundamentalists. Nothing has changed, regarding the place of the Bible in Baptist life. Difference in interpretations of the Bible continue, as they always have.

11. The most forgotten dimension of the controversy by the moderates: That moderates are defined by the two decades of struggle. One understands the moderate longing to get "beyond" the controversy, but the truth of the matter is that moderates are who they are because of what they both resisted and affirmed in the controversy. Moderates will "forget" or "get beyond" at their peril.

12. A moderate hero who should never be forgotten: Cecil Sherman. He was right more times in more ways on more issues than any other single person. I am grateful for him, for his courage, for his tenacity, for his wisdom, and for his leadership.

13. The most overlooked dimension of the controversy: The doctrine of God. Alan Neely, another of the many moderate heroes of the war, said correctly that the controversy was "fundamentally an argument about God." He meant, I think, that fundamentalists were mired in a concept of God that was exclusive, intolerant, and legalistic, while moderates pleaded for God's inclusiveness, forgiveness, and acceptance.

14. One of the biggest victories for the SBC fundamentalist leadership: The triumph of creedalism in SBC life. Even some moderates, under the influence of that triumph, long for a "statement of what we believe." It is a dangerous itch. Let it itch. Don't scratch it.

15. The most pathetic people in the controversy: Those who said, "Plague on both the fundamentalists and the moderates," and who serenely stayed out of the line of fire. Next to the most pathetic are those mega-church pastors who waited to see who would win before they cast their sails toward the winning fundamentalists. If moderates had won, these ambitious pastors would have gone with moderates.

16. People who have never heard enough "thank yous" from moderates: Old-line SBC leadership that helped launch the new moderate organizations and then gladly stepped aside: Duke McCall, Grady Cothen, Jimmy Allen, Carolyn Crumpler, Foy Valentine, Randall Lolley, and a few others who have been too often derisively labeled "the good old boys (and girl)." They were indeed a group of good old boys and girl.

17. I'm glad to be done with the fundamentalist leadership of the SBC that transformed some good, basically conservative denominational agencies into a bastion of fundamentalism. The new SBC is not even close to my Baptist identity. The Cooperative Baptist Fellowship and the Baptist Alliance are much closer. It feels good to be able to embrace the larger Baptist tradition and the larger Christian community.

18. I hope moderates will grow more and more into issues of social justice while keeping their Bibles open and their hearts warm. My prayer is that moderates will take seriously what Jesus took seriously. Baptists of our ilk have been big on missions and big on personal devotion, and that is very good. We need to become bigger on justice issues.

19. I hope moderates will not dumb down our worship simply because dumbing down is the fad and draws crowds. I hope moderates will never get stuck again on issues of size, but I also hope that we will explore the possibility of being Baptist with other Baptists, especially American Baptists, Canadian Baptists, and some African American Baptists.

20. The biggest nonsurprise of the controversy: Historic Baptist principles regarding the importance of the individual, the centrality of the local church, religious liberty and the separation of church and state, anti-creedalism, and the priesthood of all believers may be more important at the turn of the century than at any time since Baptists began in seventeenth-century England.

CBF and Baptists in 2010[1]

I note three interrelated trends that will impact Baptists and CBF by 2010.

Creative Baptist localism

1. Among moderate Baptists, *creative Baptist localism*—which got a huge shot in the arm by the fundamentalist-moderate controversy—will continue to increase in strength. "Creative Baptist localism" means that an increasing number of local churches have rediscovered their true Baptist church polity—congregationalism. These churches will certainly not let a national body dictate to them. They will be empowered to follow the leadership of Christ as they understand it. This is one of the happiest consequences of the controversy, and it is pregnant with implications for moderate Baptists. CBF must heed and encourage this creative localism, as it has done for the last ten years. If not, it risks being shunned by local churches who have finally found their ecclesiastical legs.

2. More Moderate Baptist churches will be excluded from existing associations, state conventions, and the SBC. The creed adopted by the SBC in Orlando will be the whipping stick.

3. Many mixed (containing both moderates and fundamentalists) local Baptist churches who are struggling with their relationship to the SBC will either sever that relationship, suffer division with new smaller moderate churches being formed, or become solidly franchised Southern Baptist churches. The first decade of the controversy (1979–1990) occurred at the national level. The second decade (1990–2000) focused on state conventions. The third decade (2000–2010) will be in some ways the most painful of all, a bit of trench warfare in the local churches.

4. More women—but not scores—will serve as pastors of local moderate Baptist churches.

---

[1]David Wilkinson, editor of *Fellowship: Newsletter of the Cooperative Baptist Fellowship* asked Nancy T. Ammerman, Cecil Sherman, and me to submit brief articles describing trends that would impact CBF by the year 2010, the end of the second decade of CBF. This article is the published version of what I wrote. The article appeared in *Fellowship: Newsletter of the Cooperative Baptist Fellowship* 11/1 (January/February 2001): 4-5.

Self-Conscious Baptist Regionalism

1. *Self-conscious Baptist regionalism,* an extension of the localism described above, will flourish in the future. Ecclesiastical "McDonaldism," where each outlet is like all the others, is surely on the decline. The Texas and Virginia Baptist conventions are primary examples of this trend in their relationships to the SBC. CBFers should not think, however, that divorcing one national group means that regional bodies are ready to marry another newer denominational franchise.

2. The Texas and Virginia conventions will be regional denominations, partnering with but also in friendly competition with national CBF.

3. This self-conscious regionalism trend can be observed in emerging mainstream Baptist groups and in state CBF organizations. These groups (Texas Baptists Committed, Mainstream Baptists of Oklahoma, etc.) appear to have some of the greatest momentum in moderate Baptist life today. Don't lose sight of the fact that their focus is regional, not national.

Likewise, some state CBF organizations appear to have no intention of becoming submissive satellites of national Fellowship. Moderate Baptists must remember that there is no such thing as *"The* CBF Baptist *Church."* We have witnessed *"The* Southern Baptist *Church"* emerge equipped with cardinals, creeds, and codes of ethics. The independence of state CBF organizations will not permit that development.

4. In several states some moderate Baptists and their churches will give up on the old state convention. They will form rival state conventions or allow the state CBF organizations to become de facto moderate state conventions.

5. New moderate associations may be formed with theological rather than geographical boundaries. These new associations will have more inclusive policies on matters of baptism, accepting Christians of other denominations into their churches without "Baptist baptism." If new associations are not formed, it will be a tacit confession that associations are no longer needed. For many moderate Baptists, state CBF organizations will replace the older associational pattern.

A Humble Denominationalism

1. All of the above argues for a *humble denominationalism* among moderate Baptists. Fortunately, the Baptist denominational pyramid has been inverted for us. Before 1980, the dynamic flow of things was from the denomination at the top to the local churches at the bottom. Today, and

more so in 2010, the dynamic flow will be from the churches at the top to the denomination at the bottom.

2. Inherent in a *humble denominationalism* is the fact that national CBF must be a cheerleader for diversity, not uniformity. Moderate Baptists are not the kind of people who tell each other what to believe, how to behave, or where to give kingdom money to be Baptist kosher.[2] If that attitude is subverted by the passing of years and a burgeoning bureaucracy, the Fellowship will be a bland annual meeting of smaller numbers by the year 2010.

3. In 2010, because of this *humble denominationalism*, national CBF will function as a conduit and a catalyst. It will function as a conduit for very diverse Baptist congregations and individuals to "cooperate" in the areas of missions, theological education, campus ministry, chaplaincy, and other such ministries. The CBF will also serve as a catalyst for moderate Baptists, challenging them to take seriously what Jesus took seriously and to honor the messy, often chaotic, but always indispensable Baptist vision of freedom.

---

[2]This line, probably the most creative one in the article, really should be in quotes because I got it in a telephone conversation from friend Hardy Clemons.

A Bibliography
Baptist Books That Have Been Important to Me

Introduction

I want to issue an apology before I write another word. My superb editor, Edd Rowell, requested that I put the following list of books together at a time when I was swamped with other writing responsibilities and near the end of his copyediting of this book. I acceded to his request, but I did so with full knowledge that the urgency of the request meant that I would certainly overlook some books that have been important to me. I am sure I will look back on this list in unbelief that I failed to list other books crucial to my life as a student of the Baptists. The reader should understand that these are merely *some* of the Baptist books that have been important to me.

The Baptist books that are important to me come in many shapes and sizes and genres. Some primary sources that are very crucial to my understanding of Baptist life are not the books that I would recommend to the laity or even to clergy who are beginning their reading in Baptist studies. Nonetheless, these primary sources have shaped my understanding of who Baptists are.

Some scholarly secondary sources have also been crucial for my own interpretation of who Baptists are. These, too, may not be ones that I would direct beginning students to for their first reading of the Baptist story.

A third group of Baptist books that have been important to me are those that constitute an introduction to Baptist life. These are books for laity and clergy who have little background in Baptist studies. These are the people I have been very concerned to reach with the Baptist story, so I have tried to pay attention to books that would be helpful to them.

Thus, I have divided the Baptist books that are important to me into three groups: primary sources, scholarly secondary sources, and books for beginners. Because I have concentrated my studies on white Baptists in America, and especially in the South, the reader should not be surprised to find more of these books pertaining to that particular group of Baptists.

Primary Sources

Backus, Isaac, *A History of New England, with Particular Reference to the Denomination of Christians Called Baptists*. Three volumes. Boston: printed by Edward Draper, 1777. Second edition. With notes by David Weston. Two volumes. Newton MA: Backus Historical Society, 1871. Indispensable for understanding Baptist life in the U.S.

Benedict, David, *Fifty Years among the Baptists*. New York: Sheldon and Company, 1860. Reprint: Little Rock AR: Seminary Publications, 1977. Interesting, often humorous, source for Baptists in America during the first half of the nineteenth century.

Clarke, John, *Ill Newes from New England: or, A Narrative of New-Englands Persecution. Wherein Is Declared That While Old England Is Becoming New, New-England Is Becoming Old. /etc./*. London: printed by H. Ellis, 1652. Reprinted (with "The Baptist Debate of April 14-15, 1668") in *Colonial Baptists, Massachusetts and Rhode Island*. The Baptist Tradition. New York: Arno Press, 1980. In my judgment, this is the single most important book by a Baptist in America in the seventeenth century.

Edwards, Morgan, *Materials towards a History of the Baptists* (1772). Prepared for publication by Eve B. Weeks and Mary B. Warren. Danielsville GA: Heritage Papers, 1984. For the serious historian, not because of its artistry or correctness, but because it is often all that we have.

Fosdick, Harry Emerson, *The Living of These Days, an Autobiography*. New York: Harper, 1956. One of my favorite Baptist autobiographies.

Gaustad, Edwin S., editor. *Baptist Piety: The Last Will and Testimony of Obadiah Holmes*. Grand Rapids MI: Christian University Press, 1978. Formative for understanding Baptists in Colonial America.

Gillette, Abram Dunn. *Minutes of the Philadelphia Baptist Association, from A.D. 1707, to A.D. 1807: Being the First One Hundred Years of Its Existence*. Philadelphia: American Baptist Publication Society, 1851. First tricentennial edition with expanded indexes and illustrations. Springfield MO: Particular Baptist Press, 2002. I learned to appreciate the importance of this book when I wrote a dissertation on the role of Baptist associations in denominational life in America from 1707 to 1814. While a listing of them would be impossible, the circular letters distributed by the associations up to 1814 in America constitute an untapped cache of Baptist theological documents, and I have read many of them with great profit.

Helwys, Thomas. *A Short Declaration of the Mystery of Iniquity (1611/1612)*. Edited and introduced by Richard Groves. Macon GA: Mercer University Press, 1998. A pivotal book for understanding early English Baptists.

Leland, John. *The Writings of the Late Elder John Leland, Including Some Events in His Life, Written by Himself; with Additional Sketches, &c. by L. F. Greene.*

Edited by Miss L. F. Greene. Lanesboro, Massachusetts. New York: printed by G. W. Wood, 1845. Reprint: Gallatin TN: Church History Research & Archives, 1986.

Lumpkin, William Latane. *Baptist Confessions of Faith*. Chicago: Judson Press, 1959. Revised edition: Valley Forge PA: Judson Press, 1969. This is one of the most-used books in my Baptist library.

McLoughlin, William G., and Martha Whiting Davidson, editors. *The Baptist Debate of April 14-15, 1668*. Bound with *Ill Newes from New-England* (1652) in *Colonial Baptists, Massachusetts and Rhode Island* (see at John Clarke, above). Edited by Edwin S. Gaustad. A most overlooked primary source that conveys much about seventeenth century Baptists in America.

Robertson, A. T. *Life and Letters of John Albert Broadus*. Philadelphia: American Baptist Publication Society, 1901.

Semple, Robert Baylor. *A History of the Rise and Progress of the Baptists in Virginia*. Richmond: published by the author, 1810. Edited, revised, and extended by George William Beale. Richmond: Pitt and Dickinson, 1894.

Smyth, John. *The Works of John Smyth, Fellow of Christ's College, 1594–1598*. Two volumes. Tercentenary edition for the Baptist Historical Society, with notes and biography by William Thomas Whitley. Cambridge UK: Cambridge University Press, 1915.

Williams, Roger. *Christenings Make Not Christians, or, A Brief Discourse concerning That Name Heathen, Commonly Given to the Indians, as also concerning That Great Point of Their Conversion*. London: printed by Jane Coe for I. H., 1645. (Original in the British Museum.) Reprint: *Roger Williams's "Christenings Make Not Christians," 1645. A Long-Lost Tract Recovered and Exactly Reprinted*. Edited by Martyn Dexter. Providence RI: S. S. Rider, 1881.

Scholarly Secondary Sources

Barnes, William Wright. *The Southern Baptist Convention: A Study in the Development of Ecclesiology*. Seminary Hill TX: published by the author, 1934. Often reprinted, most recently as *A Study in the Development of Ecclesiology: The Southern Baptist Convention*. BaptistWay series. Dallas: Baptist General Convention of Texas, 1997. In my judgment, this is one of the most prophetic books on Southern Baptist history ever written. Wright predicted in 1934 much of what happened to Baptists in the last two decades of the twentieth century.

Brackney, William Henry. *The Baptists*. New York: Greenwood Press, 1988.

_____. *A Genetic History of Baptist Thought, with Special Reference to Baptists in Britain and North America*. Macon GA: Mercer University Press, 2004.

_____. *Historical Dictionary of the Baptists*. Lanham MD: Scarecrow Press, 1999. I have a lawyer's bookcase next to my desk in my office at my home. I reserve one small shelf for Baptist books that I consult often. This book is on that shelf.

Copeland, E. Luther. *The Southern Baptist Convention and the Judgment of History: The Taint of an Original Sin.* Lanham MD: University Press of America, 2002. Searing and uncompromising, Copeland has written one of my all-time favorite books on the history of the SBC.

Flynt, Wayne, *Alabama Baptists: Southern Baptists in the Heart of Dixie.* Tuscaloosa: University of Alabama Press, 1998. I consider this the very best state Baptist history ever written.

Gardner, Robert G. *Baptists of Early America: A Statistical History, 1639–1790.* Atlanta: Georgia Baptist Historical Society, 1983. The Morgan Edwards of the twentieth century, Robert Gardner placed all historians in his debt with this meticulously researched history. It is always close by to any research I do on Baptist history in early America. Because of the technical nature of the book, it would never be a best seller.

George, Timothy, and David S. Dockery. *Baptist Theologians.* Nashville: Broadman Press, 1990. Revised edition: *Theologians of the Baptist Tradition.* Nashville: Broadman & Holman Publishers, 2001. This volume contains some extremely valuable essays.

Goen, C. C. *Revivalism and Separatism in New England, 1740–1800. Strict Congregationalist and Separate Baptists in the Great Awakening.* New Haven CT: Yale University Press, 1962. Reprint: Middletown CT and Scranton PA: Wesleyan University Press; dist. by Harper & Row, 1987.

Hinson, E. Glenn. *Soul Liberty: The Doctrine of Religious Liberty.* Nashville TN: Convention Press, 1975. Here is maybe the best "study course book" ever produced by the SBC publishing house. It deserves to be updated and republished so that Baptists can regain their soul on this issue.

Hudson, Winthrop Still, editor. *Baptist Concepts of the Church: A Survey of the Historical and Theological Issues Which Have Produced Changes in Church Order.* Chicago: Judson Press, 1959. A very valuable book of essays, though I disagree with Hudson's interpretations at some crucial points.

King, Martin Luther, Jr. *Why We Can't Wait.* New York: Harper & Row, 1963. Often reprinted, most recently with a new afterword by Jesse L. Jackson, Sr. New York: Signet Classic, 2000.

Leonard, Bill J. *Dictionary of Baptists in America.* Downer's Grove IL: InterVarsity Press, 1994. Only an arm's length away, it is one of the few books on my Baptist shelf in my lawyer's bookcase beside my desk at home.

_____. *Baptist Ways. A History.* Valley Forge PA: Judson Press, 2003.

Lumpkin, William Latane. *Baptist Foundations in the South. Tracing through the Separates the Influence of the Great Awakening, 1754–1787.* Nashville: Broadman Press, 1961. The remarkable and thrilling story of the Separate Baptists never ceases to put me in touch with some of my deepest Baptist roots.

Marney, Carlyle. *Priests to Each Other*. Valley Forge PA: Judson Press, 1974. I have some "favorites" in Baptist history. Numbered among them are John Clifford, Walter Rauschenbusch, William Carey, Clarence Jordan, Martin Luther King, Jr., and Carlyle Marney.

McBeth, H. Leon. *The Baptist Heritage. Four Centuries of Baptist Witness*. Nashville: Broadman Press, 1987. I used this as a textbook in my courses in Baptist history.

McLoughlin, William Gerald. *New England Dissent, 1630–1833: The Baptists and the Separation of Church and State*. Two volumes. Cambridge MA: Harvard University Press, 1971. A model of brilliant scholarship.

Miller, Samuel H. *The Life of the Soul*. New York: Harper & Brothers Publishers, 1951. The former dean of Harvard Divinity School and an American Baptist, Miller taught me about the meaning of "Baptist Spirituality" in this book and in his *The Life of the Church*.

Newman, Stewart A. *A Free Church Perspective: A Study in Ecclesiology*. Wake Forest NC: Stevens Book Press, 1986. I find Stewart Newman to be a soul brother in his interpretation of Baptist life.

Payne, Ernest A. *The Fellowship of Believers: Baptist Thought and Practice Yesterday and Today*. With a foreword by H. Wheeler Robinson. London: Kingsgate Press, 1952. One of the first books on Baptist thought that I read. It has remained pivotal for me since my seminary days.

Stricklin, David. *A Genealogy of Dissent: Southern Baptist Protest in the Twentieth Century*. Lexington KY: University Press of Kentucky, 1999. A delightful book that deserves a far larger reading audience than it has received, this book, along with those by Rufus Spain, John Lee Eighmy, and George Kelsey, taps into my twin interests of Baptist history in the South and Christian ethics.

Thurman, Howard. *With Head and Heart: The Autobiography of Howard Thurman*. Harcourt, Brace & Company. 1979. One of the great Baptist mystics who combined contemplation with action.

Tull, James E. *Shapers of Baptist Thought*. Valley Forge PA: Judson Press, 1972. Reprint: Reprints of Scholarly Excellence (ROSE) no. 8. Macon GA: Mercer University Press, 1984. I have always considered Tull's book to be a model of how to do theological biography of Baptists.

Wardin, Albert W., editor. *Baptists around the World: A Comprehensive Handbook*. Nashville: Broadman & Holman Publishers, 1995. An encyclopedia of information.

White, B. R., *The English Separatist Tradition: From the Marian Martyrs to the Pilgrim Fathers*. Oxford and New York: Oxford University Press, 1971. Very important to my understanding of Baptists as emerging from the Separatists of England.

White, B. R. *The English Baptists of the Seventeenth Century*. The Baptist Historical Society, 1983. Revised and expanded edition: Didcot UK: Baptist Historical Society, 1996. This is exceedingly valuable for understanding

Baptists in their first century in England. In addition, the subsequent books in this series by Raymond Brown, J. H. Y. Briggs, and K. W. Clements have also been helpful to me.

Baptist Books for Beginners

Beasley-Murray, Paul. *Radical Believers: The Baptist Way of Being the Church*. Baptist Union of Great Britain, 1992. With a title that I admire, this is an interesting and helpful presentation from the British Baptist perspective.

Cook, Henry. *What Baptists Stand For*. London: Carey Kingsgate Press, 1947. Retains its value after a half century of use.

Deweese, Charles W., editor. *Defining Baptist Convictions: Guidelines for the Twenty-First Century*. Foreword by Walter B. Shurden. Franklin TN: Providence House Publishers, 1996.

Hays, Brooks, and John E. Steely. *The Baptist Way of Life*. Way of Life series. Englewood Cliffs NJ: Prentice-Hall, 1963. Revised edition: Macon GA: Mercer University Press, 1981.

Humphreys, Fisher. *The Way We Were: How Southern Baptist Theology Has Changed and What It Means to Us All*. Revised edition. Foreword by Walter B. Shurden. Macon GA: Smyth & Helwys Publishing, 2002.

Robinson, H. Wheeler. *Baptist Principles*. London: Carey Kingsgate Press, 1925. Fourth edition, edited by James Henry Rushbrooke. London: Carey Kingsgate Press, 1925. Reprint: London: Carey Kingsgate Press, 1960.

_____. *The Life and Faith of the Baptists*. London: Kingsgate Press, 1946; 1927.

Maring, Norman H., and Winthop S. Hudson. *A Baptist Manual of Polity and Practice*. Valley Forge PA: Judson Press, 1963.

Mullins, Edgar Young. *The Axioms of Religion: A New Interpretation of the Baptist Faith*. Philadelphia and New York: American Baptist Publication Society, 1908. Maybe the most influential interpretation of the Baptist identity in the twentieth century.

Oates, Wayne E. *The Struggle to Be Free*. Philadelphia: Westminster Press, 1983. The autobiography of one of Baptist's most significant scholars in the twentieth century.